ARAB WOMEN

Indiana Series in Arab and Islamic Studies

Salih J. Altoma, Iliya Harik, and Mark Tessler, general editors

ARAB WOMEN

Old Boundaries, New Frontiers

EDITED BY

JUDITH E. TUCKER

Published in association with
the Center for Contemporary Arab Studies,
Georgetown University, Washington, DC

INDIANA UNIVERSITY PRESS

Bloomington and Indianapolis

The paper used in this publication meets the minimum requirements of American National Standard for Information Sciences—Permanence of Paper for Printed Library Materials, ANSI Z39.48-1984.

 ™

Manufactured in the United States of America

Library of Congress Cataloging-in-Publication Data

Arab women : old boundaries, new frontiers / edited by Judith E. Tucker.
    p.   cm. — (Indiana series in Arab and Islamic studies)
    "Published in association with the Center for Contemporary Arab Studies, Georgetown University, Washington, DC."
    Includes bibliographical references and index.
    ISBN 0-253-36096-X (cloth), — ISBN 0-253-20776-2 (paper)
    1. Women—Arab countries—Social conditions. 2. Women—Arab countries—Economic conditions. 3. Feminism—Arab countries.
I. Tucker, Judith E. II. Georgetown University. Center for Contemporary Arab Studies. III. Series.
HQ1784.A72 1993
305.42'0917'4927—dc20   92-33583

1 2 3 4 5 97 96 95 94 93

CONTENTS

Part 3 Politics and Power

Part 4 Gender Roles and Relations

INTRODUCTION

Judith E. Tucker

A collection of papers on women in the Arab World must presuppose some shared context and set of concerns among women in an area stretching from Morocco in the west to the Arab Gulf in the east, an area of considerable diversity of geography, of economic base, and of social class. Does this Arab World, indeed, provide a shared context for women? Is there a shared history and culture that privileges the Arab World, as the seat of a particular gender system, as against, say, an Islamic World on the one hand or the more familiar category of a nation-state on the other? We begin with the assumption here that the Arab conquests of the seventh century A.D., which made Arabic the enduring lingua franca of the region (outside of a few linguistic redoubts), created a parallel cultural unity or at least a geographic zone within which an educated person might feel culturally at home even as he or she traveled vast distances. The political vicissitudes of the centuries, which repeatedly divided this territory in different ways, did not obliterate this shared culture. In the nineteenth and twentieth centuries, the drive to unite in order to face European threats led many Arabs to fashion out of this shared language and culture the potential for a new political unit—the Arab World—as the basis for political solidarity. This world was not, and is not, synonymous with Islam. Most Arabs are Muslims, but some are not, and more of the world's Muslims live outside the Arab World than within it. That Islam is an important part of Arab culture is indisputable, and religion, or at least a shared religious history, has often been invoked as a prime basis for unity. Probably more important, however, has been the political imperative. As the region divided into a plethora of nation-states in the twentieth century, pan-Arabism fought the centrifugal tendencies of the independence period by promoting Arab identity. Many intellectuals helped merge cultural history with political exigency to sustain at least the idea that the inhabitants of the region where the Arabic language predominates are, despite their diversity, bound into a singular cultural unit with, by extension, a particular gender system.

One could argue that the diversity of the region militates against any useful generalization: women's lives—their access to power and economic resources as well as their social and legal standing—surely vary from one community or class to another. It is a mark of the coming of age of women's studies in and about the Arab World that we now recognize that diversity: facile assumptions about the monolithic role "Islam" or Arab culture plays in the seclusion, disempowerment, and oppression of women no longer pass as the accepted academic discourse on the topic. Have we now emerged into a world where infinite varieties of experience and shades of meaning preclude any discussion of gender at a culture-wide level? As we shall see below, the debates and discussions that took place at the Georgetown symposium in the spring of 1986, giving rise to this book, suggest that this diversity is underpinned by a certain shared understanding of how gender, as a social category rather than a biological given, has been constructed in the region known as the Arab World, and how, as a result, the women of that region define the issues of concern to them. Certain themes do indeed recur. On the other hand, one could also take the position that Arab women do not have concerns or problems that are really all that different from those of women in other parts of the Third World or, indeed, in the world as a whole. That gender-based oppression and, therefore, the analyses and strategies of feminism are pretty much the same everywhere is an attractive proposition providing, as it does, a ready-made basis for transnational and intercultural solidarity. Most of the contributors to this volume, as western and western-educated Arab women, have had to come to terms with the fact that western women's experiences, however, do not necessarily provide a universal framework for analyzing gender oppression elsewhere in the world.[1] Many of the misunderstandings that have developed between women in the West and in the Arab World can be traced, I believe, to our assumption that the symbols and content of women's oppression are constant across cultures, that how women look and act has a similar meaning everywhere, that the issues of women's liberation as they developed historically in the West should prove to be the same in the Arab World. On the contrary, the specificity of the western historical experience, the particularities of the gender oppression we have encountered in the dominant culture incubated in northern Europe, have shaped our basic beliefs about gender and our reading of the meaning of gender in other societies. There are certain benchmark aspects of a society that we, as western-trained feminists, tend to search out as a measure of the position of women. Legal equality, reproductive freedom, and the opportunity to express and fulfill the individual self whether through work, through art, or through sexuality recur as central topics of feminist inquiry. But are these the natural universals of feminism?

If we take the chapters which follow as a whole, we find that women who study the Arab World, taking their cue from the concerns expressed by women within the region, focus on somewhat different aspects of the gender system in the Arab World in keeping with the specificities of the history and present circumstances of the region. What are the issues that resonate in today's Arab World? First, there is concern with the way gender issues are treated in the region, discourses that invoke Islam, those that dwell on "authenticity" and "tradition," and those that are self-consciously feminist. Second, there is the issue of women's economic activities, not so much as a problem of the lack of economic participation or legal disability, but rather of social constraint and marginality. Third, there is the issue of political power, again not as an issue of the lack of access or legal obstacle, but rather as an arena where the troubled course of relations between nationalism and feminism must be resolved. Finally, there is the issue of domestic and social relations where the social and psychological aspects of gender relations are developed and lived most concretely: the changing nature of these relations reflects the importance of the family and community in any approach to gender questions.

This is not intended to be an all-inclusive list of the relevant gender issues. Among the missing, for example, is the entire issue of the state and gender in the Arab World, an issue which is just beginning to receive the attention it deserves.[2] This list may also reflect a geographical bias. The Arab countries of North Africa are not well represented among the papers published here. Interestingly enough, however, the several North African participants at the conference did not dwell much on their differences from their sisters in the Arab East; indeed, they tended to stress the economic, political, and cultural similarities, and called for the development of a truly pan-Arab feminist movement.

Gender Discourses

Certainly the current discourse on gender in the Arab World frequently invokes Islam as a guide to gender organization, and much of the literature on women in the area still assumes an "Islamic" culture that has everything to do with gender roles. But there is actually little agreement on what even the central texts of the religion have to say about gender. The Qur'an, the basic revelation of the religion, is rather vague or so all-encompassing on most gender questions as to offer only very general guidance on the subject. The *hadith*, the collections of accounts of the historical sayings, life, and times of the Prophet Muhammad, are not much more help because their number and variety allow for a wide range of interpretations. They are a useful historical record, perhaps, of the evolution of establishment religious thinking on gender as they do reflect how members of the 'ulama (the Islamic clergy who compiled the collections of *hadith* in the early centuries of Islam) thought about, and sought to impose, notions of gender in changing historical circumstances. The body of Islamic law, the *shari'a*, again the product of 'ulama discourse, does contain certain rules for governing gender relations, particularly within the family. Some of these are well known: the permitting of polygyny, the provision of unilateral divorce without grounds for men only, the assignment of all child custody rights to the father and his family all prejudice women. On the other hand, Muslim women, whether married or not, were (and are), unlike their European counterparts, full legal personae with unabridgeable property rights. Is Islam, then, nothing more than a set of rather contradictory indications of gender roles which can be selected and interpreted to suit the demands of each social class and era? Fatima Mernissi has argued that there is a certain transhistorical Muslim view of female sexuality as dangerous and destructive in its power, as in need of close male supervision and control.[3] Barbara Stowasser demonstrates that modern Islamic thought on gender questions has focused on certain other themes, female domesticity and its implications being perhaps the most important, although conclusions concerning the specific social requirements of Islam have differed over time and place.

The difficulty of isolating any one "Islamic" discourse on gender is further complicated by the close association between Islam and the quest for cultural authenticity in different contexts. Stowasser discusses the views of currently active fundamentalist groups who have given a rather conservative "Islamic" view of gender new life by making it the centerpiece of an Islamic authenticity locked in conflict with western imperialism. This entwining of gender and anti-imperialist discourses in the Arab World has a long history. The European colonial and imperial powers that intervened in the Arab World in the nineteenth and early twentieth centuries often claimed that the advancement of women was a special concern of, and justification for, their intervention and rule.[4] Women in "native" society were degraded, a condition that could only be ameliorated through the good offices of European governors. The fact that colonial states did not, in fact, actively pursue policies that worked in any real way to "liberate" women, much less to provide basic services to women in the areas of health and education, changed little in the equation of colonialism with an imposition of western gender roles: the emergence of a politicized "tradition" opposed to colonial positions on gender was inevitable. In Algeria, for example, despite active female participation in the War of Independence, the fashioning of an indigenous discourse on gender stressed the superiority of the traditional roles of women as wives and mothers and made the wearing of a veil synonymous with Algerian patriotism.[5]

An anti-imperialist gender discourse need not be explicitly Islamic. On the contrary, in the Palestinian case discussed below by Julie Peteet, the Palestinian leadership and most Palestinian communities are generally careful not to invoke Islam, a potentially divisive issue in a national movement of people of mixed religious background. The cult of female domesticity, and the special role women play in the definition of cultural authenticity and the distinction of "them" and "us," is rooted in custom and a "tradition" of social practice and social values with little explicit religious reference; the fine line between "tradition" and religion is maintained.[6] Many of the features of "authentic" gender roles are similar, of course, to the new "Islamic" writing on gender although the importance of national identity and culture, not Islam, holds center stage.

This close historical relationship between the development of nationalist movements in the Arab World and the elaboration of ideas on gender, as well as the tendency to view women as the repository of tradition and authenticity, has dogged the development of a feminist voice in the region. Mervat Hatem's chapter suggests many of the impediments to the growth of an independent feminist discourse: it has been very difficult to steer the straits between the rocks of authenticity and nationalism and the shoals of western feminism. A feminist movement or movements in the region, to be both meaningful and successful, must find a voice independent of current political projects yet fully in tune with indigenous needs and realities.

Women's Work and Development

The growth of a modern capitalist economy and its extension to almost all areas and sectors of the Arab World underlies many of the changes women have experienced, and are experiencing, in the Arab World today. The literature on women's economic activities has tended to focus on two kinds of questions. First, what kind of impact does this sort of economic growth have on women's participation in the economy: does the scope or character of women's economic contributions change in any significant way? Second, how has the custom of sexual segregation intersected with the demand for female participation: have distinct patterns of female employment tended to emerge? The idea that economic "modernization" gradually brought women out of the "traditional" confines of a *harim* or a peasant family into a "modern" labor force is no longer an accepted generalization: new research suggests far greater complexity in the process.

The stereotype of the traditional sheltered woman who contributed little to economic life outside the home fits poorly with what we now know about women, at least in Arab urban history. A range of urban occupations were open to lower-class women, including peddling, cosmology, midwifery, entertainment, and domestic service, many of which took women out of their houses and into the thoroughfares of the city. Upper-class urban women, as members of wealthy and powerful families, were often important holders of urban real estate. All the available studies of sales and purchases of urban real estate, *waqf* (property endowed ostensibly for some religious or charitable purposes) transactions, inheritance records, and merchant activities, as they were recorded in the various *shari'a* courts, arrive at similar conclusions: upper-class women owned considerable property, controlled large amounts of money, and managed some businesses themselves.[7] Margaret Meriwether's contribution on women's work in nineteenth century Aleppo not only underscores the scope of women's involvement in the "traditional" economy, but also examines the ways in which this activity changed in the course of the nineteenth century.

The economic changes of the modern period did not necessarily spell improvement for all women nor raise the level of participation in the economy. As Meriwether demonstrates for Aleppo, certain crafts that employed women, notably textiles, faltered in the face of European competition. The modern industry that emerged in the twentieth century did not compensate for this displacement: women's participation in industrial production in the Arab World is remarkably low, and both economic and cultural factors seem to play a role.[8] Whether in a poor quarter of Cairo or in a Moroccan village, the ideal woman has been the woman who remains at home caring for her husband and children. If a woman has to work, it is better to keep out of public view and away from men: laundering, spinning and weaving, the raising of small animals, and other home-based activities win social approval.[9] This is not to suggest, of course, that lower-class women do not often participate in other ways in today's urban economy. Evelyn Early's chapter on *baladi* Egyptian businesswomen describes both the range of activities and the complexity of the connections with the wider economy that characterize the work of the many women of Cairo's busy "informal" economic sector. The basic insecurity, low remuneration, and devaluation of much of this work, however, reveals the costs to women of relegation to the "informal" sector.

The importance of economic factors to the development of female work patterns, on the other hand, has been made abundantly clear in the wake of some of the economic changes of recent decades. As male workers migrated to the Gulf from Egypt, Jordan, and the Occupied Territories (the West Bank and Gaza) in response to a demand for labor in the oil-producing countries beginning in earnest in the 1970s, women entered factories as replacement labor, or, in some cases, migrated themselves. The ways in which such an economic change intersects with social and political change to alter work patterns is perhaps most dramatic in the Palestinian community in the West Bank and Gaza. Souad Dajani aptly stresses the need to understand the larger socioeconomic and political context in which women find themselves. Palestinian women face the long-term emigration as well as temporary migration of significant numbers of men, the economic shock of integration with the Israeli economy with resulting inflation, water and capital shortages, and the erosion of family ties. Economic necessity has pushed many of them into the labor market, but the underdevelopment of educational and training programs, as well as health facilities, has made their work particularly burdensome. Dajani reminds us that the patterns and the implications of female labor must be located in each specific context. In addition, the changes in consciousness among the women who find themselves not only in the labor force but also, in many cases, the mainstays of their families and their communities cannot be overemphasized. Once women have taken on new kinds of daily activities, we can expect their ideas about their own social and political roles to change. As women's entry into the formal labor market pushes against the old boundaries, their access to formal political power invariably becomes an issue.

Politics and Power

In the study of women and politics today, most writers are careful to avoid viewing society as a public/private dichotomy in which politics belongs to the public world of men and family belongs to the private world of women. A striking feature of political life in the Arab World, in some cases right up to the present, is the permeability of the boundaries between the public and private spheres.[10] Whereas formal politics—the public institutions that have the power to make and enforce decisions about society—have excluded women until relatively recently, a range of informal political activities, undertaken at the family or community level, have always been critical to the political system. Despite the fact that the ideal of female seclusion and the practice of sexual segregation is ingrained in the Middle East, women have not been entirely closed off from political power, thanks to a multiplicity of techniques of influence-mongering and manipulation. The political importance of marriage alliances, for example, given that marriage arrangements are often controlled by women, has accorded women considerable power in the sphere of informal politics. Still, there is much reason to believe that this informal road to power is gradually narrowing as the sphere of formal politics expands.

Women have not been strangers to other kinds of political activity, including the peasant revolts, urban uprisings, and the street demonstrations that were and are so important to the nationalist movements of many Arab countries. In Egypt, for example, as Margot Badran illustrates, women of middle-class background participated in street demonstrations and the political mobilization of other women in the Egyptian Revolution of 1919. But although women participated actively in various struggles of national liberation in Egypt and elsewhere, they have not necessarily been rewarded with access to formal political power or greater sensitivity to women's issues. As Badran points out, activist Egyptian women were even barred from attending the opening of the Parliament they had struggled for: the only women allowed through the door were the wives of ministers and other prominent officials.

In Egypt, such exclusion, coupled with the many socioeconomic changes in upper-class lifestyle, including urbanization, educational reform, and improved transportation, incubated a self-consciously feminist movement—the first in the Arab World. The Egyptian Feminist Union (EFU), led by Huda Shaarawi, directed its energies toward reforming the national political agenda in such a way as to take women's concerns into consideration: it lobbied for political rights, educational opportunities, and legal reform, particularly of marriage and divorce laws. It is Badran's contribution not only to document the history of this prototypical movement, but also to give major credit for introducing feminist ideas to the women who led the movement, rather than to a handful of sympathetic male intellectuals.

Although the EFU was successful in part (women do have at least legal access to the political process and to political office in Egypt), it also encountered, as have all subsequent feminist movements, the tensions which have plagued the relationship between the nationalist and feminist movements throughout the region. The EFU began in strong alliance with European feminism, and only gradually moved toward its eventual endorsement of an Arab feminism with nationalist resonance. The very existence of a European feminist movement was a problem, both in the imposing of its agenda on Arab feminists (the struggle against the veil is a good example), and in the unfortunate association of feminism with the West and thus with everything the nationalist movement stands against. In many cases, Arab feminists have dealt with this problem by working within the nationalist movement, by trying to expand the political agenda of nationalist movements to include women's issues rather than establishing independent women's organizations.

Both Sondra Hale and Rosemary Sayigh examine this phenomenon, albeit in very different contexts. Hale's study of the Sudan Communist Party (SCP), which was one of the strongest mass-based political parties in the region in the 1950s and 1960s, shows how many members of the Women's Union of the Party, although extraordinarily active in their outreach to other women through educational and health programs, were not able to gain an independent voice in the Party. In fact, according to Hale, the Women's Union found itself in the position of providing a "women-as-Greek-chorus" for approval of the Party's policies. The opportunity to use the strength and broad base of the party to fashion a committed indigenous feminist movement was lost.

Similarly, according to Sayigh, the Palestinian movement has dealt with feminism very gingerly. The involvement of women in the movement in Lebanon, as social service workers, organizers, and even occasionally as fighters, could not but result in greater freedom of movement for women and higher levels of political activity. Such changes did not, however, bring women into decision-making positions within the Palestinian movement. The General Union of Palestinian Women, part of the Palestine Liberation Organization, has lacked the autonomy to formulate and promote women's issues effectively, apparently because of the belief that women's issues must take a back seat to the demands of the nationalist movement.

The idea that women's issues, at least as they might be formulated by an independent feminist movement, would promote tensions and derail the political struggle for national or social liberation is deeply rooted in the thinking of much of the male leadership today. There is debate about the best current strategy among feminists themselves: in part 1 of this volume, Hatem clearly takes a position for the establishment of a fully independent women's movement as central to the promotion of women's issues while Dajani, in part 2, appears much more sanguine about the prospects for change within the existing structures. What the issues are and are not needs to be explored with reference to the realities and perceptions of gender roles and relations, and how they are changing, in the region.

Gender Roles and Relations

The construction of gender roles and relations at a concrete level by social institutions, the question of how these roles and relations are changing, and the ways in which these relations and criticism of them find literary expression constitutes the fourth broad area of current concern. Many of the papers in this volume assume the centrality of the family and community to the elaboration and enforcement of particular notions of male and female behavior, as well as to the question of how women and men should interact. Although almost all studies of and discussions about Arab women, whether they revolve around the issues of dominant gender discourses, economic participation, or political access, make certain assumptions about the social and psychological aspects of gender, this area is still relatively neglected in the feminist literature on the Arab World. It may well be that the tendency of some of the existing social and psychological literature to view women as the quintessential victims of Arab society or to dwell on the exotic or shocking (female circumcision, veiling) has discouraged feminist scholars. The problem of "otherness" as a dominant conceptual approach to Arab society is discussed in the context of studies of the Arab family in my chapter, which begins the final part of this volume.

The importance of the family to the daily construction of gender roles and relations is never questioned. We actually know, however, very little about the ongoing evolution of the family in any specific context. There has been a tendency to assume the existence of a "traditional" family, a family defined and regulated by Islamic law, that has remained unchanged throughout the centuries. In my discussion I review the historical evidence that suggests considerable diversity of family structure and gender relations, at least in the city of Cairo and the town of Nablus, from class to class. Although all the families studied were governed by the same Islamic laws regulating marriage arrangements, marital relations, divorce, child custody, polygyny, etc., the urban poor placed far less weight on marriage arrangements, married their women at more advanced ages, and countenanced fairly high rates of divorce. There is no one traditional family, just as there is no one traditional social life for women. The ideal of female seclusion was clearly observed primarily in the breach by the urban poor, whose women could ill afford to keep off the streets and out of the market. We need to keep in mind that our ideas about traditional gender roles and relations are not based, by and large, on much historical evidence, and we therefore should proceed with caution in any discussion of change.

Just as we have come to recognize the many varieties of gender relations of the past, so we need to stress the importance of context in any discussion of the current transformation of gender relations. Susan Davis explores the specific social and economic setting of ongoing change in gender relations in a Moroccan town. In her account, the vision of a typically "Arab" or "Islamic" pattern of domestic relations recedes in the face of her study of the way adolescents adapt their views of gender relations and their behavior to the new mobility and experiences they have. If there is anything here which may be typical of much of the region, it is the speed of this change, a speed that parallels the rapid pace of socioeconomic change in the Arab World as a whole. It is less clear that this kind of change in the attitudes and behavior of adolescent girls will survive their marriages and integration into female domesticity. Variations in the definition of gender roles and relations, over the course of a lifetime or in response to economic or political imperatives, have probably always occurred throughout the history of the region.

Although we still have very few studies of the social and psychological aspects of gender relations, discussions of women's writing often yield insights into their own views on gender. There has been a good deal of attention paid to the women artists and writers of the twentieth century when women clearly began to play a central role in the development of new art forms, including poetic free verse, the novel, and painting and sculpture. The chapter by Evelyne Accad demonstrates how women novelists have developed their ideas about gender in the Arab World over the last few decades. According to Accad, an overwhelming concern with the existential issues of personal freedom in the 1950s and early 1960s first gave way to a more focused treatment of gender issues and a faith in political solutions for the oppression women suffered on a personal level. Most recently, the limitations of both nationalist policies and male views on the reform of gender relations have emerged as themes. Arab women novelists appear to be growing more forthright in their criticism of the prevailing arrangements. We cannot assume, of course, that the views of gender relations expressed by educated women necessarily resonate in all social circles, but it seems that such questioning and criticism has, at least, a solid middle-class audience.

Conclusion

The title of this volume, the notion of old boundaries and new frontiers, posits the present as a time of change, of tension, of strain for women in the Arab World. The "old boundaries" are not, however, the boundaries of some mythic traditional universe, nor are the "new frontiers" the brave new world of the modern West. Rather, the boundaries this volume examines have been drawn by the specific historical experiences of the various parts of the Arab World. Some of these boundaries appear to be common to much of the region.

The weight of Islam and authenticity in gender discourse, a certain distance from the idea that women can work in public space, the restriction of women to indirect access to power, and a definition of gender roles that emphasizes female domesticity all reflect a past in which the gender system undergirded a family-based organization of access to wealth and power. These boundaries were, and are, more fixed in some parts of the Arab World than in others, but they are at least recognizable features of public discourse and social organization almost everywhere.

The new frontiers are, I believe, the ways in which the ideas about gender and the realities of women's lives are changing. It is true that women, at least some of them, have much better access to education, to satisfying work, and, to a lesser extent, to political power. In many places, political mobilization of the population as a whole has at least brought women into mass politics. These gains did not, of course, come automatically out of a period of social, economic, and political change but were, in many instances, hard won by women themselves and their male allies. These gains also help place some women in a position from where they can participate in the ongoing debate about the meaning of gender in Arab society. There is the very real possibility that Arab women could sustain a powerful pan-Arab women's movement, one which could give real meaning to the dream of an authentic indigenous feminism.

NOTES

1. See Rosemary Sayigh, "Roles and Functions of Arab Women," *Arab Studies Quarterly* 3, no. 3 (1981), 258–74.

2. See Mounira Charrad, "State and Gender in the Maghrib," *Middle East Report*, no. 163 (March-April 1990), 19–24.

3. Fatima Mernissi, *Beyond the Veil: Male-Female Dynamics in a Modern Muslim Society* (Cambridge: Schenkman, 1975). See also Fatna Sabbah, *Women in the Muslim Unconscious*, trans. Mary Jo Lakeland (New York: Pergamon Press, 1984).

4. For information on colonial policy in Egypt, see Judith E. Tucker, *Women in Nineteenth-Century Egypt* (Cambridge: Cambridge University Press, 1985), chap. 3, pp. 102–31.

5. Nora Benallegue, "Algerian Women in the Struggle for Independence and Reconstruction," *International Social Science Journal* 35, no. 4 (1983), 703–17.

6. Rema Hammami, "Women, the Hijab and the Intifada," *Middle East Report*, no. 164/165 (1990), 24–28.

7. Gabriel Baer, "Women and Waqf: An Analysis of the Istanbul Tahrir of 1546," *Asian and African Studies* (Jerusalem) 17, nos. 1–3 (1983), 9–28; Abraham Marcus, "Men, Women, and Property: Dealers in Real Estate in Eighteenth Century Aleppo," *Journal of the Economic and Social History of the Orient* 26, no. 2 (1983), 137–63; Judith Tucker, *Women*, chap. 2, pp. 64–101.

8. Earl L. Sullivan, *Women in Egyptian Public Life* (Syracuse: Syracuse University

Press, 1986); Nadia Haggag Youssef, *Women and Work in Developing Countries* (Berkeley: Institute of International Studies, 1974).

9. Susan Schaeffer Davis, "Working Women in a Moroccan Village," in Lois Beck and Nikki Keddie, *Women in the Muslim World* (Cambridge: Harvard University Press, 1978), pp. 416–33; and Andrea Rugh, "Women and Work Strategies and Choices in a Lower-Class Quarter of Cairo," in E. W. Fernea, ed., *Women and the Family in the Middle East* (Austin: University of Texas Press, 1985), pp. 273–88.

10. Cynthia Nelson, "Public and Private Politics: Women in the Middle Eastern World," *American Ethnologist* 1 (1974), 551–63.

I

Gender Discourses

I

WOMEN'S ISSUES IN MODERN ISLAMIC THOUGHT

Barbara F. Stowasser

The customer of religious bookstores, streetvendors' stalls, and publishers' outlets in the Middle East today gains the impression that the titles available on "women in Islam" are more numerous than those on any other single topic, and that they sell briskly. A veritable avalanche of publications, ranging from biographies of the wives of the Prophet to primers for the contemporary Muslim girl and wife, from theoretical discussions of women's place in contemporary society to pamphlets on Islamic dress and the evils of makeup and "embellishment," indicate that women's issues have become a major concern in contemporary Islamic Middle Eastern culture.

On the basis of their doctrines, assertions, and intentions, i.e., their ideological orientation, the authors of this literature can roughly be divided into modernists, conservatives, and fundamentalists or integrists; and it is worthwhile to note that the bulk of this voluminous literature is produced by the latter groups, the conservatives and the fundamentalists. The criteria by which these divisions are made here consist in the writers' philosophical stance toward the nature of Islam, their view of its role in social development, and their understanding of social reality. The modernists among them perceive Islam as a "dynamic" religion, and they emphasize its "openness" and "permissiveness" as legislated in the scriptures (Koran and Hadith) which allow them to consider the factors of time and societal change in their interpretation. To the modernists, therefore, contemporary social concerns are eminently compatible with the flexible blueprint of original Islam as realized in the way of life of the early Muslim community. They distinguish this early, open, and pure Islam from its later manifestations which resulted from the wars of

This paper is based on research done in Jordan and Egypt in 1985 funded by a Fulbright-Hays Training Grant and a Social Science Research Council fellowship. Its writing was made possible by a 1986 Georgetown University Summer Research Grant. A shorter version of this paper was published in *Arab Studies Quarterly*, vol. 9, no. 3 (Summer 1987).

expansion, the internationalization of Islam, and a host of ultimately damaging acculturation processes. In their efforts to show the compatibility of modern social and political ideas with early Islamic norms—i.e., in their efforts to legitimize these ideas in Islamic terms—the modernists rely on an individual interpretation of the scriptures (*ijtihad*) and deemphasize the *shari'a* as well as the processes that led to its formation, especially the process and principle of community consensus. The conservatives, on the other hand, view Islam as an inherited, balanced system of faith and action which is both based on the scriptures and interpreted by the verifying authority of community consensus. Spokesmen of this community consensus are, of course, the lawyer-theologians. The core of Islam is the *shari'a*. The conservatives' understanding of Islam, then, provides for some adaptation of the scriptures to the needs of the age; but the processes involved require consensus-building and institutionalization, not only individual effort, and thus have to unfold within the boundaries of Islamic law. Ultimately, the emphasis is on balance and stability. Traditional customs (*'adat*) are sanctioned in Islamic terms. In their perspective, balance, even if it be achieved through compromise, is more important than the ideological purity of the system and its application. As for the fundamentalists, they insist on the "static" and immutable nature of Islam as legislated in the scriptures. Everyday reality is judged as being either right or wrong, "righteous" or "sinful." The objective and absolute criteria by which this distinction is made are the eternally valid norms and laws laid down in the Koran and interpreted in the Prophet's Sunna. According to the fundamentalists, then, social reality and social development have no influence *on* religion, while religion unilaterally shapes and guides them from above. There is one holistic Islam which, revealed to and lived by the Seal of the Prophets, Muhammad, is the final and all-inclusive religion of mankind. As Absolute Truth, valid for all times, places, and nations, it does not undergo or adapt to change. Even though it was revealed in human time, it is not historically conditioned by it. Thus, individual religious thought as interpretation of the scriptures plays a crucial role in social development. It spells out the divinely established, eternally valid order and thereby ensures that society lives righteously by the Word and the Law of God. Religious thought thus shares in the features of God's revelation which are directive power and immutability. Society may lag behind in hearing and adopting the ideal blueprint thus conveyed; but what is real is always the message, not its temporary, frail, and fallible realization and application. The less society conforms to the ideal, the more urgent is the fundamentalists' demand for change and purification.

In presenting the interpretations of contemporary Muslim thinkers and writers on women's issues, this paper deals with "religious ideas" in two meanings of the term: first, ideas as religious norms and, second, ideas in the sense of interpretative thoughts of the religiously committed concerning those norms. This paper's aim, however, is not to engage in scripturalism for its own sake. As an outsider to the Islamic order, its author observes and must take into consideration that "religious ideas" are linked with social reality in mutually affective relationships. We as observers do not share our pious Muslim writers' *belief* that religious ideas shape social reality from above, but view these ideas as existing in a state of tension with this reality, shaping it and being shaped by it in turn. Methodologically, this approach owes much to Clifford Geertz's definition of religion as a cultural system of symbols[1] in which "religious patterns" (made up of clusters of such symbols) are "frames of perception, symbolic screens through which experience is interpreted" while also being "guides for action, blueprints for conduct."[2] Religious interpretations share in bearing this double aspect. As modes of "symbolic formulation" they, like the system they formulate, grow out of experience by which they are shaped, while perceiving wider truths and norms which they expound in order to influence and shape that experience. The symbolic dimension merits our great attention and effort. But it is understood that its presentation here will tell only one part of the story, while other parts will emerge from the chapters in this volume that deal with the factual dimension—social reality.

Interpretational Approaches

Despite the differences in their doctrines and intentions, the interpreters of women's issues in Islam today share an ethical-religious ("symbolic") approach insofar as they purport to simply state what is "legislated by God" on this subject and hence is "truly Islamic." This approach translates into a shared technique in that the interpreters base their argumentation on the Koranic text and on the Hadith. Regardless of sophistication, learning, or aspirations, the argumentation remains couched in scripturalist terms and concentrates on the theoretical interpretation of the eternally valid word of God and the Sunna of the tacitly inspired, infallible Prophet and his collectively inspired Companions. As bases of their paradigms, contemporary Muslim interpreters use a very small number of the hundred or so Koranic verses that deal with women's issues. Most important among them are 2 (*Baqara*):228 and 4 (*Nisa*):34 (on status); 2 (*Baqara*):282 (on witnessing), 33 (*Ahzab*):59 and 24 (*Nur*):31 (on clothing and public behavior), and 33 (*Ahzab*):33 (on segregation and staying in the house). The fact that the resulting paradigms of the "truly Islamic" status of women vary widely should, however, not be surprising. Both the Koran and the Hadith have through the history of Islam been highly adaptable sacred texts. In the case of the Koran, its directives are general, broad, and flexible in most cases; therefore, they could be translated into the terms of a specific social reality by each generation of interpreters. Concerning the Hadith, it was both a record of the way of life of the early community and a dynamic vehicle of the process of Islamization.[3] In this latter capacity, it mirrors the growth and development of Islam and contains an abundance of contradictory traditions from which later interpreters chose various details to substantiate their varied teachings.

Scripturalist interpretation is much more than a pious technique. It is a vital mechanism for the functioning of religion. The importance of religion, to return to Geertz's definition, consists in "its capacity to serve, for an individual or for a group, as a source of general, yet distinctive, conceptions of the world, the self, and the relations between them. . . . Religious concepts spread beyond their specifically metaphysical contexts to provide a framework of general ideas in terms of which a wide range of experience—intellectual, emotional, moral—can be given meaningful form."[4] In its understanding of reality, religious perspective differs from the common-sensical and from the scientific one. Unlike the former, it "moves beyond the realities of everyday life to wider ones which correct and complete them," and unlike the latter, it "questions the realities of everyday life not out of an institutionalized scepticism . . . but in terms of what it takes to be wider, non-hypothetical truths."[5] One such symbol of faith is the ideal of the united, unified Islamic community, the *umma*.[6] As such, this ideal continues to prevail in the contemporary literature on women's issues, which lacks local specificity and consistently speaks to the problematic of "the Muslim woman," not the Egyptian or the Jordanian or the Turkish Muslim woman. By carefully scrutinizing the available literature, it may be possible to establish a set of regional coordinates within which Muslim writers take into special consideration those problems that plague their region most (family disintegration because of male and/or female labor migration; working mothers; country-urban migration resulting in uprootedness and alienation; overpopulation; unemployment, etc.). The intent of this literature, however, is a different one. As a literature of faith, it means to speak, indeed has to speak, in terms of Islamic unity and to address women's concerns as a pan-Islamic issue.

The status of women in Muslim society is an entity of faith (a "symbol") and thus has implications for the religion of Islam as a whole. Whether the interpreters intend to "modernize" women's status or whether they want to maintain or reestablish a threatened "traditional" or "original" order, they are in all cases dealing with issues that go beyond the women themselves and involve concerns such as political legitimacy, human rights questions, and the like. It is not surprising, therefore, to find that the literature produced by the conservative and fundamentalist interpreters is pervaded by a mood of anguish and disorientation that stems from the discrepancy between ideal reality and everyday experience. Their ideal order is one of freedom, lawfulness, social equality, economic justice, affluence, unity, and victory; its social structure is patriarchal, its women are veiled and excluded from the public sphere. Everyday reality, on the other hand, is marked by oppressive economic, political, sociodemographic, and cultural problems which must be played out in a world that has shrunk to domestic dimensions; the patriarchal structures are neither solid nor unquestioned any longer, as women are gaining access to education, the professions, and to institutionalized political power. In anguished rejection and calling for action, the conservative and fundamentalist thinkers take a defensive stand against modernity, which they perceive in terms of westernization and, hence, cultural contamination. The restrictive tenor of their injunction against women's education (other than in the "suitable" fields) and participation in public life must, then, be understood from the point of view of societies undergoing traumatic changes, often in dire poverty and hopelessness, for whom ideal symbol and actual reality no longer fit together. As they purport to quote the norms and guidelines provided once and for all time by the religious scriptures, these spokesmen's goal, implicitly, is to map out a strategy of resistance against the changes of modernity, perceived as cultural rape committed by outside enemies and their clients in the Islamic world. If cultural authenticity—*asala*—sign of God's favor and source of dignity, is to be preserved, cultural change must be withstood. Such anguish is missing in the works of the modernists; for them, the clash is softened by their acceptance of a changing world.

With regard to women's questions, the lines that separate the modernists' (reformists') exegesis from that of the conservatives are fairly clearly drawn; they are much less clearly drawn between conservative and fundamentalist thought. Here, the difference is mainly one of mood, of tone, of decibel, as much as it is of engagement and emphasis on the need to act, and to act now.

As for the religious establishment, the *'ulama*, proponents of mainstream orthodoxy, most often support the policies of their governments, even though they may speak differently in private and may even undermine in practice some of those official policies. This writer's research in Egypt and Jordan indicates that, at least in these two countries, few of the establishment *'ulama* belong to the modernist camp. Most are conservatives, and a small number speak the language of the fundamentalists. This is certainly related to the fact that the fundamentalists, such as the members of the jam'iyyat in Egypt, oppose government policy in their political, economic, and social platform, which the *'ulama*, as salaried servants of the state, cannot afford to do. Regardless of ideological orientation, however, the *'ulama* are set apart by their knowledge of the *shari'a* and their familiarity with the correct procedures in tafsir (exegesis), Hadith criticism, and fatwa (legal opinion) writing. As professionals in these fields, they are critical of individual ijtihad (individual and partial interpretation of the sources) that lacks serious consideration both for the principle of consensus (*ijma'*) and for the traditional law codes. This attitude continues to shape Islamic conservatism, which most *'ulama* support; it has also led to conservative attacks on the *ijtihad* methods of the modernists, most of whom are lay thinkers.[7] Because of the fact that the theological conservative stance agrees with the fundamentalist one on women's issues, however, the latter's individualist approach, as well as its high degree of politicization, have on the whole escaped similar attacks.

The Modernists

Modernism is alive in the Middle East today, but it appears weakened and is less influential than it was just a few decades ago. The modernists or reformists are the proponents of the back-to-the-Koran and onward-to-modernity school of thought that was given shape and cohesion at the turn of the century by the Egyptian theologian and legal authority Muhammad Abduh. While Abduh and his disciples taught that Islam is compatible with modernity, they did not go very far in their proposals for changing and modernizing the status of women. Here, Abduh's, and later Rashid Rida's, theoretical-theological argumentation was much more advanced than their application of that theory to women's questions. Their theoretical breakthrough consisted in the fact that they separated—in the Koran and in the *shari'a*—the *'ibadat* (religious observances) from the *mu'amalat* (social transactions) of which family law is a major part.[8] Their purpose in making this distinction was to establish that while the *'ibadat* do not admit of interpretative change, the *mu'amalat* allow for considerable interpretation and adaptation by each generation of Muslims in light of the practical needs of their age. This led them to some modernist Koranic interpretation in the area of women's rights within the family. These interpretations, however, were put forth not for the benefit of women in and of themselves but in order to bring about a moral rebirth of Islamic society.

Abduh saw the remedy against the moral disintegration of Muslim society and, especially, the Egyptian society of his time in the "re-Islamization" of the family.[9] He proceeded from the premise that women's status is causally linked with the well-being or decay of social life as a whole, and that this truth was demonstrated to the Muslims in the Koranic revelations. The community, however, "takes of the revelation only that for which it is ready," and so this truth was disregarded as the people reverted to the ignorance of the Jahiliyya, to which they added the licentiousness and animal drives they had learned from the Franks. "See how we have become an argument against our religion!"[10]

Among the reform measures which Abduh proposed were, first, the education of women in the obligations and rights established for them by their religion. "How can a nation prosper in this life and the next when one half of its members are like beasts of burden, neglecting their duties toward God, themselves, and their relatives?"[11] Second, he called for the education of the men "in the true meaning of Islam" which would make them give up all selfishness, material greed, power hunger, and love of tyranny; they would then begin to deal with their wives in the spirit of "love and compassion" and equality, as enjoined by the Koran.[12] "Know that the men who try to be masters in their houses by oppressing the women beget but slaves for others."[13] Third, this would lead to the reestablishment of righteous marriage as "solemn covenant," which is part of the natural order of being,[14] as well as to a reconfirmation of the "exact equivalence" of the spouses. In this God-willed, natural order the man is charged with "leadership" to protect domestic life and well-being, and is to the wife as the head is to the body. He merits this leadership because his physical constitution is stronger, more perfect, complete, and beautiful, as is the case with the males in all species (recognizable in the human species in man's beauty of beard and moustache). This physical constitution in turn is linked to a stronger mind and sounder perceptions, along the lines of *mens sana in corpore sano*. Woman's role in this natural order is to be in charge of all domestic affairs, for which she has to be trained in order to cope with all modern exigencies. Man is in charge of all work outside of the house. Therein consists the "exact equivalence" of the spouses.[15]

As he described the oppression of women by men in his own society in terms of a poison that affected society in all of its aspects, Abduh emphasized several manifestations of this oppression, most importantly among them the practice of polygamy. It was this theme that led him to his most daringly innovative Koranic interpretations and *fatwas* in which he called to abolish polygamy in Islam. He argued that while polygamy was a sound practice among the righteous early believers, it had developed into a corrupt practice of unbridled lust, without justice or equity, in his own time. "A nation that practices polygamy cannot be educated. Religion was revealed for the benefit of its people; if one of its provisions begins to harm rather than benefits the community . . . the application of that provision has to be changed according to the changed needs of the group."[16] "Exceptions will always remain possible—as in the case of a barren wife—but must be decided upon by a judge. There is no impediment to this in religion. What prevents [its implementation] is merely custom (*'ada*)."[17] Abduh was equally concerned with the harmful effects of divorce on public morality. He described the inequities of the divorce system on women at great length and in passionate language. But instead of engaging in innovative *ijtihad* on this issue, he merely exhorted the men to mend their ways and live up to their religiously sanctioned obligations toward their wives, former wives, and children. As for women's rights to divorce, he merely stated that a wife may request divorce with a judge if there is "harm" to her from her husband, such as unlawful neglect, unlawful beating, abuse, etc.; in these cases, the burden of proof rests with the wife.[18]

Abduh's ideas have been presented here in some detail for several reasons. His methods of *ijtihad* remain the staple of modernists to this day while continuing to be rejected by the conservative thinkers, especially the *'ulama*, even though the great lecture hall at the Azhar now bears Abduh's name—a contradictory symbol of sorts. As for the fundamentalists, they are still so agitated by his methodology as well as his doctrine that they accuse Abduh of collusion with imperialist circles.[19] Second, the issues identified by Abduh remain important today and are far from resolved. Third, what Abduh's interpretation shares with contemporary thought is the fact that his interest lay clearly with the weal of Islamic society as a whole and not with women's rights *per se*. Like Rashid Rida,[20] whose work on these issues he influenced profoundly, Abduh was concerned with reform in the sense of correction, amendment, and restrengthening of the Islamic order. Like all other, later writers on women's issues, including even the nationalists and socialists among them, he saw women's liberation from male oppression as an essential precondition for the building of a virtuous society, and not as liberation for the benefit of women.[21]

Abduh's and Rida's theoretical stance on the adaptability of the rules of *mu'amalat* by each successive generation was developed by the Egyptian journalist, lawyer, and politician Qasim Amin, author of *Tahrir al-Mar'a* (The liberation of women, 1899) and *al-Mar'a al-Jadida* (The new woman, 1900).[22] Of these two works, the second was written as a rebuttal to the attacks on the first; in reality, however, it goes far beyond it in its call for modernity and marks an ideological shift in Qasim Amin's attitude toward western culture in general and secularism in particular. In *al-Mar'a al-Jadida*, Amin demanded women's rights to higher education in all fields, in preparation for professional careers, either in "cases of need" (such as for bachelor women, widows, childless women, and the like) or "to benefit the family."[23] He identified women's education as a life-long pursuit of gathering experiences, applying knowledge, and participating fully in all social activities.[24] More importantly, he saw this freedom to work and to grow as women's "natural right" which flows from their intellectual and spiritual equality with men.[25] Women's freedom to him had become a question of human rights; it was within this context that he perceived its importance for the progress and perfection of society as a whole.[26] This secularist approach to women's issues was the result of Amin's increasingly positive attitude toward the West; Europe and, especially, America to him provided the model which the East should follow, since "the countries where women enjoy freedom and all their rights . . . lead all other nations on the path of perfection."[27] The more the East imitates the West, the better off it will be; to speak of European morality as "corrupt" and of Islamic civilization as "spiritually superior" is merely wishful thinking, the revenge of the impotent, a "lullaby."[28]

Unlike this pro-western work with its use of western sources and its secular arguments, Amin's first book on women's issues, *Tahrir al-Mar'a*, reflects the ideology and methodology of Islamic reformism and shows the influence of Abduh (which has led some, including the editor of the complete works of both men, to assert that Abduh wrote some of its chapters).[29] All proposed reforms are here justified in Islamic language and are presented as a return to the original order of Islam. Reform will be made possible through the education of women, which is their right, as they were created as the spiritual and intellectual equals of men. Education is the magic process that will transform the women from the pets, the servants, and the possessions they are in the urban middle and upper classes of Egypt into full human beings.[30] In this way, they will become full partners for their modern, educated husbands whose attraction they will be able to hold once they have learned to clean and groom themselves properly; more importantly, they will be transformed into competent and knowledgeable mothers capable of shaping a better generation of children.[31] All they require, however, is an elementary education supplemented by ongoing contacts with real life outside of the home, through which they will acquire practical minds and freedom from superstition.[32] Women's education has to include physical training in order to combat the prevailing problems of obesity, anemia, and premature aging.[33] As Qasim Amin lashed out against the *hijab* as the main barrier to women's growth and the main source of their ignorance, he used this term in the sense of seclusion in the home, sexual segregation, and the face veil. He insisted on women's right to mobility outside of the house and demanded adaptation of *shar'i* veiling (which leaves face and hands uncovered) as the only truly Islamic garb.[34] To ensure that this form of dress would not lead to general corruption was men's responsibility; Amin called upon the men to learn to control themselves rather than merely to rely on the women to remove temptation from their paths.[35]

Beyond an elementary education, women must also be given the same rights as men in the choice of their marriage partner.[36] Polygamy is a destructive "custom" that must be eradicated and may lawfully be forbidden by the ruler as a measure taken "in the public interest."[37] Divorce for men should be established according to a new government-legislated procedure that would involve a judge, witnesses, and a divorce document, and women must be awarded greater rights in initiating divorce along the lines of Maliki—not Hanafi—law in Egypt.[38] These measures in their totality would strengthen the Muslim family in spiritual, cultural, and economic terms; thus, they would fortify the nation as a whole and enable it to stand up in the battle against the exploitative powers of the West.[39] In this battle, Amin perceived the theologians and jurists as backward and selfish and hence not just as useless, but as presenting a major national handicap.[40]

It is significant that of Amin's two works on women, only *Tahrir al-Mar'a* is easily available and continues to be cited in Islamic women's literature today. Its main themes remain controversial, but its argumentation on the basis of Islamic sources and within the framework of Islamic culture continue to make it accessible and meaningful to Muslim thinkers, if only as the goal of their attacks. Thus, its ongoing controversiality, as opposed to the now obscure and neglected status of *al-Mar'a al-Jadida*, is an important indication of the structure, the argumentation, and the language of the contemporary Islamic dialogue on women. Only criticism of the western model and arguments clad in Islamic language are admissible and taken seriously today.

The modernist school of thought continues to bear the imprint of Abduh's argumentation and Amin's choice of crucial issues. Prominent among the later modernists was Mahmud Shaltut (d. 1963), Rector of the Azhar and ally of Gamal Abdul-Nasser, who opened the doors of the Azhar to women, albeit on a different campus and in disciplines other than the traditional religious ones. Shaltut insisted that the Muslim woman has the Islamic right to be educated because of her creation as man's partner and her status as his equal in religious responsibility.[41] New issues, however, now came to be emphasized in addition to the traditional modernist ones. Shaltut argued for women's right to political participation because the Prophet sought and received the women's *bay'a* (pledge of allegiance) in Medina.[42] In the question of polygamy, however, Shaltut differed from the modernists preceding him. Not only did he insist that polygamy is "a part of Islam and sanctioned by the *shari'a*," but he also called for state support of polygamous families among the poor. Yvonne Haddad is undoubtedly right when she links this stance with Shaltut's overriding concern for social justice in Islam, which had to clash with the 1945 proposal of the Egyptian Ministry of Social Affairs to introduce legislation restricting the number of wives to one except in cases of the husband's established and proven means to support two or more.[43]

An important voice in contemporary Islamic modernism is Muhammad Ahmad Khalaf Allah, whose books *al-Qur'an wa-Mushkilat Hayatina al-Mu'asira* (The Koran and the problems of our contemporary life, 1967) and *Dirasat fil-Nuzum wal-Tashri'at al-Islamiyya* (Studies in Islamic systems and legislations, 1977) represent a further stage in the development of modernism. Dr. Khalaf Allah first gained fame—or notoriety—in 1947–48 with his dissertation, *al-Fann al-Qisasi fil-Qur'an* (The art of storytelling in the Koran), under Shaykh Amin al-Khuli, which was rejected, under pressure from the Azhar, by Fuad University (now the University of Cairo).[44] He obtained his doctorate with another dissertation and embarked on a career of teaching and writing; at present, he is the editor of the influential journal *al-Yaqza al-'Arabiyya* and thus an important modernist voice in Egypt today. He was prominently involved in the formulation of the 1985 personal status law in Egypt. His methodology is that of individual *ijtihad*. Concerning law reform, he maintains that the majority consensus of all citizens, as voice of the public interest, does and should lead to civil legislation on the basis of the *shari'a*.[45]

Khalaf Allah maintains that the Koran gives women political rights which they freely exercised during the Prophet's lifetime but which were then disregarded by the early caliphs. Most notable among these is the right to elect the head of state. Women who demand the franchise, therefore, are merely asking that their legitimate Islamic rights be returned to them.[46] The Koran not only gives women the right to work, including the right to work outside the home; rather, women in Islam are under a social and religious obligation to work, as no development is possible without women's participation in the work force.[47] The Koran does not prescribe a particular "Islamic dress" for women.

Of the two verses revealed on this topic, one (33:59) prescribes a garment that helped to distinguish the free woman from the slave in seventh-century Arabia, while the other (24:31) demands modesty, but does so from both sexes (24:30–31). These verses on dress, then, were revealed as a call for reform of public conduct and etiquette in the early community against the still prevailing customs of the Jahiliyya. Clothing styles, however, change with the times and with social conditions, just as do the rules of etiquette and the norms of public behavior. Similar developments are observable in other practices, such as in warfare, where the Koranic norms on martial participation and the sharing of the spoils are now no longer applied.[48] In marriage, Muslim women have the right to choose their husbands, even from among the members of the other Religions of the Book. On the question of polygamy, Khalaf Allah opines that this Islamic practice may be necessary at certain times; he stipulates that it is the right of Muslim society to legislate whether polygamy is in the public interest at any given time or not.[49] The notion of man's "superiority" over women, commonly argued on the basis of Koran 2:228 and 4:34, is—according to Khalaf Allah—an incorrect one which resulted from a faulty interpretation of the texts. What the Koran says on man's status in respect to the woman merely concerns his role as head of the family. The family is a unit of production in which tasks must be organized and distributed; to do so is man's responsibility as the family's provider and protector.[50] In the matter of divorce, women have a share in the decision to divorce, but to a lesser degree than men. Even so, these limited rights represent a great step forward for women, when compared to the practices of the Jahiliyya.[51]

Khalaf Allah's interpretation, then, is in the modernist tradition, as he relies on a form of historicized *ijtihad* that considers both the factor of historical change and the concept of a changing "public interest." He finds the notions of progress and modernity as well as their manifestations compatible with and sanctioned by the early Islamic norms as they existed before the beginning of the medieval acculturation processes that eventually "polluted" them and led to the stagnation and backwardness of the Islamic world.

Khalaf Allah's main concerns no longer lie with women's right to education, but with their right to participation in public life. Like the modernists/reformists before him, he does not tangle much with family structure, and does not propose to undo the patriarchal order of Islam. It is noteworthy that this has been the orientation of Islamic modernism as a whole. With some ingenuity, the modernists could very well construct an Islamic paradigm on the basis of the Koran which provides for *full* social equality of the sexes, including equal personal status rights, if they were to take their method of *ijtihad* and their emphasis on "the public interest" to their logical conclusions.[52] Social reality does not yet warrant such a step. Khalaf Allah, like the modernists before him, sees reform on women's issues as centrally important to the reform of society as a whole, and his vision includes women's participation in the public sector (politics and work). As for women's rights and women's freedom for women's sake, as individual human rights questions, they are none of his concern.

The Conservatives

The conservatives argue differently from the modernists. Formally, they reject the historicized *ijtihad* as well as the admissibility of such concepts as "the public interest." Instead, they maintain that the scriptures legislate what custom, in turn, has long established: the social and legal inequality of women and men. Full participation and leadership in political and religious life, as well as control of the family (including superiority of spouse over spouse) are given to the man because he is strong, and not to the woman, because she is weak. This God-willed order is laid out in the Koran,[53] clarified in the Hadith, and codified in the *shari'a* which remains binding. Not all conservatives, however, remain satisfied with the reaffirmation of the continuing validity of the Holy Law. Especially among those conservatives who are more knowledgeable about customs than legal matters, we find voices that propagate women's lower status in often pseudo-scientific laymen's terms. The aim is to go beyond women's social and legal inferiority to enumerate the physiological and psychological factors which prove the equity of this God-willed order.

When Qasim Amin called for women's education and entrance into society at large, Tal'at Harb, the Egyptian nationalist who later founded Bank Misr, responded by arguing against women's emancipation, which he saw as just another imperialist plot designed to undermine Egypt's social structure, her religion, and her morality.[54] As part of his argument, he furthermore pointed toward the absurdity of the notion of women's emancipation, since women comprehend and perceive less than men.

> All revealed laws agree that the woman is weaker than the man, that she is his inferior in body and comprehension, and that 'men are superior to women.' Thus, men rightfully have supremacy over women . . . and women's submission to men is part of God's order.[55] . . . Women were created for men's earthly pleasures and in order to take care of domestic affairs; God did not create them to attempt to defeat the men, nor to give opinions or establish policies. If God had wanted to do so, He would have given women courage, intrepidity, chivalry, and gallant audacity, which is not the case. And if women wanted to behave like men and carry heavy burdens to be his equal . . . would this not be a shirking of the duty assigned them by the Almighty?[56]

Women were created constitutionally different from men. The heart of the female weighs only four-fifths that of the male (at birth), her respiratory organs are weaker, and western science has furthermore established that the average weight gain of the brain of the female infant is less than that of the male. In constitution and physique, women resemble children. Like children, they are emotional and, lacking analytic insight, are given to unbalanced mood shifts, from joy to sorrow, from pain to pleasure, from hatred to love.[57] Most importantly, women menstruate while men do not. Menstruation is *adhan* (Koran 2[*Baqara*]:222), which carries the connotation of both hurt and pollution. "The woman is afflicted with menstruation, with childbirth, with pregnancy and delivery, with the raising of children ... with a deficient constitution."[58]

This notion of women's constitutional, psychological, and intellectual weakness was taken to its natural limits by Abbas Mahmud al-Aqqad, a misogynist Egyptian writer and intellectual who had fallen out of love with western culture when he published two books on women's status in Islam in the fifties: *al-Mar'a fil-Qur'an* (Women in the Koran) and *Hadihil-Shajara* (This tree). These books gained wide popularity, were repeatedly reprinted, and some of the ideas are still quoted in the contemporary conservative Islamic literature on women.[59] According to Aqqad's interpretation, women's childlike qualities are destructive. Women desire what is forbidden; they are ignorant, curious, weak-willed, and unable to resist temptation.[60] Women's disobedience and love of rebellion are but functions of their dependency on the male. Even the female will and female patience are negative qualities, as women do not use these powers except to refuse. Will that manifests itself as obstinacy is feminine, whereas will that equals decisiveness is masculine. Even woman's power over the man is not born of female strength, but merely follows from the sexual desire in the male. Thus, her influence over him results from his weakness and bad habit, just as tobacco and wine only have power over him who is addicted.[61] Women are intellectually inferior to men. Aqqad supports his argument by drawing upon historical examples: while women have prepared food since prehistorical times, all the great chefs are men; while women have been dressmakers since the beginning of history, all the great designers are male.[62] Occasionally, one hears of a great woman scientist, such as Marie Curie; but in her case, she was really her husband Pierre's student and assistant to the end. At best, these "achievers" among the women are extraordinary exceptions.[63] Peace will reign in the world at large and in the small world of home and family only when the woman ceases to demand the rights of a falsely pretended "masculinity" and begins to claim her real rights, those of femininity and motherhood.[64]

Undoubtedly due to the pressures of social change and women-related governmental policies, the conservative stance on women's inferior nature began to be replaced after the fifties by a different one that stipulated not the inequality of the sexes, but rather their equality. This equality, however, was perceived as based on the immutable and complete difference in the nature of the sexes, which is part of God's plan for the world. By being completely different—as night is from day—the sexes are mutually complementary. By virtue of her anatomy, the woman is predestined to perform only one task—the noblest of all tasks—which is to bear and raise children. Her special profession was designed by the Almighty Himself as a sign of honor for the woman when He gave her an innate nature in which emotionality prevails over rationality.

> The Prophet said about the women that "they were created from a crooked rib; the most crooked part is its highest portion, and if you were to straighten it, you would break it (the breaking signifying divorce)—so enjoy her as crooked as she is." He was not blaming the woman when he said this, but was defining women's natural disposition and the preponderance of emotions over rationality, with which God has distinguished them in contradistinction to the male in whom rationality surpasses the emotions. Neither man nor woman are inferior to the other. The "crookedness" in the Hadith does not imply any corruption or imperfection in woman's nature, because it is this crookedness of hers that enables her to perform her task, which is to deal with children who need strong compassion and sympathy, not rationality. The words "the most crooked portion of the rib is its uppermost part" signify the compassion the woman feels for her child, and the supremacy of her emotion over her rational mind. On this basis, her "crookedness" has become a laudatory attribute for the woman, because this "crookedness" is in reality woman's "straightest" qualification for her task.[65]

Woman's domesticity bears a golden halo of religious significance. Her work in the home and her role as supportive wife and loving mother were designed by God Himself in her honor. To attempt to change this God-willed order of task-distribution and to compete with the male who toils outside of the home is sinful and will lead to the corruption of the whole order of being.[66] Only as wife and mother will a woman achieve rank, honor, and even her selfhood. What women do or are in the West has no relevance for Islamic society except as a warning example. In any case, there is no need to imitate the West, since women in Islam were given by God Himself the highest rank occupied by women in any culture on this earth.[67] Western interference on these issues, therefore, must be explained not just as colonialist attacks designed to disturb and weaken the Islamic weal. On an even more important level, these attacks are disturbances created by an inferior culture. This is most clearly recognizable in connection with the criticism which the West—and especially its Orientalists—hurl at Islam with regard to the institution of polygamy. Psychologically and biologically, polygamy preserves women's mental and physical purity, permits the sexes' sound natural disposition to flower, and protects the female.[68]

When the woman leaves the house on a necessary domestic errand, she has to wear the veil. The conservative thinkers in Egypt, Jordan, and Syria appear to have reached a consensus on how to interpret the Koranic verses 33 (Ahzab):59 and 24 (Nur):31, that is, how to define "Islamic dress" (zayy shar'i or zayy islami). Only very rarely does one or the other of them prescribe the wearing of the face veil.[69] For the overwhelming majority, Islamic garb consists of a garment and a headcover that hide the woman's body except for face and hands. To be truly a Muslim woman means to wear this dress; failure to do so means that the woman's faith has been shattered and that she will surely be punished by God. This is so, first, because she transgresses when she fails to wear the veil and, second, because she becomes guilty of corrupting all the males who come in contact with her and whose unbridled lust she incites.[70] But her "best *hijab*" is her home.[71]

The conservative Islamic literature differs from the modernist most importantly on the issues of women's participation in public life and women's right to work. While the modernist demands both of these rights for her with the argument that this is what original Islam provided for the woman, the conservative unconditionally and categorically rejects both the argument and its implication. Conservative literature generally uses moral issues to substantiate the righteousness of its call for woman's domesticity. The woman outside of her home, away from her male relatives, is *fitna*, a source of social anarchy. She loses her crown (her chastity) when she leaves her throne (her house) in order to mix with men in the places of lowly lust called work places. If she knew what she gives up and what she gets in return (a salary paid by Satan) she would weep blood.[72] Such a course of action is acceptable only if there exists a true, established need for her to work, if she comports herself with all modesty when outside of the home, and if she gives up her work and returns to the home at the very earliest possibility. Indeed, it is the duty of the state and/or of the community at large to help the woman to save her body, her morals, and her reputation by forcing her to return to domestic life. If the state paid her one-fourth of her salary as a pension, she could easily save the remaining three fourths because she could go without those new clothes, makeup, expensive meals outside the home, etc.[73] Hadith and Koran in conservative interpretation both teach that the Muslim woman is forbidden to mingle with strange men, and hence may not work outside of her home. The Koranic verses most frequently quoted in this context are 33 (*Ahzab*):33 (which bids the Prophet's wives to stay in their houses); 24 (*Nur*):31 (which requires Muslim women to refrain from displaying their beauty and ornaments except to their relatives); and 33 (*Ahzab*):33 (which forbids the Prophet's wives to engage in pagan *tabarruj*, the displaying of their charms).

The social anarchy created by women working outside of their home is most disastrous and most keenly felt inside of the family, because it plays havoc with man's *qiwama*, "guardianship" (over the woman). The Koran legislates in Sura 4 (*Nisa'*):34 that "Men are the guardians and maintainers of women, because God has given the one more than the other, and because they support them from their means. Therefore the righteous women are devoutly obedient, and guard in (the husband's) absence what God would have them guard. As to those women on whose part ye fear disloyalty and ill-conduct, admonish them (first), (next) refuse to share their beds, (and last) beat them (lightly); but if they return to obedience, seek not against them means (of annoyance): for God is Most High, Great."[74]

> A working woman's husband is selling his *qiwama* for five dirhams. . . . She takes away his manhood in exchange for a mere portion of her salary. Not only will he find himself forced to take care of the child and to cook on those nights when she has to work, he can also no longer ask her where she has been when she comes home after dark, or who that is who is calling her on the telephone all the time. . . . It is she now who has the right to ask him to tone down his voice, etc. By permitting his wife to work, the man loses his dignity, his substance, his willpower. The Hadith says that "Women make up the majority of the inhabitants of Hell, because of their ingratitude towards their husbands." This ingratitude is compounded manyfold if the woman contributes part of the household expenses.[75]

Even more dangerously, the family as an institution may become doomed to extinction. Working women shirk their religious and social duty in postponing marriage; thereby, they harm Muslim society as a whole since they fail to have children. In consequence, men err in like fashion. Why, indeed, should the men get married if they have scores of unveiled working women to keep them company?[76] History provides warning examples on this issue; it teaches us that great empires, like the Greek and the Roman, began to decline at exactly that time when women began to leave their houses.[77]

Much more harmful than women's work outside the home, however, is women's involvement in politics, and not only because it necessitates late working hours and intimate intermingling of the sexes. This issue is more serious because it goes clearly against the directives of the religion of Islam. Both the Koran and the Hadith forbid women access to public leadership positions. The issue is clearly stated in a Hadith in Bukhari which says that "a people who have appointed a woman to be their ruler will not thrive."[78] This Hadith was adopted and supported by the consensus of the early Muslim community and signaled the exclusion of women from all public positions of power (judgeship, military leadership, etc.)[79] Even 'Aysha's role in the Battle of the Camel, public though it was, does not represent an exception to women's seclusion from public affairs. 'Aysha was simply bitter and bent on avenging Uthman's death, be it by herself. The Companions did not support her in this scheme, all the less as the Prophet had predicted this unfortunate event. Therefore, 'Aysha ultimately acknowledged her mistake and repented. Not only public leadership, but even the franchise are forbidden to women by Islamic standards, because to participate in an election will imply to stand for election; the former will be construed as a means to the latter, and thus "the end disqualifies the means."[80]

It is in particular the question of women's access to political power that forces conservative thinkers to deal with the notions of democracy, equality, and freedom. The women's question here most clearly becomes a symbol of a larger ideological orientation that, going beyond it, addresses the political and social order of Islam as a whole.

We believe that it is . . . not necessary to speak further about the rights which Islam has provided for the woman, since this is a clear matter . . . , nor about these good eastern traditions of ours which do not grant women the right to stand for election . . . in accordance with religion and its directives. Rather, we want to discuss the defects of the supporters of women's right to political candidacy, by which we mean democracy, equality, and freedom, which allegedly should belong to everybody. There is a fine line between freedom and anarchy which we must strive to preserve, as otherwise disaster will follow. Democracy and equality do not consist in the fact that everybody obtains what he wants at the expense of religion and the common weal; rather, they consist in general rights and duties . . . which prevent that people oppress each other, and through which each citizen can confidently obtain the wages of his labor for which he is qualified in terms of nature, abilities, and talents.

This democracy, and the equality and freedom that go with it, do not empower each citizen to obtain any work he desires, no matter how insignificant. How, then, about political representation? Political representation is the highest form of public sovereignty. Therefore, we see that standing law codes and public ordinances define the conditions of access to governmental positions, no matter how lowly—which is necessary to guarantee smooth operations. The duties of the judiciary and the administration are, therefore, defined by conditions which prevent that every man apply to be a representative in parliament or a senator. If equality were absolute, it would turn into oppression . . . and pervert sound practices, since God did not create men as equals in nature, talent, ability, and qualification. But God has said that ". . . It is We Who portion out between them their livelihood in the life of this world: and We raise some of them above others in ranks . . ." (43 [*al-Zukhruf*]:32). He also said: "And in no wise covet those things in which God hath bestowed His gifts more freely on some of you than on others . . ." (4 [*Nisa'*]:32). And concerning men and women, He said: "And women shall have rights similar to the rights against them, according to what is equitable; but men have a degree over them" (2[*Baqara*]:228).

This is what the Koran confirms, in these and other verses, which to us is a confirmation of how things really are, besides being God's ordinance.[81]

The conservatives by their very nature feel called upon to stem the tide of social and political change. Their interest in women's issues must be understood within this context. By designing an ideal Islamic social paradigm that keeps women in their traditional place, these larger goals are indirectly addressed as well. The argument with contemporary Muslim conservatives is no longer just women's incapability of rational conduct. The tenor has shifted to one of panic concerning the future of the traditional social and political order in the Islamic world. As they endeavor to delegitimize development, the conservatives seek to establish a "holding pattern" on the basis of the religiously sanctioned, consensus-supported models of the past.

The Fundamentalists

The fundamentalists are scripturalist activists. They insist on a strictly literal interpretation of the scriptures and thereby often bypass and disregard the work of centuries of theological experts. Instead, they translate the sacred texts directly into contemporary thought and action. Fundamentalism in Islam is, of course, not a new phenomenon but has a long tradition reaching back to the Middle Ages. John Voll's definition of fundamentalism considers its main characteristics, as observable through Islamic history, in the following terms: fundamentalism stresses the transcendent nature of God and places emphasis on His ethical commands; it insists on a literal application of the scriptures in all situations and locations and thus stresses Islamic unity in thought and practice rather than accept diversity in local customs; and fundamentalism aims at maintaining the authenticity of the Islamic tradition by rejecting "borrowed" innovations or customary adaptations that have developed over time.[82]

Fundamentalists, then, are very seldom legal or theological experts. The rank-and-file fundamentalist supports the *shari'a* as an emotional issue and clamors for its reapplication in all Islamic countries and all areas of life. But his knowledge of it is hazy, and he is not clear on what a "return to the *shari'a*" would entail in practical terms: whether the medieval *madhahib*'s codes would be revived in their entirety or whether a new Koran-based *shari'a* would have to be written, and, if so, how, by which authorities, and the like.

As laymen, the fundamentalists rely on individual interpretation of the scriptures (*ijtihad*), not on tradition or community consensus. In this fashion, they shape for themselves a scripture-based platform for action that is designed as a coherent and compelling plan for the socio-moral reconstruction of Islamic society, which is the goal of their activism. The motivation here appears to be something both bigger and more desperate than the desire to preserve the status quo. In touch with the modern world, usually politicized, the fundamentalists see themselves as the conscience of Islamic society. As they condemn deviations that endanger the "Islamic way of life," they see reform as a process of getting rid of foreign (most often equated with pagan or *jahili*) practices. This is the road that will lead to the salvation not only of Islam, but of mankind.

The fundamentalists' blueprint for a just society differs from the conservative one on issues such as social equality, economic justice, and political legitimacy. It is only in the area of woman's role in society that they both speak in similar language insofar as they both emphasize woman's natural and God-given domesticity, glorify the status awarded to her in Islam, and predict certain doom to befall the Islamic world if the woman deserts or is lured away from her traditional place in society. It is therefore on this topic that a dialogue is possible between the fundamentalists and the conservatives, as made evident in the literature by mutually borrowed expressions and points of argument. Even so, the fundamentalists' idiom remains recognizably different; it is informed by global issues, pits Islamic authenticity against foreign conspiracy, and sees Islamic strength not in established Muslim tradition but in the scriptures themselves. To the fundamentalists, the so-called liberation of women is one of the characteristics of contemporary society which demonstrate that Muslims have strayed from the teachings of Islam. Women's emancipation is a deviation borrowed from the materialist West where its features are adultery, illegitimate children, venereal disease, and women so hardened by professional competitiveness that their reproductive organs have gone into a state of recession where they are unable to conceive and have turned into *al-jins al-thalith*, "the third sex."[83] At the basis of this deviation, the fundamentalists perceive an ongoing global Judeo-Christian conspiracy that combines the motivations and techniques of the Crusades with the goals of Zionism. The West, in a neocolonialist effort, has pitted itself against the East; it has chosen to launch its attacks against Islam on many different fronts, most notable among which is the Islamic family structure.

According to several treatises available in Cairo today, Egyptian fundamentalist interpretation distinguishes between the first campaign strategy of the "British imperialist crusader conspiracy" conceived by Gladstone against the Koran and the Ka'ba, and a second strategy, added later, against the Muslim family as the more critical goal of frontline attack. In their war against the latter, the imperialists concentrated on the education of Muslim children in Christian schools with the aim of implanting doubt, undermining the children's faith, and leaving them neither Christian nor Muslim. Most crucial for the success of this war was to draw the Muslim girl away from her faith; thereafter, she was taught "how to get the upper hand over the man," estrange him from his religion, and raise her children in un-Islamic ways. This line of attack of western imperialism was the more perfidious of the two, as the family is the cornerstone of Muslim society, and Islamic strength stands and falls with it. To achieve their goal, the British imperialists further promoted an end to the segregation of the sexes and called for restrictions in divorce procedures and polygamy.[84]

The women's movement in Egypt was and is seen as but a continuation of these hostile imperialist policies, and its leaders as spokesmen of the enemies of the country. The Egyptian feminist Nazli Fadil's links of friendship with Lord Cromer are seen as having enabled her to put pressure on Qasim Amin, thus drawing him into the web of traitors against Islam and making of him a mouthpiece of imperialism. Huda Shaarawi, who took off her veil in public in 1923 and went on to found the Egyptian Feminist Union, was none other than Muhammad Sultan Pasha's daughter. He had received high decorations from the British as well as large sums of money for his collaboration with them. In the forties, as the Americans joined the British as a colonialist threat, American support for the Feminist Congress held in Egypt in 1944 was seen as coinciding with American plans for the foundation of the state of Israel in the heartland of the Arab Muslim world; it was, especially, Mrs. Roosevelt who was involved in both of these activities and personified their linkage.[85] No feminist is regarded as having been more devious and corrupt, however, than the beautiful Durriyya Shafiq, founder of the *Ittihad Bint al-Nil*, or Daughter of the Nile Union.[86] A true client of imperialism, she is said to have been celebrated on her many trips abroad for the damage she did to the Muslim family at home by way of her militant demands for women's political rights, the introduction of European divorce law, and the abolishment of polygamy in Egypt.[87] Her personal links to Zionism were established by the fact that she retained contacts with Israeli feminists even during the years of the Arab boycott of Israel in the fifties. While she was nothing but a lackey of imperialism, she and those like her were seen as proof that the feminist parties were connected with the imperialist enemies of the nation and of Islam from the very start, and must be opposed at all cost.[88]

To adherents of this perspective, indirect political involvement of the enemy through traitorous servants of his cause is a great danger to Islam, but foreign ideologies represent another, possibly even greater threat. In undermining Islamic family structure, no ideologies are seen as more dangerous than the theories of Durkheim, Marx, and Freud, three Jewish writers (whose Jewish background is accepted as proof of their natural membership in the Zionist conspiracy against Islamic values). Muhammad Qutb, a fundamentalist thinker and writer whose books are widely read not only in the Arab world but by Turkish fundamentalists as well, is erudite and sophisticated in his definition of the dangers presented by these foreign "determinists."[89] His ideas have been popularized by less knowledgeable fundamentalists for whom these thinkers have become little more than catchwords that aid to personify the forces of darkness launched at Islam from the West. Occasionally, Darwin and/or Sartre are included in this list of enemies whose intention it is not only to debase Muslims, but man.[90]

Against the onslaught of these hostile armies without and within, the fundamentalists see the Muslim woman who follows her traditional role of loving wife and nurturing mother as a soldier fighting a holy war for the sake of Islamic values. Her conduct, her domesticity, her dress are vital for the survival of the Islamic way of life. Culture, religion, and morality stand and fall with her. She is strong—"he who believes her to be a weak creature is mistaken . . . she who in past centuries bore the age's hardships, the father's oppression, the husband's tyranny, the burden of pregnancy, the pain of menstruation, the bitterness of suckling, in contentment and serenity, is no weak creature . . . . She is the measure of the community; who wishes to know the secret of a people's progress or backwardness, let him inquire about the woman's influence on the character of their men."[91]

Social Reality and a New Fundamentalism

At the beginning of this paper, religious symbols and everyday reality were said to stand to each other in mutually affective relationships, and the tension between them to inform the mood of the symbols' "formulation." The interpretations of the status of women in Islam here described corroborate this statement.

The modernists, for the most part, represent the well-to-do, westernized, urban, intellectual elite and are sympathetic both to modernity and to western ways; they formulate the symbol of women's status in acculturationist terms. Because of their economic, social, and cultural minority status, their influence on Islamic society at large is limited and their efforts remain marginal in overall terms, even though their voice has been and continues to be important, especially to the members of their class.

The conservatives are led and guided by the religious establishment. On the basis of this writer's work in Egypt and Jordan, it appears that the spokesmen of conservatism as well as their constituencies are tied to or live in the small towns as well as the traditional quarters of the big cities, where life has not yet been drastically altered by modernization. Here, the teachings of the *'ulama* and traditional custom continue to be regarded as "right." The conservative message is especially attractive to older people who deplore the fast pace of change in contemporary society and culture, as well as to the young of traditional background who do not feel comfortable with modernity and for whom modernity holds no promise, while traditional custom (rather than political action) provides a safety catch in cultural, spiritual, and even economic terms. By their devout religiosity, the conservatives are culturally differentiated from the westernized political and economic elites of their country; if this cultural factor is activated by disadvantageous governmental policies, especially in the areas of economics and social privilege, opposition to state authority is then most naturally expressed in Islamic language, and a shift to fundamentalism can occur. In the area of women's questions, this shift does not bring about a significantly different attitude except in tenor, language, and argumentation, as identified above.

The rural areas are a different matter altogether, and it is significant that neither conservative nor fundamentalist writers refer to rural women. Village society is conservative; but the conservative Islam here professed and observed is shaped by custom to a larger degree than by the guidance of the *'ulama*. The rural women labor in the fields, outside their home, as they have done for millennia. Their way of life, then, does not mesh with conservative (or fundamentalist) teachings on women's status. This is indicative of a much larger problem that involves the participation of the rural areas in the formulation of Islamic norms as well as in their application. It is significant in this context that, for instance, women's Islamic rights to inherit and to bequeath property are very seldom applied in the rural areas. Within the scope of this paper, however, it suffices to point out that it is only the modernists (especially Qasim Amin) who speak of the women in the villages; however, they present them as models of health, strength, and independence, in other words, in acculturationist and utopian language. As for the conservatives and the fundamentalists, they completely disregard the women in the countryside—who represent to this day the majority of Muslim women—in their formulation of women's issues in Islam. Based as it is on political, economic, social, and educational factors, the city-oriented bias of traditional Islamic culture thus continues to prevail in contemporary Islamic thought. Social reality affects the formulation of religious symbols; but the countryside has so far not been granted a voice in the city-grown formulation of what is and what is not "Islamic," which is indicative both of the nature of Islamic interpretation and of its limitations.

As for fundamentalism, it is to a large degree an urban phenomenon today whose spokesmen—most of whom are young, recently urbanized, disenfranchised, and aware of the world at large—are in the position of having to cope with modern life without the economic and educational endowments enjoyed by the modernists. (This writer's research data indicate, however, that the lower-middle-class frame of reference is more characteristic of Egypt than it is of Jordan.) For the fundamentalists, the clash of expectations, fed by knowledge of modern concerns and modern skills, with the daily reality of poverty, frustration, and alienation leads to a formulation of social/economic/political issues in a more anguished and politicized Islamic language than is found among the modernists and conservatives.

In view of a greater identification with religion, coupled with increased literacy, professional ambition, and political awareness on the part of Muslim women today, the question is whether the fundamentalists will be able to maintain their position on "woman's status in Islam" in the future, or whether they will have to rework it to include for her a role in public life. Conservative thought may even have to borrow some of that language, if these trends continue. At least in Egypt and Jordan, young Muslim women (of whom only a small number appear to be activist) are becoming increasingly visible as they regularly participate in the Friday prayers in the mosques and the celebrations of the feast days. These women in Islamic dress are becoming literate in the Islamic scriptures, even though they may be students of secular disciplines or young professionals. As they read and discuss Koran and Hadith in women's study groups, they take as their models the founding mothers of Islam, those women who participated in the early religious wars and were part of the advance cadres of Islamization. With those early pioneers as their examples, the contemporary women see their efforts as crucial for the survival of Islamic morality and their work as redemptive,[92] even though it may involve a career. In Egypt and beyond, Zainab al-Ghazali is an important role model, at least for the more activist. With her commanding presence, her fundamentalist political credentials, and her profound knowledge of the Islamic sources, which add up to acknowledged public leadership in fundamentalist circles, Zainab al-Ghazali has few equals at the present time.[93] The future will show if others will follow her, if fundamentalism will move to sanction women's role in the public sphere, and if it thereby will become attractive to larger numbers of women.

These religiously committed women, like their secularist sisters before them, emphasize the importance of the collective good over the benefit of individual liberation and self-realization; hence, they neither entertain the notion of "women's liberation" nor do they see themselves engaged in a struggle against men. Family concerns and their own traditional roles remain centrally important to them. At the same time, they are invading public space in increasing numbers in the name and with the symbols of Islam.

NOTES

1. Clifford Geertz, *The Interpretation of Cultures* (New York: Basic Books, 1973), pp. 91ff.

2. Clifford Geertz, *Islam Observed* (New Haven and London: Yale University Press, 1968), p. 98.

3. Barbara Freyer Stowasser, "Religious Ideology, Women, and the Family: The Islamic Paradigm," in *The Islamic Impulse*, ed. Barbara Freyer Stowasser (Washington, D.C.: Center for Contemporary Arab Studies, 1989 reprint), pp. 263ff.

4. Clifford Geertz, *The Interpretation of Cultures*, p. 123.

5. Ibid., p. 112.

6. Bassam Tibi, *Der Islam und das Problem der kulturellen Bewältigung sozialen Wandels* (Frankfurt am Main: Suhrkamp Taschenbuch Verlag, 1985), pp. 20ff.

7. Muhammad Abdul-Fattah al-'Inani, (Ra'is Lajnat al-Fatwa bil-Azhar [President of the Fatwa Committee of al-Azhar]), "Hukm al-Shari'a al-Islamiyya fi Ishtirak al-Mar'a fil-Intikhab lil-Barlaman," in *al-Harakat al-Nisa'iyya wa-Silatuha bil-Isti'mar*, ed. Muhammad 'Atiyya Khamis (Cairo: Dar al-Ansar, 1978) pp. 101ff.

8. Cf. John L. Esposito, *Women in Muslim Family Law* (Syracuse: Syracuse University Press, 1982) pp. 129–30 and Malcolm H. Kerr, *Islamic Reform* (Berkeley and Los Angeles: University of California Press, 1966), pp. 189ff.

9. Muhammad Abduh, *al-Islam wal-Mar'a fi Ra'y al-Imam Muhammad 'Abduh*, ed. Muhammad 'Imara (Cairo, n.d.), pp. 136.

10. Ibid., pp. 83, 105–6, 57.

11. Ibid., pp. 58–59.

12. Ibid., pp. 105ff.

13. Ibid., p. 69.

14. Ibid., pp. 75ff.

15. Ibid., pp. 61–67.

16. Ibid., p. 117.
17. Ibid., p. 118.
18. Ibid., p. 96.
19. Muhammad Fahmi Abdul-Wahhab (member of Shabab Muhammad [Youth of Muhammad]), *al-Harakat al-Nisa'iyya fil-Sharq wa-Silatuha bil-Isti'mar wal-Sahyuni-yya al-'Alamiyya* (Cairo: Dar al-I'tisam, 1979), p. 13.
20. Cf. Muhammad Rashid Rida, *Huquq al-Nisa fil-Islam* (Damascus: al-Maktab al-Islami, n.d.), passim.
21. Yvonne Y. Haddad, "Islam, Women, and Revolution" in *Women, Religion, and Social Change*, ed. Y. Y. Haddad and E. B. Findly (Albany: State University of New York Press, 1985), p. 279.
22. Both reprinted in *al-A'mal al-Kamila li-Qasim Amin*, ed. Muhammad 'Imara, vol. 1 and 2 (Beirut: al-Mu'assasa al-'Arabiyya lil-Dirasat wal-Nashr, 1976).
23. Muhammad 'Imara, op. cit., vol. 2, pp. 168ff., 172.
24. Ibid., pp. 201ff.
25. Ibid., pp. 136ff., especially p. 140 and p. 144.
26. Ibid., pp. 156, 184ff.
27. Ibid., p. 194.
28. Ibid., pp. 213–14.
29. Muhammad 'Imara, op. cit., vol. I, pp. 139ff.
30. Muhammad 'Imara, op. cit., vol. II, pp. 20–25.
31. Ibid., pp. 29ff.
32. Ibid., pp. 35–37; 54ff.; 68.
33. Ibid., p. 58.
34. Ibid., pp. 43ff.
35. Ibid., p. 49.
36. Ibid., pp. 84ff.
37. Ibid., pp. 89ff., 93.
38. Ibid., pp. 104, 107ff.
39. Ibid., pp. 65ff.
40. Ibid., pp. 73ff.
41. Mahmud Shaltut, *al-Islam 'Aqida wa-Shari'a* (Cairo: Dar al-Shuruq, 1983), pp. 223ff.
42. Yvonne Y. Haddad, *Contemporary Islam and the Challenge of History* (Albany: State University of New York Press, 1982), p. 57; cf. Mahmud Shaltut, *Min Tawjihat al-Islam* (Cairo: Dar al-Shuruq, 1983), pp. 128ff., 195ff.
43. Yvonne Y. Haddad, *Contemporary Islam and the Challenge of History*, pp. 64–65; Mahmud Shaltut, *al-Islam, 'Aqida wa-Shari'a*, p. 194.
44. J. Jomier, O.P., "Quelques positions actuelles de l'exégèse coranique en Egypte" in *Mélanges* (Institut Dominicain d'Etudes Orientales du Caire, 1954), pp. 39–72.
45. Interview with Dr. Khalaf Allah by this writer on August 15, 1985.
46. Muhammad Ahmad Khalaf Allah, *Dirasat fi l-Nuzum wal-Tashri'at al-Islamiyya* (Cairo: Maktabat al-Anglo al-Misriyya, 1977), pp. 189–93.
47. Ibid., pp. 193–98.
48. Ibid., pp. 198–99.
49. Ibid., pp. 200–206.
50. Ibid., pp. 206–8.
51. Ibid., p. 208.
52. Barbara Freyer Stowasser, op. cit., p. 294.
53. For example with regard to the issue of women's status: 2 (*Baqara*):228; 4 (*Nisa*):34; with regard to witnessing: 2 (*Baqara*):282; polygamy: 4 (*Nisa*):3; divorce: 2 (*Baqara*): 227, 230–232; 65 (*Talaq*):1 and 2; inheritance: 4 (*Nisa*):11, etc.

54. Muhammad Tal'at Harb, *Tarbiyat al-Mar'a wal-Hijab* (Cairo: Matba'at al-Taraqqi, 1899) pp. 2–7; cf. Thomas Philipp, "Feminism and Nationalist Politics in Egypt," in *Women in the Muslim World*, ed. Lois Beck and Nikki Keddie (Cambridge, Mass.: Harvard University Press, 1978), p. 279.

55. Muhammad Tal'at Harb, op. cit., pp. 10–11.

56. Ibid., p. 19.

57. Muhammad Kamil al-Fiqi (Former Dean of the Faculty of Arabic and Islamic Studies, Azhar University), *La Tazlamu al-Mar'a* (Cairo: Maktabat Wahba, 1985), pp. 47–50.

58. Ahmad 'Isa 'Ashur, "Huquq al-Mar'a fil-Islam" in *al-Harakat al-Nisa'iyya wa-Silatuha bil-Isti'mar*, ed. Muhammad 'Atiyya Khamis (Cairo: Dar al-Ansar, 1978), p. 56.

59. Al-Fiqi, op. cit., pp. 113–19.

60. Abbas Mahmud al-'Aqqad, *al-Majmu'a al-Kamila li-Mu'allafat al-Ustadh*, vol. 4 (Beirut: Dar al-Kitab al-Lubnani, 1975), pp. 20, 30.

61. Ibid., pp. 31–34.

62. Ibid., pp. 15–16.

63. Ibid., pp. 17–18.

64. Ibid., p. 154.

65. Muhammad Mutawalli al-Shaarawi, *Qadaya al-Mar'a al-Muslima* (Cairo: Dar al-Muslim, 1982), pp. 32–33.

66. Ibid., pp. 7–8.

67. Ibid., pp. 15–17.

68. Ibid., pp. 39–40.

69. E.g., al-Fiqi, op. cit., p. 33.

70. Al-Shaarawi, op. cit., pp. 43–63; al-Fiqi, op. cit., p. 18.

71. al-Fiqi, op. cit., p. 34.

72. al-Fiqi, op. cit., pp. 9–12.

73. al-Fiqi, op. cit., pp. 57ff.; al-Shaarawi, op. cit., p. 18.

74. The first sentence in this verse was translated by the author; the remainder is the translation of A. Yusuf 'Ali, *The Holy Quran* (Washington, D.C.: The Islamic Center, 1978), p. 191.

75. al-Fiqi, op. cit., pp. 59–66.

76. Muhammad Zaki Ibrahim and 'Ali al-Mansur, "Mawqif al-Tarikh al-Islami min Huquq al-Mar'a al-Ma'zuma," in *al-Harakat al-Nisa'iyya wa-Silatuha bil-Isti'mar*, ed. Muhammad 'Atiyya Khamis (Cairo: Dar al-Ansar, 1978), p. 28.

77. al-Fiqi, op. cit., p. 36.

78. Through the methods of traditional Hadith criticism, Fatma Mernissi has established that this is a "weak" Hadith. Fatima Memissi, *The Veil and the Male Elite*, translated by Mary Jo Lakeland (Reading: Addison-Wesley, 1991), pp. 49ff.

79. Muhammad Abdul-Fattah al-'Inani, "Hukm al-shari'a . . . ", pp. 107ff.

80. Ibid., pp. 115ff., 124.

81. Dr. Muhammad Yusuf Musa, "Mawqif al-Shari'a al-Gharra min Huquq al-Mar'a," in *al-Harakat al-Nisa'iyya wa-Silatuha bil-Isti'mar*, ed. Muhammad 'Atiyya Khamis (Cairo: Dar al-Ansar, 1978), pp. 48–50.

82. John Voll, "Evolution of Islamic Fundamentalism" in *Islam, Nationalism, and Radicalism in the Sudan*, ed. Gabriel R. Warburg and Uri M. Kupferschmidt (New York: Praeger, 1983), pp. 115–16.

83. This is the title of a book available in Jordan that deals with issues related to working women; it is distributed by the Jordanian Ministry of Education (reportedly controlled by the Muslim Brotherhood); cf. Yvonne Y. Haddad, "Islam, Women, and Revolution," p. 287.

84. Muhammad Fahmi Abdul-Wahhab, *al-Harakat al-Nisa'iyya fil-Sharq wa Sila-tuha bil-Isti'mar wal-Sahyuniyya al-'Alamiyya* (Cairo: Dar al-I'tisam, 1979), pp. 7–12.

85. Ibid., pp. 15ff., 23–24, 27–28.

86. Durriyya Shafiq founded the *Bint al-Nil* magazine for women in 1946 and the Bint al-Nil (Feminist) Union in 1948 with the aim of working for full political equality of the sexes and increasing the literacy rate among women. Her political activism was at times militant; she succeeded in winning the vote for Egyptian women in 1956.

87. Muhammad Fahmi Abdul-Wahhab, op. cit., pp. 29ff.

88. Ibid., pp. 46–53. Many of the facts and ideas presented in this booklet by Muhammad Fahmi Abdul-Wahhab correspond in detail with portions of Muhammad Qutb, *Jahiliyyat al-Qarn al-'Ashrin* (Cairo: Dar al-Shuruq, 1980), as quoted by Yvonne Y. Haddad, "Islam, Women, and Revolution," pp. 289ff. Furthermore, this booklet is in large parts *identical* with the article "Silat al-Harakat al-Nisa'iyya bil-Isti'mar" by Husayn Muhammad Yusuf, who is a representative of the Shabab Muhammad, as is Muhammad Fahmi Abdul-Wahhab. This article was given as a paper at the 1952 conference on women's political rights, held in Cairo, and is now included in the printed proceedings of that conference, *al-Harakat al-Nisa'iyya fil-Sharq wa-Silatuha bil-Isti'mar*, ed. Muhammad 'Atiyya Khamis (Cairo: Dar al-Ansar, 1978).

89. Cf. Yvonne Y. Haddad, "Islam, Women, and Revolution," p. 291.

90. E.g., Anwar al-Jundi, *'Ala al-Fikr al-Islami 'an Yataharrar min Sartre wa-Freud wa-Durkheim* (Cairo: Dar al-I'tisam, 1979), and many others.

91. Muhammad Hilmi Nur al-Din (al-Ikhwan al-Muslimun [Muslim Brotherhood]), "Khatar al-Huquq al-Ma'zuma 'ala Kiyan al-Mujtama'" in *al-Harakat al-Nisa'iyya wa-Silatuha bil-Isti'mar*, ed. Muhammad 'Atiyya al-Khamis (Cairo: Dar al-Ansar, 1979), pp. 14 and 16.

92. Cf. Yvonne Y. Haddad, "Islam, Women, and Revolution," p. 295.

93. Interview by the author with Zainab al-Ghazali on August 7, 1985. Cf. a very similar interview in Valerie J. Hoffman, "An Islamic Activist: Zainab al-Ghazali," in *Women and the Family in the Middle East*, ed. Elizabeth W. Fernea (Austin: University of Texas Press, 1985), pp. 233–38; also excerpts from Zainab al-Ghazali's autobiography, *Ayyam min Hayati*, translated by V. J. Hoffman, ibid., pp. 238–50.

II

TOWARD THE DEVELOPMENT OF POST-ISLAMIST AND POST-NATIONALIST FEMINIST DISCOURSES IN THE MIDDLE EAST

Mervat Hatem

During the last ten years, independent and semi-independent women's groups or organizations have bloomed in Morocco, Algeria, Tunisia, Egypt, the Sudan, the West Bank, Gaza, Lebanon, and Kuwait. The regional rise of these groups is anomalous in part because the Arab oil revolution that transformed the region in the 1970s has left behind a very conservative Arab social order. The preponderant influence of the Gulf States, the widespread adoption of *laissez-faire* models of capitalist growth, the emergence of Islamism as an important social and ideological force in different societies, and the acceptance of U.S.-sponsored negotiations which respond minimally to Palestinian national aspirations, are all distinguishing social, economic, and political features of this conservative Arab social order.

In this chapter, I will discuss how some features of this social order contributed to the rise of independent and semi-independent groups and the birth of new discourses on women. The studies and journals published by these groups explicitly indicate dissatisfaction with old definitions and solutions to women's problems and express a desire for new types of changes that are at once post-Islamist and postmodernist. However, their writings and views do not completely break with the dominant nationalist approaches, which are incongruent with their independent goals and views. For this reason, the second section of the chapter will review and offer a critical discussion of these nationalist approaches and why they impede the development of new feminist discourses.

The Rise of Non-Governmental Women's Groups

Five regional and international factors explain the dramatic emergence of non-governmental women's groups and organizations across the region in the 1980s. First, there was the discrediting of the official women's organizations that dominated the region in the 1960s and the 1970s. These organizations served as representatives of regime policies *vis-à-vis* women. They developed a host of functions, which ranged from welfare in Jordan[1] to mobilization and development in Egypt, Algeria, Tunisia, and Iraq.[2] Their functions and activities were largely determined by the priorities set by the existing regimes, whether it was rational household spending and savings in Egypt,[3] birth control in Tunisia,[4] education and training in traditional occupations in Syria,[5] labor needs and/or the war economy in Iraq.[6] The close association between these organizations and official policies led to their being viewed suspiciously by rural and urban women. They never developed a legitimacy that was separate from that of the regime nor presented an agenda that could serve as a means of organizing their distinct base of support among women.

Second, there was the particular encouragement which the United Nations' Decade for Women gave to both the discussion of women's concerns and the creation of non-governmental organizations. There was, for example, UNESCO's Expert Meeting on Multidisciplinary Research on Women in the Arab World held in Tunis in May 1982[7] and a discussion of the images of Arab women in the media organized by the United Nations Economic Commission of West Asia held in Baghdad in 1983. The Association for the Development of Research on Women in the Arab World emerged from the UNESCO meeting in Tunis.[8]

Activities by the United Nations development agencies contributed to other organizational efforts among women of different classes. In the former North Yemen, the International Fund for Agricultural Development (IFAD) and the United Nations Development Program (UNDP) have started a variety of governmental and non-governmental projects aimed at reaching rural women and integrating them in agricultural development.[9] Other programs by the UNDP have contributed to the organization of Saudi women in community development projects,[10] the assistance of women's cooperatives in the Sudan,[11] the creation of women's artisanal organizations in the United Arab Emirates,[12] and the support of women's vocational training as health professionals in the former Democratic Republic of Yemen.[13] In other words, the efforts of the United Nations agencies to pursue the development goals of the U.N. Decade for Women helped to disseminate interest in the needs of women and to organize groups of women around those needs.

It is important to note, however, that Arab feminists within the U.N. agencies are critical of the approaches that these agencies use to deal with women's problems.[14] They point out that the U.N. agencies usually work with governmental agencies, especially the ministries of social affairs, which hold very traditional, bourgeois views of the needs of working-class women. They do not go beyond stressing the need for literacy, vocational training, and birth control in helping these women. Finally, the critics argue for the need to have the U.N. agencies work with the ministries of national planning for a more serious overall integration of women in different sectors.

Still, within the conservative social climate of the 1970s, these U.N. agencies and the Decade for Women were successful in introducing some changes into the lives of working-class women. More importantly, they provided middle-class Arab feminists with new national, regional, and international forums to discuss issues that were of importance to them and to push for changes in social attitudes toward women.

Third, the rising tide of Islamism in the region served to push middle-class women to organize themselves in opposition to its socially restrictive goals. It is important to note here that the rapidly changing social and economic systems of the 1970s contributed to the rise of Islamist groups whose values and demands struck a responsive chord among middle-class men and women. In Egypt, where the state was beginning to withdraw its commitment to provide employment to college graduates, the Islamist demand for a return to the old Islamic definitions of the sexual division of labor legitimized the return of women to the home at a time of large scale unemployment. The adoption of the veil by college and working women served to protect them from sexual harassment in the streets and the work place.[15]

In Syria, where an Alawite minority monopolized economic and political power, Islamism emerged as a protest movement against the exclusion of the Sunni middle and bourgeois classes from key positions. Despite official active disapproval, the widespread adoption of the veil served as a means of defying a repressive regime. Ideologically, the rejection of secularism was also used to detract from the regime's Islamic credentials and legitimacy.[16] In both Algeria and Tunisia, Islamism has emerged as an ideology distinguishing the social and political agendas of the younger generations of men and women from the older generation whose legitimacy and control of political power they challenged.[17] In addition, the severe economic crises made young middle-class men the victims of spiraling inflation and unemployment in Algeria and of the austerity measures adopted in Tunisia in 1986.[18] Violence against working women in Tunisia[19] and against unveiled women in Algeria[20] served to create a climate of fear that was designed to force women's return to the household and thus make available more employment opportunities for men.

Even more important, the Islamists have been successful in rolling back some of the gains made by women in precisely those states where the cause of women was expected to proceed the farthest, i.e., in Egypt, the Sudan, and

Algeria. These states made expedient alliances with the Islamist groups in the 1970s and the 1980s,[21] and state ideology and laws were changed to reflect the changing social and political terrains.

The process of reversal started first in Egypt. In 1976, article 2 of the constitution was amended to make the *shari'a* (Islamic law), which used to be one of the sources of legislation, *the principal* source of law making. The *shari'a* was the argument which the Islamists used to mobilize the Egyptian public against the 1979 personal status law. That law had considered the taking of a second wife as a source of harm (*Dharar*) for the first, and used this new interpretation to give the first wife new grounds for divorce. The High Constitutional Court struck down this law on a legal technicality in 1985. The law was quickly substituted with a new one that discarded the woman's undisputed right to divorce in case her husband took a second wife and gave the judge the power to interpret whether or not harm occurred in such instances.[22]

In the Sudan, the Islamization policies adopted by the Numairi regime in 1983 allowed for the hegemony of the *shari'a* over the customary and civil codes. The presence of these different sources of jurisprudence had, up until then, maximized women's capacity to seek redress from a variety of legal sources. Islamization was also used by the conservatives to invent the new crime of attempted adultery. While Islamic law had purposely required very difficult conditions to prove adultery, a new law took the unusual step of making the mere presence of any woman with a man to whom she was not married in a public place and/or in a car an indication of attempted adultery and grounds for incarceration.[23] Since 1989, the National Islamic Front has also succeeded in announcing an Islamic dress code for women that is seen as part of the continued Islamization of society.

In Algeria, the most recent family code deemphasized French civil laws, which were in use until 1983, in favor of some of the very conservative concepts found in the Egyptian personal status laws. For example, the new code stated for the first time that a woman's duty was to "obey" her husband in return for support. It also stated that a woman's right to work, if it was to be granted, must be included in the marriage contract. In other words, the new law retreated significantly from the state's prior unqualified constitutional commitment to women's right to work and to equality.[24] The erosion of popular support for the ruling FLN and the increasing popularity and political prominence of the Islamic Salvation Front since 1988 have also contributed to the reopening of societal discussion regarding women's work roles and mode of dress.

The net results of these moves toward more Islamization in Egypt, the Sudan, and Algeria were conservative and repressive in character. In creating legal systems that were deemed more homogeneous (i.e., in tune with certain conservative strands within the *shari'a*), they have eliminated sources of legal ambiguity that made women more able to maneuver in the area of personal status. Moreover, women experienced these changes negatively and felt threatened by them. This climate of fear more effectively stimulated an effort to organize secular middle-class women than any abstract commitment to women's rights. The non-governmental organizations formed by this group of middle-class women had a variety of purposes and concerns, but they were united in criticizing the new conservatism, defending the old rights which were now under attack, and pushing for new types of changes.

In the Sudan, Numairi's hostility to the radical Sudanese Women's Union in the 1970s led to the liquidation of the union and the formation of the official *Ittihad Nisa'a al-Sudan* (the Union of the Women of the Sudan) in 1971. Thus a vacuum was created which the Babiker Badri Scientific Association for Women's Studies tried to fill. The association, formed in 1975, focused on issues of concern to women that the official union did not address. Since any overtly political association would have been unacceptable to the regime, the association adopted an academic approach, focusing its attention on social problems like the conditions affecting women's work in the countryside, the change of the definitions of gender roles as they were presented in school textbooks,[25] and some customs like circumcision.

This academic approach was strengthened in 1984 by the publication of the *Ahfad* journal from the Ahfad University College for women. Like the Scientific Association, the journal published research done by women about women, their history, and the problems they faced in the Sudan.

Following the fall of Numairi's regime, the Sudanese Women's Union began the process of reconstructing itself. Its plans for the future included resuming its studies of the concerns of women. According to Fatma Ahmad Ibrahim, the president of the union and a noted figure in the Sudanese women's movement, the union's mobilization effort was going to focus on the improvement of women's rights in the family and the personal status laws.[26] But the ascent to power of a military junta (1989) committed to continued Islamization has discouraged all political efforts to mobilize women around these issues.

In Egypt, the effort to organize goes back to 1977 with the creation of small informal discussion groups. By 1979, formal committees on women had been formed as part of already existing professional associations and political parties. Women artists and reporters were the first to form a women's committee within the Reporters' Union in 1979. Its major activity was to organize debates to celebrate the international women's day and to highlight the contributions made by Egyptian women to their society and to the cause of women.[27]

In January 1982, the Constituent Congress of the Federation of Progressive Women met to discuss its program and its organizational links with the National Progressive Unionist party. The Federation of Progressive Women was committed to the defense of the accomplishments of the 1952 revolution and the deepening of those gains as part of the increased democratization of Egyptian society. It is important to note here that when the Constituent Assembly of the party met in August 21, 1976, to discuss the establishment of the party, it approved the formation of a feminist wing; however, no effort was made to start the mobilization effort among women until 1982.[28]

Finally, a permanent Committee on the Conditions of Women was created in 1984 by the Arab Lawyers Federation. The Committee was seen as "a natural extension of the Federation's interest in the discussion of human rights. It also allowed women to have their own committee within the organization and hence pay special attention to [a group that makes up] half of humanity and whose rights are largely ignored."[29]

In an interesting parallel development, *Jami'yat Bint al-Ard* (The Daughter of the Land Association) was formed in 1984 in Mansura, a town in Lower Egypt. In contrast to the abovementioned non-governmental organizations, the *Bint al-Ard* association represented the first independent (unaffiliated) women's organization to be formed during this period, demonstrating political awareness among women outside of Cairo through their separate initiative.

While this association was formed without opposition from the political authorities, Nawal al-Saadawi's *Tadamun al-Mar'a al-'Arabiya* (Association for the solidarity of Arab women) met resistance. State opposition was partially inspired by the controversial reputation of al-Saadawi, who successfully mobilized key liberal men in support of her association. Eventually, her organization was given permission to operate in 1985.

Both *Bint al-Ard* and *Tadamun al-Mar'a al-'Arabiya* view the increasing social conservatism of Egyptian society as a major concern. They have sought to establish a separate voice for women on the major issues of the day. Both have recently published their own magazines: the *Bint al-Ard* magazine and *Noon* (the Arabic letter that transforms masculine verbs into feminine ones). Both advocate less rigid definitions of Islam in fighting the Islamists, and emphasize the importance of organizing women around issues that unite them while taking note of the divisions that exist among them.[30]

In Algeria, the effort to organize dates back to 1980 when *Les Journées d'études et de réflexion sur la femme algérienne* (Studies and Reflections on Algerian Women) was organized in Oran.[31] This eventually became a basis for a women's club which continued to operate until 1985, when it was closed down by the university.

In March 1989, academic women at Algiers University constituted themselves into a new society on such issues as women and work and women and reproduction, which they called *Présence de femmes*.[32] In addition, they organized other activities to celebrate women's contributions to the arts and the Algerian revolution.

Palestinian women's organizations developed in response to the Israeli occupation and its policies, which have led to the alarming deterioration of the economy as well as the supply of key services. Here, new women's groups and organizations like *Lijan al-'Amal al-Nisa'i* (Women's Work Committees) in the West Bank (in operation since 1978) and Mary Khass's Mothers Understanding Methods of Schooling established themselves as self-help organizations to supply women with social services critical to the society. Both supplied women with training, day care, health, and employment services. They encouraged women to run these committees and to take responsibility for themselves and their children.[33]

While both organizations see the importance for women of the national struggle, they are not interested in subordinating women's cause to the national one. The latter approach is the one adopted by the Palestinian women's organizations affiliated with the PLO. These groups have focused attention on the distinctiveness of women's positions in the struggle for nationhood. In a document prepared for the Second General Conference of the Women's Work Committees in the occupied territories, the organization argued that Palestinian women suffered from a triple oppression: national, class, and sexual oppression.[34] In another publication, they argue that Israeli internment policies have contributed to the spread of female-headed households. It is estimated that one man in six has been arrested by the Israeli authorities at least once.[35] Consequently, women have experienced new pressures which these organizations emphasize as key in discussing the situation of Palestinian women.

Finally, the organization of women's groups in Kuwait, Tunisia, Morocco, and Lebanon was shaped by the particular history and demands of women in those states. Among the Gulf States, Kuwait has moved the farthest to integrate women in the public arena, especially in the areas of education and employment. It was not surprising that these changes inspired Kuwaiti women to begin to demand the right to vote. Since 1984, the Women's Cultural and Social Society of Kuwait, which brought together upper-and middle-class women, has attempted to mobilize women and to lobby key political figures on the issue of extending voting rights to women.[36] Kuwaiti women's participation in the resistance during the Gulf War strengthened their claims. The promises made by the government in that regard remain, however, unimplemented.

In Tunisia, there has been disappointment over the fact that progressive personal status laws have not, by and large, contributed to the change of negative attitudes toward women. This, combined with the rise of Islamism, has been a key factor responsible for the organization of the Tahir al-Haddad Cultural Club in 1984 and the publication of *Nisa'a* in 1985. (Tahir al-Haddad was the first male advocate of the liberation of women in Tunisia.) Both forums introduced discussions of the way in which personal experiences are also political experiences, a perspective that is new to the region as a whole. They also emphasized the importance of understanding these experiences as part of a broader social and political concern for development and democratization. During its first year of publication, *Nisa'a* discussed the issues of sexism, violence against women, sexuality, desegregation, and the conservative backlash against the 1956 Tunisian personal status law.[37]

A women's committee was also created in the Tunisian Human Rights Organization in 1985. As part of its activities, the committee planned a large-scale campaign aimed at the defense of the rights of women against numerous attacks. The campaign was to include the following activities:

> (1) Circulating a petition that declares support for women's equal access to work, education, civil and political rights, divorce, guardianship (*wilaya*) of children after the husband's death, and the enhancement of the inheritance rights of single female offspring; (2) organizing a series of debates on these issues by the different regional branches of the association; (3) discussing some of these issues on TV and radio programs; and (4) concluding the campaign with a big demonstration as a manifestation of popular support.[38]

More recently, there emerged two other groups. One, the Tunis Association of African Women Researchers, was formed in 1989 to "highlight the role of women in development . . . and create favorable gender focused development."[39] The second was *Nisa'a Dimuqratiyat* (Women Democrats), which "works to integrate women in society and to build up a new society based on men and women working together."[40]

In Morocco, a similar questioning of existing definitions of gender began with the publication of *Lamalif* ("No") and then *Thamaniya Mars* ("March 8"), founded in 1983. Both publications maintain a critical leftist orientation, but stress the distinct character of women's struggles. However, the former seems more academic and focused on the national scene, while the latter aims at reaching a larger public and linking the local Moroccan struggle with the international one.[41]

Finally, the Institute of Women's Studies in the Arab World was formed as part of the Beirut University College in 1973. "Since the old Beirut College for Women had provided women with higher education for fifty-five years before, the creation of the institute was designed to maintain a relationship between the new university and its active Arab alumnae."[42] Its major concerns seem to be largely academic, with its goals including the following: "(1) Establishing contacts between those interested in the affairs of women within and outside the Arab world; (2) Increasing the awareness of Arab and other societies regarding the conditions of Arab women and how these have changed as a result of modernization; and (3) Advocating the need for liberating and integrating women in development so that they can advance in different arenas."[43]

The institute has largely been engaged in the documentation of writings on Arab women and in compiling bibliographies of works written in Arabic, English, and French. It publishes a quarterly newsletter, *al-Ra'ida* (The pioneer), in English, which is largely concerned with covering the contributions of pioneering women (past and present) and analyzing their works. The interest in pioneers along with the fact that the newsletter and many of its publications are in English, give it a distinct elitist orientation. It is not clear what effect the journal has had, if any, on the Lebanese scene. The newsletter has been successful in providing English-speaking women with information about one another.

In view of this regional picture, one can safely say that the rise of independent non-governmental feminist groups in many Middle Eastern states constituted a new development. They presently exist in Morocco, Algeria, Tunisia, Egypt, the Sudan, the West Bank, Gaza, Kuwait, and Lebanon. The proliferation of these organizations in the last two decades indicates that they are not a transient, but a lasting trend that seems to address a real need. The publication of women's journals and/or studies on the status of women in Morocco, Algeria, Tunisia, the Sudan, Egypt, Kuwait and Lebanon, that discuss social issues and attitudes which affect women, offer numerous examples of a different feminist consciousness and modes of analysis offered by a new generation of Arab women.

On the whole, these emerging groups and their organizations reflect the greater confidence of Arab middle-class women, who feel comfortable in applying their social science skills to develop critical analyses of their societies and their position within them. The only possible exception to this characterization may be the Kuwaiti Women's Social and Cultural Society, where upper-class women have played the dominant role. As a result of its membership, this Kuwaiti non-governmental organization tended to work closely with governmental organizations in calling for and convening the first (1975) and second (1981) regional conferences on Gulf women.[44] While these conferences and their publications served to document the prevalent older modes of thought (legal, religious, literary, and social science) regarding Gulf women, the studies it presented by Arab male researchers as well as those of Arab and Gulf women agreed on the desirability of a new goal, that of integrating women in the development process.

The new women's journals and/or studies on the status of women published by these non-governmental groups reflect changes in some of the approaches used in indigenous writings on women. For instance, the new women's journals break with the old middle-class concept which located their primary interests within the family and focused on such things as childrearing, fashion, cuisine, and housekeeping. They attempt to cover current social and political events that interest and affect women. They also offer more sophisticated perspectives on women's personal lives, and especially on how life in patriarchal societies distorts a woman's definition of herself and her relationship to society.

It is interesting to note that non-governmental women's groups have been missing in both the conservative Gulf States of Qatar, the United Arab Emirates, Saudi Arabia, Oman, Jordan, and the former North Yemen as well as the radical mobilizing states of Iraq, Libya, Syria, and the former South Yemen. Both the conservative and the mobilizing states share a hostility to independent women's groups. These groups are considered threatening in conservative regimes because they challenge the rigid control of women. They are considered subversive of radical regimes because they challenge the societal consensus about which societal goals are appropriate for the mobilization of women.

Because the views of the new independent and semi-independent women's associations in the region reflect the adoption of new approaches and perspectives often on top of the old nationalist assumptions, strategies, and goals, I want to devote the final section of the paper to a critical discussion of the key nationalist approaches that continue to exercise influence on all the regional discourses on the liberation of women. My purpose here is to begin a thorough critique of some of the conservative uses of nationalism, which all approaches utilized in different ways, to control the change in the status and the role that women can play in their societies.

Key Nationalist Approaches Used in the Discussion of the Liberation of Women

The Modernist-Nationalist Discourse

The modernist-nationalist approach represents the *oldest* discourse used for the discussion of women's position in Arab society. It was developed largely as a response by key Arab intellectuals to the colonial challenge. Given the attack on Islam by the European orientalist scholars and colonial administrators, who identified it as the cause of the oppression of Arab women, this discourse offered a nationalist defense of the religion along with the adoption of western definitions of new rights for women in modern societies. Modernist critics who simultaneously defended and criticized Islam included thinkers like Rifa'ah al-Tahtawi, Qasim Amin in Egypt, and Taher al-Haddad in Tunisia, and feminist women, like Malak Hifni Nassif, Huda Shaarawi in Egypt, Nazirah Zein Ed-Din in Lebanon, and Bechira Mrad in Tunisia. All exonerated Islam from the charge of oppressing women and placed the blame on the failure of Islamic society to live up to its religious ideals. They then proceeded to support new interpretations of the religion which accommodated some western assumptions about the modern roles of women. In this way, the orientalist attack from without was generally internalized by Middle Eastern intellectuals in these defensive modernist discourses on women.

In this debate on the role of women, the modernists did not question the idea that Islam is relevant to the new modern society, but focused their discussions on how major reforms like the extension of education and employment to women would show the capacity of Islamic societies and its old sexual division of labor to adjust to the needs of a modern society within their own boundaries. Their primary goal, which continues to be attractive to Middle Eastern intellectuals (both men and women), was to develop a synthesis that would successfully preserve the structure of the Islamic family (and its gender roles and relations) and increase the social acceptance of women's education and work, which are western indices of modernization.

The emerging modern patriarchal systems allowed women increased public participation in education and employment, but kept the asymmetrical definitions of gender roles and relations within the family, which western modernization theories accommodated. Middle Eastern modernization combined new public roles for women with the culturally specific concepts of male leadership (*Quwamma*) over women, the assumption of women's diminished mental and religious capacity (*Naqisat 'Aql wa Din*) in comparison to men (and hence their exclusion from key religious, judicial, and political positions), and finally a female familial obligation to obey (*ta'at*) men. This did not represent a form of distorted modernization. On the contrary, it was a very good reading of what the development of modernization in the West was associated with. Western modernization did not begin by extending the principles of liberty and equality to women.[45] These were only applicable to men. Even when the struggles of women expanded these public principles to include women, the family remained as a social arena where patriarchy (and gender inequality) was firmly entrenched.

Despite their accurate copying of what western modernization was about, the modernist nationalists experienced their own personal and social dilemmas in defining how to manage these changes. Shaped by distinct class backgrounds and different social and political agenda,[46] all the modernist nationalists from Qasim Amin and Taher al-Haddad to Gamal Abdul-Nasser and al-Habib Bourguiba showed great ambivalence regarding the impact of the roles assigned to women in modern society (whether it was capitalist or socialist) on the Islamic character of the family and/or society. Despite their secular definition of religion as social practice, they did not want to abandon the Islamic definitions of gender, but to reformulate them in some new ways.[47] In instances where these efforts contributed to conflict, most were never forceful in their defense of the new roles for women. Even al-Habib Bourguiba, who was the Arab world's most modernist leader, argued in 1969 for the need to put modernization "in perspective" and warned that too much reform would lead to "a loosening of our morals."[48] Nasser showed his ambivalence more passively. His official commitment to the integration of women in the public sphere did not start at home. His wife remained absent from public view and only played the most traditional functions of wife and mother in a period when new expectations and attitudes were gaining ground.[49]

In evaluating the contributions which the modernist-nationalists (whether men or women) made, it is important to give them credit for having undermined both the old sexually segregated patriarchal systems and the limited social changes introduced by bourgeois feminism. In their place, they created a new social climate and a political economic system that accepted women's rights to public space, where they were expected to pursue public activities like education, work, and some forms of political participation, especially suffrage.

The acceptance of women's right to public space had significant implications for all women. Those who try to trivialize the effects of desegregation by pointing out that the majority of peasant and working-class women were never secluded ignore the social stigma and the sexual harassment that working-class women suffered under the old system. As women's right to public space became recognized, the conditions under which they worked and socialized improved for all, even though these conditions differed from one class to another.

The discourse produced by the modernist nationalists was problematic in more than one way. First, it presented itself as having completely liberated women. As a result, a whole generation of modernist women were persuaded that they were clients of these states. Meanwhile, these states continued to be silent on changing the remaining forms of gender inequality in the family and the new forms of inequality that emerged in the work place and the political system. In other words, the modernist-liberal discourse which stressed the public liberty of women coexisted with personal forms of subordination in the family and/or new public forms that developed in the socio/economic arenas where women were located. It adopted concepts legitimizing male leadership in the family, the work place, and the political system. This gave new reinforcement to the old belief in women's diminished mental, emotional, and religious faculties. It also showed how the emphasis on women's obedience (ta'at) to men within the family influenced the definition of the public positions they were expected to fill in the public arena. In these modern systems which professed their commitment to public equality for women, the judiciary (or at least some of its branches), the religious establishment, and the political arena remained largely the preserve of men.

Why is it, then, that these modernist states enjoyed the political and social support of some men and many women? By their own formal measures, these states seemed to be successful in what they had set out to accomplish. In addition to figures showing the increase of the number of women at all educational levels and in the formal labor force, attention was also given to the changes the state did or did not introduce in its personal status laws. Most students and supporters of modernization showed limited concern about the class-specific nature of these gains. Most of the educational and employment gains made by women under these modern states were unequally distributed. Middle-and upper-class women emerged as the largest beneficiaries, along with a very small segment of working-class women. Only the needs of urban women were accommodated. Regional differences remained very pronounced so that the women of the hinterland were the least advantaged.

Assessments of the personal status laws were also similarly judged. An emphasis on outlawing or restricting polygamy, which the modernists adopted as the western test of their commitment to women's rights, was presented as a sufficient measure of the depth of change in the family. This was, of course, a very misleading measure of change. For example, the Tunisian code, considered the most modernist in the region,[50] internalized hierarchical assumptions about gender roles in the family and used them to explain gender inequality in custody laws. Most modernist personal status laws do not challenge the hierarchical nature of the marital relationship. They accept the patriarchal nature of the family in their treatment of custody matters and do not accept the concepts of mutual responsibility and consent. In other words, even though these laws were hailed as both liberal and modernist, the changes they prescribed in gender relations within the family were more formal than substantive.

Finally, because the modernist discourse on women defended its legitimacy by presenting itself as a new interpretation of Islam, it is viewed synonymously as part of the debate on the role that Islam needs to play in society. It is not surprising, therefore, that the Islamist attacks on the failed economic and political efforts of the modernists should bring into question their interpretations of the role women should play in society.

While it is not clear that the modernist nationalists were committed to a radical restructuring of gender relations in Islamic societies, the more conservative nationalists were on more comfortable grounds presenting the feeble modernist changes in the gender arena as an assault on Islam from within. The representatives of this conservative nationalist school were often religious figures like Rashid Rida and Hasan al-Banna. They also included members of the new professional class like Mustafa Kamel, Tal'at Harb, and Muhammad Farid, and, in the 1970s and 1980s, members of organizations such as *al-Jama'at al-Islamiya* in Egypt, the Islamic Tendency Movement in Tunisia, the Islamic Salvation Front in Algeria, the Muslim Brotherhood in Syria, and *al-Da'wa* in Iraq and Kuwait.[51] These Islamist groups included large numbers of middle-class women, who supported their conservative political and social agenda. These women were very active in the grassroots organizations and the social and religious activities of the mosques. Also, whenever relative electoral freedom prevailed, some of these women campaigned and voted for Islamist candidates in Egypt and in Algeria. In Egypt, some of these Islamist women have achieved the comfortable status of being respectable public figures with their own following among men and women, e.g., Zainab al-Ghazali and Safinaz Kazim.

Since both the conservatives and the modernist-nationalists use the defense of Islamic/Arab culture as a basis of their political legitimacy, their commitment to women's rights is at best secondary. The experience of this century has shown that this particular discourse has reached its limits in serving the personal and social needs of women. The problems outlined above suggest that a new discourse would have to break with the modernist and Islamist assumptions that have crippled women in different ways. This post-Islamist and postmodernist discourse would have to deconstruct the categories of Islam, modernity, and women to begin a more fruitful discussion of the changing lives of women of different classes, of different ethnic groups, and of different regions.

The National Liberation Discourse

Whereas in the previous nationalist discourse the discussion of women's new rights to education and work was part of the process of creating new modern societies, the national liberation approach dealt with women as part of the struggle for economic and political decolonization. Most Marxist theorists view the process of national liberation as a process of transformation that roots a new (socialist) society in the womb of the old (capitalist) one. If one looks at the definitions of women's roles in the liberation struggles that have taken place in the Middle East (like the Algerian and the Palestinian struggles), one is struck by their modesty. While women became increasingly involved in the resistance and politics, their activities did not collide with previously existing gender expectations. They were usually involved in the occupations traditionally associated with women, like nursing, cooking, carrying weapons, and hiding people. They implemented plans and goals worked out by others but they did not participate in the discussions leading to the adoption of new goals or in the planning of operations. Instead of introducing new roles for women, the old ones were imbued with new respect.

Commitment to radical social change aside, the Algerian and the Palestinian liberation organizations resisted significant changes in personal values women were expected to uphold. The preoccupation with women's honor as part of the definition of a respectable wife was not challenged despite the brutal treatment to which women fighters were subjected. Those fighters, like Djamila Boupasha, who were raped by members of the French military police, were used to show the barbarism of the French colonial administration, but they were not accorded the same social or national recognition that was extended to those who avoided that fate. To become respectable and whole, they needed to be married and that part of their history needed to be forgotten. Here, it is very important to understand why the Palestinian and the Algerian struggles were torn between the need to introduce some change in gender roles and the need also to avoid it.

Despite the differences that exist between the Algerian and the Palestinian struggles, both movements faced enemies that denied their very existence as peoples with distinct cultures and national aspirations. The French settlers claimed that Algeria was part of France, not the Arab world, and Golda Meir claimed that the Palestinians did not exist. This negation of one's cultural and national existence made changes in that culture both desirable and fearful. While the mobilization of women in the struggle was needed, it had to be reconciled with the equally important task of cultural preservation. The results were contradictory expectations of women, who were to take on new public tasks in the struggle, but without challenging the old value systems or the roles they played in the personal arena.

While one needs to understand the circumstances that led the Algerians and the Palestinians to elect this particular approach to integrating women in the national struggle, it is clear that in choosing this approach they succeeded in controlling the radicalizing consequences of women's political engagement. In contrast, Amilcar Cabral emphasized the importance of treating one's culture as a living thing whose interaction with the surrounding environment allowed it to constantly change and grow.[52] The static approach to culture which the Algerian and the Palestinian national liberation struggles used traced its intellectual heritage to Franz Fanon, who was the theoretician of the Algerian struggle. It represented a more ambiguous and conservative position on this question. In his book *A Dying Colonialism*, Fanon stressed the importance of women's participation in the national liberation struggle, but viewed the change of culturally specific gender roles with distrust as part of the effort by the colonizers to conquer colonized men.[53] With Algerian women becoming cheap imitations of French women, Arab culture would be subverted from within, paving the way for the final subjugation of the colonized.

It is curious that Fanon did not see the incorporation of colonized men in the colonial economy and educational system in the same way. While men were expected to interact with their changing environment, women were relegated to the task of being the conservators of the traditional culture, which was deemed important for the national struggle. Other than frustrating colonial designs, it was not clear what concrete benefits women derived from being defenders of tradition. In this part of Fanon's discussion, women were not important autonomous actors. They were key because they were part of the primary contradiction between men as colonizers and men as colonized. The emphasis on the unity of men and women in the struggle for decolonization postponed the critical questioning of the inequalities of power between men and women in these patriarchal cultures.

This suggests the need for a reexamination of the dialectic of liberation (meaning transformation and change) and the definition of cultural or national identity as the maintenance of old (patriarchal) rules and roles. Without the questioning of the latter, the promise of radical changes in the postcolonial societies will remain unrealized.

The Dependency Discourse

In contrast to the two other nationalist discourses on gender inequality, this discourse stands out as the distinctive intellectual contribution of a new generation of Arab women trained in the social sciences. It represents their radical nationalist views of how gender inequality is part of the larger social/national problems. It also tries to place the basic needs of working-class rural and urban women at the center of the discussion. Like the other nationalist discourses, the dependency discourse subordinates the problems of women to those of their postcolonial society, especially development. The literature produced by Arab women on "women and development" begins with a structural analysis of underdevelopment and its relationship to gender inequality. It critiques the capitalist international division of labor that relegates the peripheral states to underdevelopment and argues that in societies where the *basic needs* of the majority go unmet, demands for sexual equality and new rights for women will continue to be blocked.[54] Conversely, movement toward development, especially under socialist conditions, can be expected to provide a more hospitable climate where gender inequality will be seriously tackled. This attempt to relate gender inequality to other political and economic sources of global and national inequality is the key insight offered by this discourse. These theorists emphasize the problems of large-scale poverty and political repression facing their Third World societies. Whereas a certain degree of capitalist development was possible in western countries, the stagnant nature of capitalism in underdeveloped societies could not offer a similar growth potential. Given these different political and economic contexts, the struggle for sexual equality in Arab societies was going to be different from similar struggles taking place in the already developed liberal democracies.[55]

Analytically, this new discourse, which stressed survival and underdevelopment as the key problems confronting Arab women, had a number of serious flaws. First, its preoccupation with the systemic problem of underdevelopment and its effect on women gives the impression that underdevelopment was the original or the single cause of gender inequality in the Middle East.[56] Gender inequality and patriarchal domination existed in precapitalist societies[57] and also continues in the developed capitalist societies.[58] To assume that the fight against underdevelopment was also a fight against gender inequality oversimplified the complexity of patriarchal domination.

Second, the analytical emphasis on how underdevelopment perpetuates the Middle East's dependence and increases its vulnerability to influence from the developed western societies led many to focus their studies only on how the West participates in actively oppressing Arab women. While it is true that colonial and postcolonial forms of western capitalist and patriarchal control have reinforced and strengthened the patriarchal character of Arab societies, Middle Eastern patriarchies should not be reduced to only those aspects of their political economies and societies that serve colonial or postcolonial interests. This ignores the role played by the indigenous patriarchal rules and their relative autonomy.

Because the existing literature on women and development largely concerns itself with the issues of economic and political survival, it presents a dehumanized and degrading picture of Middle Eastern women, whose other social and sexual needs are ignored or treated as unimportant. Despite the serious and genuine concern which most of these writings reflect for women, their neglect of these other social needs and rights shows a serious bias in their analysis of everyday life. Arab women appreciate and have fought for liberal marriage and divorce laws.[59] They put a value on egalitarian marital relations within the family.[60] They appreciate the autonomy that work allows them.[61] To assume that economic concerns preclude other sexual, emotional, and psychological needs cannot be justified on any theoretical or empirical grounds. By not linking the study of the sexual and psychological relations of patriarchal society and the economic/political relations of capitalism, these analysts have presented unidimensional characterizations of the problem.[62] They privilege the broad national concerns of the society in their definition of the legitimate concerns of women.

Conclusion

The three above-mentioned nationalist discourses deal with women's issues as part of the general problems confronting Arab societies, whether these are problems of modernization, national liberation, or development. They depersonalize women's problems by emphasizing the importance of introducing macro changes in these societies, which they claim will improve the public conditions under which women operate. They avoid any discussion of the personal, familial norms for women, which in fact significantly influence public attitudes. The approaches do not discuss how these public and personal problems are produced by the existing Arab patriarchal systems (of which Islamic law is one component).

Despite the widespread dissatisfaction of women's groups with the results of regional efforts to deal adequately with these problems, their attempt to break with these nationalist approaches has been stalled. Women's incorporation in the body politic as citizens was premised on their acceptance of nationalism as the only acceptable discourse. The present ideological struggles between the discredited modernists (who failed to deliver development to younger generations of men and women and the lower middle classes) and the ascendant Islamists (who claim that there is an Islamic solution to these problems) make it difficult to develop an independent discourse. The political and the ideological choices that this struggle offers are old and tired concepts and roles that cannot be expected to deliver new solutions. In this sense, the crisis of Arab feminist discourses is a reflection of the real crisis facing Arab societies.

NOTES

1. The activities of the Jordanian Women's Union serve as an example of the official welfare functions. See Suhair Sulti al-Tal, *Muqadimat Hawl Qadiyat al-Mar'a wa al-*

Harakat al-Nisa'iya fi al-Urdun (Beirut: al-Mu'assasat al-'Arabiyat lil-Dirasat wa al-Nashr, 1985), chap. 4, pp. 130–44.

2. Bassam Tibi, "Mas'alat Tahrir al-Mar'a fi al-Mujtama' al-'Arabi," *al-Tali'a* 4, 11 (November 1968), pp. 78–79; Juliette Minces, "Women in Algeria," in *Women in the Muslim World*, Lois Beck and Nikki Keddie, eds. (Cambridge: Harvard University Press, 1978), pp. 168–69; Mark A. Tessler with Janet Rogers and Daniel Schneider, "Women's Emancipation in Tunisia," in *Women in the Muslim World*, Beck and Keddie, eds., pp. 142–43; Suad Joseph, "The Mobilization of Iraqi Women into the Wage Labor Force," *Studies in Third World Societies* 16 (June 1981), pp. 69–85; Amal Sharqi, "The Emancipation of Iraqi Women," in Tim Niblock, ed., *Iraq: The Contemporary State* (London: Croom Helm, 1982), pp. 74–87.

3. "Rabat al-Bayt: Kayf Yumkinaha Muwajahat al-Ghala'a," *al-Ishtiraki* 10 (June 12, 1965), p. 9; "Ila al-Qayadat al-Nisa'iya: al-Idikhar min Ajl al-Rakha'a," *al-Ishtiraki* 11 (June 26, 1965), p. 7; UNESCO, Expert Meeting on Multidisciplinary Research on Women in the Arab World: Final Report, Paris: SS-82/Conf. 804/11, 10 (February 1983), pp. 1–27.

4. Tessler, Rogers, and Schneider, pp. 142–43.

5. The Syrian Arab Republic, *Munjazat al-Ittihad al-'Am al-Nisa'i: 1980–83* (Damascus: Maktab al-Thaqafa wa al-'Ilm al-Markazi, n.d.), pp. 18–23.

6. Joseph, pp. 69–85; Shariqi, pp. 74–87.

7. UNESCO, Expert Meeting, pp. 1–27.

8. Ibid., p. 25.

9. Susannah Tarbush, "Women, and Development in Rural Yemen," *The Middle East* (March 1985), p. 34.

10. UNDP, *Journey to the Future: UNDP and the Arab World* (New York: UNDP, 1984), p. 49.

11. Ibid., p. 53.

12. Ibid., p. 58.

13. Ibid., pp. 20, 27.

14. Discussions with Fatma Khafagy, Program Officer for Women's Development at UNICEF in Cairo, Egypt, and Farida Allaghi, also of UNICEF in Riyadh, Saudi Arabia, during the Center for Contemporary Arab Studies Symposium, "Women and Arab Society: Old Boundaries, New Frontiers," Washington, D.C., April 10–11, 1986.

15. Mervat Hatem, "Egypt's Middle Class in Crisis: The Sexual Division of Labor," *Middle East Journal* 43, 3 (Summer 1988), pp. 416–20.

16. Interviews with veiled and unveiled Syrian women as part of a preliminary study of the past and present history of Syrian women, December 1987-January 1988.

17. Emna Bil Haj Yahia, "Islamisme Radical et Droits de Femmes," Presentation to the Faculty of Law Students at Tunis in February 1988, p. 1; Ben Wilkinson, "All Change in Chadli's Algeria," *The Middle East* (April 1984), pp. 20–21.

18. Islamic Society of North America, *The Movement of Islamic Tendency in Tunisia: The Facts* (September 1987), p. 9; "In Algeria: Unequal before the Law?" *The Middle East* (April 1985), p. 54.

19. Hayat Qurbi'a, "Min Wahy Ahdath Sousa: al-Ma'touh Fina wa Mina," *Nisa'a* (April 1985), p. 6.

20. Fayqa Mujahid, "Ghadab al-Nisa'a al-Jaza'iriyat," *Noon* (August 1989), p. 22.

21. Gilles Kepel, *The Prophet and Pharoah* (London: al-Saqi Books, 1985), chap. 5; Ahmed Abdalla, *The Student Movement and National Politics in Egypt* (London: al-Saqi Books, 1985), chap. 9; Pascale Villiers Le Moy, "Numairi Plays the Islamic Card," *The Middle East* (February 1984), pp. 22–23; Wilkinson, "All Change in Chadli's Algeria," pp. 20–21.

22. For a more detailed discussion of the Law and the circumstances surrounding it, see Mervat Hatem, "The Enduring Alliance of Nationalism and Patriarch in Muslim Personal Status Laws: The Case of Modern Egypt," *Feminist Issues* 6, 1 (Spring 1986), pp. 19–43.

23. Interview with Dina Sheikh El-Din Osman (Head of the Department of Commercial Law, University of Khartoum).

24. "Unequal before the Law," p. 55.

25. Jami'yat Babiker Badri, *Murshid al-Mar'a al-Rafi'a* (Omdurman: Jami'yat Babiker Badri, 1984); Babiker Badri Scientific Association for Women Studies, *Synopsis: Proceedings of the Workshop African Women Speak on Female Circumcision* (Omdurman: Babiker Badri, 1984).

26. Al-Sayidah Ibrahim, "Interview with Fatima Ahmad Ibrahim;" *al-Watan al-'Arabi* (January 31—February 8, 1986), p. 74.

27. Iqbal Baraka, "Ba'd Ashr Sanawat: Matha Qadamat al-Mar'a lil Mar'a?" *Sabah al-Khayr* (March 8, 1982), pp. 22–23.

28. *Al-Mu'atamar al-Ta'ssissi li-Ittihad al-Nisa'i al-Taqadumi* (Cairo: 1982), p. 24.

29. Ingie Rushdy, "al-Lajnat al-Da'imati li-Awdah al-Mar'a bi Ittihad al-Muhamin al-'Arab Tatlub," *al-Ahram* (November 30, 1984), p. 12.

30. Angela Davis, "Women and Sex: Egypt," in *Women: A World Report* (London: Oxford University Press, 1985), pp. 338–42.

31. Fatima Hakiki and Claude Talahite, "Human Sciences Research on Algerian Women," in *Social Science Research and Women in the Arab World* (Paris: UNESCO, 1984), p. 83; Abdel Qader Jaghlul, ed., *al-Mar'a al-Jaza'iriya* (Beirut: Dar al-Hadalha, 1983), pp. 234–36.

32. Fayqa Mujahid, "Nisa'a 'Arafa," *Noon* (May 1989), pp. 20–21.

33. The Women's Work Committees in the Occupied Territories, Report to the Second General Conference of the Women's Work Committee in the Occupied Territories (March 1983), p. 2; Informal meeting with Mary Khass, Nairobi 1985.

34. Ibid.

35. "Palestinian Women—An Unheard Voice," *Palestine/Israel Bulletin* 9, 1 (January 1986), p. 1.

36. David Ottaway, "Feminists Seek Voice in Kuwaiti Politics," *The Washington Post* (April 14, 1984), p. A 21; Sarah Graham-Brown, "Why Kuwaiti Women Want the Vote," *The Middle East* (October 1985), pp. 7–9.

37. *Nisa'a*, no. 1, 2, 3 (1985).

38. "Nisa'a wa Anba'a," *Nisa'a* (August 1985), p. 3.

39. Society for International Development, "Report on Middle East and North Africa Region: Tunis Symposium," 64th Governing Council Meeting, November 17–18, 1989, Document 1, p. 7.

40. Ibid., p. 8.

41. *Nisa'a* (December 1985), p. 2.

42. Ilham Kalab, *Hiya Tatbukh, Huwa Yagra'* (Beirut: Ma'had al-Dirasat al-Nisa'iya fi al-'Alam al-'Arabi, 1983), p. 5.

43. Ibid., pp. 5–6.

44. Al-Jami'yat al-Thaqafiyat al-Ijtima'iyat al-Nisa'yat, *Dirasat 'An 'Awda al-Mar'a fi al-Kuwait wa al-Khalij al-'Arabi* (Kuwait: al-Jami'yat al-Ijtima'iyat al-Nisa'yat, n.d.), preface; al-Jami'yat al-Thaqafiyat al-Ijtima'iyat al-Nisa'yat, *al-Mar'a wa al-Thanmiya fi al-Thamaninat*, vol. 1 (Kuwait: Sharikat Kazima lil-Nashr wa al-Tarjama wa al-Tawzi'a, 1982), pp. ii-iii.

45. Carole Pateman, *The Sexual Contract* (Stanford: Stanford University Press, 1988), chap. 1.

46. Juan Cole, "Feminism, Class and Islam in Turn of the Century Egypt," *International Journal of Middle East Studies* 13 (1981), pp. 387–407; Jean Lacouture, *Nasser: A Biography* (New York: Alfred Knopf, 1973), p. 112.

47. Souad Halila, "From Koranic Law to Civil Law: Emancipation of Tunisian Women Since 1986," *Feminist Issues* 4, 2 (Fall 1984), p. 29; Abdelkader Zghal, "The Reactivation of Tradition in a Post-Traditional Society," in *Arabic Society in Transition: A Reader,* Saad Eddin Ibrahim and Nicholas Hopkins, eds. (Cairo: The American University in Cairo Press, 1977), p. 596; Muhammad 'Imarah, *Qasim Amin wa Tahrir al-Mar'a* (Cairo: Dar al-Hilal, 1980), chap. 5.

48. Tessler, Rogers, and Schneider, p. 147.

49. Lacouture, p. 112.

50. Hamida Bishri Bilhaj, "Ashkal al-Tamyeez did al-Mar'a min Khilal ba'd al-Nusus al-Qanuniya," *Nisa'a* (August 1985).

51. Kepel, Chap. 5; Wilkinson, p. 21; Ottaway, p. 21.

52. Amilcar Cabral, *Return to the Source: Selected Speeches of Amilcar Cabral* (New York: Monthly Review, 1973), pp. 42–45.

53. Frantz Fanon, *A Dying Colonialism* (New York: Grove Press, 1965), pp. 38–39.

54. Nawal al-Saadawi, Fatima Mernissi, and Mallica Varjarallion, "A Critical Look at the Wellesley Conference," *Quest* 4, 2 (Winter 1978), pp. 101–5; Nawal al-Saadawi, "Creative Women in Changing Societies: A Personal Reflection," *Race and Class* 22, 2 (Autumn 1980), pp. 163–64; Sarah Graham-Brown, "Feminism in Egypt," *MERIP Reports* 95 (March-April 1981), pp. 24–28.

55. Laila Abdul-Wahab, "Development of the Situation of Egyptian Women during the International Decade of Women (1975–1985)," unpublished paper, p. 7.

56. Laila Abdul-Wahab, Draft Working Paper for the Arab-African Seminar held in Cairo, February 25–28, 1985.

57. Mervat Hatem, "Sexuality and Gender in Segregated Patriarchal Systems: the Case of Eighteenth and Nineteenth Century Egypt," *Feminist Studies* (Summer 1986).

58. Zillah Eisenstein, ed., *Capitalist Patriarchy and the Case of Socialist Feminism* (New York: Monthly Review Press, 1978).

59. Fatiha Akeb and Malika Abdelaziz, "Algerian Women Discuss the Need for Change," in *Women and the Family in the Middle East*, Elizabeth Fernea, ed. (Austin: University of Texas Press, 1985), pp. 18–23; Huda Shaarawi, *Mudhakarat Ra'idat al-Mar'ah al-'Arabiya al-Haditha* (Cairo: Dar al-Hilal, 1981), pp. 360–64.

60. Barbara Lethem Ibrahim, "Cairo's Factory Women," in *Women and the Family in the Middle East*, Fernea, ed., p. 298; Safia Mohsen, "New Images, Old Reflections: Working Middle Class Women in Egypt," *Women and the Family in the Middle East*, Fernea, ed., pp. 64–67.

61. Ibid.

62. Lourdes Arizpe and Marysa Navarro, "Further Comments on Tinker's 'A Feminist View of Copenhagen,'" *Signs* 7, 3 (Spring 1982), pp. 714–16.

III

AUTHENTICITY AND GENDER
THE PRESENTATION OF CULTURE

Julie M. Peteet

This article explores the relationship between gender and class structures and the construction of cultural authenticity in a Middle Eastern society.[1] Discussion of this relationship is cast in a theoretical framework that integrates a political-economy perspective with a cultural and ideological interpretation of ethnographic data.[2] The historically specific political-economy of a moment shapes the contours of culture and ideology; in turn, societies respond to these forces in a variety of ways, exerting a creative force on the parameters of the social formation. This article investigates one dimension of how a people in the process of national formation have responded to political and sociocultural upheaval by assertively and creatively renegotiating the meaning of central cultural complexes in an attempt to construct cultural authenticity.

The Presentation of Culture

During the course of ethnographic research one must scrutinize those elements of culture people strive to present. Indeed this is often the first aspect of doing ethnography; most ethnographers have faced the frustrations of trying to proceed beyond the "ideal," which informants initially present. Yet this initial ideal presentation in itself constitutes an integral component for understanding other cultures. Beyond those aspects of culture for which people feel they must strive, it reveals selected dimensions of their interaction with external forces and the power structure within which such a relationship is organized. The ethnographer plays a role in this relationship, representing, in a generalized fashion, forces external to the people being studied. The presentation of culture is a means of establishing a social relationship with others and a form of communication; in such a case, ethnography is a form of dialogue. The focus on how culture is presented assumes an added imperative in colonized or recently decolonized societies, where definitions of and control over cultural content and meaning can assume paramount importance. Control over the ethnographic process and presentation of self and community is not only the preserve of the more powerful cultures who have tended to protect their rights to privacy and determine the way they choose to be presented.[3] What are thought of as less powerful and less autonomous components of a world cultural system may exert control over the presentation of culture precisely as a means of addressing powerlessness in the face of other dominant sociopolitical systems.

Roger Keesing argues that in colonial or postcolonial situations culture may become a "thing" to be articulated and objectified to an alien once situated within the colonial framework of domination and more or less distanced from it.[4] Objectifying culture asserts cultural identity vis-a-vis colonial rule, and gender constructs are an integral component of this assertive process. Among the Kwaio Solomon Islanders, Keesing discovered that women's life stories were tantamount to "commentaries on virtue," embodying the ideal elements of precolonial, indigenous culture, and were purposely made available to the ethnographer. "In the elevation of 'custom' to the level of 'political symbol' women's performance of ritual and custom assumed prominence in Kwaio's determination of what they wanted the ethnographer to know."[5]

Among the Palestinian exile community in pre-1982 Lebanon, potential appeals to a past tradition were superseded by, or in some cases accompanied by, the quest for an innovative culture in response to continuous crisis and intermittent but frequent external assault. This was a community engaged in a two-decade long process of cultural reconstruction. They were not resurrecting traditional culture but rather consciously devising a blend of old and new to form a "culture of resistance." Cultures of resistance are built upon "expressions of ethnic identity and group solidarity . . . retained in part from precolonial traditions, but they are also reshaped, altered, and created anew," and involve "a long process of redefinition of cultural identity, widening in scope from narrower village . . . to larger and larger groups, coupled with a growing awareness of the commonality of exploitative situations and of solidarity in the face of oppression."[6] The concept of cultures of resistance has been neglected in the analyses of societies striving for independence and autonomy in the wake of colonization and yet in delving into the topic one must be aware of their duplicity,[7] their contradictory potential for progress and regression.

In the process of reconstructing cultural forms the ideal may assume a prominent, guiding position. Specific elements of culture are reinterpreted in a process of extraction and then close scrutiny. In the Palestinian "diaspora" some cultural elements associated with defeat have been left behind or reinterpreted and are given a new meaning, reinforcing the notion that while symbols themselves remain potent, their meaning is variable, negotiable, and subject to reinterpretation in specific sociohistorical instances. The changing concept of honor is an apt example. A readily visible and traceable transition has taken place in the meaning of this central cultural complex of Arab society[8] from personal, localized, and familial-based definitions of honor expressed in women's behavior, to one encompassing national aspirations and based on the individual's stance as a nationalist. In 1967, significant numbers of West Bank Palestinians fled the advancing Israeli army citing fears for their kinswomen's honor.[9] Palestinians who fled in 1948 expressed a similar reaction to Israeli military advances and their own subsequent defeat. By the early 1980s, younger Palestinians, the *jil al-thawra*,[10] were quick to criticize this concept of honor. The national honor lost in the 1948 and 1967 defeats was being restored by militant political action expressed in new and popular idioms. The concept of *'ird* (honor) was enmeshed with *ard* (land) as a play on words and meanings. *Sharaf* (honor) refers to the reputation and social standing of an entity larger than the family, usually the community and its defense and protection, sexual or otherwise, while *'ird* (honor) refers to the sexual behavior of women. The Palestinian resistance movement, as an expression of national rather than clan and village loyalties, fostered new symbols of a Palestinian culture of resistance. One such symbol was the slogan *al-ard abl al-'ird* (land before honor), a direct challenge to the primacy of honor (*al-'ird*) as residing in kinswomen's behavior. This was a selective, conscious renegotiation of the meaning of a salient cultural complex; the form (honor) remains the same, but the content and meaning have been dramatically altered.

A central component of the presentation of culture, particularly in societies with a colonial history, is the question of authenticity. Some contend that it is less an indigenous concept and more a cultural construct of outsiders, a discourse about what westerners strain to discover in non-western societies.[11] But as observers of formerly colonized societies recognize, authenticity is a crucial concept in the cultural rethinking that often accompanies decolonization and independence.[12] Nevertheless, authenticity is not only a question in countries and cultures with a colonial past or that are under assault in some ways.[13] A more fruitful discussion ensues if the parameters of the debate are shifted from a polarized western/non-western phenomenon to one where the concept of authenticity is examined within cultures, focusing on their specificity.

In the contemporary Middle East, authenticity is a buzzword that carries a potent political and symbolic content and apparent class and gender dimensions. It can be a discourse about others within the society, the preserve of an elite who designate certain sectors of society (such as women, peasants, and tribespeople) as their public, performative representatives without, however, vesting much power in this assignment.[14] Such assignment determines what category of people (and material things or artifacts) represents the authentic component of a society. Authenticity is the burden of those sectors of society, and the cultural artifacts specific to them. These sectors may also be distant from contact with other cultures and underrepresented in the power structure assigned to represent the "folk" and the "culturally pure" ideal of the largely idealized past.

The presentation of culture is a communicative act, a means of initiating and establishing the parameters of dialogue with outsiders. It is a statement asserting existence, especially where historical and political existence and cultural specificity have been denied. It also displays the cultural values and kinds of social relationships its purveyors wish to perpetuate, internally as well as externally. Indeed, its interpretation and analysis should be solidly located in a sociopolitical context. A message is conveyed through this medium that may communicate a refusal to accept another's definition of existence and culture, and it may be an attempt to transform the power spectrum by making one's own definition of the situation the prevalent one. It is, equally, a negotiation of situation calculated to affect reality. Thus, the presentation of culture is more than a drama expressing old or new cultural ideals and elements and forms of social relationships. As a performative genre it does not necessarily transcend, displace, or even comment on the order of reality but is a communicative medium to shape reality, to construct it in order to achieve specific ends. In the Palestinian case, where social fragmentation is pervasive, the presentation of culture extends well beyond the exterior; in response to national fragmentation it is an internal affirmation of culture and contributes to the construction of a sociopolitical unity.

"Tradition" is a primary component in the construction of authenticity possessing a salient mobilizing appeal. The conscious veiling of women in Algeria during the struggle for independence was a "language of refusal,"[15] but the veil can also constitute an active, seemingly progressive weapon in the contest for political and cultural autonomy. Women donned it to cloak themselves in anonymity in order to carry out covert military assaults on the French in Algeria. Yet, conversely, it can also represent an attempt to revert to an idealized past. In Iran in the late 1970s, veiled women were both symbols of opposition to the Shah's regime and active participants in the political events leading to its dissolution. The same veil that symbolized a militant, female activism now is used to circumscribe women's presence in the workplace and confine them to the home as well as to regulate and control male-female interaction. Thus, tradition is not a set of static cultural complexes but displays a remarkable flexibility in activation, content, and meaning according to historical time and place. Indeed the same phenomenon or symbol, such as the veil, may be used in seemingly contradictory ways within the same society during proximate historical periods. Therefore, an authenticity based on tradition is not necessarily a passive, mutely adopted reversion to tradition. The use of tradition can be both calculated and creative. It can represent an active language of refusal and militancy to overcome cultural denigration, and be a means to reclaim autonomy. Among the Palestinians, traditional forms and symbols have been imbued with new meaning both to express and to activate strategies to transform their position in the larger sociopolitical equation.

Gender and Authenticity

The thematic elements of a Palestinian authenticity revolve around the dialectical experience of the "diaspora" and a militancy derived from a refusal to accept defeat. Women, hardly remote or immune from the vicissitudes of exile and militancy, play a central role in expressing the tragedy and hardship of the diaspora yet they also prominently display the sacrifices and progressive social change necessitated by militancy. There is still ambiguity as to why it is often women, whether visible or not, who may be assigned the task of representing culture. Are they, as primary transmitters of culture through their reproductive and mothering roles, repositories of tradition? Do women communicate messages? Women represent the status and power of their group, exhibiting its wealth and upholding its honor. Traditionally, as Middle Eastern men gained in wealth their kinswomen often were secluded or veiled as a sign of prestige.[16] In addition, the piety of a man is often displayed in his wife's modest and circumspect demeanor and clothing. Displaying modernity is also a task accorded women. Western clothing, higher education, white-collar employment, the vote can be signs of modernity that women visibly display, yet they can be accompanied by a continued denial of personal autonomy and equality of legal rights.

Are women metaphors that transcend social discontinuities to form the basis of a social language intelligible to believing Muslims? Gustav Thaiss contends that in the discourse used by the Islamic opposition to the Shah's regime in the 1970s, women were metaphors for the integrity of the Islamic community, expressing its purity in an idiom common to Muslim culture—the honor and chastity of women. On the one hand, women were metaphors for attacks on the community of believers—the Iranian Muslim community as a once pure but now violated woman. On the other hand, the polluting and dangerous nature of women serves as a metaphor for the forces that lead men to deviate from the path of Islam.[17]

Those who present culture to outsiders and who embody valued cultural attributes in an idealized form are persons designated to offer a representative sample of what is considered culturally significant in a society's interaction with external forces. An examination of a few selected facets of Palestinian society in pre-1982 Lebanon will illustrate that the role of gender in the search for an authentic tradition holds a dual meaning for women. This is an instance where the quest for an authentic society and culture was an integral component of a community's creative dynamic in response to assaults on its basic foundations. In this case both class and gender are salient features in an authentic presentation of culture. Women's representation of culture is somewhat striking when juxtaposed to a past practice of semi-marginality in *public* life. In contemporary Palestinian society in Lebanon there was a division of labor for presenting culture: on one hand the resistance cadres, usually middle class and knowledgeable of foreign languages, and on the other the mass of camp people, poor and of peasant origins. Women figured prominently in both categories.

In pre-1948 Palestinian villages, visitors were received and hosted in the village guest house, a largely male preserve. By contrast, in Palestinian camps, whose population is composed of these same peasants and their descendants, women are integral to the presentation of their societies; they present and are presented as "commentaries" on various dimensions of the Palestinian condition.

Mothers of Martyrs and Militants

In pre-1982 Lebanon, Palestinians were vitally aware of the implications of presenting their culture to outsiders. Their readiness to present their culture and the calculations that accompanied it were a means of reclaiming the past and asserting control over their own future. Like the Kwaio, Palestinians were in the process of objectifying their culture in order to present it to outsiders. During the ethnographic encounter, the embeddedness of women's lives in the political matrix was immediately apparent. The manner in which women presented their lives to outsiders and the content of their discourse were located in the historical and political context of the specific instance of ethnographic research. Palestinian women viewed their own lives as commentaries on suffering and militancy. They embodied the dialectical experience of national dispossession and resistance. Indeed, in the beginning it was difficult to elicit anything other than historical-political information from them, as women tended to perceive their role in speaking with outsiders as one of conveying the misery of exile and the sacrifices and glory of national resistance. The setting defined the nature of the dialogue; in such a situation, women felt compelled to represent the collective experience and situation and tended to downplay personal experiences. Once I was able to elicit personal stories (the home was a much better place to talk), it became clear that the presentation of their lives was divided into fairly clearly demarcated historical periods. Major life events, such as marriages, births, graduations, illnesses, deaths, employment, etc. are juxtaposed with the major events of Palestinian sociopolitical history. The war and subsequent exile of 1948, the years of waiting in the 1950s and early 1960s, the 1967 war, the rise of the Resistance movement, and the Lebanese civil war of 1975–76 were the markers around which women organized the presentation of their lives. Thus women do not perceive or present their lives as solely localized or personal affairs, but situate themselves in the local, regional, national, and international matrix reflecting their own individual experience of political events—a patent case of the political as personal.

The relating of life stories, recollections of historical events, and the solicitation of opinions on political matters were often occasions for dramatic performances that affirmed community consensus and served as vehicles of socialization in heritage.[18] One evening in early 1982 I visited Um Yasser,[19] a fifty-year-old mother of ten and wife of a full-time guerrilla in Ain al-Helwah camp. I had planned to discuss with her the events of 1948 and to elicit her perceptions of women's role in the national movement. Three of her daughters and two of her sons gathered around the colorful cotton sleeping cushions spread out on the floor to listen to her stories. They interrupted now and then to clarify a point and in the process garnered details of their family, village, and cultural history. For instance, I asked her how much she had received as her *mahr* (bride-wealth). When she said about two hundred Palestinian pounds, her eldest son said he thought that was a lot of money at the time. She proceeded to tell him and the other children that it was a substantial amount of money, enough to cause her husband's family to consider it carefully. She is a Bedouin, and customarily they did not marry their daughters to peasants. Therefore her family felt justified in asking for a rather steep *mahr*. Her children would frequently ask her to clarify her story of how they left in 1948. They had heard the story many times, but each time new details emerged; old ones were repeated for the umpteenth time. Sometimes she would direct her dialogue to her children, explaining kin and village relations when mentioning a person from the past. Her stories of 1948 and the fighting around her village kept alive the heritage of her children, conveying to them the experiences of a generation of Palestinians who experienced the exodus firsthand.

On another occasion when I visited Um Yasser, several of her woman neighbors came over to chat with us. I thought this an opportune time to ask her a few questions about the situation of women in the national movement and in the camps. Her neighbors felt at ease to intersperse their own comments when they felt it would better clarify issues. All had their own experiences of events to add, reaffirming what another had said but adding personal touches. In this way individual experiences became integral parts of a collective experience reaffirming the community consensus. When Um Yasser expounded upon a topic as she did when I inquired about the situation of women in the movement, the other women cleared the verbal stage and a hushed silence fell over the room. Some of Um Yasser's statements would evoke supportive interjections from what now resembled an audience—"By God, we have our rights now," "The Resistance has given us our rights," and "Young women today are lucky—they are free to come and go, to marry whom they please." Her descriptions of the years of early hardship in the makeshift camps evoked knowing and empathetic interjections—"By God, how we suffered" and

"Thank God we survived." Elderly, ordinary women, nationalists but not formally affiliated to any political organization, most often conveyed the sense of tragedy and suffering because they had experienced it firsthand over the last forty years.

What elements of culture and tradition do women convey and are they expected to convey in the presentation of Palestinian society? A pervasive quality or ethos of contemporary Palestinian culture is militancy (*nidal*), whose concrete expression is found in the PLO with its myriad sociopolitical institutions and military wing, and in the idea of steadfastness, the quality of facing and remaining undaunted in the face of national adversity. The quest for a peculiarly authentic "Palestinianism" assigns women contradictory positions; they have been appointed on the one hand to provide a commentary on suffering and tragedy and, on the other hand, to be commentators on, or a measure of, militancy. "Mothers of martyrs" combine elements of both. Women who have lost sons in battle are highly respected for their sacrifice. They are collective mourners epitomizing the continuing high losses in a militant refugee society, yet they defy the often seemingly insurmountable forces that have resulted in their dispossession, having made the ultimate sacrifice— their children. The stature accorded the mother of the martyr is a communal expression of the solidarity attendant on national conflict. Delegations of activist women visit her on religious and national holidays, giving gifts of sweets. During national celebrations, marked by rallies and large public gatherings, she is usually seated in the front near the leaders, a position of honor that indicates respect for her new status as one who has made a substantial contribution to the national endeavor. Speeches by political leaders extol her virtues as the mother of all Palestinians. She is frequently visited by social workers who try to remain abreast of her financial and medical needs. These public, almost ritualistic, demonstrations of solicitude underscore how women's reproductive capacity has been endowed with political meaning, representing and serving as a commentary on both suffering and the requisite sacrifices of militancy.

Is there a relationship between women's representation of culture and class? More specifically, is this an instance where class and gender intersect? My ethnographic observations of Palestinian society in Lebanon led me to note a rather consistent pattern whereby lower-class women, usually the most powerless and in this case vulnerable sector of society, are more readily assigned the task of being testimonials to the tragic dimension of culture. Indeed, it could hardly be otherwise, for mothers of martyrs are infrequently anybody other than poor camp women; the young men who join the military are overwhelmingly of camp origin. Yet occasionally one encounters middle-and upper-class mothers of martyrs. A distinction must be drawn between the camp mother of the martyr and the urban middle-and upper-class mother of the martyr. The following incident illuminates these differences and their meaning. Madame Farah, a middle-class Palestinian whose only son, a university student, was killed in battle, exclaimed to his friends at his funeral: "Why take my son, take someone else's! What do we have to do with this resistance movement!" To voice such sentiments in the camps would violate the norms of community participation in shouldering the burdens of the diaspora and involvement in the national movement. It would immediately set one apart from the rest of camp society, many of whose members have undergone precisely such a traumatic experience or, at the least, share the potential for such a loss. It is at the funeral of martyrs that camp mothers are praised as the "mother of all young men," highlighting communal solidarity and affirming the enmeshment of her sacrifice in the larger sociopolitical matrix. Rather than blaming the Resistance for the loss of their sons, the camp mothers are likely to locate the cause of their deaths squarely with the forces that killed him. To blame the Resistance was considered shocking. One's attention is drawn to the class disparities in upholding and exemplifying the more violent and sacrificial aspects of the national movement. One mother sees herself not as having contributed something but as having something taken from her; the other mother feels, and is encouraged to feel, that she personally has made a contribution. She voices herself in the first person singular—"I sacrificed my son for the cause," "I gave my child," "I've made a contribution to the cause."

In the division of cultural representation, lower-class women are testimonials to sacrifice and tradition, whereas middle-and upper-class women represent progress. An indication that the camp mothers of the martyrs were assigned to represent the tragic and sacrificial dimension of society to the outside was the practice of taking journalists and delegations to visit them as one of the primary components of their "tour" of Palestinian society. Along with the social institutions constructed and managed by the national movement, mothers of martyrs were a salient component of the presentation of culture. To visit them was to witness and partake in the drama of presentation, the staging of culture, and the outward manifestation and conscious manipulation of representations that poignantly capture the Palestinian dilemma.

As an anthropologist, it was assumed that I would want to meet mothers of martyrs, wives of martyrs, and activist women. Naturally I wanted to meet these women, but not everyone could understand my interest in ordinary women as well.[20] By "ordinary," I refer to women who were not formally politically active and had not experienced numerous losses. But even ordinary camp women were presented as the epitome of Palestinianness. Visitors to the camps are frequently told that these, the mass of poor camp women, are the ones who "really suffer" and bear the brunt of the refugee conditions. The more numerous the children she has borne and raised the more an ordinary woman is held up as a representative of the Palestinian experience of exile. During crises, staying in the camp and not fleeing attack is described and valued as a militant act. Ordinary women also perceive themselves as bearers of a new culture of militancy. Indeed women, particularly housewives, described their whole lives as a form of struggle, their discourse pervaded by political and military terms. Women use such a lexicon not only when the situation seems to solicit it, as in the presence of outsiders, but in conversing among themselves as well. The position accorded ordinary women clearly points to a class division of labor in the representation of exile society. Ordinary camp women shoulder a heavier burden of exile than do their urban middle-and upper-class counterparts. Collective traumas such as the Sabra-Chatila massacres and sieges of the camps weigh more heavily on camp women. Moreover, the resistance displayed by camp residents during these incidents is subsequently incorporated into the Palestinian collective consciousness. Camp women are then lauded both as victims, representing the victimization of a whole people, and conversely as survivors who continue to bear children amidst extreme poverty and insecurity and try to hold their families together in the face of powerful forces of dispersal. Urban middle-and upper-class women simply do not share this representational assignment or the repeated trauma of assaults. Camp women have few options in deciding whether or not to accept this designation; it has become an inevitable and pronounced aspect of their daily lives.

Whereas the celebrated "mother of the martyr" poignantly reveals and represents the continuing tragedy of the Palestinian exile community, the female fighter/worker/political activist represents the adoption of an active stance, a direct and consciously undertaken challenge to the political equation. Although both the mother of the martyr and the activist represent the active refusal of a people to adopt a passive stance and disappear from the political and historical scene, the militant also represents social progress, a vital component in the process of sociopolitical transformation. Women activists who achieve recognition for heroism are called "true strugglers" while mothers of martyrs are the embodiment of "true suffering."

Activist women, women employees, and those enrolled in vocational or literacy training projects are also included in the presentation of society to others. Like the mother of the martyr, they are high on the list of what should be displayed for visitors. To those outside Palestinian society, they are held up as examples of the extent to which exile and militancy have transformed society, compelling the casting aside of traditional cultural norms. Female activism is touted as a hallmark of the progressive dimension of Palestinian society.

The class division of labor that suffuses the presentation of different aspects of Palestinian society is most readily discernible in the case of the mothers of the martyrs. But it is not simply a matter of poor camp vs. middle-class urban women. Gender itself is a primary component, intertwining with class in a complex way. Middle-class women, who prevail among women activists, represent women's new (although limited) access to power and the Resistance's implementation of a debatably progressive policy on women. They are publicly visible during conferences, as members of Palestinian delegations to international conferences, and in press interviews. Welcoming and hosting visiting delegations provides the opportunity for them to display women's inclusion in the national movement. However, a middle-class activist was quick to point out: "Be careful of the official line. The Resistance is aware that foreigners judge it by its ideas and programs on women. So they put on a good face about women when foreigners come." Thus women themselves are aware of their centrality in the presentation of culture. Camp women, more often involved in literacy and vocational training projects, and workers in resistance-sponsored industries in the camps, are presented to outsiders as part of the tour of resistance institutions. They are meant to display the movement's capacity to build projects to advance the developmental infrastructure and draw women into it in an attempt to dilute family-based control over their public participation.

Any discussion of authenticity must include at least a cursory reference to the centrality of notions of reproduction and motherhood. This takes on an added imperative in a society engaged in a protracted and violent conflict. Palestinians, both inside Israel and outside, know their high birth rate increasingly constitutes a weapon in a long-term war of demography. However, the birth rate issue has the potential to become controversial within Palestinian circles, though it has yet to erupt in open confrontation. Men can often be heard to glorify women's role in reproduction, jokingly stating that women should produce as many children as possible for the sake of the national cause. Some women also voice such sentiments—"Raising children is a contribution to the cause."[21] But the rhetoric is not necessarily carried over into reality. Women are not denied access to birth control, though neither are they encouraged to practice it. Women activists and health personnel gently counsel the spacing of children to improve the health of mothers and their children. The subject has not yet become a topic for debate, though as younger women have smaller families the rhetoric may one day become more than just rhetoric.

The visual arts often reflect tension between definitions, identities, and expectations of women. Palestinian poster art, a popular medium for expressing political sentiments, captures and renders the duality of women's representation and cultural assignment. A common theme is the mother, in traditional Palestinian dress, carrying both child and gun. The depiction of pregnant gun-carrying women lends visual expression to the most fundamental duality.[22]

Even as mundane a topic as clothing can reveal much about the reconstruction of a society and the role women play in expressing authenticity. Traditional Palestinian embroidery, colorful and intricately designed, has passed through a renaissance of sorts in the last decade. Camp women have been trained in the art of embroidery, and many produce fine pieces at home for sale through Resistance-sponsored co-ops and small workshops. Costly salon pieces adorn the homes of urban Palestinians, and both middle-and upper-class women display Palestinian culture by wearing traditional dresses. Middle-aged and elderly peasant women continue to wear the dresses as their normal everyday clothing; the urban middle class and the elite have adopted them as a symbol of nationalism and a reclamation of the past and future, whose artistic expression they find rendered in traditional clothing. The introduction of a primarily peasant art form into the wardrobes and homes of the bourgeoisie affirms the emergence of a distinctly Palestinian cultural unity in spite of geographic fragmentation, a phenomenon not without precedent in Palestinian society. The *kuffiyah* (black-and-white or red-and-white checked kerchief), a largely peasant form of headdress, was donned by urbanites during the 1936 Rebellion in Palestine as a symbol of defiance and national solidarity;[23] Christian urban women were reported to have veiled in a similar gesture of national unity.

Conclusion

Is women's involvement in the search for a secular, seemingly progressive tradition necessarily a positive phenomenon for them? Can it not also place a heavy burden of representation on women, a representation that is subject to controls? It is apparent that we must ask to what extent women's representation of progress and authenticity is a concept of self developed by women and to what extent it is an imposed one defined more by others. Women are increasingly in a position to decide for themselves what they desire to represent. Yet they do not actively oppose the assignment of cultural representation.

Palestinian women do not represent only tradition. They may stand as symbols of progress. But, it may be argued, this does not allow women to escape the burden of representing authentic culture; it simply expands the parameters and contents of authenticity.

NOTES

1. This chapter is based on data collected for the author's dissertation in anthropology during fieldwork in Lebanon in 1980–82. Funding for writing was obtained from the Diana Tamari Sabbagh Foundation.

2. *Anthropological Quarterly* (Self and Society in the Middle East) 58 (1985) is composed of articles that adhere to an integrated approach often absent in Middle East anthropological literature.

3. See Laura Nader, "Up the Anthropologist—Perspectives Gained from Studying Up," in Dell Hymes, ed., *Reinventing Anthropology* (New York: Vintage Books, 1974), pp. 284–311, for an interesting discussion about studying the power spectrum in the U.S.

4. Roger Keesing, "Kwaio Women Speak: The Micropolitics of Autobiography in a Solomon Island Society," *American Anthropologist* 87(1985): 37.

5. Ibid.

6. Mina Davis Caulfield, "Culture and Imperialism: Proposing a New Dialectic," in Hymes, ed., *Reinventing Anthropology*, pp. 203, 204.

7. Ibid.

8. There is a voluminous body of literature on the honor/shame complex in Middle Eastern and Mediterranean societies. See among others: Lila Abu-Lughod, *Veiled Sentiments: Honor and Poetry in a Bedouin Society* (Berkeley and Los Angeles: University of California Press, 1986); Richard Antoun, "On the Modesty of Women in Arab Muslim Villages: A Study in the Accommodation of Tradition," *American Anthropologist* 70(1968): 671–97; Anton Blok, "Rams and Billygoats: A Key to Mediterranean Code of Honor," *MAN* 16(1981); Michael Meeker, "Meaning and Society in the Near East: Examples from the Black Sea Turks and the Levantine Arabs," *International Journal of Middle East Studies*, 7(1976): 243–270; Fatima Mernissi, *Beyond the Veil: Male-Female Dynamics in a Modern Muslim Society* (New York: Schenkman Publishing Co., 1975); J. Peristiany, ed., *Honor and Shame; The Values of Mediterranean Society* (Chicago: University of Chicago Press, 1966); Jane Schneider, "Of Vigilance and Virgins: Honor, Shame and Access to Resources in Mediterranean Societies," *Ethnology* 10(1971): 1–24.

9. Peter Dodd and Halim Barakat, *River without Bridges: A Study of the Exodus of the 1967 Palestinian Arab Refugees* (Beirut: Institute for Palestine Studies, 1969).

10. *Jil al-thawra*, the generation of the revolution, refers to those Palestinians born in the diaspora who grew up during a period (roughly speaking, in Lebanon from 1969–1982) when the Resistance movement exercised its open, armed presence and exerted a considerable influence over the daily lives of most camp Palestinians.

11. Richard Handler, "Authenticity," *Anthropology Today* 2 (1986): 2–4.

12. See Issa Boulatta, "Challenges to Arab Cultural Authenticity" and Kamal Abu Deeb, "Cultural Creation in a Fragmented Society," in Hisham Sharabi, ed., *The Next Arab Decade* (Washington, D.C.: Center for Contemporary Arab Studies, Georgetown University, 1988).

13. R. Handler aptly notes that the concern with authenticity is not confined to those societies studied by western anthropologists when he writes that "the same constellation of cultural ideas which allows a soft drink to be marketed as the 'real thing,' with the suggestion that those who chose it thereby gain a real or authentic existence, underlies the anthropological search for authenticity." Op. cit., 2.

14. For a discussion of tribal representation in Jordan see Linda Layne, "Self-Representation in Jordan," *American Ethnologist* 16, 1 (1989).

15. Pierre Bourdieu, "Guerres et Mutation Sociale en Algérie," *Etudes Méditerranéennes* 7 (1960): 25–37, quoted in Eric Wolf, *Peasant Wars of the Twentieth Century* (New York: Harper & Row, 1969), p. 225.

16. See Gerda Lerner, *The Creation of Patriarchy* (New York: Oxford University Press, 1986), chap. 6, "Veiling the Woman," pp. 123–40, for an account of the veil's early association with the formation of class society and its signification of prestige.

17. See Gustav Thaiss, "The Conceptualization of Social Change through Metaphor," *Journal of Asian and African Studies* 13(1978): 1–13 and Fatna Sabbah, *Women in the Muslim Unconscious* (New York: Pergamon Press, 1984) on the Islamic conception of woman as a source of desire that leads men astray from the path of righteousness.

18. For an engaging discussion of lower-class Cairene women's narratives and their cathartic effect in the process of self-affirmation, see Evelyn Early, "Catharsis and Creation: The Everyday Narratives of Baladi Women of Cairo," *Anthropological Quarterly* 58(1985): 172–81.

19. All names are pseudonyms.

20. For accounts of ordinary Palestinian women and political conflict, see Julie Peteet and Rosemary Sayigh, "Between Two Fires: Palestinian Women in Lebanon" in Rosemary Ridd and Helen Callaway, eds., *Caught Up in Conflict: Women's Response*

to Political Strife (London: Macmillan, 1986). This volume includes similar articles on Cypriot, Irish, Turkish, Iranian, Israeli, and Breton women.

21. See Peteet, ibid.

22. See J. Peteet, "Women and the Palestinian Movement: No Going Back?" *Middle East Report* 138(1986): 20–24, for a discussion of the politicization of women's domesticity.

23. Walid Khalidi, *Before Their Diaspora: A Photographic History of the Palestinians 1876–1948* (Washington, D.C.: Institute for Palestine Studies, 1984), p. 203. Photo 250 shows detainees during the 1936 Rebellion garbed in traditional dress. The caption reads: "Traditional dress was worn by urban detainees as a gesture of defiance."

II

Women's Work
and Development

IV

WOMEN AND ECONOMIC CHANGE IN NINETEENTH-CENTURY SYRIA
THE CASE OF ALEPPO

Margaret L. Meriwether

The impact of the world market and capitalist development on Middle Eastern women has generated considerable literature. One central issue in this literature is the impact of these changes on the productive activities of women and on their access to and control of critical economic resources. In rural areas, women's productive activities have inevitably been affected by the transition from subsistence to market economy, from production of food crops to production of cash crops, from communal or hereditary usufructuary rights to private ownership of land, and from the household as a unit of production and consumption to the household as a unit of consumption. In urban areas, the division between work place and residence and the new conditions of the market have similarly affected the value and availability of different kinds of economic resources and tended to devalue the labor that women have done or the resources that they have controlled, and to deny them control over more socially valued resources. The conclusion reached by many researchers on this issue is that women have often lost the authority and power, as well as the choices, that were available to them in the precapitalist economy. The research has revealed the fallacy of the belief that westernization, modernization, and economic development have brought an automatic improvement in the lives and status of Middle Eastern women. Clearly, the reality is much more complex, and making meaningful analyses/conclusions from the diverse experiences of Middle Eastern women is not easy.

Doing justice to the complexity of women's experiences under changing global economic conditions requires a closer look at the historical experiences of Middle Eastern women in the early stages of the long-term process during which the Middle East was more and more closely integrated into the global economic system. Both the time framework in which this process occurred and regional conditions—traditional economic organization, the particular relationship to the forces of the world economy, the responses of local actors—affected the degree of autonomy an area could maintain and its ability to control its own development. These in turn affected the extent of social dislocation and its impact on women.

Egypt is as yet the only area of the Middle East where the issue of the impact of the world market and capitalist development on women in the nineteenth century has been systematically explored. Judith Tucker has shown how the transition from subsistence economy to statist industrialization under Muhammad Ali initially created a demand for female labor in both agricultural and industrial production, while at the same time, it changed women's role vis-à-vis the household economy. After the failure of Muhammad Ali's industrialization program and the transition to an export economy, the demand for women's labor in new enterprises declined. Meanwhile, rural and urban society were so much changed that women were unable to play the kinds of roles in production or control the kind of resources that they had in the past. Judith Gran has shown that, in later stages of this process, upper-class Egyptian women found their options and activities greatly expanded, while women of the urban lower middle classes experienced just the opposite.[1]

The Egyptian case, however, was special in the speed and thoroughness with which Egypt was integrated into the global economic system and its economy and society transformed. In Syria, where there was no Muhammad Ali to enforce a radical restructuring of government, economy, and society, the pace and extent of the integration into the world economy and the degree of change varied. Areas like Lebanon, where an export economy quickly developed around the production of silk, underwent a similar transformation.[2] In the interior, however, the old caravan cities, which had historically been centers of international and regional commerce and local production, were affected by these changes, but the consequences for the local economy and society were different. In particular, at least in the early stages of this process, the impact on the productive work of women and their control of economic resources differed in important respects from the Egyptian case. It is the experience of Syrian women in the first half of the nineteenth century that will be explored in this paper through a case study of Aleppo. In order to set the context, it is necessary to describe the stages of economic change in Aleppo in the eighteenth and nineteenth century.

Stages of Economic Change

Aleppo's commercial fame before 1750 rested on its role as the hub of an international trading network linking the East with Europe. Iranian silk and other eastern goods passed to Europe through Aleppo, while English woolens were distributed throughout Syria, Iraq, and southern Anatolia. More important to the economic vitality of the city, however, were its other economic roles. Aleppo was part of what one historian has called an "Ottoman world market."[3] In this system, it was a major transit center through which the products of Iran, India, and the Far East passed to Istanbul, and the produce of the Balkans and Anatolia to Iraq. It was also an important center of production and exported the products of its own workshops and countryside. Ultimately, Aleppo's prosperity depended more on trade within the Empire and on local production than on trade with Europe.[4]

After 1750, European economic dominance became more clearly established. While a definitive study of Aleppo's economic history from 1750 to 1914 has yet to be written, it is possible to identify three stages (1750–1830, 1830–1860, 1860–1914) of economic change during this time which mark turning points in Aleppo's integration into the European-dominated world economy.[5]

The first stage, 1750–1830, was characterized by a clear shift in the nature of the trade with Europe. With the decline of the silk trade after 1750, Aleppo was no longer the middleman in commerce between Europe and the East. Instead it became an exporter of raw materials (especially cotton) and importer of European manufactured goods. Trade with Europe, particularly France, expanded rapidly in the late eighteenth century.[6] The consequences of this new economic relationship with Europe were limited, however, in large part because trade with Europe still played a relatively small role in the overall economy of the city and the province. Until the 1820s, trade with Europe was balanced by the continued prosperity of trade with the Empire and the East and the continued demand from these sources for Aleppo goods.[7] Coffee, tobacco, and local textiles, all central to the caravan trade, continued to earn large profits for local customs, and the wealth of the merchants engaged in this trade was apparent.[8]

By the 1830s, however, the impact of the expanding European economy could no longer be easily absorbed, and the traditional economy began to feel the effects. The end of the Napoleonic wars, the quickening tempo of the Industrial Revolution, and the development of steam navigation brought renewed European pressure on and involvement in the Middle East, including northern Syria. These external developments coincided with a series of internal crises in Aleppo during the 1820s which left Aleppo vulnerable to outside forces.[9] The 1830s marked the transition to the second economic stage, the establishment of the "colonial economy" in Aleppo. The decisive event which marked the beginning of this stage was the Egyptian occupation in 1831. Its most important long-term consequence for Aleppo was the revival of trade with Europe, especially England. Direct trade between Aleppo and Great Britain was re-established in 1828.[10] British merchants were attracted to Aleppo because they considered Aleppo "by far the most important interior depot" of Syria, the key to selling British goods throughout northern Syria, southern Anatolia, and Iraq.[11]

This second economic stage saw the continuation of the exchange of Syrian raw materials for European manufactured goods, a pattern already established in the late eighteenth century. What was new about this stage was the extent to which trade with Europe dominated Aleppo's economy and set the conditions under which other sectors of the economy operated. The sheer growth in the volume of trade between 1830 and 1860 was largely responsible for Europe's dominant position.[12] The consequences of increased trade with Europe were felt throughout the economy. As the figures on imports and exports indicate, one of the most serious consequences was the growing trade deficit, which was no longer offset by the strength of the eastern trade.[13] Aleppo's exports to Europe—grain, wool, cotton, gallnuts, and pistachios—did not earn enough profits to pay for the manufactured goods that were imported, even as prices for these commodities rose between 1835 and 1870 in response to the increase in European demand. The trade deficit meant a large bullion drain, which resulted in serious fluctuations in the currency. Inflation also became a serious problem. In addition, two other major consequences were apparent. The dominance of European trade in the economy stimulated the production of cash crops like cotton, wheat, and sesame seeds. It also led to the decline of local production, particularly textiles, and the displacement of eastern and local goods by European goods in the markets.

Despite these characteristics of a colonial economy, the transition to such an economy was not complete, and the consequences of this change not as disruptive as in Egypt. As Aleppo's commercial relationship with Europe stabilized in the second half of the nineteenth century, Aleppo's economy entered a third stage, which might be called a modified colonial economy. Aleppo continued to be a major transit center, not simply an exporter of raw materials and importer of manufactured goods. At least one-third of all goods imported into Aleppo, including manufactured goods from Europe, were re-exported to those areas with which Aleppo had traditionally had strong commercial links.[14] Aleppo also remained a point of export for goods from as far away as Iraq and Iran. Aleppo merchants were found in cities all over Anatolia and Iraq engaged in facilitating this trade.[15] The type of goods and their ultimate destination had changed, but they were carried through the traditional commercial networks, which remained under the control of members of the indigenous population. To some extent this trade offset the trade deficit with Europe.

Moreover, Aleppo continued to export some locally manufactured goods. Although the textile industry declined, after a point it stabilized, and Aleppo's weavers could compete in certain markets, supplying finished goods to Anatolia and Egypt throughout the rest of the century.[16] Aleppo's largest trading partners at the end of the nineteenth century were Turkey and Egypt rather than any one of the European countries.[17] The city also never came to rely exclusively on a single cash crop, as Egypt did, instead exporting a variety of raw materials.

That Aleppo's economy retained certain strengths from its traditional commercial and productive role and was not transformed completely into a colonial economy does not mean that the consequences of economic change in the city and province were easily absorbed. It does mean that the impact of the integration into the world economy was highly selective. Some groups were little affected by it; others were able to adapt; while still others suffered greatly from the consequences of unemployment, underemployment, high prices, shortages, and low wages. The rebellion of 1850 was a clear symptom not only of unresolved political conflicts of an earlier period, but also of the social tensions generated by economic change and the uneven burden of this change. Women were no exception. The effect of these changes on the productive activities of women and their control of economic resources was determined by their relative position in the class structure and by the particular relationship of these activities and resources to the organization of labor and distribution of resources in the society. The remainder of this paper will examine the most important consequences of integration into the world economy—the shift of resources to real estate, the crisis in textile production, the commercialization of agriculture, and inflation—and how they affected women in different classes.

Upper-Class Women and Property

The initial stage of economic change, 1750–1830, coincided with the acceleration of a striking trend in the eighteenth century, the rush to buy property. Several factors that grew out of the general political and economic environment of the Ottoman Empire in the eighteenth century help explain this trend. On the one hand, it reflected a renewed period of urban growth and development as a result of new resources coming into the city. In the eighteenth century, economic and administrative changes in the Ottoman Empire put more money in the hands of local notables, who were then searching for outlets for this cash. They found an outlet partly in taxfarming, which was a lucrative investment and a means of exercising a new kind of power through the control of rural surpluses.[18] Taxfarming, however, was a precarious investment, and many of these notables were clearly searching for more secure and stable investments. Property represented that kind of investment. Rural property was in short supply, since most agricultural land was state-owned. While they purchased what rural property they could, primarily vineyards, orchards, and mills, most turned their attention to urban real estate.[19] This choice of investment reflected another reality of the period: the uncertainty that economic change and political instability brought. For the timing of this movement toward the investment in property was likely not a coincidence. It represented a strategy of seeking more secure and diversified investments in a time of change. The effect was to enhance the importance of urban property in the total configuration of resources which these notables controlled.

Women as well as men owned urban property. Islamic law gives women important rights with regard to property. Marriage and inheritance laws are both designed to provide women with some basic economic security. Therefore, women from those classes prosperous enough had access to their own resources and a modicum of economic independence guaranteed by Islamic law. Inheritance laws gave women rights to a portion of the estates of their male relatives, and, thus, women had a share in the family resources. Marriage laws stipulated that the *mahr*, which was given by the husband's family to the bride and was usually used to purchase jewelry and household goods, remained solely the property of the woman. In addition, any property that the woman brought with her at the time of the marriage and any property that she subsequently acquired remained hers. Theoretically, her husband had no control over it.

Women were property owners of some importance in the eighteenth and nineteenth centuries, even as property was growing in importance as an investment. The best evidence of this lies in the participation of women in the real estate market. In 1770, 59 percent of all property sales involved women as either buyers or sellers; in 1800, 67 percent; and in 1840, 53 percent. However, the percentage of women involved in property sales is less important than the reason why they were buying and selling property, how they obtained access to the property, and what kind of property they controlled.[20] For example, it is possible that women's involvement in the real estate market simply reflected pressure that was put on women to give up property that they had inherited. For many property-owning families, a significant part of the family patrimony was tied up in urban real estate, and there was a sense of the importance of keeping that property together.[21] If this were the case, then in the majority of sales involving women, they would be sellers, the sales would involve inherited property, and the person buying the property would be a male relative. Clearly, some sales followed this pattern, although that was true also of the sales of some men.[22] In the majority of cases, however, women were engaged in property transactions in their own right. Women bought property as well as sold it. Some of the property which they sold had been acquired by inheritance, but much of it had also been acquired by purchase. There was not a significant difference from men in the kind, value, and location of the property that women owned.[23]

The fact that women were actively engaged in the real estate market throughout the period between 1750 and 1850 is important evidence of their economic position. Nevertheless, legal title to property does not prove that women ultimately controlled the property and that economic control was transformed into meaningful authority and status within the family unit. In many areas of the Middle East, female ownership of property was a legal fiction; control of the property remained in male hands.[24] One nineteenth-century European resident of Beirut claimed that female ownership of property was a strategy employed by property-owning males to avoid the threat of confiscation in an unstable political environment. Property was registered in the woman's name because the authorities would then hesitate to confiscate it.[25] However, although this was undoubtedly true at times, evidence from the involvement of some women in *waqf* in Aleppo strongly suggests that women did manage their own property and make decisions about its disposition.[26]

A large number of *awqaf* were set up in Aleppo in the eighteenth and first half of the nineteenth century, and a significant number of the endowers of these *awqaf* were women. In the decades from 1770 to 1820, the number of new *awqaf* averaged about seventy-five per decade. In the first two decades, men established about ten more *awqaf* than women; however, in the next three decades the pattern was reversed. In the period after 1820, the number of new *awqaf* fell off, but women and men were equally represented among this smaller group of endowers.[27] Moreover, the nature of these *awqaf*—the kind of property and its value, how it was acquired, the amount of property, and the type of *awqaf* (i.e., *khayri* or *dhurri*)—was similar for men and for women. The major difference was that no woman created a *waqf* as large as the dozen or so largest *awqaf* established by men, which ranged from fifty to over a hundred pieces of property. The largest *waqf* established by a woman during this period was that of Saliha bint Muhammad Taybi, which included a couple of dozen pieces of property.[28]

The most significant aspect of women's involvement in the establishment of *awqaf*, however, was the set of arrangements that they made for the administration of the endowments. In all but a few cases, women appointed themselves as the administrators (*mutawalli*) of the endowment for their lifetimes. That meant that they actually managed the property and the payment of the income to those people or institutions designated to receive it. Moreover, the endower's female children and descendants were usually included among the possible future administrators. In a few cases, the endower restricted the office of administrator to female descendants, at least until there were no more female descendants. At that time, the male descendants of their female descendants would be eligible.[29] However, such cases were rare. More often, future administrators were to be drawn from the most worthy descendants of the endower, male or female. Women, therefore, were not specifically designated as administrators, but theoretically had an equal chance with male descendants. By contrast, male endowers were more likely to favor their male descendants. These arrangements were not just legal fiction. Women appeared frequently before the *qadi* in their role as administrators of endowments, making arrangements for rental or repair of *waqf* property and for the collection or payment of income.[30] Women also brought suit on occasion to claim their right to be considered the most worthy descendant of an endower and therefore their right to be administrator of the endowment, and they often won these suits.[31] *Waqf* property was economically, socially, and religiously significant in eighteenth and nineteenth century Aleppo society. The fact that women not only created endowments but also were active managers of endowments attests to the reality of their control of property.

The distribution of the proceeds from those *awqaf* which were *awqaf dhuri-yya* is also suggestive of the relationship between women and property and of women's property to the total resources of the family. The most common arrangement for these *awqaf* funds was to divide the proceeds among the descendants of the endower, either among all of them equally or in proportion to what they would receive under the inheritance laws (i.e., females receiving half the share of males). Women's endowments sometimes followed this pattern, but more often than not they deviated from it. In many of the *awqaf dhurriyya* set up by women, the designated beneficiaries were other women, either daughters, sisters, mothers, or nieces, and in a couple of cases, manumitted female slaves. If they did set up the endowments for their male and female descendants, women were more likely to leave their income equally distributed among their male and female heirs. Men's endowments, on the other hand, tended to favor the males. The difference is quite important. On the one hand, it shows that female property was used for distinctive purposes and was not treated as part of the family patrimony. The disposition also suggests that women played a role in providing for the future security of other women. At the same time, it suggests that women did have the right, and acted upon it, to manage and make decisions about their own property, that it was theirs and under their control.

Among property-owning families, therefore, women legally owned and actually controlled property. Although it represented perhaps only a small part of the total family resources, it still meant some economic security and independence for the woman who owned it. It provided her with a means of taking care of herself if necessary and of providing for certain of her relatives as she perceived the need. Moreover, during this period of economic change, as property took on a new importance in the economy of the upper classes, women were able to retain their control of a valuable economic resource. In effect, then, upper-class women's experiences during this period of change paralleled those of the class and family to which they belonged. As the family prospered, so did they. If the family fortunes declined, so did theirs. Wealth was not redistributed within the family in such a way as to deprive women of their control of important resources; in the face of changing and uncertain circumstances, they retained their relative economic power and authority.

Lower-Class Urban Women and the Crisis in the Textile Industry

The kind of resources over which women of the propertied upper class had control were unaffected by the changes of the first half of the nineteenth century. For women from other parts of the urban population, however, the economic transition that Aleppo was undergoing had a direct, and largely negative, impact on their role in production. The productive activities of women from the lower strata are not very visible. Even the legal sources, the best sources on the activities of women, ignore those areas of the economy where women's work was essential, since they concentrate on property issues and on formal economic structures like the corporations. Piecing together the fragmentary evidence, however, gives a fairly clear picture of the general impact of economic change on the work of women, if not the details.

In the late eighteenth century, production was still dominated by hierarchically organized and highly specialized craft corporations, which regulated volume, price, and quality of goods, controlled membership and training, and were responsible for social control and social welfare among their members.[32] Women were naturally excluded from membership in these corporations, which meant that they received none of the benefits or protection that men engaged in similar productive activities could expect. Interestingly, however, women were sometimes able to influence corporation membership or receive income from it. This situation arose because of the way that corporation membership was regulated. Admission into the corporation was controlled through the issuing of *gedik*. An individual wishing to practice a particular craft was required to obtain a *gedik* which gave him the right to practice the craft in a particular shop or workshop, such as a *qasariyya*. In practical terms, the *gedik* referred to the particular tools, equipment, or physical space necessary to perform the job, but it also implied the right to practice the craft as well. Moreover, the *shaykh* of the corporation actually owned the raw materials and the finished products of the corporation, but the *gedik* included a contractual arrangement about how the raw materials and profits would be distributed among the members of the corporation.[33] The *gedik* was treated like property, and, at least among some corporations, it was inheritable. If a craftsman died with male heirs, at least one son had the right to follow his father in the practice of the craft and inherited the *gedik*. If he died without male heirs, however, the rights to the *gedik* passed to his female heirs. Since women could not exercise the *gedik* directly, they were allowed either to sell the *gedik* to a craftsman for a fair price or to retain the legal ownership and "rent" the *gedik* to members of the corporation. That is, the percentage of raw materials attached to that *gedik* was shared among these members. The legal owner would receive a share of the proceeds as "rent." Women were also able to transmit the *gedik* to their sons.[34] Because the *gedik* was treated as real property and because Islamic inheritance laws permitted women to inherit, this anomalous situation arose where women could influence the transferral of productive rights or benefit from the activities of a corporation, even though they were excluded from participation in the craft.

The system of corporations was one of the principal victims of the process of economic change that Aleppo underwent in the first half of the nineteenth century. The decline of the corporations went hand-in-hand with the competition from European manufactured goods and the changing tastes generated by new products. Some of the crafts disappeared entirely, such as that of the pipe-makers, who were put out of business by the introduction and growing popularity of cigarettes.[35] Others survived, but were seriously weakened by the loss of markets and access to raw materials.

The greatest casualty of these changes and the one whose decline was directly linked with changes in the productive activities of women was textile production. Textiles had been the most important local product. Aleppo textiles, especially the gold- and silver-embroidered cloth, brocades, and a striped cotton-silk fabric called *alaja*, had been famous throughout this part of the Ottoman Empire. In the late eighteenth century, about one-fourth of Aleppo's corporations were concerned in one way or another with the production of textiles, and they produced at least ten different kinds of cloth and finished goods.[36] The production of these goods was shared by a number of different corporations. For example, the production of *alaja* involved twelve different steps, each controlled by a different corporation.[37] Not all steps of the process were controlled by the corporation, however. In cotton production, spinning was not controlled; rather it was a cottage industry carried out by women in their homes.[38] No statistics exist for how many women were involved in these activities, but the extensive output of the textile workshops indicates that their numbers must have been considerable. The wages were undoubtedly extremely low, but the work provided women with some productive activity that could be performed in the home within the domestic context, and it was an activity on which the cotton weavers and wholesalers were dependent.

The decline of textile production had a major impact on the city, given how important textile production had been, but the impact on women was proportionally much greater because of the particular nature of the change in production. The exact timing of the decline in the textile industry is impossible to pinpoint without adequate production statistics. It is safe to assume that the decline was already underway by the first decade of the nineteenth century. The rapid increase in the volume of French textile imports in the last years of the eighteenth century inevitably had an effect.[39] The final blow, however, was the Egyptian occupation. Government monopolies on raw cotton, silk, and wool, which were shipped off to supply Egyptian mills, left local craftsmen short of raw materials during this period.[40] Furthermore, Egyptian encouragement of European trade, especially British trade, with Syria quickly flooded the markets with textiles that competed directly with local production, especially with the more ordinary cotton cloth. Silk textiles were less affected by direct competition, but changing tastes and economic austerity lessened the demand for luxury products.[41] The number of shops that handled British and French goods in the city market was eighty-two by 1840; the number handling Aleppo goods was fifty.[42]

Equally damaging was the Egyptian policy of conscription. The Egyptians began forcible conscription of men from the towns and villages of Syria in 1835. During that year, three separate levies were conducted in Aleppo, first among the urban population and then the entire province. Similar levies took place in 1836, 1837, and 1838, and to add insult to injury, they usually occurred during Ramadan.[43] The number of men who were taken from Aleppo is unclear. A quota was supposedly set at 10 or 15 percent of the male population, but the levies were accompanied by great irregularities, and many more men were taken than were actually required by the army.[44] Richard Wood claims that after one levy the streets of Aleppo were empty of men, and he describes a dramatic scene of women marching through the closed markets, bewailing the loss of their menfolks and demanding that something be done to stop the conscription.[45] Women took the lead in protesting conscription. They not only marched through the streets of the city, but even entered the coffeehouses to berate the men who were left for failing to stop conscription.[46] The city lost not only men who were drafted, but also additional men who fled in large numbers to escape conscription. Some of them went with their families and never returned. Conscription fell most heavily on the working classes of the city, since the well-to-do were usually able to buy their way out of the military. Many observers commented on the negative effects on the city of the loss of the productive population, and the large number of weavers who were taken was specifically mentioned.[47]

The extent of this decline in textile production was apparent in both the declining number of craftsmen and the declining number of looms. One observer said that the number of weavers in Aleppo dropped from between sixteen thousand and twenty thousand to two thousand by 1844.[48] Bowring estimated that six thousand were engaged in textile production in the 1830s.[49] The total number of looms in the city by the mid-1830s was four thousand. These four thousand looms equalled the number of looms operating in Aleppo during a very severe economic crisis in the middle of the eighteenth century.[50] The number of looms producing *alaja* declined from six thousand in 1829 to seventeen hundred in 1838, five hundred of which had been shifted to cotton weaving.[51]

Although the decline in the textile industry was significant, it did not disappear completely, and indeed stabilized after 1840. According to Bowring, there was some sign of revival in production by the end of the 1830s, a revival due to the increased demand for stuffs from Aleppo's market region. While British goods remained cheaper, Aleppo's manufactured cloth had a reputation for being more durable and so it increased in popularity, giving certain kinds of British cloth a run for their money.[52] Dominique Chevallier suggests that this persistence in textile production in face of the stiff competition from Europe was an act of resistance to the economic encroachment of Europe by the local population.[53]

This stabilization, however, did not do women engaged in textile production any good. What accompanied the decline in the 1830s was a restructuring of production. Cotton cloths were now woven not from local raw materials spun into thread by a cottage industry, but rather from imported twists and dyes.[54] The huge demand for imported twists and dyes reflects how extensively these materials were used in local production. The American consular agent in

Aleppo wrote a letter to the American consul in Beirut urging the Americans to get involved in supplying these goods to meet the rising demand in Aleppo.[55] The effect of this was to put the cottage industry out of business, and women lost this vital productive function. The looms continued to be operated by men and even children, but women apparently did not take over weaving responsibilities.[56]

Moreover, no other sources of employment appeared at this time to absorb the labor of women. Unlike Egypt and Lebanon, where women also lost productive functions, the economy did not evolve during this period to create new areas of employment for women. In Egypt, women were drafted to work in the textile mills set up by Muhammad Ali as craft production declined. When his industrialization scheme failed, women found employment in the ginning mills and cigarette factories that appeared in Egypt in the middle years of the nineteenth century.[57] In Lebanon, the growing silk industry employed women.[58] It was not until the late nineteenth century that changes in the nature of production, the emergence of textile factories on a larger scale, and the development of new cottage industries combined to again provide substantial employment for women in textile production.[59]

The change in the nature of the textile industry in Aleppo and the loss of employment by women came at a time when the lower classes of the population were experiencing considerable hardship. Inflation was a fact of life in the 1830s and 1840s. The cost of living rose dramatically as a result of the pressure on supplies created by Egyptian demands and of the increasing dependence on imported goods. Housing prices and rents remained stationary, but the prices of other necessities rose rapidly, and on some items, like grain and fuel, they more than doubled. The government fixed prices on retail goods, but these prices were largely ignored.[60] The government itself compounded the problem by imposing monopolies on production, from the "butcher's stall to vegetables, from the fish-market down to clay."[61] The low prices that the government paid the producers discouraged production, which created shortages. In addition, a large percentage of what was produced was taken by the government to feed, clothe, and supply the army, and this also contributed to shortages and higher prices.[62] The cost of living may have risen as much as 100 percent while wages remained stationary. Labor shortages, created by conscription, corvee labor, and flight, meant that rates of employment were high, but had little effect on wages. The higher cost of living, combined with a much higher tax burden, created real economic hardship for much of the population. The loss of income from women's work compounded an already serious problem.

Like upper-class women, working women shared in the fortunes of their class. The artisans and small craftsmen of Aleppo bore the burden of the changing economic organization of society. Women of this class shared the burden, but also suffered from its effects in a special way. The disappearance of spinning under the impact of direct competition from Europe deprived women of a major productive activity at a time when the economic plight of their families as a whole worsened.

Rural Women and Commercialization of Agriculture

The diverging experiences of urban women in the early nineteenth century had a parallel in the experiences of rural women. In this case, however, the differences were not class-based, but rather were dependent on the degree to which commercialization of agriculture took place. Sources on the productive activities of rural women are even sketchier than for lower class urban women. Even noted female observers like Gertrude Bell later in the nineteenth century, someone who lived in the Middle East for many years and spoke the language, left the impression that the countryside was curiously devoid of women. However, from a knowledge of the general patterns of change, it is possible at least to suggest some hypotheses about what happened to rural women during this period.

Rural areas of northern Syria were basically similar to peasant societies in other parts of the Middle East and other parts of the world. The basic social unit was the peasant household, which was a unit both of production and of consumption. Division of labor was by sex and age, but tended to be complementary, and all tasks, including those performed by women, were vital to the survival of the family. The exact division of labor varied from village to village and perhaps within the village according to relative economic standing. In all villages, women were engaged in fetching water, gathering firewood, taking care of animals, and gleaning, as well as producing necessary goods, like clothing, and processing food. In some areas, they were engaged in field work.[63] Women were also observed doing the heaviest kind of manual labor, including digging ditches.[64]

Women were not simply workers. They controlled the products which they produced and were owners of some critical resources. Women sometimes owned animals, processing equipment, trees, and agricultural implements. Furthermore, women sometimes held usufructuary rights on land. Under the existing system of land tenure, most agricultural land was either owned by the state or formed part of a religious endowment. Peasants rarely owned land, but they did have legal rights to cultivate the land. These rights were similar to private property in that they could be bought and sold, rented, and passed on to one's heirs. They also could not be taken away from the producer by either the state, its agents, or the administrator of the endowment. They were bought and sold like property in the law courts, and women as well as men were engaged in buying and selling these titles. Of the forty-five such sales between 1770 and 1830, twenty-four involved women, as either buyers or sellers.

The way in which Aleppo was integrated into the world economy suggests that the changes of the first fifty years of the nineteenth century altered this rural society in a highly selective way. The organization of labor and therefore the work that women did was affected in the short-run by the Egyptian occupation. Ibrahim Pasha's efforts to increase production and rebuild deserted villages undoubtedly affected the division of labor within those peasant households that moved to take advantage of the opportunities that the government offered them. It seems likely, for example, that women would have been required to take on an even greater amount of labor in these relatively underpopulated villages whose lands needed to be reclaimed after years of neglect. Conscription and the use of forced labor had a similar effect. Draftees were taken from villages as well as from the working population in the city. Although there are no reliable figures on how many were drafted, seventeen hundred were reportedly taken from the villages of the province in 1837, enough that village proprietors complained to the Egyptian authorities about the effects on production of losing so many able-bodied males.[65] In the countryside the fear of the draft led many others to flee to the relative safety of Ottoman territory in order to avoid conscription. Sometimes men took their families with them. At other times, whole villages fled to escape the punishment of the Egyptian recruiters. The consequences of such a policy would have been similar to what happened in Egypt. Women were forced to assume a greater burden of responsibility than before. They had to perform the productive labor of the men as well as their own and take on responsibilities for the family and for dealing with the outside world that formerly were the prerogatives of males.[66]

In the case of Aleppo, unlike Egypt, these developments represented a temporary condition rather than a long-term change in the nature of rural society. Conscription went into effect in 1835; by 1839, the Egyptians were gone. Although the Ottoman government also introduced conscription, it was less frequent and less systematic, and involved many fewer recruits relative to the population. How many left during this period and never came back and how this might have affected demographic patterns is not known. There is no evidence of major changes in the rural economy, however, that would suggest that these policies had long-term effects.

More important in the long run was the commercialization of agriculture that took place as increased European demands for raw materials and foodstuffs continued. Commercialization occurred in cotton, silk, grain, pistachio, and gallnut production, as rising demand and rising prices led to increased production. However, this commercialization was limited to certain areas of the province and coexisted with the survival of subsistence agriculture. Silk was grown only near Ayntab and Antioch, cotton near Kilis, and, later, tobacco near Latakiyya. Most of these cash crops were labor intensive (i.e., both male and female labor was used). In silk production, for example, women were responsible for the worms, and during harvest season, entire families were hired to get in the crop. As throughout the world, wages paid to women were less than those paid to men.[67] The production of these cash crops also affected women's work in another way. Even if women themselves did not work in the raising of crops, they would have to assume greater burdens at home as men were drawn away to work in the fields of large landowners engaged in commercial production. As men increasingly assumed the role of wage laborers and women were left behind, the nature of the peasant household was radically altered. The separation of home and work place undercut the role of the home as a unit of production. It is likely that here, as elsewhere, this change tied women to the domestic context and devalued the labor that they did.

Generally, however, in contrast to what had happened in Egypt and Lebanon, where a major transformation of the rural economy was underway by the middle of the nineteenth century as a result of the development of cash crops and other changes in the economy, the dislocation of labor and the commercialization of agriculture was still limited by the middle of the nineteenth century. The work of most women was still carried out within the peasant economy, and the forces of the market had only intruded into rural regions in a circumscribed way. Even where women had become wage laborers during certain parts of the year, this coexisted with a traditional nexus of social relationship and work in the village and within the kinship unit.

Conclusion

The first fifty years of the nineteenth century brought major economic changes to Aleppo, as commerce and production were affected more and more directly by the pressures generated by the forces of the global economic system. However, these changes can be more accurately described as an adaptation of traditional commerce and production to changing global conditions rather than a full integration into the world market. Through continued access to and control of traditional markets and sources of supply, the merchants and producers of Aleppo were able to respond to changed conditions on their own terms and to retain a certain degree of autonomy. As a result, the social consequences of this transition to a new world economy were less far-reaching in Aleppo than in many other parts of the Middle East. Aleppo's greater stability after 1850 was a sign of renewed and continuing prosperity and adaptation to the existing conditions, without major upheaval in its social structure.

Some groups, however, felt the effects much more acutely than others. The impact of these changes on women varied greatly by class and geography. While upper-class women continued to own and manage key resources and to play a vital role in the family economy, and therefore continued to exercise considerable authority within the kinship unit, women in other groups of the urban population suffered the greatest loss as a result of these changes. They shared the hardships inflicted by underemployment, low wages, and inflation generally, and at the same time, lost their vital role in textile production. In rural areas, some women were relatively unaffected by these changes, while others were forced to shoulder a heavier burden because of the commercialization of agriculture and the absence of men that resulted from conscription, corvee labor, and demand for wage labor. This additional burden was imposed on women at the same time that the social context in which they had traditionally performed their productive activities was changing. Thus they had more work to do at a time when that work was valued less.

Part of the significance of the diversity of women's experiences in the early years of the nineteenth century lies in the way it may help explain one of the striking features of the conditions of contemporary Middle Eastern women: the wide gap between the lifestyles, freedom of choice, and options available to women at the upper levels of society and those at the lower levels. The gap is especially obvious in education and the work force. Women are well represented in universities and in the professions. Yet they make up a relatively small percentage of the labor force in other areas, and, where resources are stretched, girls are increasingly being denied access to primary and secondary education. The causes of this situation involve a highly complex interaction between economic conditions, social structure, political pressures, and dominant attitudes and values. But the cause is also partly historical. The situation needs to be understood partially in light of the diverging experiences of women in the early stages of global integration, which affected their relative freedom to take advantage of new opportunities that later opened up to them. Where women were able to control key economic resources, they retained greater influence within the family unit and therefore greater control over their own lives and choices. Where women were deprived of productive activities and found their labor devalued, they lost their relative power within the family, and their options and freedom of choice were restricted by both economic conditions and social constraints imposed by the family.

NOTES

1. Judith Gran, "Impact of the World Market on Egyptian Women," *MERIP Reports* 58 (1977): 3–4; Judith Tucker, "Egyptian Women in the Workforce: An Historical Survey," *MERIP Reports* 50 (1976): 6–8; idem, "Decline of the Family Economy in Mid-Nineteenth Century Egypt," *Arab Studies Quarterly* 1 (1980): 245–71, *passim*.

2. Dominique Chevallier, *La société de Mont Liban à l'époque de la révolution industrielle en Europe* (Paris: 1971).

3. Afaf Marsot, *Egypt in the Age of Muhammad Ali* (Cambridge: Cambridge University Press, 1984), p. 1.

4. Ralph Davis, *Aleppo and Devonshire Square* (London: Macmillan, 1967), pp. 39–40. For a recent discussion of Aleppo's economy in the early modern period, see

Bruce Masters, *Origins of Western Dominance in the Middle East: Mercantilism and the Islamic Economy in Aleppo, 1600–1750* (New York University Press, 1988).

5. The following discussion of economic change is very summary in nature. I have covered this subject in much greater detail in a recent paper, "The 'Decline' of Aleppo in the Nineteenth Century: A Reconsideration," presented to the twenty-third annual meeting of the Middle East Studies Association, Toronto, Ontario, 16 November 1989.

6. Paul Masson, *Histoire du commerce français dans le Levant au XVIIIe siècle* (Paris: Hachette, 1912), p. 325.

7. Christina Phelps Harris, *The Syrian Desert: Caravans, Travel, and Exploration* (New York: Macmillan, 1938), p. 76.

8. Herbert Bodman, *Political Factions in Aleppo, 1760–1826* (Chapel Hill: University of North Carolina Press, 1963), pp. 37–38 and 41; Margaret L. Meriwether, "The Notable Families of Aleppo: Networks and Social Structure," Ph.D. dissertation, University of Pennsylvania, 1981, p. 161 and chapter 2, *passim*.

9. Chief among these crises was a major rebellion against the Ottoman government in 1819, a severe earthquake in 1822, and a cholera epidemic in 1823. The death and destruction which resulted from these led to major depopulation and disruption of commercial and productive life. For details of these see Bodman, *Political Faction*, chap. 4 and Meriwether, "Notable Families," chap. 2.

10. John Bowring, *Report on the Commercial Statistics of Syria*, 1840, reprint (New York: Arno Press, 1973), p. 88.

11. Ibid., p. 77.

12. In 1835, sixty-seven European ships arrived at Iskanderun, Aleppo's seaport, and unloaded merchandise valued at 177,840 pounds sterling. The same number of ships departed, carrying merchandise from Aleppo valued at 75,968 pounds sterling. By 1860, Aleppo's imports from Britain alone totaled 820,438 pounds sterling, and exports to Britain totaled 319,725 pounds sterling. See "Gross Returns of British and Foreign Trade at Principal Ports of the Consulate of Aleppo, 1835," FO 78/293, pp. 29 and 33, Public Record Office, London; "Commercial and Industrial Report of Aleppo, Syria, 1860," *Dispatches from U.S. Consuls in Beirut, 1853–1908*, vol.4, Record Group 84, National Archives, Washington, D.C.

13. The gap between the costs of exports and imports is apparent in the figures in the preceding footnote.

14. Bowring, *Commercial Statistics*, p. 87.

15. "Commercial Report on the District of Aleppo for the Year 1871," *Dispatches from U.S. Consuls*, vol. 8.

16. *Dispatches from U.S. Consuls in Aleppo, 1835–40*, vol. 1, p.6.

17. Great Britain, Foreign Office, Historical Section, *Syria and Palestine* (London: HMSO, 1920), p. 152.

18. Margaret L. Meriwether, "Urban Notables and Rural Resources in Aleppo, 1770–1830," *International Journal of Turkish Studies* 4 (Summer, 1987).

19. Meriwether, "Notable Families," pp. 162 and 177–79.

20. Abraham Marcus has looked at the role of women as property owners in mid-eighteenth-century Aleppo in "Men, Women, and Property: Dealers in Real Estate in Eighteenth Century Aleppo," *Journal of the Economic and Social History of the Orient* 26 (1983): 137–63.

21. Meriwether, "Notable Families," p. 210.

22. Ibid., p. 212.

23. This analysis of property sales is based on samples of property sales taken from the archives of the *mahkama shari'ya* of Aleppo (henceforth MSA), Mudiriyyat al-watha'iq al-tarikhiyya, Damascus.

24. Mona Hamman, "Women and Islam," *MERIP Reports* 95 (1981), p. 28.

25. J. Lewis Farley, *Two Years in Syria* (London: Saunder and Otley, 1858), pp. 38–39.

26. A *waqf* (pl. *awqaf*) is a religious endowment in which land or another revenue-producing resource is put into a perpetual trust. Originally the income from the endowment was to be used for religious or charitable purposes (*waqf khayri*). Another form of *waqf*, called *waqf dhurri*, was later established, under the terms of which the income from the *waqf* was designated for members of the endower's family.

27. The figures and the following analysis are based on the 465 *waqfiyyat* found in the *mahkama shari'ya* archives. There were actually more *awqaf* created during this period, which al-Ghazzi found. See Kamil al-Ghazzi, *Nahr al-dhahab fi tarikh halag*, 3 vols. (Aleppo: Maronite Press, 1923), 2:534–631. However, these *waqfiyyat* were not found in the archives. Therefore, for purposes of analysis, I have had to ignore them.

28. MSA 129: 134–37, 18 Rabi' al-awwal 1200.

29. MSA 175:174–75, 17 Ramadan 1227.

30. MSA 140:132, 20 Rabi' al-awwal 1207; 230:56, 21 Rabi' al-thani 1239.

31. MSA 206:175, 25 Jumada al-ula 1240.

32. Gabriel Baer, "The Administrative, Economic, and Social Functions of Ottoman Guilds," *International Journal of Middle East Studies* 1 (1970): 28–50; idem, "Monopolies and Restrictive Practices of Turkish Guilds," *Journal of the Economic and Social History of the Orient* 13 (1970): 145–65; Abdul-Karim Rafeq, "The Law Court Registers of Damascus as a Source for the Study of Craft Corporations," in *Les Arabes par leur archives*, ed. Jacques Berque and Dominique Chevallier (Paris: Centre National de la Recherche Scientifique, 1976); Meriwether, "Notable Families," pp. 31–34.

33. MSA 140:358, 11 Muharram 1210; 144:18, 24 Shawwal 1211.

34. MSA 107:524, 20 Dhu al-Qa'da 1188; 139:46, 6 Sha'ban 1205; 140:6, 28 Safar 1206.

35. al-Ghazzi, *Nahr al-dhahab*, 3:388.

36. Meriwether, "Notable Families," pp. 32–33.

37. Muhammad Sa'id al-Qasimi, *Qamus al-sana'at al-shamiyya*, 2 vols. (Paris: Mouton, 1960), 1:39–40.

38. Rafeq, "Law Court Registers," p. 149; Tucker, "Egyptian Women," p. 7.

39. Masson, *Histoire du commerce français*, p. 235.

40. Werry to Lord Ponsonby, 26 July 1835, FO 876/1, pp. 10–11.

41. Ibid., p. 21; John Murray, *A Handbook for Travellers in Syria and Palestine*, 2 vols. (London: John Murray, 1858), pp. 611–12.

42. Bowring, *Commercial Statistics*, p. 80.

43. Richard Wood, *The Early Correspondence of Richard Wood*, ed. A. B. Cunningham, Camden Fourth Series, vol. 3 (London: Office of the Royal Historical Society), pp. 69–70, 79; Bowring, *Commercial Statistics*, p. 122; Werry to Lord Ponsonby, 15 December 1837 and 30 January 1838, FO 876/1.

44. Bowring, *Commercial Statistics*, p. 112; Werry to Lord Ponsonby, 15 December 1837, FO 876/1.

45. Wood, *Early Correspondence*, p. 79; al-Ghazzi, *Nahr al-dhahab*, 3:363; Bowring, *Commercial Statistics*, p. 88.

46. al-Ghazzi, *Nahr al-dhahab*, 3:363.

47. Bowring, *Commercial Statistics*, p. 88.

48. Henri Guys, *Un dervish algérien en Syrie: Peinture des moeurs musulmanes, chrétiennes et israélites* (Paris: Bureau de l'Orient de l'Algérie, 1854), p. 78.

49. Bowring, *Commercial Statistics*, p. 83.

50. al-Ghazzi, *Nahr al-Dhahab*, 3:301.

51. Bowring, pp. 20–21.

52. Ibid, p. 84.
53. Dominique Chevallier, "Un exemple de résistance technique de l'artisanat syrien aux XIXe et XXe siècles," *Syria* 39 (1962):301.
54. Bowring, *Commercial Statistics*, p. 84.
55. *Dispatches from U.S. Consuls in Aleppo*, vol. 1, 20 November 1837.
56. Bowring, *Commercial Statistics*, p. 84.
57. Tucker, "Egyptian Women," pp. 7–8.
58. Foreign Office Historical Section, *Syria*, pp. 112–13.
59. Ibid., p. 114.
60. Bowring, *Commercial Statistics*, p. 123.
61. Wood, *Early Correspondence*, p. 80.
62. Werry to Lord Ponsonby, 26 July 1835, FO 876/1.
63. Bowring, *Commercial Statistics*, p. 123.
64. Curtis, pp. 141–42.
65. Werry to Lord Ponsonby, 30 January 1838, FO 876/1.
66. Tucker, "Decline of the Family Economy," pp. 263–66.
67. Bowring, *Commercial Statistics*, p. 133.

V

GETTING IT TOGETHER
BALADI EGYPTIAN BUSINESSWOMEN[1]

Evelyn Aleene Early

Introduction

In Cairo, young, traditional, urban women—*baladi* women—with diplomas tend to work in shops or government offices, but many other *baladi* women work in the informal economic sector in such occupations as vendors, creditors, service providers, and expeditors. The economic activity of the informal sector is considerable, but is rarely reported in Egyptian economic indicators. Although they do not sit on boards of directors of international corporations, *baladi* women *do participate* in international and national markets and labor migration. Their lives are buffeted by winds such as those of Gulf States' labor policies and those of Egyptian inflation. *Baladi* businesswomen work at the intersection of the domestic and the public, the informal and the formal economy, the *baladi* and the modern (*afrangi*). They frequently bridge the two sectors to expedite bureaucratic snags of family jobs, or to sell imported goods door to door.

In this chapter I examine the culture of businesswomen in traditional Cairo, and look at three cases: a vendor, a merchant, and a creditor assistant. My analysis depends heavily on the naturally situated social discourse of everyday work narratives and other informal social performances. During my ethnographic research in the seventies and eighties in the traditional quarter of Cairo, Bulaq Abu 'Ala, I marveled at the *baladi* women's energy in promotion of their marketing and social opportunities. The quarter of Bulaq is a ten-minute walk north of the downtown Hilton in Cairo, but many of its one-room flats in three-story mud brick buildings have neither running water nor electricity. Selected as an industrial site by Muhammad Ali in the early nineteenth century, Bulaq rapidly lost the spiffy vestiges of a medieval elite Mamluke suburb to become a grimy popular quarter with textile, spinning, iron foundry, and dye factories. An early twentieth-century traveler described Bulaq as a "Vulcan's Empire" and as a hotbed of resistance to the British occupation: "An urchin hangs on to the chain of a smith's bellows whilst others are engaged in filing and adjusting. . . . Dealers in old iron offer you all sorts of objects for which you have no use: dented mudguards, out-of-date engines, enormous rusty wheels and even boilers . . . . [Bulaq is] already conscious of its power and has several times set fire to trams and buses, plundered work-shops, and raised the scare of strikes. Heedless of the river god, it hammers away, forging proletarians" (Leprette 1939: 253, 255).

Contemporary Bulaq still provides critical lathing and foundry services. Contractors in sleek cars edge along streets past donkeys and ducks and their occupants leap out to commission factory molds or intricate woodwork. Shoppers from all over Cairo crowd the famed second-hand Wikalat al Balah market in Bulaq to buy spare car parts or clothing. The Nobel Prize-winning Egyptian novelist Naguib Mahfuz's *Wikalat al-Balah* has immortalized the life of a young proprietress of a scrap metal yard and her secret narcotics agent admirer/protector posing as a crippled beggar.

As the inflation of the late seventies following the *infitah* (the economic "opening up" of the post-Camp David era) hit Egypt full force, *baladi* people became more hard pressed to make ends meet. When I returned to Bulaq in the 1980s, I found that more older women had begun to work in the informal economic sector, and that most men had either left to work in the Gulf or had taken to moonlighting in coffeeshops or workshops. Some had even devised a third source of income such as renting out a food cart.

The Culture of *Baladi* Work: The Traditional
Urban Egyptian Woman's World View

Baladi is a rich cultural concept which is based on a series of *baladi:afrangi* (traditional:modern) oppositions, which contrast *baladi* people as downtrod-den, destitute (*galaba*) and *afrangi* as pampered (*dala'ain*). There are *baladi* ways and there are *afrangi* ways to earn a living, practice religion, celebrate a wedding, cure a disease, talk to a friend, or solve a problem. *Baladi* people see themselves as authentic, astute, honorable, religious, nationalistic, simple, personal, and hospitable as opposed to *afrangi* people who are spoiled, gull-ible, dishonorable, non-religious, Franco philistic, materialistic, artificial, and stingy (Messiri, 1978).

The above are neat symbolic oppositions of a cultural anthropologist. While they are implicit in the *baladi* identity as celebrated by Egyptian media and by *baladi* people themselves, some may not always be explicit. However, piety, authenticity, destitution, and savvy were traits that my friends in Bulaq often used to contrast their society with those of places such as Zamalek, an *afrangi* quarter just across the river. Bulaqis feel that *afrangis* ignore the most basic of human obligations: to assist and to pray for others.

Afrangi people don't rally to help a neighbor in distress; *baladi* people do. Here,
if there is a problem, the whole house turns out. . . . *Afrangi* people do not take
religion seriously. When the people in a place like Zamalek bury their dead,
they just put them in a car and haul them away. They don't know how to walk
in a proper funeral procession. If a procession passes them, they don't even stop
to read the *Fatiha* (the opening verse of the Quran) and they don't even walk
a few blocks with the procession as we do here to show our grief for the family.

The *baladi* way of life is popularly associated with authentic Egyptian culture of the days when the *ibna al-balad* ("sons of the country") defended
Egypt against French and British occupiers. *Baladi* generosity and good humor
("lightness of blood") are glorified in Egyptian films, and modern, highly
educated Egyptians speak admiringly of the "tough and resourceful *baladi*
Egyptians."

Baladi people see themselves as *galaba*, and when they become frustrated
they intone such phrases as, "What should we do, we're destitute, and at the
mercy of X," where X is a greedy landlord, recalcitrant bureaucrat, market
inflation, whatever. The Saudi Arabian husband of a Bulaq woman sent her
parents money when his wife gave birth. The father remarked: "My daughter
was *galaba*, but God gave her a great chance when she married Hassan."

The narrow lanes of non-zoned *baladi* quarters in medieval and central
Cairo wind around workshops and markets peppered in amongst dwellings.
Domestic activities such as cooking and industrial activities such as welding
frequently spill over into the lanes already crowded with donkey carts and
herds of goats. Landmarks such as a distinctive mosque or famous food shop
are more important than street names. The *baladi* ethos is unstructured and
detail-specific. A Bulaq resident once categorized grocery stores for me as
follows:

> In a *baladi* grocery, there are a few things scattered about on the shelf, rather
> disordered, with a lot of dust. The proprietor knows his goods and prices piece
> by piece. He offers customized service such as placing orders in baskets lowered
> from balconies. In an *afrangi* grocery everything is sorted neatly with price tags
> and there is a large stock of each item. One must go to the store and purchase
> in an orderly way.

Baladi women relish duping the less astute *afrangi*. One day as we consoled
a neighbor who despaired of receiving her veteran's widow's pension, a
woman recounted hitching a ride with an *afrangi* man:

> My friends and I were on our way to visit my daughter Amal. As we stood by
> the side of the road a well-dressed, *afrangi* man offered us a ride in his car. We
> were several, and not afraid to ride with him. Maybe he wanted some money
> to help with gas, maybe he was being nice, maybe he wanted some fun. But we
> were old women! My neighbor started to chat and discovered the man was in
> the army. Straightaway, she asked how she could secure her son's early release

from the army. He gave her the name of a person to see and advised her what to say. At the end, we got down a block from Amal's (so that the man could not trace us), thanking him nicely. We never paid for our ride, and in addition, we received some good advice! (Early 1992: 106–7)

The narrative account both consoled the neighbor and celebrated the savvy of *baladi* women whose wits compensate for limited resources.

Baladi is a cultural, not a class, concept. There are extremely wealthy Egyptians who do not abandon simple *baladi* dress, housing, and consumption styles, and spend extra income on food and hospitality. However, in the rampant consumerism of the eighties, *baladi* and *afrangi* distinctions began to crumble. *Baladi* Egyptians began to buy European design furniture and the latest Paris fashions.

Baladi Women in National and International Society and Economy

Traditional Egyptian women worry not only about weekly village market prices, but also about the cost of imported goods and about international labor migration. Egypt staffs much of the Arab world with physicians, engineers, teachers, and (un)skilled labor. *Baladi* women are routinely involved in national and international economic and bureaucratic networks. To help a relative or to make a commission, a woman may hustle such employment as a taxi-driving job or a Saudi construction job through her social networks. She may finance a family member to go to work in the Gulf, or buy goods to resell herself from middle merchants returning from a foreign shopping trip. A *baladi* woman may also obtain documents to travel abroad to work, usually as a domestic. She may also forage for extra income within the local bureaucracy. At the mother-child health (MCH) clinic where I researched medical practices, one woman of strong character negotiated with clinic officials on behalf of neighgorhood women wishing to raise an orphan baby, for which they received a stipend from the Ministry of Health. The women paid her to expedite the placement of a Ministry orphan with them.

Women's historic economic role when the family was the basic unit of production in cottage industries has changed with the advent of wage labor (Gran 1977; Friedl 1989; Tucker 1985). In Bulaq today, the main economic role of women is in the market place as merchants and creditors. Sometimes, when a husband dies, a woman takes over the family workshop. Some women work in textile, pharmaceutical, and other factories, but jobs are limited and a woman often waits to replace a retiring family member. Young women who have diplomas queue the requisite period of more than three years for guaranteed government office jobs.

Baladi work is regarded as informal, individualized work where one shows initiative, while *afrangi* work in formal, bureaucratic, and industrial sectors is boring work with little freedom. Bulaqi women speak of the *afrangi* schedule kept by a woman office worker who goes home for lunch and a nap, unlike the *baladi* woman street vendor who keeps long hours and may even make a pre-dawn visit to a wholesale market. They see the factory worker's life of some of their daughters as one without freedom, where one is tied to a machine. *Baladi* women are proud of their freedom. Sawsan Messiri reports the following self description of a *baladi bint al-suq* ("woman of the market"):

> *bint al-suq* . . . implies a character-type associated with the nature of the job—buying and selling fruits, vegetables, butter, fish, and so on. . . . Such work requires foresight and intelligence; it is said, "One *bint al-balad* equals twenty men in trading." In contrast, a woman employee in the government is "bound" to her desk and hence lacks experience and is unaware of the world about her. (1978: 532)

This *bint al-suq* has developed into a female character type acceptable within the traditional *baladi* value system. A street, food stand, or cafe vendor, the *bint al-suq* is known today as a *mualimma*—a tough "street woman" who is respected and feared by all and who is untouched by innuendoes of loose morals reserved for other "street women." A *mualimma*, also the word for teacher but never confused, talks roughly and curses as if she were a man, and deals sternly with customers. A popular story claims an Egyptian coffee-house proprietress barred an army general from her establishment shortly after the 1967 defeat by the Israelis, with a stream of expletives that this "pimp of the Israelis" would never darken *her* door. Tough in the street and shop, a *mualimma* reverts to her other "more womanly" self at home. When I asked a woman if we had met before, she replied: "Oh, you don't recognize me now because you last saw me when you bought bread in my shop where I was a *mualimma* wearing black and acting tough; now you see me as a normal housewife."

Bulaqi women develop strategies for mobility, investment, credit, and savings. Mothers, seeing glutted government and service sectors, encourage their children to enter blue collar work or at least to marry a skilled laborer whose salary far exceeds the pittance paid in office and government jobs. One woman exclaimed to me: "What use is a *muwazaff* (office, white collar worker) these days! He makes less than a hundred pounds (a month) while a *sana'i* (skilled worker) makes at least four to five hundred. None of my daughters will marry *muwazaffin* !"

Lucrative work or a strategic marriage are women's two best chances for economic mobility. They, or their families, employ cold realism when they choose their marriage partner from the foreign Arabs crowding the marriage scene of Cairo. In the seventies, many *baladi* families were so economically pinched that they overcame the cultural discomfort of marriage with a foreigner. Besides, Saudis—the major group seeking wives in Egypt—were good Muslims. Foreigners seek an industrious wife; *baladi* women, an escape from the poverty cycle. Women learn via rumor networks of potential suitors for their daughters. Some families fared worse, marrying their daughters to wealthy old local codgers; these marriages had high failure records, and some young women escaped through suicide.

Baladi women invest any extra money in gold, both a bank on their arm, and a hedge against inflation and divorce. They treat jewelry much as stocks and bonds and pawn it for a worthwhile, or a mandatory, investment. Women often take the lead in such major family investments as renting a new flat, which requires key money, or buying furniture. Women obtain credit for investments via the informal economic sector from area merchants or from a popular savings association (*gamaiyya*). Women (and men) pay, say, ten pounds each month to the association organizer, and receive the lump sum of one hundred pounds once in the ten month cycle. The woman who forms the association determines when everyone takes her or his payment. First is not always best; a woman calculates payment to coincide with a major expense such as a wedding. These associations are viewed as a way to avoid frittering money away on daily trifles. Sometimes a *baladi* woman uses her money savings share to launch herself in the informal economic sector of credit and finance.

Everyday Social Discourse

The naturally situated *baladi* social discourse of everyday narratives and other social performances is a major source for my analysis of *baladi* business.[2] Scholars have begun to pay increasing attention to the different forms of talk which constitute a researcher's data. There are the "formal" discourses of ritual, epic tales, written texts, and so on. There are the "informal" forms of the everyday narrative and the mundane social, and so on. Naturally situated social discourse is invaluable in cultural analysis. (See, for example, Abu Lughod 1987; Basso 1984; Bauman 1986; Briggs 1988; DelVecchio Good/ Good/Fischer 1988; Friedl 1989; Geertz 1983; Glassie 1982; Labov and Waletzky 1966; Stahl 1977; E. Turner 1987; V. Turner and Bruner 1988.)

Discourse is a particularly powerful cultural source when, as with a narrative, it simultaneously captures the uniqueness of such biographic events as finding a job or supporting a family, and the shared nature of cultural understandings about *baladi* savvy or kinship obligations. In my analysis of Bulaqi work culture, accounts of a woman supporting herself while her husband is away, or of a woman investing egg money in trade, provide a rich optic on the intersection of the domestic/personal with the market/public.

Elsewhere I have discussed the role of the everyday narrative and other social performances in linking such cultural ideals as honor or fate with personal experience, and in providing an arena for personal expression and catharsis (Early 1982; 1985; 1987). One of the best ways to understand the lofty ideals of culture is to locate them in the nitty gritty of praxis (Bourdieu 1977; Glassie 1982; V. Turner 1988). In a discussion of illness narratives, I noted:

> The narrative, like a ritual performance or ceremony, conveys social intent and endorses a state of affairs. . . . Narratives are set off from a conversation, not as a tale or myth would be set off, but rather as a stylistically recognizable part of everyday explanations. Stylistically, they are set off from conversation, while being embedded in it. . . . Narratives place explanations in everyday life; they provide a rich context in the Egyptian case for interpreting *baladi* cultural categories, whether of poverty or health. (Early 1982: 1491–92)

Illness narratives and commentaries on disease progression and surrounding events in the patient's life situation are one genre of narrative discourse on religion, work, family, and so on. In the last ten years, there has been a flowering of literature on the narrative as a special form of social discourse situated in everyday life and conveying cultural truths in personal form. (See the references on naturally situated discourse cited above.) In this paper my use of narratives about business, set off with such framing devices as "I'll tell you how it was," is a straightforward attempt to let *baladi* women speak for themselves.

Everyday narratives allow a woman to "work out" a problem at hand *in the context of her life and her social support system.* The *baladi* woman contextualizes her understanding of work, everyday economic and household maintenance problems, mobility, and the international economic system within her own unique biographic situation. Accounts valorize tough and powerful women money lenders as well as ordinary women plugging away as mere street vendors. Within the narrative arena, Cairene women compare notes on how to use resources and to negotiate favors best. In such cozy settings the women not only empathize with each other as they swap war stories, but they also provide advice from their personal stores of experience and anecdotes. In such settings, women trade diverse tips, from where to find jobs to where to sew school uniforms.

Here, I present three businesswomen who were energetically plying their trade when I first met them in Bulaq in the mid-seventies: a street fruit vendor, a house-to-house cheese merchant, and a creditor "helper-expeditor." All three began business after the social dislocation of labor migration; all three balanced kin obligations with self-support. Each possessed different material or social capital, and different access to markets. Each had a different tale, but they were all active participants in the informal economic sector. Many other *baladi* women work in the informal sector as seamstresses, bread bakers, or even day laborers.

Three Baladi Businesswomen: Vendor, Merchant, Creditor Expeditor

Case One: Um Hanafi, Casual Vendor

We start with the simplest form of merchanting—the casual vendor, who needs only a few pounds to buy some fruit or sweets to sell in the street. Women who might otherwise never venture into the informal economic sector will resort to street vending when they are in dire straits. One such woman was Um Hanafi, the wife of a hashish dealer who was imprisoned for several years; this forced Um Hanafi to support her family. One day when a group of us were discussing ways to make money, while waiting to fit clothes at the seamstress, Um Hanafi told the following narrative set off from ordinary discourse by a typical framing device, "Let me tell you why I am sewing these dresses," to an eager audience:

> When my husband went to prison, I had no way to support myself, so I began to sell grapes in front of Gala' hospital on 26th July street. I continued selling for two years. Let me tell you how rough life was when I worked. I woke at 3 a.m., rode a cart to the wholesale market at Rod el-Farag, picked and bought fruit, and was back by 6 a.m. to pick through and clean the fruit. I sat selling fruit in front of the hospital all day, and returned home in the afternoon so tired that I would sleep at once, laying my head on anything I could find. Then I would wake and look at my watch—a plain one that I had before my husband sent me such a fancy one from Libya—and make tea and dress the children for school before leaving the house again at 3 a.m. In those days my house was very chaotic. I had no time to clean. (Early 1992: 315–16)
>
> When my husband was released from prison, he traveled to Libya to work, but for seven months he sent no money. Then he sent 43 pounds, then a hundred more, then yet another hundred. He returned the Ramadan before last, but he sent a message ahead to me, with money, telling me to decorate the house rather than keeping all the money on my stomach where it did not show. So I spent 80 pounds to buy a wardrobe, 70 pounds to stuff the mattresses, and another hundred pounds to paint the walls. The apartment looked *zayy al-ful* [gorgeous, literally "like jasmine"]. When my husband returned, I stopped selling and sat at home cooking sweets and all kinds of food for him.

(The women listening remarked that Um Hanafi's friends must have increased in those days!)

> My friends grew [in number] and so did I until I became truly fat. After two years of all the activity of marketing, suddenly sitting all the time while my husband visited, plus taking birth control pills, made me grow bigger and bigger. I became worried about the children and lost weight, but I only lost it in my face. See my tremendous buttocks. I could have an operation for excess fat where they slice it off just like a butcher. But I can not face such an operation.

After my mother-in-law returns from pilgrimage, I will travel to Libya to stay with my husband. It is better than his being angry and unhappy there, and my being here alone. I cannot sleep for worry and exhaustion preparing the children and myself for travel. I am sewing some dresses here at the seamstress, but really it is wasted energy because in Libya I will wear a *melaya laf* [the *baladi* black piece of cloth which can be draped over street clothes and over the head—but not the face—when one goes out] over my dresses. All women married to Egyptians do that; only the servants go out in dresses, so you can tell the difference. Libyan women wear an *abaya* [cloak] over their dresses.

I miss my husband; a day is like a year. I have no one but my friends. God will be with me. When I go to Libya I will just have to make new friends.

Um Hanafi's business narrative is resplendent with the "wonders of work abroad." Her husband sends extravagant gifts such as watches and tells her not to spare money in refurbishing the flat. Work abroad assumes a miraculous aura for those left at home to recount apocryphal narratives of some son, husband, relative or friend who has lived in the Gulf or Libya, earned piles of money while enjoying a house provided by his company (some stories add drivers and cooks!), and returned with heaps of gifts for all. While migrant laborers from Egypt probably scrape and save to buy the fancy appliances and clothes that are *de rigueur* for the returnee, those left behind can hope. After all, they see the summer tourists from the Gulf throwing their money about in Cairo; is there not more where theirs came from?

Um Hanafi never attempted any but the safest business of street vending, while our other two businesswomen below diversified. Having no close kin to help finance her forced Um Hanafi into what was the least profitable business. Although all three women were involved in international labor and market networks, only Um Hanafi actually chose the alienation of living abroad, where, as she said, she would have no friends, as a better option than living alone in Bulaq. It was a sign of her desperation that she, unlike most women with Egyptian husbands abroad, decided to travel to live with her migrant laborer husband.

Case Two: Um Muhammad, Merchant: Village to Cairo to Saudi Arabia

Um Muhammad was born in a northern Delta village three hours from Cairo by train. She left home for Cairo in the fifties to marry her husband, a peasant turned civil servant functionary. Using money earned selling sandwiches in her home village to which she had returned for two years in the early sixties after a quarrel with her husband, Um Muhammad began to sell cheese and ghee house to house in Cairo, on credit, in the mid-sixties. Pinning her hopes on her son Muhammad, she used her profits from her trade to help finance his marriage and work abroad. When Um Muhammad became too ill to work, she depended on her son's support.

Her village to Cairo to Saudi Arabia saga is not unusual. With increased land fragmentation, agriculturalists have crowded Cairo and its expandable service sector; from there, they have looked to lucrative Gulf or North African employment, often performing unskilled labor that nationals avoid. One of my friends, Zakiyya, and her husband, who lived in rural Menoufiyya in the Delta, ran a home grocery with cigarettes and tea to supplement earnings from grain and water buffalo. Frustrated with the meager income left after splitting farm proceeds with his extended family, Zakiyya's husband traveled to Libya to work in construction.

When I met her in 1974, Um Muhammad's trade was thriving. She returned regularly to her home village's weekly market where she bought as much as she could carry back on the train. She sold cheese and ghee to neighbors at a slight profit if they paid at once, and at a larger profit if they paid by install-ment. Um Muhammad reconciled higher prices with Islamic prohibitions of interest:

> It is true that I charge more if people buy cheese or ghee on installment, but this is compensation for my patience. If customers pay a lump sum they pay less because I use their money to buy more ghee right away. After all, wasn't the Prophet a merchant? It is an honorable trade.

Later when Um Muhammad's health failed and she could no longer market weekly, her nest egg dwindled at the very time that her medical expenses soared. Her son had married and traveled to Saudi Arabia to work in a printing press while on leave from his Ministry of Culture job in Cairo. She consulted a doctor who told her that she was as strong as a horse. One day in 1982 when I visited Um Muhammad, she played a cassette tape-letter which Muhammad had sent from Saudi Arabia; hearing it moved her to recount her trials:

> My son Muhammad has traveled to Saudi Arabia to seek his fortune. In his tape-recorded letters my son tells his wife Sabah to care for me. But does Sabah do anything? No. Only a few days ago Sabah threw me out of her house. My sister Fikriyya had come from the village to nurse me. Fikriyya, her daughter, and I were staying with Sabah across the street. You remember how my husband and I vacated the sunny, airy room across the street so Sabah and my son could move there? My husband and I moved to this dank hole without windows where you see me now.
>
> I have been too sick to market in the village since last spring. Now I have spent all my money on doctor's examinations. . . . My next-door neighbor carries my water from the pump down the street and my upstairs neighbor woman brings me food from the market. My husband is of no help whatsoever. It is better for me to stay with my daughter. I become very ill from the anger which I feel when my husband and I quarrel. You heard what he said when I was too upset to record something to my son on the tape: "Don't talk; your son will think that you have died!"
>
> *Al-baraka fi al-'a'ila.* [The saving grace is in one's (natal) family]. But why

should my siblings have to care for me when my own daughter-in-law lives across the lane? When my brother-in-law's son Abdul-Wahid returned from Saudi Arabia, he brought me a dress as a present; when my own son Muhammad finally returns I will be lucky if he brings me a dress. . . . Muhammad sent his wife three hundred pounds to buy a refrigerator, but all he does is tell me in tapes "May God cure you." But I ask you, since when did words cure someone? . . . . Why did I spend so much for my son's wedding if he does not even ask for me now?

Do you remember Muhammad's engagement party in the village? What an elaborate procession of gifts we prepared to present to the bride's family! There were eight chiffon dresses, ten bottles of *sharbat*, ten kilos of sugar cones, and countless piles of macaroni and rice. What a sight we provided!

Remember how the next day we waited for the bride's family to respond to our gifts; we expected them to bring at least a length of cloth to make Muhammad a suit. When they finally appeared, I was so humiliated—since I could see that there was no cloth—that I did not even go out to meet their procession on the path with the songs and chants one should perform to greet visitors at such times. The bride's family were so embarrassed that they dropped their trays as soon as they entered the door, and ran. We inspected our presents to find nothing but *futir* [rich pastry] and some macaroni and rice and fruit. The *futir* was of such poor quality that it was soggy in the middle and stuck together. (Early 1985: 81–82)

That next summer, matters had deteriorated as Um Muhammad's physical and material resources dwindled. Muhammad was back from Saudi Arabia on vacation. When I visited her, Um Muhammad lowered her voice to confide her woes in the style typical of *baladi* personal narratives.

I am living on treatment. I made a picture of my heart last week and the doctor said that I was lucky that no more arteries were blocked and if I continued this medication everything would be fine. He told me: "Everything has its time." I asked the doctor if I could eat more than a quarter-loaf of *baladi* bread, for after all a whole loaf is not that big, and I will die when I die.

Two weeks ago the doctor prescribed new medicine, but I had no money and my husband refused to help. My son Muhammad, who overheard me, asked me what I had been complaining about to my husband. I told Muhammad that I had no money for medicine, that I wanted to go to Qasr el Aini Hospital [the major teaching hospital] for treatment, but that I could not afford Qasr el-Aini because admittance required referral from a prestigious doctor whose exams cost fifty or sixty. Muhammad told me that he would buy me my medicine, but ten days later he had brought nothing. Muhammad's wife avoided greeting me just so she would not have to ask me about my health and give me an opportunity to mention the medicine that her husband [Muhammad] promised. Finally Muhammad came to visit and I asked: "Why haven't you brought me medicine?" He responded, "Give me the empty boxes and I will get it." But he took only these two boxes.

(How did you get the other medication?) My daughter Nabila brought me the vitamin shots and pills and said she wished she could do more but her husband made her account for every piaster she spent. Nabila promised to bring me meat this Friday, but she said she could not stay because her husband becomes angry if he returns from work to find Nabila away.

I say to my son Muhammad, "Why won't you take care of me when you can see that your father is doing nothing for me?"

Um Muhammad's account reveals an intimate relation between business and kin. Relatives expect assistance from other kin successfully employed. In a world of no insurance and no retirement policies, one "invests" in the future through people. Muhammad's mother was catapulted into the informal business sector when she quarreled with her husband for gambling too much, and she returned to her home village. There, Um Muhammad supported herself selling bean and cheese sandwiches, an activity which, like Um Hanafi's, required little capital. Two years later when she reconciled with her husband and returned to Cairo, she used her nest egg plus strategic knowledge of rural and urban markets to start a cheese and ghee trade. While *baladi* women prefer to buy dairy products straight from a rural market because products are fresh and taste better, only recent migrants with access to nearby northern Delta markets and with a modicum of capital and good sense could have started a trade such as Um Muhammad's. Ghee (clarified butter) is the mainstay of *baladi* cooking—where the heavier the meat sauce is, the better!

When Um Muhammad's trade prospered, she invested in her son—a reasonable decision since her husband was a soon-to-retire ne'er-do-well. Although he continued to live with Um Muhammad after retirement, her husband contributed nothing to the household and did not expect to eat his meals at home. But Um Muhammad may have pinned too much hope on her son, Muhammad. A mother always faces competition with daughters-in-law for a son's affection and support. There were early signs of trouble during the engagement party when the bride's family did not produce cloth for a suit for the groom. Um Muhammad had been determined to find her son a bride from the "known" society of the village; Sabah had been one of the few available, but her family's meager resources had been further stretched by an ill father. In the end, it was Um Muhammad's daughters who helped her most.

Um Muhammad had also cultivated a neighborhood-customer social network from past favors of a bit of fresh cheese here and there; Um Muhammad praises the goodness of neighbors who carry her water and bring her food. Businesswomen active in rural-urban marketing have already left the simple life of kin, if that was ever simple, and entered the more complex life where kin, friend, and customer are balanced against one another. The future of such merchants as Um Muhammad in the informal economic sector is uncertain. On our last trips to Menoufiyya together, I noticed well-groomed men loading cheese and ghee into Peugeot station wagons to take back to Cairo for sale. Their station wagon could carry hundreds of kilos. Um Muhammad's back strained to carry her two baskets of some twenty kilos.

Small-scale, local merchants such as Um Muhammad may survive despite the flashy new merchants because the Um Muhammads of Bulaq provide more than the valued fresh rural dairy products; they also provide informal credit— a critical service in the marginal economy of Bulaq where a householder's budget barely covers food for the day. Meat is a special, irregular expense. Home furnishings or bulk food bought on installment are paid for, not out of the daily household budget, but from a periodic credit installment budget. *Baladi* women continually maneuver to obligate as many household expenses as possible to installment payments so that they may save part of their daily "stipend" from their husbands as a nest egg to start a small business or to hedge against divorce. Installment buying starts many a marital dispute because husbands recognize this tactic and often sternly forbid it. The most controversial installment payments are not for cheese or oil, but for major items such as furniture or clothing. These are financed by true creditors, the *dallalat* (the plural of *dallala*), who are the *baladi* equivalent of the Sears revolving charge account. We turn now to consider the assistant of one of these *dallalat*.

Case Three: Zainab, Creditor Sidekick with Social Resources

To become a small-scale merchant requires minimal capital. To become a big-time merchant dealing in furniture and clothing orders for multiple customers requires sizeable capital from successful merchanting, inheritance, family workshop profits, or a gainfully employed relative. Although the term *dallala* simply means any "door-to-door" merchant, Bulaqis usually reserve the term for "big-time" merchant women, and I use it here for such creditors.

Since creditors need help cultivating trustworthy customers (there are no "credit checks" in the informal economic sector of *baladi* credit) and tracking down clients who owe monthly payments, they retain assistants who have social capital of dense kin and friend networks. Zainab was such a woman for the creditor Hamida. Zainab spoke of Hamida as her dear friend (*habeba*); their relationship, clearly both business and social, was what I have described elsewhere as "quasi-kin" (Early 1977). Such a mixture is typical of patron-client relations in Cairo and in southside Chicago alike. When Hamida's son was drafted, Zainab carried a homemade casserole and accompanied Hamida on her search from army camp to army camp. Zainab recruited customers for Hamida, and extracted monthly payments from them. Zainab helped Hamida cook for special occasions. Hamida in turn gave Zainab informal commissions on customers and sent Zainab's children special treats on birthdays and feast days.

As with Um Muhammad, the tides of international labor migration and of kinship affected Zainab's work as a creditor's assistant. When her husband traveled to Iraq to work as a truck driver, Zainab learned to process remittances sent from Iraq at the bank, and began to look for a way to supplement her income in between irregular payments from her husband. Zainab moved back to live with her parents in Bulaq, where her repertoire of childhood friendships, coupled with her spirited personality and perseverance, made Zainab a successful, sought-after expeditor and assistant. She was respected as a woman of her word and as a good mother. My memory of Zainab is of her talking to neighbors—either hanging out of her window or leaning against the door, or of her setting off to help someone. Zainab's dependence on social capital dictated a highly social life. While part of it was Zainab's personality— she loved the bustle of visiting and finding out the latest news—part of it was also business.

Zainab's work for Hamida was casually arranged. Zainab trooped off with a friend to the clothing and furniture markets in Wikalat al-Balah to meet Hamida. The friend decided on a purchase at the shop of Hamida's business associate and, with Hamida's guarantee to the shop owner, the matter was settled. Zainab would collect monthly installments. As with Um Muhammad, there was never any discussion of "interest," which is forbidden in Islam. Rather, Hamida simply stipulated, say, twelve monthly installments of ten pounds each to cover a purchase of one hundred pounds.[3]

Hamida's husband owned a car repair shop while Zainab's husband drove lorries for others. Hamida dangled over a dozen gold bracelets on her arm; Zainab wore dramatic gold earrings and sported a gold tooth. While patron-client relations such as Hamida's and Zainab's are stacked on the side of the patron, Zainab refused Hamida by politely "getting lost" in the back streets of Cairo if Hamida's "familial" demands became unreasonable; indeed, women remarked that someone visiting Hamida on a simple errand was often detained for hours washing dishes and cooking.

As dear friends (*habayeb*), Zainab and Hamida's business and personal relations were broken and mended via the state of "speaking" and "not speaking." One dramatic occasion was when Zainab's only son was rushed to the hospital after a fall from a ladder. At the time the two women were estranged. Hearing of the emergency, Hamida seized the opportunity for reconciliation, collected some of her friends, and swept through the streets bearing an expensive box of sweets. When the two women greeted each other at the hospital their everyday social performance signaled the discourse of reconciliation.

> Hamida: When I heard the news of your son's fall, I was beside myself and could not rest until I came to see him.
> Zainab: I am grateful for this visit. How is your family and children? I cannot get along without you.

For Zainab, a profitable work relation, as well as a social relation, was re-established.

The rise and fall of the "social capital" which Zainab brought to her business directly affected her work as creditor assistant. Zainab and Hamida became even more "connected" when Zainab's niece and Hamida's son Muhammad were engaged to be married. When Zainab's husband returned from Iraq, he disapproved of Muhammad, saying that he took too many hallucinogens, and insisted that the engagement be cancelled. Unavoidably, Zainab and Hamida broke off speaking and this condition was not to be easily reconciled with a social performance such as the above at the hospital. The social development drastically curtailed Zainab's income; one of her neighbors commented: "She lost her leg by doing that."

Zainab always maintained her dignity as she worked for the informal favors and commissions of her patron creditor. Zainab knew that she was *galaba* (downtrodden) and the expression peppered her conversations when she became dejected and exclaimed: "Why do I have to live in these filthy lanes? I am *galaba*!" or "If we weren't *nass galaba* I wouldn't have to spend all of my time in the market helping others." Zainab chafed at being forced by necessity to live in her father's house so that her husband could work abroad. It was Zainab's loyalty to her family that brought the rise and—with the termination of Zainab's niece's engagement—the fall of her business. As with Um Muhammad, life was a balance between demands of kin and friends, and manipulation of social capital to further business.

Conclusion

We have considered three traditional Cairene businesswomen with varying social and material capital, and with varying constellations of kin and friends. All three occupy the same place in national and international business: the informal (the "baladi") economic sector. However, their work and kin positions often extend from this sector to the national and international formal economic sectors and labor market.

The everyday discourse of these three *baladi* businesswomen reveals delicate, individual counterpoints of market and wage labor opportunities, with support of and demands by family and kin. Controlling differing capital and differing access to rural, national, and world markets, all three women mobilize impressive resources to lift themselves out of material penury and personal distress.

Um Hanafi, with few assets, resorted to simple vending and later opted out of business altogether to join her husband in Libya. Um Muhammad marketed successfully for years, using her rural and urban market connections. When her health failed she invested, sagely it would have seemed, in her son's ventures in the international labor market. Zainab, pushed by her husband's labor migration (as are all three "pushed" to some degree by a husband's "unavailability"), used social capital to plug into the thriving urban informal credit sector.

Each woman balances her capital and her opportunities in a work milieu without banks, insurance, and job security. Um Muhammad and Zainab were more adventurous in reaching out to non-kin in more than a straight vending relation of "buyer and seller." Unlike Um Hanafi, who confined herself to selling grapes and oranges for a set price, these two women diversified their business ties into more complex, multistranded ones of "quasi-kin" with women who mixed trade and social favors.

This chapter has been largely a cultural analysis, but understanding the *baladi* and the informal sector, interpreting what it means to be a traditional Cairene businesswoman, has located these women socioeconomically at the juncture of domestic and business worlds. The reader should draw no sweeping conclusions about Egyptian women in general from this paper, for the bulk of educated Egyptian women work as engineers, lawyers, doctors, professors, civil service employees, businesswomen in banks and corporations, and other white-collar employees. These Egyptian women would find our three *baladi* women as foreign as a non-Egyptian reader would.

Why then study the informal business sector? Will it vanish with illiteracy? Will future *baladi* women all work in government offices and private business? It is hard to say, but until the infrastructure of *baladi* society changes, it will need the Um Muhammads for short-term credit, the Hamidas for long-term credit, and the Zainabs to help find jobs. The informal economic sector maintains an economically marginal population; it will not soon vanish. Institutions such as informal credit or "savings associations" are not unique to Egypt, but culturally meaningful forms of social discourse such as "breaking off speaking" help to define those institutions.

Throughout the business of *baladi* women are woven such cultural themes as *galaba* or downtrodden—not as something to drag one down into ineptitude, but as a condition above which to rise, using one's wits. *Baladi* work culture values the astute shepherding of household resources and manipulation of the *afrangi* formal economic sector; supports the rights of kin and friend; and stipulates a rich social discourse of informal performances to articulate some of these values among *baladi* businesswomen. It should be clear that *baladi* businesswomen have "gotten it together" and that they may be far ahead of the Amway and Avon ladies of the United States!

NOTES

1. This article is based on anthropological field work from April 1974 to March 1977, and repeated revisits from 1977 to 1991, in Bulaq Abu 'Ala, a traditional, low-income neighborhood near downtown Cairo. My research was sponsored by Fulbright-Hayes, the Social Science Research Council, and the National Institute for Mental Health while I was a doctoral candidate at the University of Chicago and a research fellow at the Institute of National Planning in Cairo; by a Faculty Development grant

from the University of Notre Dame where I was an assistant professor; and by a Center
for Public Policy grant from the University of Houston-University Park where I was
an assistant professor in honors and anthropology when I wrote the first draft of this
article.

I dedicate this article to Um Muhammad. News of her death reached me as I was
finishing the final draft. I am of course indebted to her and all my friends in Bulaq for
the inspiration for this piece. In addition special thanks go to Janet Abu Lughod, Jean
Comaroff, Michael Fischer, Wafiq Ashraf Hassouna, Nawwal Messiri, Sawsan Messiri,
Mustafa Shafa'i, and Judith Tucker for discussions and suggestions on various ideas
in this manuscript.

The views in this article are solely my own and do not reflect the policy of the U.S.
government.

2. Fieldwork conditions in Cairo in the mid-seventies dictated that I not attempt to
use a tape recorder in a popular quarter such as Bulaq Abu 'Ala; I recorded all the
narratives which I heard during field work as soon as I returned to my apartment
either in a hasty taped reproduction or in rough notes. Sometimes, I jotted preliminary
notes while drinking juice at a street stand on my way home. Thus all texts of narratives
and social performances presented here are from notes which reconstruct field events as
faithfully as possible. I have freely translated my Arabic notes into colloquial English.

3. I was unable to ascertain exact interest rates charged by *dallala* in Bulaq both
because the matter was sensitive and because rates varied from creditor to creditor
and even from customer to customer—depending upon social relations.

A standard rate for a year loan was twenty percent, but rates could be as little as
five percent for friends with small purchases, and as astronomical as forty or fifty
percent for unknown customers with large purchases.

REFERENCES

Abu Lughod, Lila.
    1987   *Veiled Sentiments: Honor and Poetry in a Bedouin Society.* Berkeley:
            Univ. of California Press.
Basso, Keith H.
    1984   "Stalking with Stories: Names, Places, and Moral Narratives among the
            Western Apache." In Bruner.
Bauman, Richard.
    1984   *Verbal Art as Performance.* Waveland Press.
Bourdieu, Pierre.
    1977   *Outline of a Theory of Practice.* Cambridge: Cambridge Univ. Press.
Briggs, Chuck.
    1988   *Competence in Performance: The Creativity of Tradition in Mexicano
            Verbal Art.* Philadelphia: Univ. of Pennsylvania Press.
Bruner, Edward M.
    1984   *Text, Play, and Story: The Construction and Reconstruction of Self and
            Society.* AES proceedings. Waveland Press.
Crapanzano, Vincent.
    1973   *The Hamadsha: A Study in Moroccan Ethnopsychiatry.* Berkeley: Univ.
            of California Press.
DelVecchio Good, Good, Fischer.
    1988   "Discourse and the Study of Emotion, Illness and Healing." In *Culture,
            Medicine, and Psychiatry.* 12: 1–7.

Early, Evelyn A.
    1977   "Social Networks of Cairo *Baladi* Women." Paper presented at Middle
            East Kinship Conference, Kuwait.
    1982   "The Logic of Well Being: Therapeutic Narratives in Cairo, Egypt."
            Social Science and Medicine. 16: 1491–1497.
    1985   "Fatima: A Life History of an Egyptian Woman from Bulaq." In *Middle
            Eastern Women Speak.* Ed. Elizabeth Fernea. Austin: Univ. of Texas
            Press.
    1985   "Catharsis and Creation: The Everyday Narratives of *Baladi* Women of
            Cairo." *Anthropological Quarterly.* 172–180.
    1992   *Baladi Women of Cairo: Playing with an Egg and a Stone.* Boulder,
            Colo.: Lynne Reiner.
Friedl, Erika.
    1989   *Women of Deh Khoh: Lives in an Iranian Village.* Washington, D.C.:
            Smithsonian Press.
Geertz, Clifford.
    1983   *Local Knowledge: Further Essays in Interpretive Anthropology.* New
            York: Basic Books.
Gilsenan, Michael.
    1976   "Lying and Contradiction." In *Transaction and Meaning.* Ed. Bruce
            Kapferer. Philadelphia: ISHI. Pp. 191–219.
Glassie, Henry.
    1982   *Passing the Time in Ballymenone: Culture and History of an Ulster
            Community.* Philadelphia, Univ. of Pennsylvania Press.
Goffman, Irving.
    1981   *Forms of Talk.* Philadelphia: Univ. of Pennsylvania Press.
Gran, Judith.
    1977   "The Impact of the World Market on Egyptian Women." *Middle East
            Research and Information Project Reports* 58: 3–7.
Labov, William, and Joshua Waletzky.
    1966   "Narrative Analysis: Oral Versions of Personal Experience." In *Essays
            on the Verbal and Visual Arts.* AES 1966 proceedings. Seattle: Univ. of
            Washington Press. Pp 12–44.
Leprette, Fernand.
    1939   *Egypt: Land of the Nile.* Translated by Lillian Goar. Cairo: E. T.
            Schindler.
Messiri, Sawsan.
    1988   "Bint al-Balad." Trans. as "Self-Images of Traditional Urban Women in
            Cairo." In *Women in the Muslim World.* Eds. Lois Beck and Nikki
            Keddie. Cambridge: Harvard University Press.
Stahl, Sandra.
    1977   "The Personal Narrative as Folklore. *Journal of the Folklore Institute.*
            14: 9–30.
Tucker, Judith.
    1985   *Women in Nineteenth Century Egypt.* Cambridge Univ. Press.
Turner, Edith.
    1987   *The Spirit and the Drum: A Memory of Africa.* Tucson: Univ. of Arizona
            Press.
Turner, Victor, and Edward M. Bruner.
    1988   *The Anthropology of Performance.* Puj Publications.

VI

PALESTINIAN WOMEN UNDER ISRAELI OCCUPATION
IMPLICATIONS FOR DEVELOPMENT

Souad Dajani

The West Bank of the Jordan River, occupied by Israel since June 1967, presents a unique opportunity to study the interrelationships between two issues of current and contemporary concern—women's problems and development.

In this chapter, conditions of Palestinian women under occupation and implications for development are studied within the framework of Israeli colonization and settlement of the West Bank. In many ways, the West Bank has been transformed into a colony for the dominant capitalist mode of production in Israel, and the situation of women under occupation, therefore, reflects the impact of this colonization process. As such, in examining the conditions of Palestinian women, one should take into account new objective realities created by the Israeli colonization of various areas, such as the extent of destruction or transformation of indigenous structures (for example, the family), the degree of proletarianization of the Palestinian population (especially women), the expropriation of land and resources, and so on. Moreover, we should take into account the repressive Israeli measures that have restricted the role of women. These include military orders, measures against indigenous institutions, and individual and collective punishment.

With regard to the issue of development, I argue that those same objective conditions that have created the oppression of women under occupation have also created the conditions for women's liberation and participation in the struggle against foreign rule.

As we shall see throughout the chapter, the Palestinian woman does not divorce her struggle against sexual oppression and discrimination from the national struggle against Israeli occupation. Instead of concentrating on liberation and equality in a male-dominated society, Palestinian women recognize that their emancipation and integration into development can only come about with the liberation of the whole Palestinian people from Israeli rule and the achievement of Palestinian dignity and freedom in the context of independent statehood.

This chapter elaborates on these themes to outline the historical emergence of the women's movement in Palestine and to analyze the conditions and role of Palestinian women under occupation. The discussion focuses on women's efforts at establishing organizations and committees to enhance their position and contribute to the overall struggle against the Israeli regime. A central theme running through the chapter is the role of Palestinian women in the development of their society and the implications of their activism in the struggle for liberation and self-determination.

The chapter begins with a theoretical background to the issue and contrasts the predominantly western bourgeois view of feminism with the political and developmental concerns of Palestinian women under occupation.

Women and Development: A Critique of Western Bourgeois Understanding of Feminism

Unlike the West, where the women's movement is dominated by feminist issues, in the West Bank, the concerns and activities of Palestinian women are directed within the political framework of the struggle for Palestinian rights and national self-determination. This "inseparability" between women's issues and political concerns, so fundamental to Palestinian women, yet so incomprehensible in the West, was highlighted in particular during the 1985 Nairobi Conference on Women. We may recall the threat issued by the United States delegation that it would walk out, should the event become too "politicized" and delve into issues "not of unique concern to women." The term "political," as it applies to Palestinian women in this instance, involves a discussion of their plight with reference to the effects of Israeli colonization of their land.

Although the threatened walkout did not materialize, this perceived contradiction between politics and women's issues has permeated an understanding of the women's movement and has specific implications for the place of the Palestinian women in this struggle.

The Western Bourgeois Understanding of Feminism

As the Nairobi and other international conferences have revealed, an organized women's movement appears to be developing mainly along the lines of a western understanding of women's problems and their solutions. However, it is apparent that the experience of women in many Third World countries is radically different from that of their western sisters, and western concepts and ideologies relating to feminism are rather inapplicable to their lives. It is necessary to examine the basis of the Western conception of feminism and show how and why this may compromise and limit women's struggle—both in the West and in the Third World, but particularly in the Palestinian territories occupied by Israel.

Western feminist ideology can hardly be described as monolithic. It includes several different perspectives, ranging from the conservative to the Marxist, with the latter quite radical in its outlook and analysis. The predominant trend, however, is toward the "liberal" feminist line,[1] whose essential characteristics can be summarized as follows:

A basic feature of liberal feminism is its perception of women's problems largely in terms of "sexism." According to this view, women experience discrimination, low pay, poor jobs, and other indicators of inequality due to male domination (of the family, the economy, politics). Such feminists argue that the solution to women's problems could be achieved through economic independence, access to better jobs and privileges, equal pay, equal rights, and general freedom from male domination.

Most of the proponents of this view are middle-class, white western women who have already achieved some basic rights and equality, but look forward to greater freedom and independence. After acquiring some higher education, securing a job or getting married, and being imbued with the individualistic western measures of success, these women see the way to greater achievements and success blocked by "men" and sexist attitudes in society.

The prevalence of these attitudes in the West can be illustrated by the extent to which men themselves have been influenced by this ideology. In a personal example, while working as a teaching assistant in a Canadian university in 1984, I suggested that my adult class in sociology attend the International Women's Day celebrations that were taking place in March of that year. The response from the male members of the class was invariably negative. When asked why, they responded that these events were dominated by "women's issues" and that they, as men, would not be welcome since the women were hostile and "anti-men." Similarly, the females in the class were quite frank in blaming "men" for women's problems—as the oppressors and exploiters of women. Finally, both sexes rejected the relevance of that particular Women's Day event as a topic of discussion since it concerned "Imperialism and Women's Issues." Most of the students could not understand what bearing imperialism could possibly have on women's concerns.

The same class revealed further evidence of the limits of western middle-class understanding of women's problems when the idea was suggested that in the lower classes, or among minority groups, "women's problems" are much more basic than any of the problems these students had ever encountered. Among such groups, not only women, but men as well were struggling for survival—for education, for jobs, and against discrimination (economic or racial). Women in these classes or groups have not had the luxury of their middle-class sisters, to call for better pay, more daycare services, an end to male oppression and sexism. Instead, these women have been struggling for the right to any pay, any job, just to survive. Although these students could not identify with such realities, it is here that women's issues, as well as men's, can be seen to approximate the experiences of Third World countries, particularly those existing under conditions of foreign colonization—as in the Palestinian case.

The Inseparability of the "Political"

Although the Nairobi Conference and its predecessors have proved that women, including western women, have not been confined entirely within the narrow bonds and outlook of western feminism, a clear statement on the interdependence of political and socioeconomic issues is still quite noticeably lacking. There is an understandable reluctance on the part of western feminists, in particular, to cite the "political" nature of women's problems. We say "understandable" in this context, since a recognition of the political bases of these problems invites a recognition and admission of the West's culpability in the oppression of many Third World nations (including their women). Such a recognition would also be an admission of class and racial oppression in the West itself, where both women and men in the lower classes and within minority groups lack basic rights, and experience discrimination at the hands of the upper classes and dominant groups—clearly a "political" concern.

In this sense, the experience of Palestinian women, although a special case, can hardly be described as unique, since "politics" pervades all societies and is inseparable from women's conditions. With reference to the Palestinian case, however, under the yoke of occupation, women are struggling against sexism and discrimination, against imprisonment and deportation, against homelessness and statelessness, and against Zionism.

It is within this framework, the reality of the daily struggle against foreign occupation, that one can understand the concerns and outlook of Palestinian women under Israeli rule. It is also by taking into account this specific context of foreign occupation that we can identify three central themes that recur within the Palestinian women's movement:

(1) A rejection of the western model of female liberation

(2) The link between national and socioeconomic oppression of women

(3) An emphasis on the role of an organized women's movement and its contribution to development and liberation

Undeniably, Palestinian women are also suffering from the kinds of sexual discrimination and oppression that women in all class societies must face. On the one hand, Palestinian women still confront the traditional sexist attitudes toward women that predate the occupation. These include the traditional Arab view of the role of women as housewives and mothers and the restrictions placed on their participation in public life and productive work outside the home. On the other hand, living under Israeli occupation has generated special problems for Palestinian women, in terms of their triple oppression— as women, as Palestinians, and, with their proletarianization under occupation, as newcomers to the labor class (this is elaborated below; see *al-Kateb*, 1982:14). In all, the effect of the Israeli occupation has in some cases reinforced the traditional role of women as inferior to men, where Palestinians have taken refuge in their own traditions in reaction to alien Israeli rule. Yet in other cases, the reaction to the reality of occupation has radically transformed traditional values, where conditions of life under foreign rule have forced both men and women to wage a joint struggle for survival. It is at this level that we can make sense of the perspective of Palestinian women with regard to the interdependence of women's issues and national concerns.

These women have realized that their liberation as women can only take place within a total context of social liberation from exploitation and oppression, namely in the liberation of Palestinians from colonial rule. Following the 1967 occupation of the West Bank, the structural changes in Palestinian society that resulted from the imposition of Israeli rule led to an objective transformation in the status of Palestinian women. Widespread land expropriation and the destruction and transformation of the indigenous peasant household forced increased numbers of women into the labor force to supplement family incomes. In addition, more and more Palestinian women were entering the educational system and joining women's philanthropic organizations. These structural transformations in their position generated a new consciousness regarding the roles of women as productive members of Palestinian society under occupation, and a growing awareness of their potential contribution to the struggle for equality and freedom from foreign rule.

It is important to note that the various women's organizations that have expanded or been established in the West Bank since the 1967 Israeli occupation emphasize this dual concern—the need to establish a unified and organized mass movement among women as part and parcel of the national movement (*Sawt al-Mar'a*, 1983:54), and the continued struggle of women for equality with men, including the right to an education, to work, and to receive equal wages, and an end to sexual discrimination (Tunis Symposium, 1984:54).

Therefore, in evaluating the relationship between women and development, Palestinian women equate their progress with that of their society as a whole (*al-Shaab*, 9 July 1985). They are particularly conscious of the fact that national and class oppression falls equally upon Palestinian men and women, and that there should be a joint struggle with Palestinian men against the common enemy.

To summarize, under Israeli occupation, Palestinian women, like Palestinian men, have to devote their main energies to basic survival, to resisting their occupiers, and to retaining a Palestinian identity. Struggling for the elementary right to a home, a land, and a nationality, they are unable to concern themselves exclusively with the issues which western women view as priorities—such as day care, abortion rights, higher pay, better jobs, and equal opportunities with men. Palestinian women, like Palestinian men, are exposed to exile, imprisonment, exploitation, and oppression, in addition to the daily hardships of life under occupation. For Palestinian women, the struggle for women's rights and the struggle for socioeconomic and national self-determination become one and the same.

The Effects of Colonization

This section reviews the impact of the imposition of Israeli rule in the West Bank since the 1967 occupation. Transformations that affect the position and role of Palestinian women in particular are then examined, followed by a closer analysis of women's conditions in health and education and the special circumstances of female prisoners.

Impact of the 1967 Israeli Occupation on West Bank Society

Before the Israeli occupation, the West Bank was predominantly characterized as a traditional peasant community that subsisted largely on agricultural production. Although this economy had already begun to disintegrate long before 1967 and social relationships were in a process of change, there is general agreement that one of the main effects of Israeli colonization of the West Bank has been to accelerate the transition to capitalist relations of production and the transformation and marginalizing of traditional social structures to serve capitalist economic needs in Israel. In analyzing the impact of the Israeli occupation on the West Bank, therefore, we may focus on the extent to which indigenous village social structures have been conserved and/or destroyed, and the effects of these trends on the situation of Palestinian women.

In the West Bank, traditional social structures have not been totally destroyed by Israeli colonization but have been transformed and subsumed under many social and economic spheres. The West Bank's dependence on Israel clearly illustrates this point.[2] This dependent relationship may be examined in terms of the main elements of Israeli colonization: the exploitation and expropriation of land and water resources, the proletarianization of the Palestinian people and their transformation into a migrant labor force, and the establishment of the West Bank as a market for Israeli goods. In this regard, Israel has created a "dependent" specialization for West Bank agriculture, turning it away from the main semi-subsistence sector of pre-1967 to the production of agricultural inputs for Israeli industries and for export abroad (Graham-Brown, 1979). Before 1967, peasant women played an important role along with men in agricultural production, working in the fields and contributing to the subsistence economy of the peasant household (*al-Fajr*, 8–14 March, 1981:14). Amal Samed has estimated that in 1967, 64 percent of the Arab female force of the territories worked in subsistence agriculture, compared to 34 percent of the male labor force (Samed, 1976:164).

The economic integration of agriculture under Israeli rule has forced West Bank direct producers into capitalist relations of production as a proletarianized peasant labor force for Israeli production. This process of proletarianization has affected both men and women.

Since 1967, widespread expropriation of land and the establishment of Israeli settlements have reduced the amount of agricultural land that is available to Palestinians. Even in areas that remain under Palestinian control, competition with the more technologically advanced Israeli agriculture, restrictions on the use of water resources, restrictions on marketing and the unavailability of grants and loans for Palestinian farmers, have all contributed to the deterioration of the indigenous agricultural sector (UN, 22 June, 1983:14). This has occurred in a situation where 70 percent of the West Bank Palestinian population continues to reside in villages (Graham-Brown, 1984:228). Statistics show that while in 1969, 65,200 people worked in agriculture, this figure dropped to 48,600 in 1983, representing a drop from 41.2 percent to 20.9 percent of the West Bank labor force (JC, 1985:33). Thus, one of the most significant effects of Israeli colonization has been the process of proletarianization of Palestinians "freed" from their traditional means of production, to work as cheap wage-labor in Israeli industries.

An increasing number of Palestinian males have been forced out of agricultural production and into wage-labor in Israel. The number is estimated at almost one-third of the labor force of the occupied territories (UN, 22 June 1983:19). The effect has been that it is mainly females who remain in local agriculture. One study estimates that 70 percent of agricultural work is done by women (WCSW, 1985:20), and that 57 percent of the female labor force is involved in agricultural production in the West Bank. These processes have several important implications with regard to women. On the one hand, the expansion of capitalist relationships has transformed both West Bank producers and other previously employed and unemployed Palestinians into a supply of cheap and available wage-labor. The proletarianization of women has emerged as part of this process of transformation, where women have been forced into productive work in Israeli industries along with men. This has created a new dimension to the exploitation of women, both as Palestinian women and as cheap labor (*al-Kateb*, 1982:14). On the other hand, since the Israeli occupation has not completely destroyed indigenous structures, there still persist the remnants of a peasant village economy. By 1980, only 30 percent of Palestinians earned their living from local agriculture (Graham-Brown, 1984:228). However, tied and dependent as it is on the capitalist mode of production in Israel, this economy and its traditional family structures have been marginalized and serve mainly the function of reproducing a migrant labor force for the Israeli economy. Samed describes the West Bank as a "bedroom community" (1976:164) where Palestinian males are employed by Israel and receive wages to cover their "productive" costs by day, but return to the West Bank by night to be "renewed" through indigenous social structures—mainly the task of Palestinian women. As such, the Palestinian woman, who formerly functioned as a household producer alongside men in the subsistence agricultural economy, has now been transformed into a marginal, unpaid laborer in the capitalist mode of production. Here, she is limited to the tasks of the "reproduction" of the Palestinian labor force. Samed explains this process by noting that the migrant labor system has increased the surplus value of labor for the Israeli capitalist economy, since there are few reproductive costs that have to be met by the Israeli employer (1976:159); Israel is thus saved the costs that it would incur without a migrant labor system.

Conditions of Women under Israeli Occupation

The 1967 Israeli occupation of the West Bank, as it destroyed what remained of the traditional economic basis of Palestinian society and transformed villagers into wage laborers, generated a radical transformation in the position and role of Palestinian women. Perhaps the most significant aspect of the impact of Israeli colonization on Palestinian women relates to their role in the labor force. As noted by Makhoul (1984:9), the subjugation of Palestinian women to the requirement of capitalist accumulation in Israel operates at two main levels: (1) indirect subjugation through unpaid housework, where the Palestinian woman assumes the role of reproducing the labor force for the Israeli market; and (2) direct integration through wage-labor.

In actual figures, the female labor force has increased in real terms since the beginning of the Israeli occupation and is characterized mainly by the entry of Palestinian women into the wage-labor force. Between 1967 and 1983, the number of female wage-laborers rose from 13,800 to 28,000 in the West Bank (SAI, 1983, 1985, and UPWW, 1981:24). In percentages, in 1983, 12 percent of West Bank females were in the labor force, constituting 17.8 percent of the total West Bank labor force (JC, 1985:24).

Increased land expropriation and dispossession of Palestinians has affected camp women in particular. Forcible proletarianization has made their participation in the labor force higher than that for village and urban women (*al-Fajr*, 21 May 1985). The statistics on women's participation in the labor force do not, however, take into account local agricultural production, which is unpaid and performed by women over and above their household duties, (UPWW, 1981:24 and Samed, 1976:165).

The agricultural sector is becoming the main employer of women in the West Bank. The percentage of women employed in this sector has increased from 31 percent at the beginning of the occupation to 46 percent as of 1983,

while in industry this figure ranged between 11 and 15 percent over this period
(JC, 1985:39, 41, and WCSW, 1985:20). The high percentage of women in
agriculture indicates that with the increased rate of male proletarianization
and employment as wage-labor in Israel, women tend to replace men as agricultural workers in the West Bank. Their work in Israeli agriculture usually
takes place through the illegal labor market and involves seasonal work as
cash croppers and in food-processing industries (Samed, 1976:159,165; JC,
1985:65). Moreover, women, who generally receive the lowest wages, are
subject to more exploitation and are the first to be fired (UPWW, 1981:26).

These general statistics on female labor in the West Bank suggest the following implications for Palestinian women under Israeli occupation. First, the
very fact that women's proletarianization has occurred indicates the degree
of disintegration of the traditional village community and its various socioeconomic structures. Thus, the traditional Palestinian village, whose residents
already faced problems of unemployment and high emigration rates, has now
been reduced to dependence on Israel and on the market system. In addition,
the village has been transformed into a community of women and children,
where the men return only at night from work in Israel. The combined effects
of the proletarianization of men and the increased dependence on Israel have
been severe in their effects on the traditional family structure. As Samed notes,
the Palestinian family remains as one of the few indigenous institutions to
survive the destruction of Palestinian society under occupation, and assumes
a new importance in preserving and maintaining the Palestinian identity
(1976:161). Under occupation, however, traditional family roles are being
continuously transformed and strained.

On the one hand, growing economic need has forced women into the labor
force to meet the rising costs of living. On the other hand, with the men
either at work in Israel, or deported or imprisoned at the hands of the Israeli
authorities, or else forced to emigrate abroad, it is the Palestinian women who
now have to bear the responsibilities of holding together a secure and stable
family under the continuous pressures of life under occupation. Many writers
agree that one of the significant effects of the Israeli occupation and its integration of the West Bank economy has been to increase the burdens on women to
provide for the family (Haddad, 1980:163; al-Kateb, 1982; UPWW, 1981:30).

It is significant to note that the demographic distribution of males and
females in the West Bank reveals a low ratio of men to women, especially in
the productive 30–64 age group. Most of those who emigrate (about 17,000
in 1980 and 15,800 in 1981: UN, 22 June 1983:19) are single males (41
percent in 1982) which means that many women on the West Bank remain
unmarried (estimated at 22 percent in 1984: WCSW, 1985:15). This surplus
of women, especially in the 30–49 age group, has significant implications for
the role of women, who are traditionally prepared for family life and who
must now enter into the labor force and various social activities in order to

secure a living. These changes in family composition and the increased number of women in the labor force have several important implications for the role of women in development, as will be seen in the final section of this chapter.

As for conditions of Palestinian women in other spheres, the Israeli occupation has had a significant impact on female education and health.

Education

Education is essential both to instill the skills and knowledge needed to join the labor force and to contribute to development by allowing greater participation in sociopolitical activities and organizations. Early on, Palestinian women came to realize that education provided a weapon to struggle against the colonization of their land and to improve their conditions in society. Christian missions established schools throughout Palestine, beginning in the mid-nineteenth century (Jammal, 1985:8).

Following the Israeli occupation of the West Bank in 1967, and with the mounting pressures and costs of daily life, families became increasingly aware of the need to educate their daughters to assume productive roles in society. While in 1967 74.3 percent of West Bank females had no education (CBS, 1968), fifteen years later females accounted for 45.1 percent of school enrollment (figures for 1981–82, al-Najah, 1982:140). In addition, females account for 42.1 percent of total university enrollment in the occupied territories (1982–83) and form 52.7 percent of the enrollment in literacy programs offered by the voluntary associations (Katbeh, 1982:156). However, these higher figures may be somewhat misleading when one realizes that female enrollment is especially high at elementary levels but drops off at the preparatory and secondary levels.[3] Furthermore, the higher percentage of females at West Bank universities reflects the fact that many males travel abroad to study, while females are forced to remain in the West Bank. Thus, in 1983, only 35 percent of secondary school students in the West Bank were women, compared to 44 percent at the elementary level and 37.9 percent at the preparatory levels (WCSW, 1985:38). The high rate of attrition can be traced to poor and deteriorating educational conditions at government schools, the lack of qualified teachers, their low salaries, over-crowding, and inadequate facilities that resulted from Israeli occupation policies restricting educational development (1985:29). Israel has tried to encourage vocational (rather than academic) training for women, in order to provide them with the necessary "skills" to enable them to be absorbed in the wage labor force that serves the Israeli economy.[4]

In summary, it is evident that education for Palestinian females in the West Bank suffers from certain constraints resulting from both neglect and repression at the hands of the Israeli authorities, and the economic and social pressures that force women out into the labor force at a very early stage in their education. Conditions under occupation have meant that illiteracy among

Arab women still remains high, especially in rural areas. Of equal significance, however, is the fact that those who do manage to complete their higher education may be confronted with unemployment.[5]

Nevertheless, women's groups in the occupied territories are increasingly concerned with improving the educational standards of Palestinian women, demonstrating their awareness of the vital link between education and development. They tend to regard education both as the key to solving problems specific to women (such as enhancing their ability to pursue equality and equal rights) and as part of women's national responsibility, to contribute to the development of Palestinian society. Particular emphasis is placed on the need to develop and orient education for both Palestinian males and females in terms of specific Palestinian conditions. This includes vocational training and literacy programs, confronting the problem of drop-outs, imparting the skills and knowledge that would enable the graduate to find work, while at the same time contributing to basic sectors needed to develop Palestinian society (especially in agriculture).

Health

Conditions under occupation have direct implications in terms of the health status and health care of the female population in the West Bank. In this paper, the subject is referred to as it illustrates general living conditions in the West Bank, and more specifically as it illustrates the conditions of females under Israeli occupation.

If we keep in mind that approximately 70 percent of the West Bank population consists of women and children, who are also considered the highest risk group because of their vulnerability to communicable and contagious diseases (Giacaman, 1982:11), then a study of the epidemiological setting of health and illness, or the environmental factors affecting health issues, is particularly relevant. This is especially so because it is usually women and children who are left in the homes while men go out to work as laborers in the Israeli economy.

As the Special Committee of the World Health Organization (WHO) has repeatedly emphasized, the health status of Palestinians has been adversely affected by numerous environmental problems. These include the salinity of the water supply and nutritional deficiencies due to the lack of essential foodstuffs (7 May 1984:7, 9). According to the Special Committee, these problems are compounded by specific Israeli policies, such as the refusal to allow the digging of wells, which "adversely affect" the health conditions of Arabs in the occupied territories (7 May 1984:2).

Apart from the fact that Israeli colonial policy has been to appropriate control over land and water resources from the Palestinians—resources which are being exploited for Israel's benefit—an examination of several features of the immediate environment reveals their effects on sanitation and health standards in the West Bank.

With regard to services and living conditions, we may note that Palestinians suffer from the results of overcrowding in homes (Giacaman, 1982:11; UN, 22 June 1983:9), and that specific services are limited or lacking. For example, the Special Committee estimates that in 1983, 36 percent of dwellings in the West Bank lacked sanitary toilets and 40 percent were not linked to electrical supplies (28 April, 1983:8). Rita Giacaman aptly points out that in general, environmental conditions in villages and rural areas are considerably worse than the cities and that, for example, running water is available in only 44.6 percent of all town dwellings and 29.3 percent of village households (data for 1981; Giacaman, 1983:13).

Other indicators show that, while in 1981, 88.1 percent of households in West Bank towns had an electric refrigerator, only 33.6 percent of village households had one (SAI, 1982, table 27/15). Also, keeping in mind that there are over four hundred villages in the West Bank, only 22 percent of these were found to have "potable and safe running water."

Without entering into further detail, it becomes evident that many essential elements of a healthy and sanitary environment are lacking, especially in village and rural areas of the West Bank. This has obvious implications in terms of prevailing health problems, where the high incidence of infectious and communicable diseases that strike particularly at children and youth is noted (WHO, 7 May 1984:9; especially gastroenteritis and respiratory diseases). Such diseases are compounded by the effects of malnutrition. This in turn reflects the poverty and generally unsatisfactory environmental conditions that result from the dispossession of Palestinians and the loss of their traditional means of livelihood under Israeli rule (WHO, 7 May 1984:7; *Kifah al-Mar'a*, 1984:58).

As for existing health services to cope with prevailing health problems, these services are particularly lacking in village and rural areas. Furthermore, they tend to be curative and hospital oriented, which means that they are extremely costly and unsuitable in meeting the actual health needs of the population. While there are over 90 mother-child health centers in the West Bank, these are not evenly accessible throughout the region, where only 26.6 percent of West Bank villages have access to such centers. Moreover, most health clinics are located around hospital areas (that is, urban areas), and therefore they are not easily accessible to the rural population where they are most needed (WHO, 14 May 1984; 8 May 1984; 7 May 1984).

Illustrating this point, in 1983, only 40 percent of West Bank women gave birth in hospitals, while most of the remainder did not even have access to qualified midwives. Thus, there is a high incidence of complications, as well as infant and maternal mortality (14 May 1984; UPWW 1981:32).

This general description of health conditions in the West Bank reveals the poor living standards under occupation, particularly in the village areas where the majority of the population still resides. Moreover, it illustrates the inadequacy of health services in dealing with the problems of women and children, thus affecting the woman's ability to cope with the hardships of daily life under Israeli occupation. In addition to her household role of "renewing" the male labor force and/or working as an unpaid laborer in local agriculture, she also has to cope with providing adequate nutrition for her children and some measure of health care to meet her needs (as well as her children's). With the men abroad, deported, or detained, it is often the women who are forced to run the household and bear the responsibility of providing both economically and socially for the family. A deteriorating standard of health can only complicate the "double burden" that the Palestinian woman is forced to endure under Israeli rule.

Female Prisoners

Before concluding this section on specific conditions of life under Israeli occupation, a few words may be said concerning another aspect of the situation of women under Israeli rule—the conditions of female prisoners.

Palestinian women, like their male counterparts, are subject to detention, imprisonment, deportation, and death in response to their resistance activities against the occupation regime. Thus, since the beginning of the occupation, some 1,250 women have been arrested or detained in Israeli prisons, and 48 have been deported (figures until 1981, WCSW, 1985:60). Moreover, 80 percent of women detained are between 15 and 29 years of age, and over 92 percent of those who received life sentences are also in their productive years (WCSW, 1985:54). As for those deported, many are women who had assumed leadership roles in their communities and had been active in various organizational spheres.

The ever-present threat of detention or arrest creates a feeling of insecurity among both Palestinian men and women: families fear for their daughters as much as for their sons, husbands fear for their wives, and whole families are disrupted when the remaining female breadwinners are also subjected to detention or house arrest.

Perhaps one encouraging consequence of such brutal oppression at the hands of the Israeli authorities is the heightened political consciousness among women and their added determination to struggle against the occupation and fight for their legitimate national and social rights. Many women's organizations have established committees in villages, towns, and camps to defend prisoners and to come to the aid of families of prisoners and martyrs. This sense of community belonging and cooperation helps contribute to the continued *sumud* or steadfastness of the Palestinian people on the land. Even within the prisons, women mobilize to resist demoralization, to fight for better prison conditions, and to keep in sight the ultimate goal of the struggle for national self-determination. Women in prison face violence, threats, and abuse; yet they struggle to keep their spirits high. They continue to educate and motivate themselves to continue working, both as women and as Palestinians, whether inside the prison, or in the community after their release (WCSW, 1985; *al-Shaab*, 11 October 1984).

A Historical Sketch of the Palestinian Women's Movement

In order to situate the struggle of Palestinian women in the West Bank in a historical context, we may briefly examine the emergence and development of an organized Palestinian women's movement beginning with the early part of the twentieth century. Currently, as in the past, the organized women's movement has expanded mainly in response to the national threat: the Zionist colonization of Palestinian land, the threatened loss of Palestinian identity, and the forcible disintegration of the Palestinian community.

As early as 1884, even before the emergence of an organized women's movement in early Palestine, Palestinian women from rural areas were already struggling alongside Palestinian male peasants against the first Zionist settlements (Jammal, 1985:8). Meanwhile, in the urban areas of Palestine in the 1920s, educated middle-class Palestinian women were becoming involved in various social activities and establishing committees and organizations to address national and social concerns.

In 1920, women joined the widespread uprising to voice opposition to the British Mandate and continued Zionist immigration; and in 1921, Palestinian women established the first Arab Palestinian Women's Union in Jerusalem, organized around national concerns. Shortly thereafter, a number of women's groups and committees emerged to unify and coordinate women's efforts in expanding the political and social struggle against Zionist settlement and British Mandate policies.

"Feminist" concerns did not preoccupy the Palestinian women. From the start, these women were concerned with social and political issues directly related to the foreign colonization of their land. However, there was a difference between the outlook of urban and rural women in this regard. Rural women, who were directly affected by Zionist colonization, actually fought with their menfolk to defend their land and livelihood. Urban women, on the other hand, despite their participation in delegations and demonstrations, directed their energies toward relief and charitable activities. Gradually, however, their activities began to incorporate political ends, as the fragmentation of the Palestinian community progressed. For example, during the First Arab Women's Congress of Palestine in 1929, in which 300 women participated, and which has been described as a "bold step to take" in view of traditional restrictions against women (*al-Fajr*, 8–14 March, 1981:8), Palestinian women reaffirmed their national goals and struggle. Women also participated in the 1936–39 revolt and organized various activities to help the revolutionaries, both by fighting and by securing food and medical care for the fighters and wounded. Again, in 1947, before the creation of the State of Israel, women participated in demonstrations against the Partition Plan.

After 1948, Palestinian women directed most of their energies toward relief and services within the framework of charitable societies and organizations, to cope with the huge influx of refugees and help the people deal with the effects of dispossession. Thus, during the period 1948–67, many new charitable societies were established, whose services included orphanages, literacy programs, health programs, and the like, to meet the needs of a dispossessed people and to contribute toward the preservation of Palestinian culture and identity.

In 1967, the Palestinian community was once again disrupted by the Israeli occupation of the West Bank and Gaza Strip. The new realities of living under occupation generated a different set of concerns for women.

The following section examines the nature of the organized women's movement that emerged in the West Bank after 1967 and its new priorities and directions in the face of foreign colonial rule.

The Role of Palestinian Women's Organizations in the Occupied West Bank

Women's organizations in the West Bank can be divided into two types. The first includes the "formal" and officially registered charitable and voluntary societies that operate within the framework of the Union of Charitable Societies (which has three regional branches in Jerusalem, Nablus, and Hebron). Many of these societies existed before 1967, although some were not officially registered until 1965, while a few were established after 1967 (Giacaman lists six such societies: n.d.:7). The second category includes the various "informal" women's committees spread throughout the West Bank, which started with the creation of the Women's Work Committee in Ramallah in 1978.

Both these types of women's groups are examined below in terms of their membership, perspective, and activities.

Charitable Societies

There are about sixty women's charitable societies in the West Bank which are included within the framework of the Union of Charitable Societies. In general, their activities constitute an extension of pre-1967 efforts and include newer functions involving primarily education, health, and social welfare (WCSW, 1985:17, and Tunis Symposium, 1984:8).

The accessibility of these societies is limited by their location mainly in the major cities and towns (Giacaman, n.d.:7). Moreover, these societies concentrate largely on relief services, although since 1967 there has been a shift away from these services into new roles more suited to changing conditions and needs. Many of these societies, in other words, were forced to take on what were viewed as their new responsibilities under occupation. Giacaman, for example, notes a change in the perspective, composition, and activities of the women's movement in the West Bank. These changes included a new emphasis on "self-help," literacy programs, vocational training, and attempts to address the problems of working and rural women, all of which came to balance the purely "relief" services of the past (i.e., helping the poor and needy; Giaca-man, n.d.:11). She does note, however, that such changes could not material-ize fully within the framework of the traditional organizations, which, she points out, were generally unable to emerge from their charitable role to encourage development and self-reliance. This became the task largely of the more recent groups that emerged after 1967, that is, the various Women's Committees and their branches throughout the West Bank.

Giacaman and others do point to one or two exceptions to the "charitable" role of the older societies. One of these exceptions is that of the well-known In'ash al-Usra Society (Family rejuvenation society) in al-Bireh. This society was established in 1965 as a response to the needs of the large refugee popula-tion for relief and services. However, not long after 1967, women realized that what was needed involved more than "relief." It was essential to enable Palestinian women to become independent, productive beings, contributing to their families, and to the development of their society. In'ash placed a special emphasis on "self-help" instead of mere "relief," by setting up a number of vocational training programs and productive and marketing activities (Giaca-man, n.d.:11, and Shabbas, 1984:4). In'ash also continues to emphasize the role of Palestinian women in the struggle to preserve Palestinian culture and identity in the face of continued Israeli occupation.

Some of the problems that confront women's societies may be located in the nature of the activities themselves. For example, with more emphasis on "relief" than on productivity, these societies have generally been unable to equip and train women to assume productive and developmental roles in society. In addition, by concentrating themselves mainly in urban areas, they have not adequately mobilized rural and village women, nor addressed their specific problems under Israeli occupation. Similarly, they have not sufficiently addressed the problems of working women, a growing concern in view of the increased proletarianization of Palestinian women under Israeli colonial rule. Moreover, where productive activities do exist, difficulties are often encoun-tered in the marketing of the produce, and vocational training, though more widely available, is still insufficient (for example, see *al-Shaab*, 31 August 1985 and UPWW, 1981:6).

Since these societies fall under the supervision of the Israeli Deputy of Social Affairs of the occupied territories, they are subject to long procedures concern-ing permits, registration, and projects, and face interference and obstacles in obtaining funds from abroad. Some of the female activists (such as Um Khalil, President of In'ash al-Usra) have been arrested or detained. There are frequent restrictions on and disruptions of cultural and social activities.

Women's Committees

By the early 1970s, the specific conditions of life under Israeli occupation forced Palestinian women in the West Bank to become aware of the need to change their roles to focus on their new concerns: working women, women in rural areas, and the need for vocational training, education, and health care.

To this end, the first of the Women's Committees was established in 1978, as an extension of the work of charitable societies, but within the context of the new realities confronting women under Israeli occupation. In contrast to the formal and traditional charitable societies, Women's Committees may be described as "non-traditional" and "unofficial" groups (WCSW, 1985:17). Their members are mostly women from the villages and the refugee camps of the West Bank whose experience of the daily problems of Palestinian women under occupation is particularly acute.

There are four different groups sponsoring Women's Committee efforts in the Occupied Territories:

(a) Women's Work Committees
(b) Women's Committees for Social Work
(c) Palestinian Women's Committees
(d) Working Women's Committees

Each of the four committees corresponds to and identifies with one of the four major factions within the Palestine Liberation Organization (PLO). These include Fateh, the Popular Front for the Liberation of Palestine (PFLP), the Democratic Front for the Liberation of Palestine (DFLP), and the Communist Party. Although ideologically distinct, the goals and activities of these committees tend to overlap, as they all stress the need for productive work and educational and vocational training for women. They also focus on the need to involve housewives and help them become more productive members of the society. In addition, they stress the importance of cultural activities, helping working women achieve their basic rights, and combating illiteracy (WCSW, 1985:18; Kifah al-Mar'a, 1984:70).

More important, these Women's Committees aim at creating a unified mass women's movement to reach all classes of Palestinian women. The goal is to mobilize women to defend Palestinian national rights and to struggle for national self-determination, in addition to defending the rights of women and improving their socioeconomic position in society. Such goals derive from the basic perception of the Women's Committees that it is through strengthening the role of women in the national struggle that the role of women in society may be developed (WWC, 1983:4).

Due to the general overlap in perspective, membership, and activities of the various Women's Committees, this chapter limits the description to the first of these groups—the Women's Work Committees.[6]

The Women's Work Committees

Women's Committees in the West Bank started with the establishment of the first Women's Work Committee (WWC) in Ramallah in 1978. As Giacaman explains, it was the general unwillingness of educated, politically committed, and nationalist women to be absorbed within the framework of the traditional charitable societies that led to the creation of this type of women's committee (n.d.:16, and Shabbas, 1984:5).

Like those that followed later, the first WWC stressed its orientation away from charitable activities and toward the creation of an organized women's movement. Instead of regarding themselves as an alternative to other women's organizations, the WWCs perceived their role as lying in cooperation and coordination with other groups around the central issue of the national struggle. In this respect, they also stressed the specific concerns of women, and concentrated on trying to organize women around their own problems: literacy, health, production, day care, and so on, as a step toward addressing political concerns. Special emphasis has been placed on the problems of working women (union representation, better wages, rights to holidays and leaves) and fighting against women's triple oppression under Israeli occupation (Tunis Symposium, 1984:54; *al-Kateb*, 1982:14).

The WWCs are organized within the general framework of the Union of Women's Work Committees, but unlike the charitable societies, they are not centralized or urban-based. Instead, they have branches in towns, camps, and villages of the West Bank and represent all sectors of Palestinian society. They include in their ranks women from all walks of life over fifteen years of age (Giacaman, n.d.:19). While the regional office is located in Ramallah, WWCs have established committees in Jerusalem, Qalqilya, Hebron, Jenin, Bethlehem, Tulkarm and Nablus in the West Bank and one in Gaza (Tunis Symposium, 1984:54). Each of these WWCs has branches in the surrounding villages and subcommittees in the refugee camps. The WWCs' main focus on villages stems from the underlying belief that "if things improve in the village, the whole society will improve" (*al-Fajr*, 22–28 February, 1981:10). Aware of the detrimental effects of the Israeli occupation, particularly on the traditional village economy, WWCs emphasize the priority of economic and social work as the first step to realizing the mobilization of women around political issues (WWC, 1983:4).

Thus, based on the perspective that strengthening the role of women in the national struggle is inextricably linked to improving their role and position in society, the main goals and activities of WWCs may be summarized as follows (WWC, 1984:4–9):

(1) Mobilizing all women, including villagers and housewives to work to improve their socioeconomic position, increase their educational level, and develop their role in the national struggle.

(2) Training women for productive work through vocational training centers, cooperatives, productive projects, and marketing household goods.

(3) Coordinating with workers' unions to achieve and defend women's rights for holidays, leaves, better wages, etc.

(4) Raising women's educational standards and instilling political awareness through literacy programs, lectures, debates, and refresher courses.

(5) Helping achieve solutions to women's social problems: establishing kindergartens, joining unions, aid for poor and needy families, health guidance (coordination with health institutions and health personnel), mother-child health centers, health insurance, and first-aid courses.

(6) Teaching the history of the Palestinians and the national issue.

(7) Reviving national and cultural traditions, through exhibitions and cultural activities.

Some of the problems faced by the various groups of WWCs include the general problems faced by all women's organizations in the West Bank: obtaining funds, confronting traditional attitudes toward women's participation in public life and, especially, harassment by the Israeli authorities. Due to their unofficial and non-traditional status, these WWCs also face problems with regard to finding adequate space to conduct their activities and plan their programs.

To conclude this section, we should emphasize that the organized women's movement under Israeli occupation, though concerned with specific problems of women, has never lost sight of wider national concerns. In the view of Palestinian women, it is the Israeli occupation which is responsible for many of the economic and social problems endured by Palestinian men, women, and children in the West Bank. It is only through a struggle on two fronts simultaneously—for national self-determination and for an improvement in women's conditions—that a just society can be achieved. The organized women's movement in the West Bank, therefore, believes that it is impossible to separate the women's struggle from the social and political struggle for Palestinian rights.

Implications for Development

The preceding sections reviewed different aspects of the conditions of Palestinian women under Israeli occupation in the West Bank. This final section, therefore, attempts to analyze the role of Palestinian women in the development of the West Bank.

In this context, we may once again review and compare the western women's view of development as articulated in the Nairobi Conference, as it concerns specifically women's issues. Here, we note that the western middle-class approach to women's problems tends to take a "packaged" and "programmed" form, defining the specific women's issue and developing an isolated "program" to deal with it, separated from other concerns. Although this is not a reflection on western feminism as a whole, the problem with such a strategy is its failure to take into account the totality and specificity of the social context of women's problems.

The "Forward Looking Strategies" of the 1985 Nairobi Conference illustrate the western approach to the role of women in development. In their press releases, western women, particularly those from the United States, asserted that economic development is better served by the "more efficient use of scarce resources." In this view, women's contribution to economic development, although already substantial, could be supported and advanced by improving their health, education, and job opportunities. As such, both the responsibilities and benefits of economic development would then accrue to the members of the society as a whole, including its women. "The underlying premise of the development strategy the U.S. delegation hopes the Conference will adopt is one which recognizes that the economic participation of women in development is essential to balanced economic development."[7] While we may agree with the basic premise that it is necessary to improve women's conditions in order to extend their participation in development, the limitations of such a strategy under certain conditions should be pointed out. In the case of the Palestinian woman, as shown above, the most obvious limitation is the absence of national independence. Opportunities for national and economic development do not exist, and are quite contrary to conditions of colonial rule and foreign occupation. This is evident if we define "development" in the Palestinian case as the establishment of a self-sufficient and viable economy with Palestinian control over vital resources (land, water, capital, and labor) and a halt to the integration of the West Bank into the Israeli economy.

Under such conditions, the increased participation of Palestinian women in the labor force and their improved educational and social opportunities are neither conducive to nor do they serve the economic development of Palestinian society. On the contrary, as has been amply documented in the case of the West Bank, the Israeli economy is profiting from both female and male proletarianization and participation in the work force. As this example illustrates, simply defining economic development in terms of increased female participation fails to take into account the political and economic realities underlying development. As both Palestinian women and men are aware, the first priority must be to end the occupation before undertaking an indigenous program of national and social development.

There is an inextricable link between women's issues and political concerns. The western strategic view, and its single-targeted "program" approach (for example, aimed at raising educational or health standards among women) is limited in its ability to address the totality of women's concerns within specific historical circumstances.

In analyzing the specific elements of the Palestinian woman's role in the development of the West Bank, we must bear in mind the conditions created by the Israeli occupation of the West Bank since 1967, and its effect on the situation of Palestinian women. This objective reality, which has increased women's oppression, may also be turned to their advantage, to create the conditions both for their liberation and for the development of Palestinian society.

The Israeli colonization of the West Bank has had an impact on all spheres of women's lives. The expansion of capitalist relations of production to the West Bank has accelerated the proletarianization of the Palestinian population, including its women, and has resulted in the integration of the West Bank economy into Israel. This integration and consequent dependency has in turn affected the structure of indigenous Palestinian institutions, especially the village economy and the traditional family. As noted earlier, the Palestinian woman under Israeli occupation bears an increased burden and responsibility in her new economic role (as wage-earner) and her continued familial role as wife and mother. Even here, with men at work in Israel, deported, arrested, or abroad, women are increasingly under pressure to hold the family together and preserve a sense of Palestinian identity and community ties. In the sphere of health, the Palestinian woman has also been affected by the Israeli occupation, where the inadequacy of health services and deteriorating living conditions in the West Bank is evident. In general, absenteeism in the educational system can be traced to the inadequate educational system under Israeli occupation and to the family hardships that women encounter, including the need to work to supplement family incomes.

However, in spite of all these difficulties, or perhaps because of them, Palestinian women are forced into taking the initiative to improve their condition. It is the reality of living under foreign occupation and the specificity of Israeli strategy and measures in the West Bank that have deeply penetrated the consciousness of Palestinian women with the realization that their problems as females cannot be separated from the total context of living under foreign rule.

In the absence of national liberation, it is inevitable that Palestinian women link the improvement in their conditions to the general improvement of Palestinian society. Their efforts at "development," therefore, concentrate on strengthening the sense of community responsibility and activity, creating and reinforcing indigenous infrastructures and continuously resisting Israeli colonial rule. We may describe the two facets of women's development efforts as *sumud*, or remaining steadfast on the land, and their resistance to Israel's creeping annexation of the West Bank.

The disintegration of the traditional Palestinian family under Israeli occupation has forced many women into the wage-labor force, as well as into higher education and the professions. Because of the shortage of males, many women, especially in their productive years, have remained unmarried. Such destructive changes in the family and labor structure under occupation have in turn served to push women into improving their education and into greater participation in public life. Greater integration in public life has generated a sense of national consciousness among women and the general willingness to work in an organized setting to improve their condition and to contribute to the welfare and development of Palestinian society. Numerous women's charitable societies and women's committees have emerged under these conditions. This organized body of the women's movement addresses the problems of Palestinians under occupation through the dual strategy of promoting *sumud* and resistance of the Palestinian people, while at the same time addressing specific women's concerns.

Regarding the issue of labor, the entry of Palestinian women into the labor force as wage-laborers in Israeli industry and agriculture under occupation has established the conditions for forging a link between Palestinian men and women under occupation, as a proletarian class in direct confrontation with Israeli capital. This link has significant potential for conducting the Palestinian struggle on both the political and socioeconomic fronts, rather than simply as a struggle of either men or women against exploitation and repression.

At another level, even the ordeals of Palestinian women in Israeli prisons have been transformed to serve the Palestinian struggle. The women's struggle in prison instills in each one of them even more determination and strength to carry on the struggle against exploitation and oppression, and for national self-determination.

Similarly, women's organizations under occupation have been forced, by changing circumstances, to reflect in their activities these new realities and the combined concerns of development and the solution of women's problems. We have already noted the transition from purely relief functions to the emphasis on self-help and productivity of women in these organizations. Moreover, these societies (particularly the WWCs) place special emphasis on the need to develop a unified mass women's movement as part and parcel of national development (*Sawt al-Mar'a*, 1983:54). As Giacaman explains, charitable societies need to develop new roles under occupation, since such societies are viewed as "the only structures left that [can] possibly . . . inhibit the destruction of the social infrastructure and prepare the way for the reconstruction of the Palestinian society in the future" (Giacaman, n.d.:10).

NOTES

1. For an overview of the differences in perspectives in western feminism and the women's movement, see, for example, Juliet Mitchell, *Woman's Estate* (New York: Vintage Books, 1973) and Shulamith Firestone, "On American Feminism," in Vivian Gornick and Barbara K. Moran, eds., *Women in Sexist Society: Studies in Power and Powerlessness* (New York: Basic Books, 1971), pp. 665–87, especially the section on the stand of the National Organization for Women (NOW).

2. For more information on how the processes of integration and dependence operate in specific social sectors, see Meron Benvenisti, *The West Bank Handbook: A Political Lexicon* (Colorado: Westview Press, 1986); Naseer H. Aruri, ed., *Occupation: Israel over Palestine* (Belmont, Mass.: Association of Arab American University Graduates Press, 1983); and Jan Metzger, Martin Orth, and Christian Sterzing, *This Land Is Our Land: The West Bank under Israeli Occupation* (London: Zed Press, 1980).

3. In villages, however, female school enrollment even at elementary levels is low since schools are not available in all villages, and transportation to other areas for girls is difficult to come by.

4. Yet it is evident that women would prefer to join academic rather than vocational institutes. Female enrollment in universities is 42 percent compared to 23.3 percent at community colleges, while in 1983/84 only 13.6 percent of females entered vocational training programs (WCSW, 1985:43, and *al-Shaab*, 24 August 1985). UN 22 June 1983.

5. It is estimated that, in 1984, 2,128 female graduates (out of a total of 8,054 in the West Bank) were unemployed (*al-Shaab*, 24 August 1985).

6. Of the four Women's Committees, the Working Women's Committees are affiliated to the PCP, Women's Work Committees to the DFLP, Social Work Committees to the PFLP, and the Palestinian Women's Committees to Fatah. Of the three not described in the paper,

Women's Committees for Social Work: These were started in 1981, and like WWCs emphasize as their main goal improving the status of Palestinian women in various spheres and strengthening the ties between them. Approximately 15 branches of WCSW exist in the various towns, villages, and camps of the Occupied Territories (Tunis Symposium, 1984:63).

Palestine Women's Committees: These have branches in various parts of the West Bank. They stress the need to conduct the struggle of women in stages, from economic liberation (that is, the freedom of women from economic need) to their involvement in productive labor and activities. From there grows women's involvement in social issues: unions, associations, etc. (Tunis Symposium, 1984:82).

Working Women's Committees: First established in Jerusalem in 1981 and with 49 branches throughout the Occupied Territories, these committees have as their main goals the liberation of Palestinian women politically, economically, and socially. They too stress the vital link between realizing the national aspirations of the Palestinian people and achieving the rights of women (Tunis Symposium, 1984:91).

7. Press release, Nairobi, 1985.

BIBLIOGRAPHY

Books and Articles

Aruri, Naseer H. 1983. *Occupation: Israel Over Palestine*. Belmont, MA: AAUG Press.
Benvenisti, Meron. 1986. *The West Bank Handbook: A Political Lexicon*. Boulder, Colo.: Westview Press.
CBS. Central Bureau of Statistics. 1968. Israel, Census of Population 1967, publication no. 3, Jerusalem. Table 13, p.21; table 40, p. 56.
Giacaman, Rita. May 1983. "Disturbing Distortions: A Response to the Report of the Ministry of Health of Israel to the Thirty-Sixth World Health Assembly on Health and Health Services in the Occupied Territories," Geneva, Bir Zeit, n.d.

————. 1982. "Planning for Health in Occupied Palestine." Bir Zeit.

————. N.d. "Palestinian Women and Development in the Occupied West Bank." Bir Zeit.

Gornick, Vivian, and Barbara Moran. 1971. *Women in Sexist Society: Studies in Power and Powerlessness*. New York: Basic Books.

Graham-Brown, Sarah. 1984. "Impact on the Social Structure of Palestinian Society." In N. Aruri, ed., *Occupation: Israel over Palestine*. London: Zed Books.

————. "The Structural Impact of Israeli Colonization." January 1979. *MERIP Reports*, no. 74.

Haddad, Yvonne. 1980. "Palestinian Women: Patterns of Legitimation and Domination." In K. Nakhleh and E. Zureik, *The Sociology of the Palestinians*. New York: St. Martins Press.

Jammal, Laila. 1985. *Contributions by Palestinian Women to the National Struggle for Liberation*. Washington, D.C.: Middle East Public Relations.

JC. Joint Palestinian-Jordanian Committee. 1985. *Development of the Labor Force in the Occupied Territories*. Amman: Joint Palestinian-Jordanian Committee, publication no. 1 (Arabic). Statistics from *Statistical Abstract of Israel* and Palestinian data.

Katbeh, Samir. 1982. *Concerning Higher Education in the West Bank and Gaza Strip*. Jerusalem: Higher Education Council. (Arabic).

Metzger, Jan, Martin Orth, and Christian Sterzing. 1980. *This Land is Our Land: The West Bank under Israeli Occupation*. London: Zed Press.

Mitchell, Juliet. 1973. *Woman's Estate*. New York: Vintage Books.

Al-Najah National University. 1982. *Statistical Bulletin for the West Bank and Gaza Strip 1982*.

SAI. Statistical Abstract of Israel.
    1985. Table 27/17, p. 720.
    1984. Table 27/3, p. 705.
    1983. Table 27/3 p. 760.
    1982. Table 27/15.

Shabbas, Audrey. 27 June 1984. "Women and the Question of Palestine." UN NGO Conference on the Question of Palestine.

Tunis Symposium. 17–19 December 1984. "Women's Committees and Women's Societies in the West Bank and Gaza Strip." Tunis. (Arabic).

UN. United Nations General Assembly. 22 June 1983. "Living Conditions of the Palestinian People in the Occupied Palestinian Territories." Report of the Secretary General. A/38/278.

UPWW. Union of Palestinian Working Women in the West Bank and Gaza. 1981. *Conditions of Palestinian Women and the Role of the Women's Movement in the Occupied Territories*. (Arabic).

WCSW. Women's Committees for Social Work. *Women in Emergency Situations: Palestinian Women under Occupation*. Jerusalem. Submitted to the Nairobi International Conference Decade for Women, July 1985.

WHO. World Health Organization. 14 May 1984. Palestine Liberation Organization. Report Submitted to the World Health Assembly. "Health Conditions of the Arab Population in the Occupied Arab Territories, Including Palestine." A37/INF.DOC./4.

————. 8 May 1984. Israeli Ministry of Health Report to the World Health Assembly. "Health Conditions of the Arab Population in the Occupied Arab Territories, Including Palestine." A37/INF.DOC./2.

————. 7 May 1984; 28 April 1983. Reports of the Special Committee of Experts

Appointed to Study the Health Conditions of the Inhabitants of the Occupied Territories. World Health Assembly. "Health Conditions of the Arab Population in the Occupied Arab Territories, Including Palestine." A37/13;A36/14.

WWC. Women's Work Committee. July 1985. *Women's Work Committees in the Occupied Territories*. (Arabic).

———. Women's Work Committee Program. 1983. *The Internal Structure of the Women's Work Committee in the Occupied Territories*. (Arabic).

Newspapers and Magazines

al-Fajr. 21 May 1985. (Arabic).

al-Fajr. 8–14 March 1981 and 22–28 February 1981. (English).

al-Kateb. 1982. (Arabic).

al-Shaab. 31 August 1985, 24 August 1985, 9 July 1985, 25 May 1985, 18 May 1985, 11 October 1984, 30 September 1984. (Arabic).

Kifah al-Mar'a. 19 June 1984. By the Women's Work Committee in the West Bank and Gaza.

al-Quds. 11 August 1982. (Arabic).

Sawt al-Mar'a. May 1983. Women's Work Committee in the Occupied Territories.

III

Politics and Power

VII

INDEPENDENT WOMEN
MORE THAN A CENTURY OF FEMINISM
IN EGYPT

Margot Badran

In the 1990s one can look back on more than a century-long tradition of feminism in Egypt. Women expressed the first stirrings of feminist consciousness in the final third of the nineteenth century. In the 1890s a feminist ideology began to take shape. Early in the twentieth century, pioneering women engaged in discreet forms of feminist activism. In the early 1920s, women inaugurated an era of open, organized feminism. Egyptian women as feminists have maintained a strong tradition of independence (from the state and political parties) unparalleled elsewhere in the Middle East. They have also maintained an unbroken tradition, for although the public movement was suppressed during most of the Nasser period, and is beleaguered at the present, feminism has persisted in Egypt.[1]

This paper will survey the feminism of women in Egypt from the latter decades of the nineteenth century to the last decade of the twentieth century. In contrast to widely held views that feminism in Egypt began with men, that it was/is western, and that early feminism was restricted to upper-class women, I shall demonstrate that feminism began with women, that it has been indigenous, and that there has been broader cross-class cooperation among feminists than commonly acknowledged.[2] From the colonial era to the present day, women across the spectrum from right to left have continued to ground their feminism in Islam and nationalism, as they have persisted in challenging a patriarchy transcending, in different ways, political and class formations.[3]

Feminists in Egypt have been most successful in the public sphere and most thwarted in the private sphere. This is *not* to imply, however, a neat division between the public and private.[4] While patriarchy's control over women for the last century and more has loosened in the societal arena, it has remained more firmly entrenched within the family. This is most vividly expressed in the preservation of personal status laws repressive to women. Each generation of feminists has had at the head of its agenda the transformation of personal legislation.

There are certain considerations to bear in mind when analyzing feminism in Egypt. Egyptian feminism is closer to that of other Third World countries than to that of the West. Feminism in the Third World usually first arose following the shift from an agrarian subsistence economy to capitalism, and incorporation into the western-dominated world economy. It often became organized and publicly visible following national independence struggles. Third World feminisms, which have had distinct nationalist dimensions, and have typically incorporated religious reformism in their agenda, have had to endure from their own patriarchies the condemnation of being western, and thus at best irrelevant and at worst culturally and politically subversive.[5]

In the Third World, the time frame of feminist evolution has been more compressed than in the West. In the United States, for example, women made significant advances in education and inroads into paid work some half-century before they stepped up the suffrage movement.[6] At the start of organized feminism in Egypt, women simultaneously demanded social, economic, and political rights, sequentially spacing out their campaigns in these areas only to a limited extent. Moreover, in Egypt, as in other Third World countries, feminists have had to juggle their feminist struggle with anti-colonialist and anti-imperialist ones, a dual battle unknown to western feminists.[7]

In Egypt, as in most other Middle Eastern and Islamic countries, feminism emerged from within the urban and middle-class world where sex segregation and domestic seclusion of women were in force. Women had to work themselves out of the hold of these practices wrongly but potently anchored in Islam. In Turkey and Iran, the state assisted this process, whereas in Egypt women took the initiative largely on their own, and in this respect they were not only pioneers in their own country but they set the example in the region. Women in Egypt, furthermore, pioneered in organizing and sustaining feminist movements in the region. Egyptian feminists have had to fight for changes in the personal status laws, a struggle that has been disappointing to them, while in Turkey, Tunisia, and Iran the state did come to issue liberal personal status laws. (Later in the century in Iran, however, the state withdrew the liberal legislation.)[8]

In the history of feminism in Egypt there are two distinct stages. The first, from the final decades of the nineteenth century to 1923, was the stage of emerging feminist consciousness and early social feminism, largely invisible to male society. During this period, most Muslim (upper-and middle-class) women continued to wear the veil, a symbol and function of sex segregation and female seclusion, signaling continued adherence to inherited conventions that women with a feminist consciousness had come to see, in whole or in part, as oppressive. Under "traditional camouflage," however, women were taking initiatives in expanding their lives into public space. This was also the period when progressive men advocated the liberation of women alongside their calls for the liberation of the country.

The second stage is that of highly visible, organized activism from 1923 to the present (with the exception proving the rule). This era began when women formed their first feminist organization, soon after which two members removed their veils in public as a political act declaring their rejection of the system of female domestic seclusion and gender segregation. This announced the start of an open campaign by feminists to realize a broad program of goals they set for themselves. This was the period of national independence (albeit partial). After Egypt achieved independence, pro-feminist men turned their attention to national politics and their own careers; their former highly visible calls for women's liberation ceased (only a few among them discreetly worked for women's advancement). In 1923, the term "feminism" came into use in Egypt and women started publicly calling themselves feminists. We shall return to the issue of terminology and definitions in a moment.

Within the second stage of feminism there are four overlapping phases: (1) radical liberal feminism from the twenties through the forties; (2) populist feminism in the forties and fifties; (3) sexual feminism in the sixties and seventies; and (4) the resurgent feminism of the eighties. We shall focus on well-known leaders associated with these phases. These include Huda Shaarawi and Saiza Nabarawi, associated with radical liberal feminism; Fatma Ni'mat Rashid, Durriyya Shafiq, Saiza Nabarawi, and Inji Aflatun with populist feminism; and Nawal al-Saadawi with sexual feminism and resurgent feminism. However, within the context of resurgent feminism we shall also mention new groupings of feminists who eschew hierarchical formations that produce high-profile leaders. We shall conclude by mentioning the recent phenomenon of the new invisible feminism of individuals.

Before proceeding further we must discuss terminology and definitions. During the first stage, the term "feminism" was not used and women did not call themselves feminists. Then, as now, there was no unequivocal term for feminist. The adjective, *nisa'i/iyya*, which was used could mean "women's" or "feminist"; this could only be understood from the context. In this paper when we use the terms "feminism" and "feminist" in reference to the first stage, we employ them as analytical constructs. Women began to use the term "feminism" and to identify themselves as feminists in 1923, as we have just mentioned. The pioneers of the feminist movement who first declared themselves feminists did this in French, the everyday language of the upper class which many educated members of the middle class also knew (although Arabic was the common language of middle-class women) and the language in which the term "feminist" had first been coined.[9]

Embedded in the project of writing the history of feminist movements and forms of feminist consciousness and ideologies is the act of defining feminism. Meanings must be recovered from historical investigation itself, and thus we define Egyptian feminisms within the context of the Egyptian experience.[10] In this paper we use a broad working definition of feminism that includes an awareness of constraints placed upon women because of their gender and attempts to remove these constraints and evolve a more equitable gender system involving new roles for women and improved relations between women and men. We shall see in the discussion below the different feminist formations that have arisen in Egypt.

A major problem with what little has been written about feminism in Egypt, contributing to the misconceptions mentioned earlier, is a neglect of women's sources. Only recently has this begun to be redressed. This study is based on women's memoirs, private papers, journal articles, books, oral histories, and personal interviews with four of the six feminist leaders noted above.

The Stage of Rising Feminist Consciousness

The nineteenth century was a time of dramatic societal transformations that wrought enormous changes in the lives of all classes and both sexes in urban and rural Egypt alike. Early in the century, Egypt was incorporated into the European-dominated world market system, and in 1882 experienced the start of British colonial occupation.

By the end of the century, the lives of Cairene women of the upper and middle classes were marked by growing contradictions and strains. On the one hand, the ideology supporting female seclusion, veiling, and gender segregation remained largely in force among Muslim women, supported by family patriarchs (and elder female surrogates).[11] On the other hand, state-instigated economic, social, and technological changes ushered in new patterns of everyday life for upper- and middle-class women, which eroded these restricting practices. Architectural alterations in the houses where they were meant to spend their lives eliminated customary material buttresses of female seclusion, while new designs and use of urban space broke down tight patterns of gender segregation as well as geographical divisions by creed and ethnicity. There were new educational and recreational outlets for middle- and upper-class women. Expanded movement for both sexes within the city and country was made possible by the new carriageways and railroads. Unprecedented professional and vocational opportunities beckoned to these women. The new conditions under which women were starting to live, their new experiences, and comparisons with men in their families gave rise to a nascent feminist awareness.[12] Women such as Aisha al-Taimuriyya from the upper class and Zainab al-Fawwaz from the middle class, who were both born in the middle of the century, were the first generation to reveal this through their writings.[13]

By the 1890s, the tight grip of family patriarchy over women had been loosened by the projects and developments encouraged by the rise of the modern state, itself a new patriarchal formation.[14] But while some forms of patriarchal control within the family were eroded, others tightened. At this historical moment, some women in the cloistered world of upper- and middle-class Cairo and Alexandria deepened their feminist consciousness. We know about this expanding awareness, which was invisible to the outside world, from the memoirs of Huda Shaarawi, who recalls the debates in the first salon for women presided over by Eugenie Le Brun, a French woman and convert to Islam, who, as the wife of an upper-class Egyptian, had been thrust into the segregated harem world. The women discovered that the veil and female seclusion were not required by Islam but were merely a function of patriarchal control. They also understood that they as women had rights within Islam which patriarchy withheld from them.[15] This awareness was assisted by the Islamic modernism Shaikh Muhammad Abduh had begun to expound earlier.

Simultaneous with the emerging feminism of upper-class women, middle-class women were also evolving a feminist consciousness shaped in important ways by their expanding formal education. They attended the new schools that had begun to open for girls in the nineteenth century. (Upper-class girls were kept under the control of family-hired tutors in the harem until about the 1930s, with the exception of some girls from elite families who attended the Siufiyya School opened by Tcheshme Harem, a wife of Khedive Ismail.) As early as the latter half of the 1880s, middle-class women began to be published in men's journals and in the early 1890s, middle-class women began to found and contribute to their own women's journals.[16] The writings of many of these women reveal a feminist consciousness with a religious and nationalist dimension.[17]

The decade after the emergence of a women's feminist consciousness saw the rise of social feminism. Upper-class women founded the Mabarrat Muhammad Ali (1909) to bring medical assistance and health instructions to poor women in their own neighborhoods. Shaarawi and some other women explicitly placed this project in a feminist context, seeing it as the first step in the process of liberating the lives of lower-class women and, at the same time, expanding their own lives beyond the harem. Shaarawi's memoirs disclose the distinct nationalist impulse motivating her and other women to pioneer in public philanthropy. [18] This, not the widely visible participation of women in the 1919 nationalist demonstrations, was the first time that upper-class harem women's unconventional, extra-domestic behavior was legitimized as a nationalist act. Middle-class women also participated in social feminism through societies they founded on their own, or with upper-class women, such as Jam'iyyat al-Mar'a al-Jadida, the New Woman Society (NWS) created in 1919 (a month after the revolution broke out), which taught working-class girls literacy, hygiene, and crafts.[19] Recurringly in the history of Egyptian feminism, nationalism would legitimize women's breaking with convention and expand their practical experience at the same time.

Women of the middle and upper classes also came together in "public" (that is, outside the harem but in places exclusively reserved for women) women's lectures given from 1909 to 1912 at the new Egyptian University and in the offices of the progressive paper *al-Jarida*. Sponsored by upper-class women and given by middle-class women, Bahitha al-Bad'iyya (Malak Hifni Nasif), Nabawiyya Musa, and Mayy Ziyada, a poet and writer of Lebanese and Palestinian origin,[20] were among the speakers. In these lectures feminist consciousness was further expanded and feminist bonds among women across class lines were forged.

Bahitha al-Bad'iyya (whose untimely death in 1918 brought Huda Shaarawi to the podium for the first time to deliver a eulogy) was the first woman to make public feminist demands in Egypt. Because she was unable herself to appear before the all-male Egyptian Congress of 1911, a man presented her agenda, which included the demand that women be allowed into mosques (as in early Islam), and have access to professions, especially those in which they could cater to other women.[21] This, and her reluctance to favor unveiling, indicated her strategy of promoting women's development within the system of sex segregation, a stand shared at the turn of the century by Nabawiyya Musa, who, however, unveiled around 1909.

Nabawiyya Musa, a life-long teacher and school administrator and founding member of the Egyptian Feminist Union (EFU), argued for more education, appealing to upper-class women to finance schools for girls. She also called for better jobs for women both for their own welfare and as a nationalist strategy to reduce foreign workers and the loss of Egyptian capital. Both women argued for controls on men's tyrannical use of divorce and polygamy.[22] These demands struck at an area of patriarchal control in the private sphere where family patriarchy stood firmest and women's (patriarchally prescribed) family roles were most threatened. In this area, proponents of feminism and defenders of patriarchal principles have remained severely polarized in a century-long struggle.

While feminism in Egypt began with women in a world segregated by sex, its radical threat to patriarchy was hidden by the very barriers that obscured and obstructed its proponents.[23] When a man, Qasim Amin, made public in a widely read book, *Tahrir al-Mar'a* (The liberation of the woman, Cairo, 1899) what was the essence of Egyptian women's early feminism, patriarchal forces rose up in fury in a public counter-attack, for the moment missing the radical force evolving more invisibly.

The Stage of Public Feminist Activism

Radical Liberal Feminism

When middle- and upper-class women participated in the Egyptian nationalist movement (1919–22), in street demonstrations, political organizing, communications, and morale boosting, the patriarchy did not construe these as radical acts.[24] On the contrary, the patriarchy considered women's unconventional behavior as defensive national acts—an extension of woman as defender of the home. Despite women's crucial roles (which men needed and welcomed) in the nationalist struggle, and male nationalists' liberation rhetoric and promises to women, when the militant struggle was over patriarchy hastened to consolidate its hold and expected women to retreat to the home. While women's nationalist experience did not, itself, produce feminism (as has already been seen), it did give women valuable political experience, consolidated their claims on the nation, and quickened expectations. Women argued that patriarchal domination was akin to foreign imperialist domination and that national liberation was incomplete without women's liberation.[25]

With the achievement of (partial) independence came a new constitution and parliamentary democracy. However, the electoral law denying women the right to vote and their prevention from attending the opening of Parliament—except as wives of ministers and high officials—signaled to women that they were expected to retreat into the private sphere of house and family. Women might defend Egypt during times of crisis, but in "normal" times men must govern and command the public sphere.

Egyptian women understood the message, and after several decades of hidden feminist evolution they were prepared to act. Huda Shaarawi and Saiza Nabarawi inaugurated the era of open feminist activism by removing their veils at the Cairo train station after returning from an international feminist conference, in a bold gesture declaring their determination to put a final end to sex segregation and female seclusion in the home. Shortly before, Shaarawi had led other upper- and middle-class women in forming the Egyptian Feminist Union (EFU). It declared an agenda for political, social, and economic transformation to integrate (urban) women into public life on a level with men and enhance women's lives in the private sphere. The feminists were aware that the lives of peasant women were not confined to the private sphere, and used the presence of these women in public space to argue their case. The EFU grounded its arguments for women's rights within the Islamic modernist and nationalist frameworks along the lines already worked out in the stage of unseen feminism.

The feminism of Huda Shaarawi, Saiza Nabarawi, and other EFU feminists can be called radical liberal feminism. The act of helping finally to dismantle the system of segregation and female seclusion through the dramatic gesture of publicly unveiling—and by implication the ideology associated with this—was clearly radical.[26] The EFU feminist agenda called for political rights for women, changes in personal status laws (especially for controls on divorce and polygamy), equal secondary school and university education for women, expanded professional opportunities for women in the fields of law, medicine, and education, and new work opportunities for women in factories and commercial establishments. It called for protective legislation for workers and support systems (childcare and health care), and also demanded an end to legalized prostitution. The EFU itself trained poor women in health, hygiene, and childcare and ran a daycare center and a medical clinic for working mothers. While regular EFU tactics included lobbying government offices and leaders, petitioning, speaking, and writing, EFU women also occasionally employed more militant tactics of picketing and street demonstrations (some EFU women were even jailed briefly in 1930). Women had to act outside the formal political system. The EFU's agenda for legal, social, and political transformation was more total and revolutionary than the project of men. After independence, men quickly became locked in the scramble for power within the new parliamentary system, resulting in a protracted struggle between the Wafd, Liberal Constitutionalists, the Palace, and British authorities, and in the process most lost sight of their earlier expressed ideals of the liberation of women.

The EFU membership included upper- and middle-class women but the former were more numerous. The EFU had two journals, *L'Egyptienne* and *Al-Misriyya*, and an impressive headquarters (inaugurated in 1932), and commanded substantial funds of its own (much of it deriving from landowners' wealth, especially Shaarawi's inheritance), which helped to sustain the movement for a quarter of a century.

Feminism typically starts from where its proponents are situated within the patriarchal system, and then widens out. The first Egyptian feminists emerging from Cairo harems led an urban-based movement. Yet from the beginning, feminists were ideologically committed to lessening the patriarchal grip over all Egyptian women. In the mid-thirties, the EFU leadership accelerated its campaign for political rights for women. It also tried to extend feminist activism to the provinces. Shaarawi opened a school and health clinic in a village near Minya and a model farm in Giza in an effort to spur other EFU women to do the same. However, by then rank-and-file EFU members had grown complacent and were uncooperative, thus thwarting the leadership in its efforts to broaden the movement in Egypt.[27] The EFU met with better results in advancing Arab feminism as a whole and in 1944 the Arab Feminist Union was created in Cairo under the presidency of Shaarawi.

By the time of Shaarawi's death in 1947, the EFU had witnessed successes for women in the public sector in education and work. Political rights were not achieved and women continued to be sexually exploited through legalized prostitution. The minimum marriage ages for both sexes were raised but there was no control over men's easy access to divorce and polygamy. The latter were the bitterest disappointments of the EFU movement, Nabarawi told me in the late sixties.

Populist Feminism

By the end of the Second World War, the serious economic problems that had afflicted the lower and middle classes in the cities since the thirties remained unresolved. From the thirties onward, the Muslim Brotherhood attracted a wide following among women and men who were economically deprived. Poverty continued to plague the peasants, who still lacked the health and educational services enjoyed by other Egyptians. The new generation of feminists were moved by these conditions. Meanwhile, in Egypt there was continued and deepening political turmoil and renewed impatience with the prolongation of the British presence. In 1952, a revolution occurred and a republic was created. During the eighteen years of Nasser's rule, socialism replaced the capitalism of the previous period.

In the second half of the thirties, the EFU membership not only failed to respond to the initiative of Shaarawi and Nabarawi to serve the needs of a broader base of women but also displayed an elitist unwillingness to welcome the more active feminists of the middle class into their ranks. However, Shaarawi and especially Nabarawi were linked to a new populist feminism that the EFU itself was unable to disseminate within its own organization. With major achievements in the public sector, yet with so many pressing concerns ahead, the moment had come for a new thrust. This came from the populist feminists, predominantly middle-class women, who accelerated the campaign for political rights for women and conducted direct action among poor urban and rural women to help them achieve economic and social liberation. They also kept up the struggle to reform personal status laws.

Fatma Ni'mat Rashid, Durriyya Shafiq, and Inji Aflatun emerged as leaders of three different strands of populist feminism.[28] All three used their pens in the cause of feminism. Two founded organizations and their own journals. One wrote books and contributed to the journals of others, but as a feminist and a communist was unwilling to be subsumed within patriarchal leftist organizations and unable to create her own independent feminist organizations.[29]

The journalist Fatma Ni'mat Rashid had written for the EFU's *L'Egyptienne* and had edited its Arabic journal, *Al-Misriyya*, before breaking with the Feminist Union in 1937. In 1944, she founded the Hizb al-Nisa'i al-Watani, the National Feminist Party (NFP), whose name indicated its conscious attempt to form, for the first time, a women's political party.[30] It intended to step up the campaign for women's political rights. The NFP, which maintained close links with the Workers and Peasants Parties, also adopted a broad agenda of economic and social reforms. It worked to spread literacy and training in hygiene among lower-class women of Cairo and was the first feminist group to advocate birth control and abortion.

The NFP had a predominantly middle-class membership which consisted of lawyers, journalists, writers, and teachers. Although its membership and agenda showed a broadening feminist base, the National Feminist Party did not have the wide appeal the second populist organization elicited.

A more dynamic feminist initiative came from Durriyya Shafiq, another middle-class woman, younger than Rashid and a protegee of Huda Shaarawi, who had supported her studies at the Sorbonne. Shafiq, with the highest formal education of the feminists to date, returned from an extended stay in Paris with her doctorate in 1945.[31] Shaarawi welcomed Shafiq, but the Feminist Union members were not receptive to her. In 1948, the year after Shaarawi's death, Shafiq started the Ittihad Bint al-Nil, Daughter of the Nile Union, served by three journals she founded.[32] Shafiq's organization adopted a feminist agenda similar to that of the NFP, giving priority to political rights for women and favoring a broad social and economic program.[33]

Shafiq was far more successful than Rashid in rousing the women of the middle class. The Daughter of the Nile Union was the first feminist organization to establish a broad base in the provinces, where centers were opened for teaching literacy and hygiene to poor women. Shafiq herself was a far bolder leader than Rashid, and more directly confrontational than other feminists. In campaigning for political rights she led a women's march on Parliament and a three-hour sit-in in 1951, and later, growing increasingly impatient, mounted hunger strikes. Meanwhile, she had also taken up the campaign to transform the personal status laws begun earlier by the EFU. She ridiculed the practice of high dowries by publicizing her acceptance of a *mahr* of twenty-five piasters, and debated Azhar shaikhs on divorce and polygamy.

Meanwhile, the third strand of populist feminism further to the left was in the making, and emerged in the context of the Egyptian women's peace movement. The two principal leaders of this populist feminism of the left were EFU feminist Saiza Nabarawi (from 1947 to 1953, Vice President of the Feminist Union) and a young upper-class woman, Inji Aflatun.

Aflatun was a student with a strong social consciousness and an adamant anti-imperialist at a time when, after the Second World War, leftist groups were forming in Egypt and elsewhere. Aflatun helped found the University and Institutes' Youth League in 1945 and afterwards became a member of the National Women's Committee. She used both direct action and her pen to further the cause of women's liberation. Aflatun went to textile factories in Shubra to meet with women workers about their rights. She also drew wider attention to the economic and social problems of workers and peasants and overarching patriarchal domination of women in the home and workplace in her book, *Nahnu Al-Nisa' Al-Misriyyat* (We Egyptian women, 1949).[34] She located class and gender oppression within the framework of imperialist exploitation. Like the other feminist leaders, Aflatun also insisted on political rights for women and on improved personal status laws. Although a communist, Aflatun situated her call for women's rights within an Islamic framework. This may seem contradictory to those more familiar with western experience, but Aflatun understood the importance of religion to the masses and how necessary it was for women to locate their struggle against patriarchy within an Islamic framework. A supporter and member of leftist groups that included members of both sexes, Aflatun, in the tradition of independent feminism, understood the political imperative for women to work within their own groups in order to keep feminist goals and priorities up front.

The Harakat Ansar al-Salam, the Movement of the Friends of Peace, brought the young feminist activist Aflatun and the veteran EFU feminist Nabarawi together for the first time in 1950. Aflatun then joined the EFU youth group which Nabarawi had organized to work with lower-class women in Cairo. This gave Aflatun a framework within which to continue the activity she had begun earlier among working women in Shubra. The following year when violence broke out in the Canal Zone, Nabarawi led women in setting up the Lajnat al-Nisa' lil-Muqawama al-Sha'biyya, the Women's Committee for Popular Resistance, to coordinate women's active resistance. Nabarawi, Aflatun, Hawa Idris (an EFU member and cousin of Huda Shaarawi), Hikmat al-Ghazali (a communist whose sister, Zainab al-Ghazali, had founded the Muslim Sisters), and other women went through British lines to Ismailiyya to agitate. Later, women—feminists and non-feminists alike—from communists to Muslim Sisters, staged an anti-imperialist demonstration. During this time, women's feminist and nationalist activism occurred side by side.

Meanwhile, the 1952 revolution led by army officers took place, followed by the installation of the Revolutionary Command Council, and soon afterwards Nasser consolidated his power. The most immediate repercussions for Nabarawi, Aflatun, and other feminist militants was a clampdown on their activity in the context of a move against the left. In fact, during this period, all independent political groupings and expressions were suppressed. The Women's Committee for Popular Resistance was prohibited and the EFU youth group, seen as too leftist, was dissolved. Nabarawi, tainted for being too radical, was forced out of the EFU in 1953 by a timid membership, exactly thirty years after she had helped create the feminist organization.

However, Nabarawi and Aflatun kept up their feminist and nationalist activism through writing and less visible organizing. In 1956, with mounting tension connected with the nationalization of the canal and the tripartite invasion in the Canal Zone, the women revived their Popular Resistance Committee and gave women paramilitary and political training. However, this would be their final public activity.

The new revolutionary government under Nasser implemented a socialist program which bestowed benefits on both sexes. In 1956, an Electoral Law gave women the vote they had first asked for three decades earlier. Education and health benefits were distributed more fully to all classes and throughout rural Egypt. University education was free and all graduates were guaranteed jobs. Within this context women made gains but they still felt the effects of patriarchal domination. Women, other than tokens, did not make it to the top echelons of the government bureaucracy or professions, and they were virtually segregated in areas of work deemed more fitting for females.[35] Additionally, the state, while welcoming women it needed as workers, did not provide them with sufficient supporting services to ease the double burden they bore working in the public and private spheres.[36] Finally, the old personal status laws remained in force, symbolically and practically oppressive to women.

In the face of continued patriarchal domination, so unequivocally clear in the personal status laws, Nabarawi, Aflatun, and others formed the Ittihad al-Nisa' al-Qawmi, the National Feminist Union, appealing to a broad coalition of women across the political spectrum, but the government blocked their efforts by refusing the organization a permit. The government, which had finally granted women the vote, withdrew from them the right to organize politically. Feminist organizations (and all other independent, political organizations) were banned. The EFU was forced to confine itself to welfare work and to change its name (it became the Huda Shaarawi Association; the word "feminist" was no longer acceptable). The following year Aflatun, as a communist, was sent to prison, where she remained for four years. Shafiq was under house arrest. Rashid's feminist party was dissolved. Nabarawi was silenced. Women's activist feminism inaugurated in the aftermath of the 1919 nationalist revolution was suppressed after three and a half decades of independent struggle. However, women kept their independent feminism alive behind the scenes in Egypt (reminiscent of the early feminism of the harem), and their voice was heard internationally.[37]

Sexual Feminism

Feminism reappeared on the public scene at the beginning of the seventies, coinciding with the coming to power of Sadat and the rise of Open Door (*infitahi*) capitalism. It also coincided with the acceleration of the second wave of Islamic "fundamentalism" that had begun to make its appearance following the war in 1967 mainly among university students, women and men, of the lower middle class, many of whom had come from the rural areas. Among the women, resurgent Islamism took the form of a return to the veil (mainly a covering of the head and body but not face) and the home,[38] an instrumental reassertion of the essentializing notion of women's exclusive sexual and family roles.[39]

At the moment when some women were returning to the veil, publicly calling attention to women as essentially sexual beings, women's bodies and female sexuality emerged as a feminist issue signaling the public reassertion of feminism itself. The new feminist concern was expressed by a medical doctor and feminist, Nawal al-Saadawi, in her book *al-Mar'a wa al-Jins* (Women and sex), published the year after Sadat came to power. In this book and subsequent writings, al-Saadawi discussed in public what was most private and, indeed, taboo.[40] This took special courage and involved great risk; in fact, al-Saadawi lost her job at the Ministry of Health and soon went into self-imposed exile. Not since Qasim Amin's *Tahrir al-Mar'a* (1899) had there been such an impassioned outcry from patriarchal forces. But, as before, there was also a positive resonance among progressive women. Al-Saadawi, in fighting against the practice of clitoridectomy (among the issues she addressed), and Amin before her, in opposing the veiling of the face (each connected with the female body), demonstrated that these practices had been falsely attributed to Islam and were simply forms of patriarchal control of women.

Earlier feminists had focused only upon the sexual exploitation of poor women as prostitutes but al-Saadawi addressed sexuality more comprehensively. The sexual exploitation of women occurred in both public and family spheres and was not confined to a single (i.e., lower) class. Al-Saadawi located it in larger political and economic contexts. With the authority and clinical evidence of a doctor, and more particularly a woman doctor with a feminist consciousness, she attacked assaults on women's bodies connected with obsessive fears about female virginity and sexual purity and condemned both the public commercial exploitation of the female body and private forms of aggression against women's bodies.

Al-Saadawi publicized the physical and psychological harm done to women's bodies by clitoridectomy, arguing for its eradication. She stressed that this extreme form of patriarchal control of female sexuality was wrongly sanctioned in the name of Islam. A number of feminists in Egypt struggled to wipe out clitoridectomy, but a similar campaign by feminists in Sudan has been far more visible and widespread.[41]

Al-Saadawi pointed in public to the operation of a double standard whereby the Islamic prescription confining sexuality to the conjugal relationship was applied to women but not men. She exposed the sexual exploitation of women in the sanctity of their own homes with disturbing evidence that this was more widespread than commonly admitted. Like feminists before her she decried the public marketing of women's bodies, but rather than focus more exclusively on matters of the law and policing, she exposed the roots of prostitution and its effects in her writings, most notably her novel *Woman at Point Zero*, based on a real-life case.

Al-Saadawi bravely brought to light the subject of the sexual domination and abuse of women, placing the onus on men and society at a time when women were being increasingly told that the responsibility was theirs to cover (i.e., veil) themselves (as omnisexual beings who threaten society) and distance themselves from the public arena to safeguard morality. Meanwhile, with open-door capitalism, women's bodies were being used for commercial exploitation as seen in blatant forms of advertising. Al-Saadawi forced the "private" subject of sexuality into the open and caused the matter to be looked at in new ways. The subject remains contentious and adversaries often allow themselves to misread the content and intent of feminists in issues of sexuality. During the eighties, matters concerning sexuality became less visible but by no means insignificant. A new awareness had been raised.

New Resurgent Feminism

In the eighties, feminism in Egypt once again became public, visible, and organized. In 1985, Jam'iyya Taddamun lil-Mar'a al-'Arabiyya (the Arab Women's Solidarity Association, or AWSA), officially came into being, although the idea had first arisen earlier. The organization, under the presidency of Nawal al-Saadawi, was headquartered in Cairo with branches in several Arab countries and in some Arab communities in the West. Egyptians as members of AWSA located their feminism within an Arab framework. AWSA feminism declared, "women's active participation in the political, economic, social, and cultural life of the Arab world is essential for the realization of true democracy in Arab society."[42] It demanded an end to gender discrimination both in the family and in society. The initial members of AWSA included a wide spectrum of feminists.

The rescinding of the liberal Personal Status Law of 1979, the first major revision since 1929, which was issued by a decree from Sadat (who had been pressured by his wife), galvanized a large number of women into action the first year of AWSA's existence. The 1979 law had given women more benefits in the case of divorce and had made it easier for them to obtain a dissolution of marriage themselves. A broad feminist coalition formed the Lajnat al-Dif'i 'an Huquq al-Mar'a wa al-Usra, the Committee for the Defense of the Rights of the Woman and the Family, to fight for the reinstatement of the law. They were successful, although the law was returned with certain restrictions.[43]

While the broader feminist coalition subsequently fragmented, AWSA continued and strengthened itself institutionally. It conducted monthly seminars, organized international conferences held in Cairo, and in 1989 founded its own journal, *Nun*. AWSA feminism was highly visible and confrontational, and outspokenly critical of conservative Islamist positions on gender. In 1990 the government ordered *Nun* to cease, and the following year shut down AWSA itself. AWSA has taken the case to court and after many imposed delays on the hearings still awaits action.

Other feminist groups also formed in the mid-eighties. These were informal groups. Two comprised women in their twenties and thirties who did not attempt to register under the Ministry of Social Affairs but coalesced more informally around their publications. A third included women in their forties and fifties who organized around a specific project.

In 1984, some women who had been active in the democratic student movement of the seventies formed a study group in Cairo. Two years later the group started to issue *Majallat al-Mar'a al-Jadida* (The new woman magazine) to disseminate their feminist views. The group later formed committees to deal with various everyday needs of ordinary women in areas such as health, legal literacy, and income generation.[44] The group announced their stand in a communication in 1990: "The New Woman Group is a progressive and democratic feminist group of women who believe that while Egyptian and Arab women share with men the hardships brought about by backwardness, dependence and economic crisis, they have to carry a double burden and suffer from a variety of forms of subordination, oppression and suppression arising specifically from their position as women."[45]

The other group of women of the same generation sprang up in the provinces. In 1982 a number of women in Mansura in the Delta who had organized public protests against the Israeli invasion of Lebanon went on to form Jam'iy-yat Bint al-Ard, the Society of the Daughter of the Earth, and two years later brought out *Majallat Bint al-Ard* (The daughter of the earth magazine). The group works with women in the town of Mansura and in surrounding villages in feminist consciousness-raising and in practical, income-generating projects. The group works with local women within their own milieu dealing with needs the women themselves deem important.[46]

Meanwhile, in the second half of the eighties several professional women in their forties and fifties came together to work on a legal literacy project. Calling themselves the Communication Group for the Enhancement of the Status of Women in Egypt, they pooled their expertise to produce a booklet called *al-Huquq al-Qanuniyya li al-Mar'a al-Misriyya bain al-Nadhariyya wa al-Tatbiq* (The legal rights of the Egyptian woman in theory and practice) to make women aware of the rights the law guarantees them. A whole chapter was devoted to the personal status code and women were instructed how to write certain protective conditions into their marriage contracts. Among other issues dealt with was law and conventions concerning work.[47]

By not being officially constituted the informal groups do not risk being dissolved by the government as AWSA was. Other officially constituted feminist organizations may have survived; there simply are no cases to prove this. The contemporary climate, however, is not receptive to feminism. For reasons of expediency, and also because of uncertainties about meanings of feminism, many progressive women operate for the advancement of women within the context of their professions, eschewing labels and public identification with feminism. Thus, today in Egypt invisible and visible feminisms exist side by side.

The most striking feature of more than a century of feminism in Egypt is that women have maintained the independent feminist tradition they initiated. The feminists, who started by understanding that patriarchy, not Islam, kept women down, have made the distinction between patriarchy and Islam in arguing their cause throughout the century. They have rejected the attempts of their opponents to impose restrictions on women in the name of Islam. This has been as true of the radical liberal EFU feminists as of the most leftist of the populist feminists. Women have not allowed their feminism and Islam to be polarized, and have certainly been aware of the political consequences of this. Women as feminists used Islamic arguments in the effort to end patriarchal tyranny in the private sphere and to legitimize their full entry into the public sphere.

Both within the segregated system and outside it, women have conducted their own nationalist activities. When their nationalist activities caused them to contravene conventional behavior, they stressed their nationalism to legitimize their actions (as they did in their early philanthropic work). However, during the period of nationalist militancy, women did not have to justify their unprecedented actions in the public sphere. There was a clear (political) crisis.

Patriarchy, threatened on the national front, welcomed and encouraged women's actions. When efforts were later made to push women back into the private sphere, some women feminists marshaled nationalist arguments to justify their continued presence in the public sphere and their rights there. Throughout the entire century, feminists have placed their feminism within the nationalist context. In argument and by active agitation, they have defended the nation against foreign occupation and economic, political, and cultural imperialism. However, patriarchy has had the temerity to label feminism in Egypt as western (akin to its labeling feminism un-Islamic) in an effort to discredit feminism by undermining its national legitimacy.

Feminism in Egypt has been far less classbound than observers and critics have claimed. From the start, women of the middle and upper classes have evolved similar feminist ideologies and strategies, and have worked together to further their goals. To summarily dismiss these and assert that feminism is elitist is a patriarchal distortion.

Feminists have made most gains in the public sphere, where the grip of family patriarchy was weakened by the rising state itself, a new but different patriarchal formation. In building a modern state and society, the patriarchal state required the labor of all its citizens, and some of the needs and goals of the state and of women coincided, for example, in many areas of education and work. Therefore, the state granted some of the feminists' demands over the century, but the timetable was typically the state's. It was not in the state's ideological or practical interest—so it was perceived—in the twenties, thirties, and forties to grant women suffrage, but the new socialist state which widened citizens' rights under Nasser found it expedient to grant women the vote in the same year that it suppressed feminist organization. However, patriarchy clung to its privileges and continued to dominate in the private sphere. State patriarchy did not need or wish to challenge family patriarchy inside the private sphere. For the entire century of feminism in Egypt, personal status legislation has reflected the persistence of patriarchal domination. Despite some gains, the personal status law continues to reflect patriarchal domination.

This overview of a century of feminism in Egypt clearly demonstrates that, irrespective of political and economic formations and forms of imperialist presence and penetration, patriarchy survives and reshapes itself according to its own needs and the nature of its feminist opposition. Perhaps the most striking achievement of Egyptian feminism is that it has understood this well and has fought to maintain an independent tradition keeping alive its cause against all odds.

NOTES

1. The original paper from which this chapter is derived was presented at a symposium on Arab women held by the Center for Contemporary Arab Studies, Georgetown

University, in 1986. The paper drew heavily on my doctoral thesis, "Huda Shaarawi and the Liberation of the Egyptian Woman," presented at Oxford University in 1977, and subsequent research on Egyptian feminism. Since 1986 I have conducted further research, written several papers, and co-edited a book on Arab women's feminist writings. Work has also recently been done by others on feminism in Egypt. In this chapter I cite writings completed after my original paper for the symposium was presented. I have added to the final section on contemporary feminism, bringing it up to date. For this purpose, I drew on my most recent research conducted in Egypt under grants from the Fulbright Islamic Civilizations Program and the Ford Foundation. I wish to express my thanks for this support.

2. Juan Ricardo Coles, "Feminism, Class, and Islam in Turn-of-the-Century Egypt," *International Journal of Middle East Studies* 13 (1981), 397–407, misses the early debates of women feminists and cross-class feminist bonds among women. Thomas Philipp, "Feminism in Nationalist Politics in Egypt," in L. Beck and N. Keddie, *Women in the Muslim World* (Cambridge: Harvard University Press, 1978, 295–308) wrongly describes Egyptian Feminist Union women as being exclusively upper class.

3. For an overview of feminist positions on "the woman question" from the late nineteenth century to the 1980s juxtaposed with nationalist and Islamist positions see Margot Badran, "Competing Agenda: Feminists, Islam, and the State in Nineteenth and Twentieth Century Egypt," in Deniz Kandiyoti, ed., *Women, Islam, and the State* (Philadelphia: Temple University Press and London: Macmillan, 1991), 201–36. On articulations of feminism by women in Egypt over the period dealt with in this paper see Margot Badran and Miriam Cooke, eds., *Opening the Gates: A Century of Arab Feminist Writing* (Bloomington: Indiana University Press and London: Virago, 1990).

4. Public and private are not conceptualized as strictly split domains but are at many levels intimately interconnected, as Cynthia Nelson has demonstrated in an early article, "Public and Private Politics: Women in the Middle Eastern World," *American Ethnologist* 1 (1974), 551–65. For a recent discussion on this issue see Suad Joseph, "Women and Politics in the Middle East," *MERIP* 138, 16, 1 (Jan.-Feb. 1986), 3–8.

5. On the rise of feminism in Asian countries see Kumari Jayawardena, *Feminism and Nationalism in the Third World* (London: Zed, 1986).

6. For comparisons see Jane Rendall, *The Origins of Modern Feminism: Women in Britain, France and the United States, 1780–1860* (New York: Shocken Books, 1984) and Richard Evans, *The Feminists: Women's Emancipation Movements in Europe, America and Australia, 1840–1920* (London: Croom Helm and New York: Barnes and Noble, 1977).

7. See Jayawardena, *Feminism and Nationalism in the Third World*. Concerning the Indian experience, see Geraldine Forbes, "Caged Tigers: First Wave Feminists in India," *Women's Studies International Forum* 5 (1982), 525–36; Gail Minault, ed., *The Extended Family: Women and Political Participation in India and Pakistan* (New Delhi: Chanakya, 1981); and Gail Omvedt, *We Will Smash This Prison* (New Delhi: 1980).

8. See Deniz Kandiyoti, "End of Empire: Islam, Nationalism and Women in Turkey," in Kandiyoti, ed., *Women, Islam and the State*, 22–27; and in the same book, Afsaneh Najmabadi, "Hazards of Modernity and Morality: Women, State and Ideology in Contemporary Iran," 48–76; Eliz Sanasarian, *The Women's Rights Movements in Iran* (New York: Praeger, 1982); and Michelle Raccagni, "Origins of Feminism in Egypt and Tunisia," Ph.D. dissertation (Ann Arbor, Mich.: University Microfilms, 1982). On certain parallels with feminist experience in Egypt see Khawar Mumtaz and Farida Shaheed, *Women of Pakistan: Two Steps Forward, One Step Backward?* (London: Zed and Lahore, Vanguard Books, 1987).

9. On Arabophone and Francophone articulations of feminism in Egypt see Irene Fenoglio-Abd El Aal, *Défense et illustration de l'Egyptienne: Aux débuts d'une expression féminine* (Cairo: Centre d'Etudes et de Documentation Economique, Juridique et

Sociale, 1988). On the origins of the term "feminism," see Karen Offen, "Defining Feminism: A Comparative Historical Approach," *Signs* 14 (Autumn 1988), 119–47.

10. On this challenge see Sharon Sievers, "Six or More Feminists in Search of an Historian," *Journal of Women's History* 1, 2 (Fall 1989), 134–46.

11. Veiling, a symbol and function of female seclusion and the distancing of the sexes, began to disappear first among Christians. See Beth Baron, "Unveiling in Early Twentieth Century Egypt: Practical and Symbolic Considerations," *Middle Eastern Studies*, 25, 3 (July 1989), 370–86.

12. Ethel Klein in *Gender Politics: From Consciousness to Mass Politics* (Cambridge: Harvard University Press, 1985) argues that feminist ideology arises from concrete experiences rather than abstract philosophy. On the rise of feminism up to the time of the start of the organized feminist movement, see Margot Badran, "The Origins of Feminism in Egypt," in Arina Angerman, et al., *Current Issues in Women's History* (London and New York: Routledge, 1989), 153–70.

13. See al-Taimuriyya's *Nata'ij al-Ahwal fi al-Aqwal wa al-Af'al* (The results of circumstances in words and deeds) (Cairo: 1887/8) and *Mirat at-Ta'amul fi al-Umur* (The mirror of contemplation on things) (Cairo: circa 1890s) and Fawwaz's *al-Rasa'il al-Zainabiyya* (Zainab's letters) (Cairo: 1910), a collection of her writings. For translations into English of writings by these two women (done by Marilyn Booth) and others see Badran and Cooke, *Opening the Gates*.

14. The rise of state patriarchy offered women of the middle and upper classes opportunities for new education and certain new jobs while also withdrawing certain outlets. The state patriarchy had more adverse effects on lower-class and peasant women. On the latter during the nineteenth century, see Judith Tucker, *Women in Nineteenth-Century Egypt* (Cambridge: Cambridge University Press, 1985).

15. See Huda Shaarawi, *Harem Years: The Memoirs of an Egyptian Feminist*, trans. and introduced by Margot Badran (London: Vigaro, 1986 and New York: The Feminist Press, 1987).

16. Women's articles began to appear, for example, in the second half of the 1880s in *al-Muqtataf* and *al-Lata'if*. The first women's journal was founded in 1892 by Hind Nawfal. Beth Baron has examined the early women's press in "The Rise of a New Literary Culture: The Women's Press of Egypt, 1892–1919," Ph.D. dissertation, University of California at Los Angeles, 1988.

17. Byron D. Cannon, "Nineteenth Century Arabic Writings on Women and Society: The Interim Role of the Masonic Press in Cairo—(*Al-Lata'if*, 1885–1895)," *International Journal of Middle East Studies* 17, 4 (1985), 463–84, sees women's articles before the 1890s as being pre-feminist while I would argue that they express the beginnings of a feminist consciousness.

18. Shaarawi, *Harem Years*. For a comparative perspective on women's social feminism see Geraldine Forbes, "From Purdah to Politics: The Social Feminism of the All-India Women's Organization," in Hanna Papnek and Gail Minault, eds., *Separate Worlds: Studies of Purdah in South Asia* (Columbia, Mo.: South Asia Books, 1982), 219–44.

19. Shaarawi donated money to the NWS and equipment for its crafts workshop, and because of this was made honorary president.

20. Bahitha al-Bad'iyya and Nabawiyya Musa went to the Saniyya Teacher's Training School, and taught and wrote while still observing harem conventions. See Bahitha al-Bad'iyya, *Al-Nisa'iyyat* (Cairo: 1910), Majd al-Din Hifni Nasif, *Athar Bahitha al-Bad'iyya Malak Hifni Nasif, 1886–1918* (Cairo: 1962), and Nabawiyya Musa, *Al-Mar'a wa al-'Amal* (Alexandria: 1920). Mayy Ziyada and Shaarawi and other EFU feminists maintained links until Ziyada's death in 1941. The EFU published a commemorative volume, *Dhikra Faqida al-Adiba al-Nabigha Mayy* in 1941.

21. The year before, at the National Party Congress in Brussels, a nationalist message from Inshira Shawqi was read out by a man who commented that customs prevented her from being there in person. Shawqi's niece, Fatma Ni'mat Rashid, is one of the populist feminists discussed below.

22. Bahitha al-Bad'iyya, whose husband already had a wife before she married him, unbeknownst to her, was particularly outspoken against polygamy. She said, "the husband of two or more wives ought to be appointed Minister of the Colonies," *Nisa'iyyat*, 41.

23. On the invisible feminist activism at the beginning of this century, see Margot Badran, "From Consciousness to Activism: Feminist Politics in Twentieth Century Egypt," in John Spagnolo, ed., *Problems of the Middle East in Historical Perspective* (London: Ithaca Press, 1991).

24. Lower-class women also participated in the revolution, especially in the street demonstrations. Some of them were killed for the cause. On the tradition of lower-class and peasant women's revolts see Judith Tucker, "Insurrectionary Women: Women and the State in Nineteenth Century Egypt," *MERIP* 138, 16, 1 (Jan.-Feb. 1986), 9–13.

25. See Margot Badran, "Dual Liberation: Feminism and Nationalism in Egypt, 1870–1925," *Feminist Issues* (Spring 1988), 15–34.

26. The term "liberal feminism," associated with western experience, does not capture the radical nature of liberal feminism in Egypt, hence my term "radical liberal feminism."

27. In personal communications, Saiza Nabarawi discussed the problem of EFU reluctance to broaden its base and welcome new middle-class women into the organization and how eventually she went her separate way.

28. The term "populist feminism" seems to broadly capture this new feminism, which had different specific forms yet basic similarities, although the feminism of Nabarawi (by this time) and Aflatun was to the left of Rashid's and Shafiq's.

29. On this period see Akram Khater and Cynthia Nelson, "al-Harakah al-Nisa'iyah: The Women's Movement and Political Participation in Modern Egypt," *Women's Studies International Forum* 2, 5 (1988), 465–83.

30. See Ijlal Mahmud Khalifa, *Al-Haraka al-Nisa'iyya al-Haditha* (Cairo: 1974) and Michelle Raccagni, "Origins," 247–57.

31. Durriyya Shafiq wrote her major dissertation on the Egyptian woman and Islam, her academic interest prefiguring women's studies to become a serious academic discipline some four decades later.

32. Shafiq recounted to me her last encounter with Shaarawi before her death, saying that Shaarawi had told her to carry on the feminist movement after her. She saw herself as carrying out that mandate.

33. On Durriyya Shafiq, see "The Voices of Doria Shafiq: Feminist Consciousness in Egypt, 1940–1960," *Feminist Issues* (Fall 1986), 15–31.

34. Michelle Raccagni is preparing her translation of this book with an introduction for publication. For Aflatun see Raccagni, "Origins," 274–78 and Raccagni, "Inji Afflation, Author, Artist and Militant: A Brief Analysis of Her Life and Works" (typescript).

35. Hikmat Abu Zayd, Aisha Ratib, and Amal Uthman achieved the post of Minister of Social Affairs, but women had more difficulty achieving middle-level appointments and positions. See Clement Moore Henry, "Sexual Equality amid Professional Impoverishment," in *Images of Development* (Cambridge: MIT Press, 1980), 131–43, and Kathleen Howard-Merriam, "Women, Education and the Professions in Egypt," *Comparative Education Review* 23, 256–70.

36. See Mona Hammam: "Women and Industrial Work in Egypt: The Chubra El-

Kheima Case," *Arab Studies Quarterly* 2 (1980), 50–69; and the same author's "The Continuum of Economic Activities in Middle Eastern Social Formations, Family Division of Labor and Migration" (paper presented at the Symposium on the Sex Division of Labor, Development, and Women's Status, 1980).

37. I first met Nabarawi, Shafiq, and Aflatun during this period. All three kept the ideology of feminism very much alive and were generous with their time in transmitting the feminist heritage to all those who came to them showing concern for the preservation of the feminist past. Of the three, at that time (1967 and afterwards) only Nabarawi remained publicly active, carrying on feminist activities internationally but remaining low key at home.

38. There was a heavy concentration of Islamist women in the medical faculties who were tending to refrain from practicing medicine. The state had paid for their education, and society was in need of their services, especially in the rural areas.

39. On the construction of women as omnisexual beings see Fatma A. Sabah, *Women in the Muslim Unconscious* (New York: 1984), trans. by Mary Jo Lakeland.

40. See, for example, *Al-Mar'a wa al-Jins* (Beirut: 1975), and *The Hidden Face of Eve*, trans. and ed. Sherif Hetata (London: 1980), and *Woman at Point Zero* (London: Zed, 1983).

41. Interviews with Asma El Dareer and many other women in Khartoum and throughout Kordofan. See Asma El Dareer, *Women, Why Do You Weep? Circumcision and Its Consequences* (London: 1982). For accounts by Egyptian women (in addition to Al-Saadawi) on their personal experience of clitoridectomy, see Nayra Atiya, *Khul-Khaal: Five Egyptian Women Tell Their Stories* (Syracuse: 1982).

42. "Challenges Facing Arab Women at the End of the Twentieth Century," an AWSA publication, edited by Nahid Toubia, translated by Miriam Cooke, in *Opening the Gates*, 367.

43. See Sarah Graham-Brown, "After Jihan's Law: A New Battle over Women's Rights," *The Middle East* (June 1985), 17–20 and Nadia Hijab, *Womanpower: The Arab Debate on Women and Work* (Cambridge: Cambridge University Press, 1988).

44. Information on the group comes from an interview with Hala Shukrallah and Aida Saif al-Dawla, September 1, 1990 and from *Majallat al-Mar'a al-Jadida*.

45. Letter to women from The New Woman Group, July 1990.

46. Information on the group comes from an interview with Jihan al-Sayyid, September 6, 1990, and from the *Daughter of the Earth Magazine*.

47. The group includes 'Aziza Husain, Magda al-Mufti, Inji Rushdi, Saniyya Salih, Mervat al-Tallawi, Awatif Wali, and Muna Zulfiqar.

VIII

TRANSFORMING CULTURE OR FOSTERING SECOND-HAND CONSCIOUSNESS?
WOMEN'S FRONT ORGANIZATIONS AND REVOLUTIONARY PARTIES—THE SUDAN CASE

Sondra Hale

Introduction

The participation of women in Middle Eastern revolutionary movements or organizations, or in revolutionary movements in general, is best understood (1) in terms of the contradictions within the social structures of Middle Eastern societies which directly affect women (e.g., the rise of "fundamentalist" Islam, the entry of large numbers of women into the paid labor force, male migration from the villages, etc.); (2) in light of the attitudes of the state and dominant class toward gender alignments in these societies, as well as the relationship of the revolutionary party or mass organization to the state—part of the contradictions mentioned above; (3) within an international context, including feminist discourse; (4) in terms of the contradictions within the structures of revolutionary organizations; (5) and with consideration for long- and short-term revolutionary strategies, especially the issue of the relationship of the movement to "traditional" culture.[1,2] In this essay on Muslim Northern Sudan, I will concentrate on the contradictions within a specific revolutionary organization. Additionally, I will incorporate a brief description of the changing conditions of Muslim Northern Sudanese women, including attitudes toward gender alignments. Aspects of the international feminist debates which will be included in the discussion focus on the uses and abuses of "traditional" culture (including Islam) and "women's culture" (e.g., the *zaar*), and whether or not we may speak of "women's issues." The essay will conclude with an outline of potential strategies for women's revolutionary participation, with special reference to the transformation of culture.

There are a number of questions to be raised about the relationship of women's emancipation to liberation parties or movements. Foremost among them, in terms of the international feminist debate, is the issue of whether or not a generalized struggle against oppression dissolves other differences. It is maintained by some students of revolutionary struggle that actors lose their specificity. Maxine Molyneux, in analyzing the Nicaraguan struggle, maintains that "the universalization of the *goals* of revolutionary subjects does not necessarily entail a loss of their specific *identities*."[3] Women do not lose their gender identities. "Rather, representatives of women acquired [in the Nicaraguan case] new connotations, ones that *politicized* the social roles with which women are conventionally associated, but did not dissolve them."[4] The issue of whether or not women have collective interests is also salient in feminist discourse. Molyneux contends that "there is no theoretically adequate and universally applicable causal explanation of women's subordination from which a general account of women's interests can be derived."[5] Here I use both the terms *gender interests* and *women's interests*, reserving the former to mean those which develop by virtue of their social positioning through gender attributes. Molyneux distinguishes between *strategic gender interests*, which we would ordinarily associate with feminist concerns (e.g., abolition of the sexual division of labor, alleviation of burdens of childcare, the attainment of political equality, measures against male violence and control over women, reproductive freedom, etc.), and *practical gender interests* (domestic provision, such as the livelihood of families, and public welfare). The former are derived deductively from an analysis of women's subordination; the latter are derived inductively and arise from the concrete conditions in women's lives.[6] I use the term *women's interests* when women's issues seem at variance with the interests of men, recognizing that the theoretical distinction between these may often times be problematic.

In this essay I will focus on Sudan and on the Sudanese Communist Party (SCP), not because Sudan's main leftist party is more problematic than elsewhere, but because in many ways, it typifies leftist parties of its kind in the Third World. Moreover, since Sudan is not yet engaged in a full-scale revolutionary process, now is the time to assess the meaning and ramifications of such a process for women.

Like many feminists who work within a Marxian framework, I have not given up on the "promissory note," that implicit contract between women and socialist movements that conceived of women's liberation as an integral part of the revolution.[7] Yet, like many students of the left, I am critical of the fact that in practice socialist theory has not absorbed feminism. With respect to this critique, I have been examining liberation movements to analyze whether or not a particular movement has addressed gender (women's) interests; if the emancipation of women has been, or might best be (in terms of effective strategy) a process initiated by women or men; and whether or not the movement has emanated from women's indigenous structures. In short, are women making their own revolution in their own name, through their own cultural structures (formal or informal), or being handed it by "another revolution?"[8] In terms of revolutionary strategies this, of course, raises questions about the autonomy of women's organizations versus mixed-gender "mass" organizations.

One of the assumptions of this essay is that, once women move to change their situation, they automatically move against the entire structure of exploitation.[9] Concomitantly the process liberates the entire society. This is, however, not usually an accepted adage of most leftist revolutionary movements. Instead, the goal of most contemporary vanguard parties is to liberate the society with the *help* of women, while acknowledging that the process is not *possible* without their help.

Gregory Massell offers us a case where this theme (which we could call the *new* "orthodoxy") was somewhat different. Official post-revolution Soviet policy among highly traditional Muslims of Soviet Central Asia (1919–29) allowed, through carefully orchestrated administrative assault and revolutionary legalism, for women to be used by the Party as a "surrogate proletariat." The goal was to create a mass revolutionary ideology by undermining the traditional social order. To the Soviets, this meant the destruction of traditional family structures. The theory was that the breakdown of the kinship system could be achieved through the mobilization of the women. Women were conceived as "structural weakpoints" in the traditional order: segregated, exploited, degraded, and constrained. It was thought that, if they were mobilized, the entire exploitative structure would be altered.[10] There was, as one might expect, effective resistance to the policy. It appeared that "a revolution in social relations and cultural patterns evidently could not be managed concurrently with large-scale political, organizational, and economic change."[11] Soviet strategists overlooked the fact, however, that these were strategies carried out in the *name* of women, but not by women themselves *for* themselves.

Although I raise these questions in the context of the SCP and its policies toward women, by assessing what might be an effective strategy for women's emancipation and gender egalitarianism within Marxist-Leninist parties in the Third World (and beyond), the suggestions necessarily have much broader implications.

Partially as a response to the many failures of the western Left with regard to women, many Marxist feminists have turned, perhaps somewhat romantically, to the experiences of Third World parties and movements. On the surface of things, women in these areas have played major roles in liberation struggles and, in some rare cases, have had their goals incorporated into the revolution during the *course* of the struggle (i.e., not as an afterthought).[12] There *is* a great deal for western feminists to learn from these movements.[13]

I am suggesting only that we be less romantic and more critical. The editors of *Promissory Notes* write that scientific socialism, a nineteenth-century model, has been applied by socialist states and organizations, mainly unchanged, whether in Asian, Southeast Asian, African, European, or Latin American societies:

> The model has been applied whether a given country's social relations were taken to be feudal, tribal, or protocapitalist, whether the country had been fully colonized or not, whether the state in question had been unified or had remained fragmented. Nor did differences in the form of kinship and marriage impede application of the nineteenth-century view that located women's subordination in private property relations, whether family forms were monogamous or polygamous, involved dowry or brideprice.[14]

With few exceptions, men and women in these struggles have failed to end most patriarchal forms of domination, to reintegrate the public and private, to emancipate the self through equality, and to politicize the networks of everyday life. Except for their *public* roles in the military (in some cases), as wage-earners in the labor pool, as members of women's organizations (often serving as fronts or auxiliaries), or as members of agrarian cooperatives, most Third World women have far less autonomy than men. More precisely, they have limited autonomy in the personal, subjective spheres of their lives. Among other things, the sexual division of labor remains basically the same, with only token urban women moving into traditional male occupations in the official workforce. Domestic labor, of course, remains unchanged.[15] "What is striking, across this vast geographic, social, and historical landscape [Cuba, Nicaragua, Mozambique, Yemen, Vietnam, West Bengal, and post-Maoist China], is the extent to which the analysis used and the policies developed are similar. Thus in each place, the very same problems remain unresolved and the very same questions are left unaddressed."[16]

Muslim Arab culture, as I have argued elsewhere,[17] presents us with a unique set of problems, namely the politicization of gender, of Islam, and of their relationship to each other. These are the ethnographic, historical, political, and economic ingredients of this essay.

Economic and Cultural Background for SCP and WU Organizing

In the twenty-eight years that I have been observing and participating with Northern Sudanese women, popular images of women and of gender arrangements have been dynamic. In 1961 it was unusual to see Muslim women in very many public spheres, including the formal workforce. However, in those years there was much discussion among the intelligentsia, civil service officials, and liberal/progressive political parties around the notion that a "developing" Sudan *needed* emancipated women; the term "emancipated" was synonymous with "wage-earner" in the bourgeois liberal parlance, as well as in the Marxist vocabulary of post-colonial Sudan. Radio Omdurman and eventually Omdurman Television (government-controlled media) urged the necessity for gender comradeship in order for Sudan to develop. Media images presented the new Sudanese woman as the sophisticated consumer or respectable civil servant, most commonly as the teacher.

In previous work, drawing on mainly Northern Sudanese women as subjects, I have attempted to document changes in the productive and reproductive roles of rural and urban women concomitant to economic developments within post-colonial Sudan.[18] The growth of capital-intensive economic schemes, the rise of multinational corporations, uneven regional development, radical changes in labor migration, and the rise and fall of the fortunes of particular ethnic groups and concomitant power realignments have all precipitated political/economic crises in Sudan. Islam is only one variable, for many a kind of *deus ex machina*, called on when economic crisis seems to necessitate the manipulation of women out of the labor force, a process not dissimilar to the post-World War II United States situation.[19] Communist Party ideology has accommodated Islam, or as some members say, the Party has chosen to "co-exist" with Islam.

The class structure of Sudan in relation to Sudanese women has been similar to Egypt's.[20] Attitudes in Sudan toward the "emancipation" of women took two forms, each associated with a particular social class and with particular nationalists of the upper and upper middle classes (e.g., the Bedri and Hashmab families and, to some extent, the Mahdi family), who viewed social reform along liberal, western lines as prerequisites for independence. The "emancipation" of women (conceived of as reform in marriage and family structure, the education of girls, the entry of women into respectable jobs such as teaching, and the like) was considered essential for improving Sudanese society. The Bedris, for example, early members of a professional class, although socially and usually politically conservative, pioneered women's education in 1907. On the other hand, more "radical" nationalists of the lower middle class were demanding an end to British rule, and as a part of that nationalist struggle, tended to romanticize "indigenous" values. These nationalists generally opposed women's emancipation, arguing that it was an imitation of the West and that it would weaken the nation's basic Islamic unit— the family. These latter ideas and groups have re-emerged with vigor in the late twentieth century.

This link between feminism and liberal pro-western nationalism, on the one hand, and anti-feminism and radical nationalism on the other,[21] is not unlike the situation we see in Iran today. There is also an alignment along class lines, with feminism and liberal pro-western nationalism associated with the upper and upper middle classes (large landowners and upper bourgeoisie); anti-feminism and radical nationalism associated with the lower middle classes. Sudanese urban society reflects these patterns, with a division (although not rigid) between an upper middle-class liberal segment in which women are relatively liberated socially and a lower-class segment which follows conservative Islamic values in family life, as well as sexual mores and behavior.

Liberal and Marxist ideologies stressing the importance of getting women out into the urban work force have, in some areas of the world, led to a process of increasing marginalization of women. The particular form of accelerating underdevelopment which Sudan is exhibiting serves to combine the constraints of Islamic-reinforced patriarchy with the inherent structural inequalities of capitalism and the multicorporate variant of neocolonialism. These factors serve increasingly to marginalize Sudan's male and female workers. However, men often have their options widened, giving them greater personal autonomy, whereas women become increasingly restricted to "appropriate" jobs, losing in competition to men, sometimes after having lost their previous "rural" skills. Religion often reinforces these inequalities.

Female participation in the urban workforce increased at a regular, if somewhat slow, pace during the years following independence in 1956. Partially this was a result of the general propaganda I mentioned above, i.e., that a truly "emancipated" woman is one who earns wages. However, this image has emerged mainly as a result of Sudan's depressed economic situation in recent years. In other words, many women *have to* work outside the home for wages, although that is rarely acknowledged.

As we might expect, many women workers in Khartoum are channeled into dull, repetitive jobs with low pay. Concomitantly, their personal lives reflect a rigid division of labor. Domestic work is still "women's work." Yet the areas of their lives where they might achieve some power or have their role valued more highly have been assumed by other agencies or have lost their importance. For example, there has been a decline of homemade crafts in favor of imports. Furthermore, the socialization of children is now often assumed by the schools, media, or childcare centers. Urban workers are more isolated from other women and frequently from their own extended families, having the effect of reducing their potential for solidarity and raised consciousness. There are also the conditions with which any political organization or movement in twentieth-century Sudan has to contend.

In this century, the political process at a national level in Sudan has meant the early foundation of nationalist groups and the eventual formation of strong, sectarian-based conservative political parties, including the Muslim Brotherhood. These have competed, sometimes effectively, with Sudan's military, which has been in power for most of the period during which Sudan has been independent. Any political analysis of Sudan must take into account the power of the military, which has often thwarted "natural" historical processes.[22]

The Sudanese Communist Party and the Women's Union

This essay is not intended as a description of Sudan's political history, the SCP, or the WU; such descriptions may be found elsewhere.[23] It is intended to provoke questions and to offer suggestions emanating from a particular ideological/cultural framework. For some years I have been questioning just how revolutionary the SCP is in terms of a transformation in gender alignments. The thesis which has emerged from my work is that the patriarchal ideology, structure, and organization of the Marxist-Leninist SCP may have greatly diminished its role as an effective force for socialist transformation. From what I have been able to observe and to glean from discussions with Party members, cadres have not had an adequate understanding of "the subjectivity of oppression, of the connections between personal relations and public political organization, or of the emotional components of consciousness,"[24] not to mention issues of sexuality. These omissions, of course, are not unique to the Sudanese left. Ideas about sexuality remain taboo not only among most Third World and Islamic societies, but in most European socialist societies as well.[25]

Thus, even if the Party had succeeded in its various attempts to gain power, or even if it succeeds in the future in effecting a socialist transformation, that success will be tempered. While perhaps succeeding in politicizing the roles with which Sudanese women are conventionally associated, by not dissolving them, the Party may fail in the necessary task of reintegrating the public and private, ending the sexual division of labor and the oppression of women in their personal lives.

Until 1971 the SCP, existing in one of the world's poorest countries with a minuscule urban working class, and a very low literacy rate, and contending with Islam, the military, and zealous sectarian parties, still was reputed to be one of the largest, strongest, best organized, and most promising of all the Communist parties of the Middle East and Africa.[26]

This strength would be reason enough to test the issues I have raised above with data from Sudan. The SCP is also a good case study because Sudan has had one of the most numerically powerful women's front organizations on the continent—the fifteen-thousand-strong Sudanese Women's Union.[27] The hope for a progressive society in Sudan seemed to rest with the SCP and its strong affiliates: the women's organization and the highly organized labor unions (especially the railway workers).[28] But that potential may have been lost.

In the 1950s and 1960s, the SCP was thought to have effective strategies for mass mobilization, not the least of which was its success in organizing women. Yet, today those conditions the Party addressed on behalf of women are worse than ever before, and the failed strategies for addressing these remain basically the same. Despite greater numbers of women in the official work force, work conditions are worse than before. Although we certainly cannot attribute these conditions to the Party, we can be critical of some of the stated policies and strategies. As for the sexual division of labor, both in the wage-earning sector (formal and informal) and in the domestic sphere, it is more pronounced today than in the past. This is partially a result of the more sophisticated mechanisms and institutions of oppression which have grown out of twentieth-century colonialism and capitalism, one of which is the tight control of women's participation in the labor force.

Part of my analysis focuses on the reluctance or inability on the part of any of the progressive organizations to address such issues as the growing rigidification of the sexual division of labor, beyond encouraging more women to enter the increasingly capitalist public sector and working on reforms within that context. Also, I am raising the question of why, by the time of the 1985 coup d'état which overthrew the Numairi military dictatorship, again installed a "democratic" multiparty system, and legalized the SCP and WU, there were only vestiges of the once powerful Women's Union.[29]

The SCP, which emerged officially in 1946, was the first political party in Sudan to open its membership to women and to establish women's emancipation as one of its goals. That same year, women members of the Party organized Rabitat al-Nisa' al-Sudaniyyat (League of Sudanese Women). Among them were Dr. Khalda Zahir, the first president (also Sudan's first woman doctor), and Fatma Talib, the organization's first secretary. Founded in Omdurman by mainly urban, educated, middle-class women, the group aimed generally at improving the quality of life of Sudanese women, e.g., establishing a night school, with associated nursery, for training in literacy, sewing, home economics, health issues, and the like. The nursery later became a primary school.

The nationalist period of the late 1940s and early 1950s saw the rise and fall of a number of women's organizations and unions, with leadership struggles and factional disputes following the same pattern we saw in national politics during the last decade of the colonial regime. The organizations represented particular class interests and sectarian politics. For example, some of the leaders and members of the Women's League left the organization and joined Jamiyat Tarwiyat al-Mar'a (Society for the Prosperity of Women), also founded in Omdurman in 1947, and representing the class interests of feudal land-owning aristocrats (the Mahdists).[30]

Because the Women's League was open only to educated women, it remained small (literacy among women probably being below 5 percent at that time). In a 1983 article by al-Bakri and Kameir, these early women's organizations are characterized in this way:

> The basis of these organizations lay largely in the urban middle classes, which meant a general lack of understanding of the real needs of rural women or even

of poor urban women, let alone women in remote parts of the country such as the south. They were relatively isolated also from other political groups, such as trade unions, which represented different interests from those of traditional political associations, and which did have specific tactics for change. By the 1950s and with the intensification of the nationalist movement, a need was once again felt for a new organization for women which would raise their standard and promote their participation.[31]

In 1952, as a response to the need for a broader membership (a part of the articulated strategy of the SCP), a handful of women, most of whom were Communists, and some of whom had helped to form the League, founded Ittihad al-Nisa' (Women's Union). Again, it was a group of educated women— mainly teachers, government officials, students, nurses, and the like—and again literacy was made a condition of membership. However, once it became clear that such a requisite for membership would greatly inhibit mass recruitment, the condition was dropped.[32]

Thus, the Union, which began with five hundred middle-class women, expanded into a large mass organization, with branches throughout the country. It campaigned for equal pay for equal work, and longer maternity leave, and dealt with other problems faced by the urban worker. By 1955 the WU was publishing *Sawt al-Mar'a* (The women's voice), one of the most progressive publications in Sudan's history. It was a relatively free forum for debating such issues as female circumcision, facial scarification, etc. A constant contributor to the organ has been the leading spirit behind the Union, Fatma Ahmad Ibrahim, one of Sudan's most progressive voices for some decades.[33] Although she is a Communist with close ties to the SCP and to the Party leadership, she is also an independent thinker and struggled for the little autonomy the WU was to have.[34]

Because membership numbers were so impressive, no one seemed to realize how frail and vulnerable the Union was. That vulnerability reveals not only the difficulty of a women's organization surviving for very long in an androcentric society, but also the weak points in gender ideology, with regard to the perspectives on "traditional" culture.

One of the problems was SCP structure, partially a reflection of its gender ideology. The party and its auxiliary organizations followed the structural pattern of most Marxist-Leninist Communist parties. That is, even though the SCP, unlike many Middle Eastern communist parties, had a truly national character in its leadership, it was still not considered an autonomous unit, but rather a branch of the main (Soviet) party. Its structure reflected that relationship: it was organized into base units, local and regional offices, a central committee, and a Political Bureau. The WU was organized on the same general hierarchical principles: a central committee, local and regional cells, and little autonomy. Initially, even the leadership of the WU was chosen (either formally or informally) by the Central Committee of the SCP.

Recruitment also remained problematic. At first the Union relied on the SCP

for most of its members, a large proportion of whom were the spouses, relatives, and friends of male SCP members, creating a weak base for any organization. Such heavy reliance on the SCP for recruitment meant that few non-
orthodox socialist ideas about women filtered in; women remained tied to the
class of their male associates; and loyalty was as much to the Party as to the
Union. Eventually, however, the Union gained some strength on its own when
it began to recruit from the population at large, forming regional branches.
Membership still reflected mainly low-level and some middle-level professional
women (mainly elementary and intermediate school teachers), who had some
ties to the mainly urban male (SCP) membership.[35] However, Fatma Ahmad
Ibrahim, in an interview with me, explained the SCP and WU relationship in
this way:

> Some members of the Party do not understand that to mix Party work with the
> Union is very dangerous. We have had many problems. We have even fought
> against our colleagues . . . [we are keen] to keep the women's organization
> independent . . . from the beginning it was very clear from the Communist girls
> that the Union should be independent and not affiliated with the Party. They
> [the women of the Union] were keen to turn it into a mass organization. . . . If
> it is affiliated with the Communist Party, it will not be [one]. That is why
> the SCP wrote in its Constitution that these organizations—women's, youth,
> students—should all be independent.

Although mine is a critical account of the SCP in relation to the WU, that
is not to overlook the contributions and achievements of the Party. Warburg,
certainly not a supporter of the SCP, and one who attempts to minimize the
future potential of the Party at every turn, pays this tribute:

> while communism never succeeded in becoming a major force in the Sudan, its
> impact on Sudanese politics was nonetheless considerable, especially during
> periods of crisis. This was due to three main reasons: Firstly, the penetration of
> the SCP into the most important sectors of Sudanese society: the cotton growers,
> the railway workers and the intelligentsia, enabled the party to become an
> effective pressure group despite its relatively small numbers. Secondly, the SCP
> provided the only consistent alternative to the sectarian and factional divisions
> which harassed Sudanese politics ever since its independence. . . . Lastly, the
> leadership of the SCP, since Abdel Khaliq Mahjub became secretary-general, was
> probably the most capable leadership of any Communist party in the region. Its
> flexible attitude towards religion, nationalism, Arab unity, etc. enabled the party
> to retain its freedom of action . . . and [it] was the only political force which
> advocated regional autonomy for the South ever since independence.[36]

Warburg, who has written more extensively on the SCP than any non-Suda-
nese, ignores the women's movement, subsuming it under various catch-all
categories. The fact is that the SCP was the first party to open its doors to
women, to "teach" them the Marxist-Leninist concept of organization, and

to politicize them in the mainly male public domain. In addition to encouraging women to enter the public arena, the Party offered educated women an outlet for some of their enlightened views and opened its membership to a broad cross-section of the female population, creating a more socially heterogeneous environment for isolated and class-bound women. However, none of this related to their *private* lives: their increasingly undervalued domestic labor, lack of control over their reproductive resources, repression under the particular brand of Islam which had been developing under colonialism and capitalism, and practices such as female circumcision.

The involvement of women in *public* political activities was an integral part of the SCP program. There was, of course, a long socialist tradition for this inclusion. Yet the "women question" was secondary in the overall ideological development of the Party. As an appended form, the WU was a step-child in birth, formation, and structure. The main function of the WU, as seen by the SCP, was to recruit members for the Party in order to have a second line to call upon in crises—the "women-as-Greek-chorus" syndrome. In other areas of the world, this same process can be seen with the recruitment of women into the military or paramilitary. Algerian women were assigned to be the terrorists and saboteurs of the revolution of the 1960s, but only as *substitutes* for the dead, imprisoned, exiled, or circumscribed male revolutionaries.[37]

Among women members of the SCP or WU, there was very little consciousness-raising about their oppression as *women*, or even about their special problems as *women* workers; the individual occupational unions grappled with these much more effectively. For example, in 1952, the Union of Women Teachers sent a letter to the Director of Education of the Sudan (then British) requesting "equality of men and women teachers as regards scales, increments, stipends, and pensions," but more along the lines of *gender interests*, they requested that during transfers "in keeping with Sudanese customs and traditions each woman teacher be provided with a chaperon from her family, and that chaperons be authorized to travel in the same class as their protégées." Also in the service of *gender interests* they requested that, "since married women teachers have heavy commitments in carrying out their official duties and also acting as wives and housekeepers . . . a distinction be made between them and their unmarried colleagues, namely that they be not transferred to locations far from where their husbands live." Their twelfth request might be interpreted as serving *women's interests*: "A woman teacher in a boarding school who performs additional duties should be paid an allowance for such duties." Although these duties were not spelled out, and although we can assume that male teachers in boarding schools also performed additional duties, the nurturing attributes and domestic labor skills of women were evidently not compensated. Basically the teachers' union was requesting "wages for housework."[38]

The issues the WU members were encouraged to confront were usually not *strategic gender* issues (i.e., *feminist* issues). When the WU did deal more specifically with women's "problems" (which is how they were viewed), the activities they carried out often reinforced traditional roles instead of *building* on informal political forms that potentially could be mobilized. The SCP and WU leadership held conventional ideas about structures that could be mobilized, for the most part limiting themselves to unions, student groups, and other formalized structures.

When women of the Party or Union *did* address personal, private issues, such as division of labor within the domestic unit or violence in the household, they were either ignored or were accused of "bourgeois feminism" or "bourgeois individualism." There were always more "important" issues at hand, such as the immediate goal of subverting or overthrowing the current regime, and women were sung the familiar refrain—wait until *after* the revolution.

After an aborted leftist coup d'état in Sudan in 1971, all political parties were banned (except the government organ, the Sudan Socialist Union), and the SCP and WU went underground. Like many Communist parties elsewhere, Sudan's had always thrived underground and in crises; however, the Women's Union did not fare as well. Although the beheaded Party was badly exposed and in disarray, the WU was even worse off. Muslim Sudanese women could not easily "go underground." It has been very awkward for women from "respectable" families (Muslim *or* Christian) to go to clandestine meetings, which are usually held late at night and in dubious neighborhoods. Even if they brave these social problems, they are told by the males that their unusual presence in such locations arouses suspicion. For the most part, after the abortive coup d'état, women were asked to stay away from crucial strategy and survival meetings. They were, however, called upon for individual acts of nurturing (e.g., medical attention).

The banning and subsequent underground movement of political groups after 1971 exposed profound and potentially long-lasting problems inherent in the relationship between the SCP and the WU. The lack of politicization, splits among older conservative and younger liberal women, and the general social and political repression in society contributed to the near demise of the once powerful Women's Union. Damaging in terms of morale and structure was the fact that many members and a number of second-rung WU leaders left the organization and joined the women's wing of the Sudan Socialist Union, taking with them the organizational know-how and internal information about the SCP and the WU. Many of these women, because of the particular mode of politicization within the WU, had had little ideological commitment to the SCP, and consequently, to the WU. Furthermore, many of them had been given few chances for leadership and saw women's problems constantly being given short-shrift.

In commenting on these defections, the Central Committee of the Party in a report on the September-November 1971 session, reflected fairly typical male-biased and unself-critical attitudes by "blaming the victim," i.e., the Women's Union, for its weaknesses:

The women's movement [Women's Union] has been exposed to open subversion and corruption. And despite the facilities rendered by the state, yet the official women's organization still depends mainly on the cheap propaganda provided by the official mass media and is capitalizing on the weaknesses of the democratic women's movement.[39]

The process from 1971 until the 1985 coup was one in which the women's branch of the Sudan Socialist Union co-opted the role of the SCP's women's organization and manipulated many of its former secondary leaders, greatly affecting the future of the WU. For that reason, leftist critics have been harsh toward these women who, until the 1985 coup, formed the "vanguard" of a large bourgeois women's organization with branches throughout the country. However, this organization, too, was haunted by the past of the WU and its ideological and structural relationship to the SCP and, by the time of my field trip to Khartoum in 1981, articles referring to the "inadequacy" of the Sudan Women's Union (SWU) were appearing in the press.[40]

For some time after the decline of the WU, recriminations from the SCP (as above) and self-recriminations on the part of the WU dominated the Communist left. For the last few years, however, some members have begun to realize that the "weaknesses" of the WU may not all have been of their own making, but were, in part, an inherent consequence of the structure and ideology of the SCP: androcentric dogma that neglected women's issues, ideological rigidity, inequality in the hierarchical Party structure, and puritanical morals that had not even kept abreast of the tone in the society at large, partially a result of the policy of coexisting with traditional culture.[41]

This critique is also applicable to the WU during most of its history. Whether in terms of *strategic* gender interests or *practical* gender interests, the potential for a mass movement emanating from women themselves, as a response to their own oppression *as women*, is not under consideration by the Party nor by the Union. The Party has not reflected, in its institutions and practices, a vision of a new society, the post-revolutionary society, which could have been in process *before* the revolution. A progressive party or an independent Women's Union might have been built on extant socioeconomic, consciousness-raising, self-help, experiential, occupational, and neighborhood networks—i.e., the networks of everyday life. An autonomous WU might have chosen to deal more critically with aspects of Islam, a major point which is discussed below.

Culture and Transformation

There are two main spheres of revolutionary potential in all contemporary societies. One such sphere, which is readily acknowledged by students of revolutionary strategy, emanates from the workers, the peasants, the students, the intelligentsia, and the disaffected "minorities" or unequally developed regions. But what is left out here is an acknowledgment of the fact that "all classes of women understand what their society's division of labor by sex requires of them: the bedrock of women's consciousness is the need to preserve life." [42] Therefore, the *second* sphere of revolutionary potential emanates from indigenous structures: women's popular culture, networks, and struggles as workers in the home and in the neighborhood work place, i.e., struggles around where we live, work, and interact with one another. Collective actions to gain rights and to survive in these arenas may have profound revolutionary consequences in the sense of politicizing the networks of everyday life, the *practical* gender interests of Molyneux's model. Here I suggest four spheres of female activity which, because of their nature, may have potential for mobilization.[43] Accompanying these hypothesized spheres of potential mobilization of women, *as women*, is the contrasting strategy or perspective of Fatma Ahmad Ibrahim.[44]

(1) *The Woman Worker:*[45] Although women are often not enumerated in censuses as "workers" (i.e., if they are not wage-earners in the formal sector), they comprise a large portion of the labor force. Many of these economic activities are carried out at or near their residences or in the homes of others. This does not even include the large agrarian and pastoral labor force where the United Nations claims women play *the* significant economic role, nor does it account for the unpaid labor of social reproduction. Sudanese women are brewers, street vendors, tailors, basketmakers, weavers, potters, needle-workers, domestic servants, midwives, wedding ritual/ceremonial specialists, spiritual experts, healers, ritual mediators, musicians/singers, beauticians, shopkeepers, bartenders, prostitutes, market merchants, and the list goes on. A number of these jobs are cottage industries and are performed at home, in private, or in a closed neighborhood setting. Payment is often in kind or in goods, but many earn irregular wages.

There has never been an attempt to organize (or even to *recognize*) these workers, to institutionalize the informal networks they form, or to incorporate them into a mass movement. Often these are women "outside" the traditional boundaries of Islamic decorum and are thus shunned by the Party. Organizing, recognizing, or recruiting them would be a "cultural risk."

The WU, claims Fatma Ahmad Ibrahim, places a high priority on forming collectives where "uneducated" women[46] can learn new trades. Once recruited into these collectives, Union cadres attempt to teach literacy and then to recruit them into the Union. Fatma commented to me:

> What do women want from their Union? *Although we know what they need*, it is always better to hear it from them—even if they are ignorant. What do they want? For me I think that the first thing is to educate them. If they are not convinced, I cannot do it for them. Our experience tells us this . . . If you tell them you are going to teach them [literacy], they won't come [emphasis mine].

(2) *The Woman Merchant*: In the market place in Omdurman, a large bazaar city across the Nile from Khartoum, there was until very recent years[47] a special section of the market totally controlled and regulated by women. They were often economically autonomous, and extended this autonomy into the domestic sphere (unlike the market women of Kumasi in Ghana).[48] They were able to do this through the collective power they had built within their various kin networks as an extension of their work place. Moreover, many of them lived within walking distance of the market and were at their work place most of the day, turning the work site into a temporary residence replete with social networks. The interconnections of kinship, residential, and occupational networks gave the collectivity of the women's market the potential for mobilization. The economic rights of these women were never extended or even protected by the WU or SCP.

In describing why the WU opted from the time of the Abboud military regime to struggle in the national political arena and work on *political* rights for women over *economic* rights for women, Fatma Ahmad Ibrahim contends:

> during Abboud's time we studied all these rights and decided to try to put forward the easiest [to convince people]. We looked at economic rights, but saw them as very difficult. Even the workers [i.e., male unions] were not supporting us in this. The trade union movement was still busy with small demands of the working class [she is not including women in this designation]. *The majority of women are housewives*, so they can't go on strike or do anything to have these rights. We had decided it was better to postpone these economical rights—not to neglect them—but not to make a big fuss about them [emphasis mine].[49]

(3) *The Networks*: Another area where there have been only feeble organizing attempts by the Party is in the government schools throughout the country where thousands of female students reside in hostels, and where various self-help, consciousness-raising, emotional supportive networks, and collective economic activities are present. The same is true in the neighborhood collectives of women, some of which take the form of the *sandug* (rotating credit ring) or the *tumin* (consumer cooperative).

In my interview with Fatma, there was considerable discussion of the building of cooperatives for women, but no mention of extant neighborhood collectives and the possibility of building onto them or imitating their organizing strategies. Nor were there strategies named for organizing among female students through their daily lives in the hostels, an area where the National Islamic Front is now very successful.[50]

(4) *Women's Culture: The Zaar*: My last example is the most controversial because the indigenous form I am highlighting, the *zaar*, is seen by many Sudanese as retrogressive or as "negative customs."[51] However, I am hypothesizing that it is in the institution of the *zaar*, a spirit possession cult which is widespread in this area of north Africa and the Horn, where we see the possibility for prefigurative political forms upon which to build. This cluster-

ing of women for the purpose of helping a possessed "sister" rid herself of demons (and, in the process, make demands upon her husband or some other male relative), is a spontaneous occasion for consciousness-raising, self-help, and emotional, collective solidarity. The extra-organizational function of the *zaar* is to help women deal with their repressed state and oppressed status within the domestic sphere. It is a healing cult, one that is recognized as specializing in women's "ailments," but Pamela Constantinides reminds us that it is more than that: "it offers both the promise of cure and ongoing membership of a common interest, multi-ethnic group, and widely ramifying network of *zaar*-based contacts."[52]

Behavior encouraged in the *zaar* gives women a rare chance for uninhibited entertainment and drama. The *zaar* ceremonies which I attended were characterized by the protagonists entering states of trance wherein the possessed would engage in bawdy or lewd behavior not acceptable in Sudanese society. Also, these are often occasions for transvestism and sexual role-switching, male homosexuals sometimes acting as functionaries, and women playing male roles and being erotic toward other women. Those possessed by their spirits may also insult the males of their family and wear outlandish costumes. But the benefits are even more profound:

> There is ample evidence that women actively use this network to form friendship and patron-client relationships, to promote economic transactions, and to offer and gain services. Moreover, once established, the network tends to extend well beyond the actual activities of the cult itself. The reciprocity principle is quite strongly institutionalized in the Northern Sudan.[53]

Although we do not usually interpret supernatural rituals as prefigurative political forms, such an interpretation of the *zaar* opens our minds to the *possibility* that there are a number of extant forms upon which women may draw; some of these are already institutionalized acts of resistance. It is *not* to suggest that the revolution can or should start from the *zaar*! However, these indigenous forms, especially one such as the *zaar*, often contain qualities for spontaneous revolts. In addition to their spontaneity, they can be experiential, subjective, collective, egalitarian, and affective. The *zaar* is a mode of ending the self-subordination of women by forcing men, if only temporarily, to submit to women's demands. More important, perhaps, it also represents, if unself-consciously, attempts at emancipation of self through sexuality. At the very least, then, the *zaar* introduces issues to be addressed which we could call *women's issues*, ones which are ignored or shunned by all religio-political or "secular" political groups.

When I discussed this issue of the usefulness of the *zaar* in teaching us about ways women organize, Fatma Ahmad Ibrahim, a long-time critic of the custom, took this position:

The *zaar* is traditional culture of women and it helps in a way. But the damage is more. It encourages them to go in a direction which will not help them to realize the *real cause* of their suppression, their inequality, and their many difficulties and problems [she continued with a description of the *zaar*, saying that she has done a study of it, indicating the cleverness of the woman, the *shaykha*, who directs the ceremonies, and saying that sometimes the women get worse].... If we encourage the *zaar*, women will never know their problems, the roots, the cause, and they will never struggle against them.... The solidarity to which you refer [she was referring to what I had just said and to my writings about the *zaar*], what kind of solidarity is it? Yes, they come together ... and depart. Meanwhile they come under the influence of an ignorant woman [the *shaykha*] who knows nothing about anything.... it is dangerous ... It removes them from developing a consciousness [emphasis mine].

In her case study of Barcelona (1910–18), Temma Kaplan reveals how closely social welfare and female consciousness are linked. "The capacity of local female networks to transcend the purposes for which they were originally formed appeared as women moved further and further away from their own neighborhoods and into the spaces occupied by the government and commercial groups."[54] I am making the same argument here: that "conservative," nurturing collective actions often have potential for conversion into "public" political action, not as choruses for the "larger" national struggles, but as advocates for self-perceived *women's* interests.

Islam and the Left

Most imported leftist parties of the Third World have at least paid lip-service to the need to adapt to local conditions and traditions. All too often, however, and as evidence of leftist cultural imperialism, local customs are violated or ignored. Local customs/traditions, however, are universally observed or even preserved when they relate to the maintenance of the gender ideology, as in the role of women in Islamic societies which use Islamic law (*shari'a*). In analyzing Islam and gender relations in revolutionary South Yemen, Molyneux maintains:

The impact of religious orthodoxy on the juridical realm, in particular on Family Laws ... is a factor of the utmost significance: it is precisely within these religious codes that the position of women is defined as legally and socially subordinate to that of men. The religious influence and derivation of the codes has allowed the subordinate status of women to be legitimatized in terms of divine inspiration and doctrinal orthodoxy, and has made it especially difficult to bring about reforms in this area. Yet given the marked gender inequality in many Muslim societies and the role of Islamic orthodoxy in sustaining it, *no government that was genuinely committed to the emancipation of women could leave the Shariah and urf (customary) codes intact* [emphasis mine].[55]

As a Party attempting ascendancy, the Sudanese Communist Party has done very little tampering with the *shari'a* or with the religious traditions as they affect women—nor has the Sudanese Women's Union. Cadres exhibit a stubborn insistence on working within a particular kind of Islamic framework which divides the sexes in many spheres of life. They are concerned that such issues as a call for the eradication of female circumcision (which is *not* an Islamic dictate, but has become closely associated with Muslim traditionalism) would create a backlash from traditionalists and impede the revolution.[56]

Fatma Ahmad Ibrahim, who identifies herself as an opponent of female circumcision, takes the following position:

> The WU is trying to tell women that circumcision is not the cause of a problem, but is the result of a situation. . . . The cure is not to spend lots of money [in reference to international agencies] to convince women to stop. . . . The solution is to *educate* women, raise their consciousness . . . so they will not feel in need of circumcision to keep respect . . . there are more than 80% of Sudanese women who are ignorant and don't know what their problems are. . . . Which is the urgent problem to be solved—circumcision or ignorance? When you look at the percentage of women who are dying from circumcision or in childbirth, it is a very small percentage. But when you look at the percentage of women dying of hunger, it is very great. Which is more important [emphasis mine]?[57]

There is a tendency on the part of the SCP to relegate all gender conflicts to the realm of cultural and to consider the cultural as private. Culture, seen as superstructural, separate from the material base, is not to be tampered with; it is private, personal, and individual.

Fatma Ahmad Ibrahim describes herself as very religious and she takes some pains to appear respectable and traditional in her dress on television. She related to me the exchange she had with Abdul-Khaliq Mahjub, late Secretary-General of the SCP, which cleared the way for her to join the SCP:

> I told Abdul-Khaliq Mahjub that I was interested in joining the Party, but that I had been brought up in a religious way. For me, joining the Party would mean a contradiction. He said, "Marxism has its opinion, but as the SCP we are different. Marxism is not a belief: it is not a religion. It is a scientific ideology. We have to take from it what is suitable for us. We are not compelled to accept Marxism in its sum total. . . . *Politics have nothing to do with religion.* We believe that religion should be kept away from . . . the Party. It is a *private* thing" [emphases mine].[58]

This is a significant evasive strategy because, as we know very well, "much of the oppression of women takes place 'in private,' in areas of life considered 'personal.' The causes of that oppression might be social and economic, but these causes could only be revealed and confronted when women challenged the assumptions of their personal life."[59] Because the SCP has treated politics as something separate from everyday life (as did the Russians, Cubans, and other revolutionaries), and culture as separate from material conditions and political life, the women of the Party and the Union have led separate lives from the men. While the *theory* of the Party stresses production, the "real" world, the economic base, etc., the *practice* of men and women members widens the polarity between the private and public domains, between production and reproduction, and between the personal and political.

Conclusion

In this essay I have tried to examine the contradictions within the structure of a selected revolutionary organization, the Sudanese Communist Party. One contradiction is in the strategy of the Party, for although the SCP follows Marxist-Leninist principles of organizational structure, there is a marked departure in the strategy of dealing with the traditional religio-kinship structures of Muslim people. Sudanese women—also segregated and constrained—are, nonetheless, not viewed as "structural weakpoints" in the traditional order, as the Soviets viewed Central Asian Muslim women.[60] None of the Party literature nor my interviews indicated a view that, because of the multiple examples of female oppression, the entire structure would be altered if women were mobilized. The Party and Union are not so secularized as to aim at obliterating, through administrative assault or revolutionary legalism, the very social fabric on which the society was built. Besides, in all likelihood, such well-informed and Russian-educated Communist leaders as Abdul-Khaliq Mahjub would have known of the resistance by Muslims to Soviet social engineering. The SCP and the leaders of the WU strive to coexist with the traditional order, rationalizing that the Sudanese revolution will be based upon the concrete conditions of the society. This means that, at a very fundamental level, there is not a great deal of difference in the gender ideologies of the "Sudanese state" in general, which has never been secular, and various parties when these "concrete conditions" relate to Islam and traditional culture, the sexual division of labor, and issues of sexuality.

We have case studies of at least two entirely different socialist revolutionary strategies for dealing with indigenous culture: (1) The Soviets had aimed at *undermining* indigenous structures and (2) the SCP at *coexisting* with them. Feminist socialist principles suggest the possible efficacy of *building onto* extant indigenous forms or the necessity of the movement *emanating from* them.

In the preceding section I raised questions about the potential for a *mass* movement based on the principles and organizational characteristics implicit in some so-called "traditional" forms. So far, women in most Third World and western leftist parties and movements have been either the nurturers, the substitute soldiers, or the Greek choruses of the revolution. It is problematic whether such a strategy would lead to a totally transformed society; it may only perpetuate a bifurcated world-view.

Inadvertently, by the very nature of the relationship of the Women's Union to its "parent" group, the SCP, progressives were reproducing the relationship of power domination we find in capitalism. Because of the hierarchical and elitist nature of the Party itself, with its stress on training professional revolutionaries, an organization in which "theory" has primacy over experience, it is difficult to imagine that the subordination of women could be abolished.

A Sudanese women's movement that was *not* established as a step-child and as an organ to enhance its male counterpart might have been very effective, one emerging from extant forms "to resist an oppression which comes from inequalities of power and confidence in interpersonal relations, and from a hierarchical division of labour."[61] We are assuming that such women are potentially "sensitive and self-conscious about inequality and hierarchy in the creating of [their] . . . organizational forms." [62]

A woman's movement that emanated from, but radically transformed, indigenous structures, e.g., women's popular culture and networks and their struggles as workers in the home and neighborhood, that emanated from *both* strategic and practical gender interests, might enable Sudanese women "to make their own revolution in their own name."[63] Once women build onto these prefigurative forms, and once they move to change their situation, they automatically move against the entire structure of exploitation. To play on some phrases from Massell, they are the structural *strong* points, and nobody's surrogate.

NOTES

1. This paper represents a portion of my ongoing research in Northern Sudan, 1961–64; 1966; 1971–72; 1973–75; 1981; and 1988. These field trips were partially funded by Fulbright-Hays; American Research Center in Egypt, Inc.; African Studies Center, UCLA; American Association of University Women; National Endowment for the Humanities; and UCLA Center for the Study of Women.

2. Others have laid out similar frameworks, e.g., Norma Stoltz Chinchilla, "Women in Revolutionary Movements: The Case of Nicaragua," Working Paper No. 27, (East Lansing: Michigan State University, 1983).

3. Maxine Molyneux, "Mobilization without Emancipation? Women's Interests, the State, and Revolution in Nicaragua," *Feminist Studies* 11, no. 2 (1985), p. 228.

4. Ibid.

5. Ibid., p. 231.

6. Ibid., pp. 232–33. Molyneux has hastily concluded that women do not have collective interests. Whether derived deductively or not, the existence of unequally aligned gender arrangements may also be measured concretely, and although not homogeneous, take similar forms cross-culturally.

7. The term "promissory note" will most probably henceforth become part of our Marxist feminist vocabulary, it being the title of a new and provocative work which was published as I was revising this essay. The authors attempt to assess the relationship between women's emancipation and socialism. Sonia Kruks, Rayna Rapp, and Marilyn

Young, eds., *Promissory Notes: Women in the Transition to Socialism* (New York: Monthly Review, 1989).

8. This terminology is from the work of Judith Stacey, "When Patriarchy Kowtows: The Significance of the Chinese Family Revolution for Feminist Theory," in *Capitalist Patriarchy and the Case for Socialist Feminism*, Zillah Eisenstein, ed. (New York: Monthly Review Press, 1979), p. 338.

9. This is paraphrased from the late Eleanor Leacock, "Women, Development, and Anthropological Facts and Fiction," special double issue of *Latin American Perspectives on Women and Class Struggle* 4, nos. 12 and 13, p. 9.

10. Gregory Massell, *The Surrogate Proletariat: Moslem Women and Revolutionary Strategies in Soviet Central Asia, 1919–1929* (Princeton: Princeton University Press, 1974), pp. xxii–xxiii.

11. Ibid., p. 408.

12. For example, see Stephanie Urdang, *Fighting Two Colonialisms: Women in Guinea-Bissau* (New York: Monthly Review Press, 1979).

13. I am certainly not attempting to detract from the contributions of women to the movements in Guinea-Bissau, Algeria, Palestine, Angola, Mozambique, Eritrea, Nicaragua, Vietnam, Guatemala, and El Salvador. Additionally Cuban women are now making major contributions (see note 15).

14. Sonia Kruks, et al., op. cit.

15. Cubans, for example, developed a Family Code after the fact, and are, therefore, having great difficulty implementing changes in the sphere of domestic labor and social reproduction. Students of Cuban society are somewhat justified in a defense that maintains that Cuban revolutionaries did not have the benefit of a long period in which a vanguard party might have developed a vision of a new society, nor much of an opportunity for women to be integrated into the armed struggle.

16. Kruks et al., op. cit., p. 12.

17. Sondra Hale, "The Politics of Gender in the Middle East," in *Gender and Anthropology: Critical Reviews for Research and Teaching*, Sandra Morgan, ed. (Washington, D.C.: American Anthropological Association, 1989), pp. 246–67.

18. I carried out fieldwork on the alienated Sudanese female worker, Khartoum, summer 1981, supported by a grant from the National Endowment for the Humanities. See "'Private' and 'Public' Labor: The Sudanese Woman Worker in the 1980s—A Pilot Study," *The Ahfad Journal* (Omdurman), 2, No. 2 (1985), pp. 36–40; "Women and Work in Sudan: What Is Alienated Labor?" *Proceedings, Conference on Women and Work in the Third World* (Berkeley: Center for the Study, Education and Advancement of Women, University of California, Berkeley, 1983).

19. A closer comparison is, perhaps, the 1980s' rise of Christian fundamentalism and its atavistic image of the role of women.

20. Judith Gran, "Impact of the World Market on Egyptian Women," *MERIP Reports* 58 (1977).

21. Ibid., p. 7.

22. See "Sudan's Revolutionary Spring," *MERIP Reports* no. 135 (September 1985) for information on the military. Also, one of the best progressive pieces written on Sudan is Carole Collins' earlier article in *MERIP Reports*, "Colonialism and Class Struggle in Sudan," no. 46 (1976). Much valuable material on Sudan's military is in Ruth First's *Power in Africa* (London: Pantheon, 1970).

On April 6, 1985, the regime of Ja'far Numairi was overthrown by a military junta, which acted as a result of popular uprisings, partially led by unions and associations of professionals. At that point we could only guess as to the future of the SCP or the WU. Eric Rouleau reported at the time that "Intellectuals, political activists and trade union militants were finally able to meet again, after years of detention, exile or life

in the underground. . . . Posters, manifestos and petitions . . . [testify] to the legaliza-
tion of all political parties. . . . Where three of four major parties used to conduct their
activities in secret or abroad, there are now some forty new parties. . . . The Communist Party is the only one that has yet to come out into the open. . . . [It] remains in the
shadows, and it is difficult to determine its size and strength" ("Sudan's Revolutionary
Spring," pp. 3–4. However, while the writing of this chapter was in progress (June
1989), there was another military *coup d'état* which overthrew the democratically
elected government and installed a military junta. All political parties, political interest
groups, and professional associations were banned. All political meetings were deemed
illegal under the state of emergency. See *The Los Angeles Times* (July 2, 1989), p. 5
and *The New York Times* (July 2, 1989).

23. My information is based on many conversations and interviews with Party
members and fellow travelers, many of whom I cannot name for obvious reasons. In
my last field trip in 1988 I was able to interview Fatma Ahmad Ibrahim, head of the
Sudanese Women's Union since the 1950s, and Suad Ibrahim Ahmad, one of the most
influential women in the SCP for more than two decades. Consult notes 26, 27, 28,
and 30 for references to information on the SCP and women's organizations, especially
the WU.

24. Sheila Rowbotham, Lynne Segal, and Hilary Wainwright, *Beyond the Frag-
ments: Feminism and the Making of Socialism* (London: Merlin, 1979), p. 7.

25. The editors of *Promissory Notes* comment on the absence of discussion of sex
and sexuality in their collection of essays from all over the world. Kruks, et al., op.
cit., p. 11.

26. The strength and influence of the SCP are commented on in many sources,
including Gabriel Warburg, *Islam, Nationalism, and Communism in Traditional Society: The Case of Sudan* (London: Frank Cass, 1978). Warburg writes that "The
accurate number of SCP members is not known. According to *The World Today* (London), January 1965, there were 10,000 party members at that time" (p. 234). Fatima
Babiker Mahmoud remarks that "the Communist Party of the Sudan (CPS) is the most
influential revolutionary organization in the country and one of the leading Communist
Parties in Africa and the Middle East" in *The Sudanese Bourgeoisie: Vanguard of
Development?* (London and Khartoum: Khartoum University Press and Zed, 1984),
p. 130. For descriptions of the SCP or leftist politics in Sudan, in general, consult J.
M. A. Bakheit, *Communist Activities in the Middle East between 1919–1927, with
Special Reference to Egypt and the Sudan* (Khartoum: Sudan Research Unit, University
of Khartoum, 1968); Salah el-Din el-Zein el-Tayeb, *The Student Movement in Sudan,
1940–1970* (Khartoum: Khartoum University Press, 1971); Saad ed-Din Fawzi, *The
Labour Movement in the Sudan, 1946–1955* (London: Oxford University Press, 1957);
Carole Collins, "Colonialism and Class Struggle in Sudan," *MERIP Reports* no. 46
(1976); Alain Gresh, "The Free Officers and the Comrades: The Sudanese Communist
Party and Nimeiri Face-to-Face," *International Journal of Middle East Studies* 21
(1989), pp. 393–409; sections of Mansour Khalid's, *Nimeiri and the Revolution of
Dis-May* (London: KPI, 1985) and of Tim Niblock's *Class and Power in Sudan: The
Dynamics of Sudanese Politics, 1898–1985* (New York: State University of New York
Press, 1987); and various Communist sources, e.g., *The African Communist* (London);
Mohamed Sulaiman, *Ten Years of the Sudanese Left* (Arabic) (Wad Medani: Alfagr
Books, 1971); SCP publications, *Thawrat Sha'ab* (A people's revolution) (Khartoum:
Socialist Publishing House, 1967); *Marxism and Problems of the Sudanese Revolution*
(Arabic) (Khartoum: Socialist Publishing House, 1968); Abdel Khaliq Mahjub, *Lama-
hat min ta'rikh al-hizb al-Shuyu'i al-Sudani* (Dar al-fikr al-ishtiraki, 1960); and the
Party organ, *al-Midan*.

27. We cannot know the exact figures, but this is the estimate usually taken from

Arabic or Sudanese sources, and it is also the one I was most frequently given during my interviews in the 1960s. As for written sources, I have used Caroline Fleuhr-Lobban, "Women and Social Liberation: The Sudan Experience," in *Three Studies on National Integration in the Arab World* (North Dartmouth, Mass.: Association of Arab-American University Graduates Information Paper no. 12, 1974). She was reliant on the major source in English in the 1970s for our knowledge of the Sudanese women's movement, Fatma Babiker Mahmoud, "The Role of the Sudanese Women's Union in Sudanese Politics," (M.A. thesis, University of Khartoum, 1971), and on a booklet by Nafisa Ahmad el-Amin, *The Sudanese Woman throughout the History of Her Struggle* (Khartoum: Government Press, 1972).

28. The most useful history and analysis of the trade union movement in Sudan is ed-Din Fawzi, op. cit.

29. See note 22 for reference to the 1985 uprising (*intifada*). As for the Sudanese Women's Union, Rouleau reported that the Sudanese "Pasionaria," Fatima Ahmad Ibrahim, was ubiquitous during the uprising as an activist on behalf of women and that she addressed the first public meeting of the WU in fourteen years on April 21, 1985 (op. cit., p. 4).

30. For historical details on Sudanese women's organizations I have relied on a number of sources, e.g., Fatima Babiker Mahmoud, op. cit.; Nafisa Ahmad al-Amin, op. cit.; and some summaries of the works by Fleuhr-Lobban, op. cit. There are also the works by the head of the Women's Union, Fatma Ahmad Ibrahim, e.g., *Tariqna ila al-Tuhasur* (Our road to emancipation) (Khartoum, n.d.), *al-Mar'a al-Arabiyya wa al-Taghyir al-Ijtima'i* (The Arab woman and social change) (Khartoum: al-Markaz al-Tiba'i, 1986), and a series of her publications in *Sawt al-Mar'a* (The woman's voice) (Khartoum, sporadically from 1955 to the present). Also, Hagga Kahif-Badri, *al-Haraka al-Nisa'iyya fi al-Sudan* (The women's movement in the Sudan) (Khartoum: University Publishing House, University of Khartoum, 1980) and (in English), "The History, Development, Organization and Position of Women's Studies in the Sudan," *Social Science Research and Women in the Arab World* (Paris: UNESCO, 1984), pp. 94–112. Another good recent source in English which has a section on women's organizations is Z. B. el-Bakri and E. M. Kameir, "Aspects of Women's Political Participation in Sudan," *International Social Science Journal* 35, no. 4 (1983), pp. 605–23. See also el-Bakri and al-Haj Hamad M. Khier's paper, "Sudanese Women in History and Historiography: A Proposed Strategy for Curriculum Change," Workshop on Women's Studies in Sudan, Sudan Family Planning Association, National Council for Research, February 9, 1989. My own interpretation and synthesis of the above appeared in "The Wing of the Patriarch: Sudanese Women and Revolutionary Parties," *Middle East Report* 16, no. 1 (1986), pp. 25–30.

31. El-Bakri and Kameir, op. cit., p. 619.

32. During one of the civilian regimes in 1965, women were given the vote, but once again, literacy was a requirement, a strategy which the Women's Union supported, according to Fatma Ahmad Ibrahim, head of the WU and member of Parliament at the time. Interview with Fatma Ahmad Ibrahim, Omdurman, Sudan, July 12, 1988. Unless otherwise indicated, quotes and ideas attributed to her are from this interview.

33. Some of the information for this section, as I have indicated in the previous note, is based on my interview with Fatma Ahmad Ibrahim in 1988, but also on two interviews with Suad Ibrahim Ahmad, a leading woman Communist (Khartoum, Sudan, July 25 and 26, 1988).

34. Although I have written this essay as if the WU is a front organization for the SCP, the relationship is far more complicated than that, depending on the source. The state always managed more control over the WU than over the SCP and more easily

infiltrated the WU with its own supporters, trying to influence or force the WU away from the SCP. Also, not all of the members or leaders of the WU were Communists or members of the SCP, and there was a great struggle between Communists and non-Communists over the WU leadership. The closeness of the tie between the SCP and WU changed historically, oftentimes depending on who was elected president of the WU. In general, however, the leaders of the WU, even if closely tied to the SCP, tried, for some "unknown" reasons, but also for reasons of the survival of the group, to discount the idea that the WU was a "front" of the SCP. In my interview with her, Fatma Ahmad Ibrahim claimed that there are no differences between the SCP and the WU on women's issues: "The Communist Party gives us its full support to every detail of women's rights. This is why people think we are a part of them and we are not."

35. This critical information is from a number of confidential interviews with women Communists and/or sister travelers.

36. Warburg, op. cit., p. 166.

37. Juliette Minces, "Women in Algeria," in *Women in the Muslim World*, Lois Beck and Nikki Keddie, eds. (Cambridge: Harvard University Press, 1978).

38. This letter is reproduced in Hagga Kashif-Badri, op. cit., pp. 106–9.

39. Warburg, op. cit., p. 211.

40. "The Sudan Women's Union [a co-opted name] has recently been the target of massive criticism. Most women complain that the SWU does not reach enough of Sudan's female population, and that its achievements have been, at best, minimal." The writer, Awatif Sidahmad, was interviewing Nafisa Ahmad el-Amin, one of the former WU members and then Secretary General of the SWU and Political Bureau member of the Sudan Socialist Union, who stated that "we do not deny the fact that the SWU was inadequate for a long time" *Sudanow* (January 1981), pp. 41–42.

41. Potential new members are screened for moral behavior, especially women. Members of "ill-repute" would reflect negatively on a Party struggling within an Islamic framework. In short, women of the SCP and WU must have acceptable social reputations, supposedly to appease male Muslims in the society at large. This process of attention to "morals" and appropriate social behavior has become acute, with the population keenly sensitive to the rise in conservative Islamic sentiments. Khartoum feminists and younger members of the WU and SCP complained to me in 1988 that Fatma Ahmad Ibrahim was insisting on pulling her *tobe* over her head and face when she appears on television, and that such conservative practices from a major left feminist role model are hurting their cause (i.e., women's emancipation).

42. Temma Kaplan, "Female Consciousness and Collective Action: The Case of Barcelona, 1910–1918," in *Feminist Theory: A Critique of Ideology*, Nannerl Keohane, Michelle Rosaldo, and Barbara Gelpi, eds. (Chicago: University of Chicago Press, 1981), p. 56.

43. These ideas are part of feminist discourse and have been discussed by only small numbers of Sudanese feminists in Khartoum. The delineation of the spheres is my own.

44. Fatma Ahmad Ibrahim has not always been the head of the WU, but her views could be said to have been the most influential for over thirty years. Therefore, I contend that it is valid to present her views as representing the WU.

45. The fullest account of the urban Sudanese woman worker, including the informal sector, is by Samia el-Hadi el-Nagar, "Patterns of Women Participation in the Labour Force in Khartoum" (Ph.D, thesis, University of Khartoum, 1985).

46. Fatma used the term "ignorant women" throughout the interview, and stressed education as the central strategy of the WU.

47. This "women's market" was removed by Numairi's government as a part of regularizing and modernizing the Omdurman marketplace. However, I was informed that many of the old women still cluster in smaller groups as street vendors. For similar

information on Khartoum women merchants see Alawiya Osman M. Salih's short paper, "Women in Trade: Vendors in Khartoum Area Markets," *The Ahfad Journal* (Khartoum) 3, no. 2 (1986), pp. 37–40.

48. Market women in West Africa have been written about extensively. Here I only want to make the point made so vividly in an ethnographic film about market women, "Asante [Ghana] Market Women" (Granada Television), that through various mechanisms such as unionization, women monopolize trade in the vegetable market and wield enormous power in the public domain while remaining virtually powerless in the domestic realm.

49. It is simply not true that "most Sudanese women are housewives." They are agricultural workers, the kinds of workers in the informal sector described in the preceding section, and members of the formal workforce. It is difficult, however, to find this data simply and clearly laid out. Liberal sources are keen to show that women are *not* represented in certain sectors of the economy and do not play an equal role in development. Their calculations are, therefore, skewed to make that argument. One has to glean the information on women's economic roles in Sudan from sporadic sources, among them a number of documents which are either unpublished or difficult to obtain: e.g., Am'na Rahama and A. Hoogenboom, "Women Farmers, Technological Innovation and Access to Development Projects," Workshop no. 5 (n.d., but post-1987); Susan Holcombe, "Profiles of Women Agricultural Producers.... A Sudan Example," United Nations Development Fund for Women, Occasional Paper no. 7, 1988; Am'na Badri, *Women in Management and Public Administration in Sudan* (Khartoum: Conferences of Business and Administrative Sciences Education in the Sudan, University of Khartoum, 1987); Samira Amin Ahmad, et al.; "Population Problems, Status of Women and Development" (Khartoum: Third National Population Conference, 1987); Zeinab el-Bakri and el-Wathig Kameir, "Women and Development Policies in Sudan: A Critical Outlook," Paper no. 46 (Nairobi: Second OSSREA Congress, 1986); Salih, op. cit.; el-Nagar, op. cit.; Nur el-Tayib Abdul Gadir, *al-Mar'a al-'Amila fi al-Sudan* (The working woman in Sudan) (Khartoum: Department of Labour and Social Security, Division of Research, Information and Media, 1984); Diana Baxter, ed., *Women and the Environment* (Khartoum: Institute of Environmental Studies, 1981); Sondra Hale, "'Private' and 'Public' Labour," op. cit.; Food and Agricultural Organization of the United Nations, Interim Report, *National Conference on the Role of Women in Agriculture and Rural Development in the Sudan* (Khartoum North: January 18–22, 1987); and International Labour Office, *Growth, Employment, and Equity: A Comprehensive Strategy for the Sudan* (Geneva: ILO, 1978).

50. A University of Khartoum woman student informed me in 1988 that she was almost intimidated into joining the National Islamic Front (or at least into wearing Islamic dress) by the zealousness of the NIF women students who organized by visiting and haranguing other students in their rooms at the hostels.

51. Fatma Ahmad Ibrahim classifies the *zaar* as a "negative custom" and, in my interview with her, July 12, 1988, refused to hear anything from me to the contrary.

52. Pamela Constantinides, "Women's Spirit Possession and Urban Adaptation," in *Women United, Women Divided: Cross-Cultural Perspectives on Female Solidarity,* Patricia Caplan and Janet Bujra, eds. (London: Tavistock, 1978), p. 195.

53. Ibid., p. 198.

54. Kaplan, op. cit., p. 74.

55. Maxine Molyneux, "Legal Reform and Socialist Revolution in South Yemen: Women and the Family," in Kruks et al., op. cit., p. 201.

56. We see the same trepidation with regard to issues surrounding reproductive rights and the relationship of revolutionary movements to the Catholic Church in Central America, for example.

57. In this quote it is clear that, although she may oppose circumcision, it is not a high priority for her. She resents the outside interference and maintains that the problem is exaggerated by outsiders, i.e., westerners. She is also critical of any monies given the Babiker Bedri Scientific Society (for Women) to work on eradication.

58. Interview, July 12, 1988.

59. Rowbotham et al., op. cit., p. 13.

60. Massell, op. cit.

61. Ibid., p. 12.

62. Ibid., p. 13.

63. Stacey, op. cit., p. 338.

IX

PALESTINIAN WOMEN AND POLITICS IN LEBANON

Rosemary Sayigh

Introduction

This chapter takes its departure from questions Marxist feminists have been putting to the concepts and assumptions of the "founding mothers" of feminist scholarship. Formulations I find particularly valuable are: that western women's experiences do not provide a universal framework for analyzing gender oppression;[1] that we must provide historically and culturally specific analyses of non-western women's situations and political action;[2] and that we must listen to women telling their own struggles.[3]

A history (or histories) of Palestinian women's action in Lebanon is important because there was a period of relative Palestinian autonomy, and because of the intense women's activism that was evident in numerous fields and frameworks. Such a history is difficult because of the destruction of archives. To be useful, however, such a history should not only record official "facts" but should also ask questions of those who lived the struggle. Among the most basic of these would be: How do we explain the non-incorporation of the majority of Palestinian women in the structures of the Resistance Movement (especially the Women's Union) in spite of their strong commitment to national struggle? Testimony that this was so comes from a leading woman cadre, speaking in 1980: "The Palestinian woman has always struggled, carried arms, and taken part in uprisings. But her role in struggle has not deepened or put down roots. It remains tied to the ebb and flow of the Revolution."[4]

I shall begin by discussing the organized women's movement, its place in the Resistance Movement, its leadership, structure, programs and methods, by focusing on three sets of relations: between the women's leadership and the Resistance Movement leadership; between women within the movement; and between organized women and the women of the camps. I recognize that Palestinian women writing their own history would perhaps not choose this

175

focus, but while supporting the necessity for all oppressed groups to voice their own struggles, we face a problem of representativity with stratified societies like those of the Middle East: Who are the spokeswomen and leaders of the women's movements in such societies? How did they come to be leaders? Whom do they represent? Thus, the second part of my paper will focus on women in the camps, in an attempt to understand *their* struggles, which are not necessarily the same as those of the organized women.

Notes toward a History of the Women's Movement, 1970–1982

The contingency of women's political action, and the fact that it is seldom self-mobilized, but is promoted and constrained by other factors, means that no history of a women's movement can be written without attention to its context. State or movement policies toward women are the most crucial factor, but the historical conjuncture, economic forces, cultural traditions, and family praxis must also be taken into account. Because of the complexity of Lebanon as a political arena, its rapid shifts in the balance of forces, and the plurality of organizations making up the Resistance Movement, a proper assessment cannot be undertaken here, but we should take note of: (i) the weakness of the Lebanese state, which gave the Resistance Movement twelve years of relative autonomy and access to the Palestinian masses; (ii) continuous crisis, with explosions of violence causing loss and displacement that deepened Palestinian commitment to, and dependence on, the Resistance Movement, and weakened family control over women at the mass level; (iii) strong economic pressures pushing women into the work force; and (iv) an "open" cultural atmosphere that allowed free play to progressive as well as reactionary currents. In terms of national strategy, two contradictory trends are discernible. On the broader regional level, especially after 1973, peace initiatives displaced the "people's war" strategy that had briefly predominated in Jordan, leading to a current of demobilization; while at the Lebanese level, recurrent crisis had a mobilizing effect, with the Rejection Front continuing to call for the total liberation of Palestine in opposition to the main Fateh leadership's adoption of the concept of an "independent state." As a result, the Lebanon period was essentially one of PLO institution-building, of internal consolidation of the Resistance groups, and of increasing competition between them. Broad effects for women were gradual displacement from armed struggle but growing scope as members and officials in the various organizations, and as employees in Resistance/PLO offices.

The Lebanon period needs to be compared with the two years that preceded it in Jordan (1968–70) to understand its combination of ideological stagnation around the "women's issue" together with extensive, unguided developments on the ground. The Jordan period was characterized by a "revolutionary tide" generated by the defeat of the Arab armies in 1967 that swept away objective and subjective constraints. Women flocked to join the Resistance Movement, undergoing military training, taking part in military operations, becoming full time cadres.[5] This marked a historic "breakthrough," the symbolic importance of which, both for women and for the Resistance, should not be underestimated. For women, carrying arms signified their full participation in the national struggle on a basis of equality with men;[6] it meant promotion from the subaltern status of their mothers in the pre-1948 national movement in Palestine. However, counterreactions were not slow to arise: from the regime, which exploited women's presence in the *fedayeen* bases in its propaganda; from conservative social forces; and from families, particularly after Black September and stories of the rape of women fighters. Women militants also encountered a series of difficulties, from insufficient organizational support, discrimination during military training and occasional ridicule from men, to distrust from camp mothers who feared the effects of Resistance training on their daughters.[7] Such problems contributed to the more cautious and "pragmatic" approach to the "women's issue" in Lebanon. Whereas the Jordan period brought forth a spate of statements (even from Fateh) calling for women's equal participation in the Revolution,[8] in Lebanon this issue was never raised except by a small minority of feminist nationalists such as Mai Sayigh. The dominant thesis concerning women during the Lebanon period was that women's liberation would come through their participation in national struggle. During the same period, radical women's groups were being formed in the West Bank, such as the Women's Work Committees, which insisted that women's issues need to be defined and worked on *during* the process of national struggle, not left pending until after national liberation. In Lebanon, several factors worked toward stabilizing existing gender relations and family praxis. One was the way that discussion of women's issues was suppressed or postponed (often through their being labeled as "secondary"), even in radical sectors of the Resistance movement. Another was the weakness of the only framework that united women, the General Union of Palestinian Women (GUPW), in contrast to the strength of their commitment to the Resistance groups that separated them. The expanding economic and political recruitment of camp women by the Palestine Resistance Movement also contributed to stabilization: by appearing to constitute a radical change in gender praxis, it satisfied those calling for such change; second, by being carefully calibrated with family/community rules in terms of place, times, duration, and surveillance of women's activities, it ensured that, while changes did occur in women's lives as a result of their mobilization, these did not exceed the limits placed by public opinion.

Beginnings

Even before the transfer of Resistance movement headquarters to Beirut, we find urban Palestinian women mobilized in a number of different frameworks. This multiplicity itself calls for analysis, especially because it has resisted centralizing pressures: Is it a product of leadership manipulation? Of

competition between women introduced by position and power? Of a culturally based preference for small, familiar contexts of association?

We find three main types of framework:

(a) The PLO: a Preparatory Committee was set up in 1969 to lay the
ground-plan for the Lebanese Branch of the General Union of Palestinian
Women (GUPW). Co-opted from among prominent nationalist women (of
whom a small number were Resistance group members), this Committee also
prepared the important Second GUPW General Conference of 1974 in Lebanon. Some Union subcommittees seem to have been active before the establishment of the Lebanese Regional Branch in 1972. Forming the Union through
co-option may have brought quick results, but raised questions concerning its
capacity for developing a mass base.

(b) Two Lebanese institutions also attracted Palestinian women. One was
the *Ittihad al-Nisa'i al-'Arabi al-Filastini*, a continuation of the Tulkarm
Branch of the pre-1948 Ittihad, which was legally reconstituted in Lebanon
in 1950. Like the older Union, it had no mass basis, and undertook emergency
relief work, ran an orphanage, and represented Palestinian women at international conferences. In spite of a constitution, elections, and offices, it had
clique-like characteristics.

A second Lebanese association whose constituency was mainly Palestinian
was *In'ash al-Mukhayam*, known for its revival of traditional Palestinian peasant embroidery. In'ash drew away from the GUPW many women who wanted
to work in a non-political atmosphere. Though its membership was somewhat
broader than that of the Ittihad al-Nisa'i, it was similarly limited in terms of
class and generation.

(c) Informal groupings: Many women preferred to "help the cause" from
within a group of friends rather than as members of formal associations.
Activities undertaken by such groups have included knitting jerseys for *fedayeen*, working in Red Crescent Field hospitals, and fund-raising for needy
families. Such groups fit established kin/friend/neighbor networks, as well as
the domestic schedule of women who are primarily housewives; they grow
easily out of the established cultural pattern of women's communal work
groups. Aside from their nationalistic purposes, such informal groups offer
valued opportunities for news exchange, mutual help, and relaxation; and
they avoid the tensions introduced by formal structure, such as offices, elections, and hierarchy.

Theoretically, we should expect the GUPW to absorb the other frameworks,
as the more evolved, potentially mass-based structure. Why it was not able to
do so is a question for historical study.

Development of the GUPW

Much careful preparation went into drawing up the constitution, internal
regulations, and goals of the GUPW, and a proper history would have to

explore these carefully, even though the blueprint of an organization tells us little about its actual mode of operation. Comparing the Union to the pre-1948 Ittihad, members point to its more explicitly political role, its organic relationship to the national movement, and its more comprehensive work program, all seen as evidence of progress. However, from the perspective of the need to form a mass-based women's union, we may question whether the structure, leadership, and action program of the GUPW were appropriately chosen. The question is complicated by problems caused by the Diaspora and by crisis in Lebanon, which may be presented as making the Union's goals unrealizable. But Palestinian institutions have to be able to operate in such conditions; thus, the field is still open for critical questions concerning the way Resistance formations operated.

Like the other Popular Unions, the GUPW is linked to the PLO through the Office of Mass Organizations, and sends delegates to the National Assembly. It receives an annual budget from the National Fund.[9] Although legislative power is vested in the General Conference, the cost of travel is such that only four have been held since the Union's establishment in 1964, and participation is thus mainly limited to women sponsored by Resistance groups. This leaves direction in the hands of the thirteen-member Executive Committee (elected by the Conference), and in the permanent Secretariat that the Executive Committee supervises. A forty-member Administrative Council, also elected by the General Conference, is supposed to meet every three months to ensure that its resolutions are carried out: a useful mechanism thwarted by dispersion.

Structurally, the Union is designed to spread horizontally by forming regional branches throughout the Diaspora, and vertically to reach the mass of women in each region through three levels of committee: the central (*hay'a idariyya*), provincial, and local. Such a highly centralized structure appears necessary as a response to dispersion, but has proved cumbersome in practice. Activating it calls for a cohesive and dynamic leadership, agreed-on priorities, and mobilization programs.

For the Lebanese Branch, activation of local camp committees became a priority after the battles of May 1973.[10] This was done by members of the central *hay'a idariyya* visiting the camps to meet with women chosen by the Resistance groups. This mode of setting up committees is general throughout the Resistance Movement, but it raises questions about the representativity of local GUPW committee members, and their potential for mobilizing the mass of women, most of whom remained hostile to organizational pluralism.

The Second GUPW General Conference held in 1974 in Lebanon produced an Executive Committee quite different from the preceding one.[11] Whereas the first had been made up of known figures, leaders of national social institutions such as the Red Crescent, pre-1948 Arab Women's Union branches, and a few new Diaspora unions, the second was composed mainly of members and representatives of Resistance groups,[12] as well as a few independents and women recruited by Fateh in Jordan to build its social and administrative apparatus.[13] Closely associated in age, social origins, and political experience with the Resistance movement leadership, this corpus of women formed the second "historic leadership" of the Palestine women's movement, reaffirmed by the Third General Conference of 1980 (also held in Lebanon), with a few minor changes. Just as the basis of representativity of the Second Executive Committee changed from social institutions to Resistance groups, so also its regional center of gravity shifted from the West Bank and Gaza, cut off after 1967 by Israeli occupation, to the communities of the Diaspora.

A proper history would weigh all the factors that mitigated against the Union's Executive Committee acting as a cohesive, dynamic leadership. The Diaspora is usually cited as a primary obstacle, but it must be noted that between 1970 and 1982 more than half of the Executive Committee members were located in Beirut, without this proximity bringing positive results. Bases for conflict might be identified in generational differences: the Abu Ali study[14] found that younger women, whatever their organizational affiliation, were more critical of the leadership's refusal to implement policies of radical change in class and gender relations than older, institution-based women, who believed that women should "help" from their traditional place in the social order. Younger women cadres were much more aware of gender oppression at the mass level. It is said that Chairman Arafat intervened to ensure a certain proportion of older women on the Executive Committee.[15]

A more basic kind of division is rooted in the fact that members of the Executive Committee, as well as committees at all other levels, derive their leadership position from their organizational affiliation. They are the *mandubat* (representatives) of their organization in the Union, chosen for nationalist and partisan loyalty rather than as a result of work among the mass of women. Their closest ties are with the leaders of their organization and women comrades, not with each other. The question needs careful investigation, but close cooperation between Executive Committee members appears to have occurred only at times of exceptional crisis, such as 1975–76 and 1982, and then mainly in emergency relief work. The single issue on which Executive Committee members are said to have campaigned systematically, and as a group, was to have their chairwoman granted a place on the central Executive Committee of the Resistance Movement. Constantly promised, this promotion has been pushed aside at consecutive National Assemblies.

Active Union women constantly resolved to put partisan issues aside and work as a "real" union, but an incident recounted by one of them shows how hard this was in practice. Union women agreed to march under a single banner during one of many commemorations that punctuated life in West Beirut in the Resistance period. When they reached the assembly point it was found that one group of women was carrying their own party slogan. Some women wanted to cancel their participation, but others said, "No, let's all carry our party banners. After all, *this is our reality*." Exploration of the specific issues that split the Union during this period would illuminate the structure of women's political consciousness, and the ways in which national, sectarian, and women's issues were hierarchized.

Another basis for division was the creation of specialized subcommittees, with each member of the Executive and all other committees responsible for designated areas of action. This tended to generate "domains" and conflicts over boundaries. At a self-critical symposium held in March 1982,[16] some members suggested that "superficial specialization" should be dropped, and that instead all active members should work in a single campaign, for example adult literacy. Such a debate so late in the Lebanon period makes it clear that the Union's activities had not developed since 1970, but had rather declined.

A third line of examination could well focus on the GUPW's Action Programme. Members compare this favorably with that of the pre-1948 Ittihad, seeing it as more comprehensive, more systematic, and more politicized, whereas the Ittihad's activities had been relatively localized, ad hoc, and concentrated in the field of social projects. The GUPW Action Programme is divided into broad categories: Social, Cultural, Economic, External Relations, Internal Organization, and Information, for each of which a member of the Executive Committee is responsible through subcommittees. Membership of the subcommittees is not limited to the Union but can be recruited from the circle of the responsible Executive Committee member. The same division of labor is replicated at the provincial and local committee levels. Though mobilization of the mass of women was from the beginning a major goal of the Union, it was never clear how the Action Programme was to be implemented at the mass level. Priorities were never specified, nor detailed programs worked out. Thus Union centers in the camps did not become foci of activity for the mass of women in spite of the activism of individual members. By 1982 it was clear that types of activity undertaken by the Union at the camp level (vocational training, adult literacy, light arms training, kindergartens, embroidery production) were not being systematically pursued. Paradoxically, the same war conditions that loosened constraints over women, and made them readier to act in an organized framework, appear as a disruptive factor for the Union. War increased the difficulty of communicating between the center and the periphery, and diminished the number of trained cadres.

One of the reasons given by a leading Lebanese branch cadre in 1984[17] for the weakness of the Union's work at the mass level was the neglect of skills needed to build concrete productive, social, and cultural projects. In part this neglect is explained by the lack of a theory linking social development to national struggle that characterized the Resistance Movement as a whole. Partly it is a consequence of the primacy given by organized women to political work. Building concrete projects in the camps was seen as a necessary part of national and partisan work, but how to run them so that the mass of women would be involved was not seen as problematic. The absence of training in project organization was visible at both central and local levels, producing a characteristic shortfall between announced programs and execution. One form this took was neglect of that part of the GUPW's program which focused on developing women themselves (whether in terms of literacy, culture, productive capacities, or organizing skills); in contrast, defense training, nationalist consciousness-raising, and mother-and-child health projects were better attended to. Several of the social programs adopted by the Union were not part of its program of mass activation, but arose either in response to emergency (as in the case of the orphanage for Tell al-Zaatar children), or in response to the requirements of particular sectors (as in the crèche for the infants of married women cadres in West Beirut). The Union's twelve camp kindergartens also benefited young, unmarried women for whom they provided employment much more than they helped the housewife majority. Kindergarten hours (from 8 a.m. to 12 a.m.) do not free mothers to work outside the home; only rarely were mothers involved in after-hours activities based on kindergarten premises.

Another factor accounting for the relative neglect of mass-level projects might be found in the priority accorded to public relations and information. This is a traditional sphere of Palestinian women's activity,[18] but constraints on women traveling before 1948 limited attendance at conferences. The Resistance Movement leadership gave even greater prominence to the GUPW's role in representing women's involvement in struggle to the outside world, by encouraging Union members to visit countries that support the Movement, receive official delegations, and attend international conferences. Most national liberation movements have used women in this way, and feminists will raise the question of whether such symbolic prominence during struggle is linked to women's demobilization later. We may ask to what extent, and with what justification, information work deflected budgets and cadres away from the work of incorporating the mass of women into the Union.

The difficulties faced by the GUPW in "putting down roots" in Lebanon require careful analysis, work best done collectively by women who were closely involved. While due weight should be given to the disruptive effects of war, it should also be noted that other Resistance-affiliated institutions managed to increase their work at the mass level, while that of the Union declined. The effects for the Union of its close integration into the national movement need to be weighed, for though this was seen as a "progressive" step by organized women, it seems to have led to loss of autonomy (in comparison to the pre-1948 Ittihad) without notably increasing its power to incorporate the mass of women. The effects for the Union of intra-organizational competition is perhaps the most serious question on the agenda, for while it is argued that organization women cadres are the most politicized and most active, so that their presence in the Union should activate it, it also had the effect of turning the Union into an arena of conflict between organizations, prevented the formulation of collective women's demands, and transferred competition between the Resistance groups to the mass level, where it alienated women who, in general, were hostile to any kind of split in national unity.

Women in the Resistance Organizations

Processes of internal consolidation of, and competition between, Resistance organizations in Lebanon offered women increased scope for membership and full-time political work as cadres. The development of women's sections as recruiting bases led to an enhanced role for women members, both in partisan political work and in building the social institutions—kindergartens, clinics, vocational training centers, embroidery and sewing workshops—through which each organization manifested itself at the camp level. There was also a growing demand for female labor in PLO and Resistance offices and institutions, in ordinary civilian jobs (nurses, typists, cleaners, etc.), at a time when economic pressures created a need for additional income, and when war violence, displacement, and loss of menfolk were eroding constraints against women working. In many cases, a woman became the wage earner, the "man of the family." Through necessity, a new ethos praising women working in national institutions grew to challenge the older one of the *sitt fil-bait* (the lady in home).[19] While women workers employed by an organization were not necessarily members, they were usually "close" to it, either as friends of members, or as belonging to affiliated families.

In Lebanon, unlike Jordan, women's membership in Resistance groups was not as restricted to the educated middle classes, but spread to those living in popular quarters of cities, and eventually to the camps. The relationship between crisis and women's membership is indicated by the fact that membership was higher in camps exposed to attack, such as those in the South, or Tell al-Zaatar, than it was in more remote camps. Resistance to daughters joining mixed political formations has continued at the camp level in spite of general and strong commitment to the struggle for Return, and shows up in the family background characteristics of women members, who often come from notable or particularly poor families, and whose entry into an organization has usually been encouraged by male kin. But the relationship between crisis and women's activism is forcefully drawn in this quotation from a young camp cadre: "During the battle for the camp (Tell al-Zaatar), I worked in the clinic and the bakery along with many other young women. Before that, most girls weren't allowed by their families to work in the Resistance clinics . . . . But after the battle of Tell al-Zaatar, no mother would prevent her daughter from going out. On the contrary, she would tell her to go out and work to help her people."[20]

For the first women cadres, those who had joined the Resistance to undertake military and political struggle, it was a sort of demotion to be directed to work with other women. We sense this in the recollections of a Fateh cadre: "In Fateh I was mobilized to work with women . . . . Being a student I wasn't interested in women's movements, having the impression that they were dull, not dynamic."[21] Such cadres initially looked at camp women across a class and cultural gap that had not been diminished by preparation or experience of mass work. Camp women were conceptualized as constrained by a "lagging reality," as "passive," and as monopolized by domestic burdens. The cadre quoted above described a typical camp woman in these terms: "She doesn't really care what happens outside her home, in society or politics. It is enough for her that her husband, daughter or son is participating, not she."[22] I will argue that this was an erroneous view which absolved organized women from seeking an appropriate framework and method of involving camp women.

The consolidation of the *tanzimat* (organizations) created special roles and powers for women members, even if very few reached higher levels of command. Heading a women's section was a fairly important post, carrying extensive responsibilities and some prerogatives. Such a post involved supervising provincial and local women cadres, initiating and managing social, cultural, and productive projects, and representing the organization in the Union. It can be argued that through women's sections and special tasks, women's entry into the organizations has been controlled to reproduce a division of labor seen as "natural," whereby men formulate policy and make plans, while women execute them; and that women were as marginalized in the mixed organizations as they were in the segregated Union. Yet while organized women complained about their exclusion from higher party levels, their sense of organizational belonging (*intima' tanzimiyya*) usually prevailed. Membership represented an important political and psychological gain that they may have feared would be jeopardized by pressing "women's issues." A cadre who was asked if women would ever join an organization because of its "stand" on women replied negatively. Women join Resistance groups because of their stand on national issues. If they leave them it is seldom in protest against their treatment as women, but for other reasons.

It was mainly medium-level cadres who undertook mass work. By the late 1970s, there was a body of cadres from camp backgrounds, better qualified than higher cadres to build relations with camp women. Their work was to recruit and train local members, visit the families of their organization's martyrs, build support for their organization's "line," and rally attendance at important ceremonial occasions, such as the organization's anniversary. Such work was important in linking the *tanzimat* to camp communities; women's relatively easy access to homes, and their diplomatic skills, made them adepts.

Mass work required judgment, staying power, and careful control over comportment.[23] There were no training programs and little guidance, so that cadres had to improvise their own methods, learning how to enter camp women's networks and gradually building relations of trust with the families of girls selected as likely recruits.[24] Often a cadre would expend much time on numerous visits to gain a new member, only to lose her through marriage or migration. Many found the work too difficult, and dropped out; but by the late 1970s a number of women cadres had built themselves through trial and error into experienced mass organizers, well versed in camp social relations and etiquette. Initial reserves that camp women had had toward them, as unmarried, or as representing organizations rather than the national movement, gave way to solidarity and trust.

One question that needs to be raised, however, is the cadres' neglect of housewives in favor of *shabaat* (unmarried girls) as targets of recruitment: was this organizational policy, or a decision taken spontaneously by the cadres? There are many justifications for such a strategy: adolescence is the phase of maximum political enthusiasm; girls are better educated than their mothers, more amenable to discipline, more receptive; and girls have more time for regular activities. The problem with this approach is that most unmarried girls in camps marry, usually in their early twenties, and only a small minority remain active after marriage. There may be long term effects from adolescent party membership on gender relations, family size, and extra-domestic activity, but such effects are not likely to be strong in the absence of an overall campaign to change the division of labor within the household. A second problem arising from recruiting *shabaat* is the status barrier between unmarried and married women in camps, which makes it almost impossible for the former to mobilize the latter; for while relations between women at the camp level hardly reflect socioeconomic status differences between families, the marital status boundary is still a very real one. The cadres' focus on *shabaat* led to a double neglect of housewives, both initially, and after the formation of local cadres. The only method that effectively incorporated housewives was the holding of *nadwaat*, informal gatherings in camp homes attended by women from the neighborhood. After a short address by a cadre, which might give an analysis of the current political situation, the floor would be opened for questions and comments. Apart from the *nadwaat*, most contact between organized women and housewives took place derivatively, in passing, as cadres visited members of the family of women in their organization. It is worth noting that whereas organized women's visiting and personal networks were mainly restricted to party comrades,[25] camp women's networks were much more open, freely crossing the boundaries of organizational affiliation.

Some of the points I have been making about class, cultural, and marital status barriers between cadres and camp women are illuminated in an incident recounted some time after the withdrawal of the Resistance Movement, but which had occurred before. The woman who tells the story is a strong, highly politicized housewife, mother of nine children and wife of a low-level cadre in one of the leftist organizations. Although not a member of her husband's group, Um Khaled carried on a wide range of activities in its support, and was considered a *sadiqa* (friend):[26]

A woman cadre from her husband's organization (unmarried, from outside the camp, high in the party hierarchy) came to tell Um Khaled that they needed to use her home for a film showing. This had happened often before, but on this occasion Um Khaled objected, saying that she had just taken on new responsibilities and that it was the turn of other cadres' wives to offer hospitality.

The woman cadre went to Abu Khaled to ask him to use his authority over his wife. Abu Khaled replied that his wife was free to take her own decisions about the use of her home.

Um Khaled came home on the afternoon scheduled for the film showing to find that the woman cadre had already installed the screen and chairs in her sitting room. She was very angry, but could do nothing.

In this incident, we note that both class and party rank combine to empower a leftist woman cadre to appropriate a camp housewife's domain against her will, and invoke her husband's authority in doing so. Further analysis would lead to other questions, for example, around the way that women cadres took for granted the extra domestic burden placed on camp cadres' wives by the frequent use of homes for political purposes. During meetings in camp homes, women cadres would be served by housewives as if they were men, and extra housework would be taken up by female household members.

This incident further points to problems raised by the introduction into the camps of organizational hierarchies of rank and pay, and the clash between older forms of political mobilization, in which unpaid activists used existing social relations, and the modern form relying on salaried cadres. Where women are concerned, the Resistance Movement introduced a new status distinction, between the *mutafarragheen* (full-time salaried cadres) and the *mutabara'at* (volunteers). Sometimes this distinction was the cause of bitterness, and a decline in the readiness of volunteers to be mobilized. In the case of Um Khaled recounted above, it is possible that her refusal to lend her home for a party film showing was a political protest against the cadre concerned, and against perceived unfairness within her husband's organization.

The sudden end to resistance autonomy in Lebanon makes it difficult to predict how work among the mass of women would have developed given more time. I have raised problems that organized women were aware of, and it is probable that the self-critical trend developing in the last years of the Lebanon period (evidence can be found in the women's symposium of March 1982, referred to earlier) would have led to more effective, more coherent work based on a deeper understanding of camp women's "reality." Discussions were taking place on the conditions of working women, reform of family law, change of gender relations within the Movement, and the need for better primary health care. The fact that certain social institutions, aligned with the Resistance Movement but independent of party control, had succeeded in setting up solid projects in the field of kindergartens, vocational training, and embroidery production, meant that models of effective mass work existed, and could be built on. These institutions insisted on the importance for women in camps of acquiring skills, and gave them scope to rise to positions of responsibility, instead of remaining unskilled employees as in most of the PLO institutions. The neglect of housewives would have been remedied by the development of *nadwaat*, neighborhood committees, the national campaign to eradicate illiteracy, and the multiple initiatives generated by the mood of *istinhad* (arousal) that the Resistance Movement gave rise to.

Camp Women and Politics

When I started working in Shatila after the war of 1982, women were coping with disaster on a scale not easily described or imagined.[27] Traumatized by the massacre, mourning the loss of family, they were rebuilding homes; searching for indemnities; and facing a campaign of arrests and intimidation. All Resistance offices and most PLO institutions had closed down, the fighters and high-level cadres had left, and a high proportion of the male population was absent: killed, missing, deported, or in prison. Physical conditions added to the difficulty of daily life: rubble blocked the streets, garbage was not collected, water and electricity supplies were cut off.

Yet at a time when household concerns could well have crushed them, women from Shatila marched to commemorate the *arba'in* (fortieth day after death, a time of renewed mourning) of the massacre victims, a politically charged act carried out under the hostile watch of the Lebanese Army. They followed this up with other protest marches. If a youth was arrested, his mother would go straight to the District Army Commander to demand his release. Women crossed over into the dangerous Eastern sector to take food and clothing to men in prison, or try to find a Phalangist *waasta* (intermediary). This capacity of unorganized women to cope with unusual hardships, and their readiness to demonstrate their Palestinian identity, challenges perceptions of them as passive and restricted to a simplistically defined domestic role. If the domestic domain is completely separated from the world of politics, how is it that housewives can undertake political actions without direction? This is not a case of housewives being used by politicians as a "special brigade," but rather of spontaneous political action legitimated by cultural tradition and generations of practice.

Spontaneous political actions like these, undertaken after the withdrawal of the resistance movement, could be seen as the result of thirteen years of mobilization. Yet this cannot be the only explanatory factor, as is suggested by the accounts people give of women's participation in the strikes and battles of 1968–69, before the Resistance moved to Beirut. It is only when one listens to women's stories told in informal settings, among friends and neighbors, that one realizes that they have their own history of struggle, orally transmitted, class- and gender-specific. Most camp women know little of the "official" history of the national movement,[28] and their stories are highly localized; but precisely because they are not learned, but reproduced in daily life settings, with continual accumulation of new illustrations, they prepare women to act politically.

Women of any age in camp milieus also show high levels of political awareness, whether concerning national or community level politics. A number of factors can be pointed to as forming a basis for such awareness, which coexists with, rather than challenges, the ideology of women's domestication. Continual crisis in the Lebanese arena may give women's daily interactions there a special political charge, but the state of the *qadiya* (Palestinian cause) is an inescapable topic for women as for men. Changes brought into patterns of women's domestic and social labor by the camp habitat and migration have strengthened women's role as communicators and commentators. Whereas men usually spend the day in one work setting, women move continually around the camp, shopping, visiting, exchanging news; women hear what is going on from a wide variety of sources (children, casual contacts in the market or on the street, neighbors and friends), while men's sources tend to be more restricted and more "official" (radio, newspapers, their party "line"). Women's awareness also seems sharpened by their interstitial position, linking but not fully part of dominant structures of clan, village, and political party. This position linking socially and culturally dominant structures has laid a basis for a gender-specific type of political awareness (that of observers and commentators rather than actors) and for gender-specific types of political action (e.g., communicating between factions).

Recurrent and violent crisis has prevented women's stories of struggle from becoming "fossilized," and the listener is struck by the continuity between past and present actions. A schoolgirl defying a Lebanese Army command to lower the Palestinian flag during a Day of the Land march in Burj al-Barajneh in 1983 replicates schoolgirls demonstrating against the British Occupation in Haifa in 1947. A young woman throwing herself against a Lebanese Army tank in Sabra in May 1985 replicates the action of Juliette Zakka, killed in street fighting in Akka in 1947. As a preliminary way of examining such actions, let us group them into three broad categories: (1) those undertaken during battles; (2) those carried out within the scope of political struggle; and (3) those embedded in daily life for which Palestinians use the term *summud* (steadfastness).

(1) Palestinian women's participation in warfare is historically well established, and was particularly developed among the peasant class because of frequent feuds between villages and clans. We know that in the Great Revolt of 1937–39, peasant women in Galilee transported arms and food to the fighters in the hills, and carried explosives hidden in milk pans or vegetable baskets to the cities. Proletarian women in Haifa (probably recent migrants) kept watch at night on the sea front for landings of illegal Jewish migrants.[29] Hiding wounded fighters, and helping them to escape, was another type of action of which many examples are given, both in the Great Revolt and again after the Israeli invasion of Lebanon in 1982. Women took part in the battles with the Lebanese Army through which the camps were liberated in 1969; in

the battles in Jordan in 1970; in the siege of Tell al-Zaatar in 1975–76; and again in the Battle of the Camps in May/June 1985. During this episode, one woman smuggled ammunition into one of the camps by strapping it around her body. Such types of military action have been sustained by the kind of struggle in which the Palestinian people is engaged, in which violence is targeted directly against homes. It is said that few women fighters remained in the camps during the massive Israeli bombardments of 1982, because their presence was felt by the fighters to be a liability; yet some women worked as scouts along the confrontation lines.

(2) Women's participation in demonstrations against British occupation and Zionist immigration began even before the formation of the Arab Women's Association in 1929, the main framework for women's national political action. In the General Strike that preceded the Great Revolt, urban women took a very active part in demonstrations, collecting funds, and organizing boycotts. In Lebanon after 1948, a minority of women in camps were involved in secret political organization; spontaneous action outside the scope of parties was also undertaken, as in the case of Shatila women who threw stones at gendarmes trying to evict "squatters" in the early 1960s. Such stories were recalled during Lebanese Army oppression in the Beirut camps between September 1982 and February 1984. During this period of daily arrests, kidnappings, and attempts to prevent the reconstruction of homes, stories circulated of how women cursed soldiers breaking down freshly built walls, and of how women accosted by patrols gave insult for insult. In this context, women recalled Um 'Ali Nasariyya, a Shatila woman who had often been punished in the 1960s by the Deuxième Bureau for her nationalist activities. In March 1986, women from Shatila conducted a day-long sit-in at UNRWA headquarters to protest against the unfair distribution of house-damage indemnities. Another form of protest can be seen in the refusal by young Palestinian women passing through Amal checkpoints to hide symbols of their identity.

(3) Women's participation in the form of resistance known as *summud* grows out of their culturally and historically formed role in the reproduction of the community. *Summud* bears on women in specific ways: they are more constrained than men in terms of confinement to the community, and less able to marry out, or migrate. Certain costs of struggle affect them in gender-specific ways: women who lose a spouse are unlikely to remarry; expectation of widowhood is high, and means bringing up one's children in poverty; loss of children is socially more painful for mothers than for fathers; destruction of the home and displacement places a particular strain on housewives. Domestic labor is aggravated by war and poverty, but the division of labor in the household has hardly changed. Women have responded to this situation by claiming their family labor as a form of struggle, mobilizing themselves to endure whatever hardships their Palestinian destiny entails. Given the imbal-

ance of force between Palestinians and Israelis, it can be argued that *summud* is politically more important than armed struggle, and therefore that women's role in the national struggle is not "limited" but central.

There is another type of political action mainly undertaken by women, though sometimes old men and children also take part: moving to prevent internal conflict. Because women do not want to expose internal conflicts to outsiders, it is hard to elicit information on how their preventive action is initiated, by whom, and in what contexts. But such action took place in the Bekaa in 1983, at the time of the Fateh mutiny, when women were reported in the Lebanese press to have interposed themselves physically between the two Palestinian sides to prevent a confrontation. Women took similar action in Shatila on at least three occasions during 1985–86, when tension between Fateh dissidents and Fateh loyalists threatened to get out of hand. It is said that on these occasions women threatened to have the resistance offices closed down; if true, such a threat suggests that women's acceptance is a condition of legitimation of armed groups in the camp. A story from before 1976 lends support to this interpretation: a delegation of women is reported to have gone to Arafat after a spate of "honor" killings in Tell al-Zaatar, to tell him that if he did not stop such crimes, they would call for a reinstatement of Lebanese law and authority.

There has been discussion of the way women's entry into the resistance groups increases their consciousness of women's issues. Yet, at the same time, politicization may act in the opposite direction, by reimposing the priority of national struggle, by dissociating women's political activities from change in the sex/gender system, and by encouraging the rejection of western feminism, viewed as focused on sexual liberation and inappropriate for Arab women. Women cadres tend to impose on themselves stricter standards of behavior than non-political women: gossip and ridicule can be as sharp inside the Resistance as in society at large.[30] The final point I wish to make is that by restricting attention to organized women, and the somewhat contradictory effects for their position in the sex/gender system of their organizational membership, we tend to ignore the less articulated struggles of non-political women to modify the system. We should at least take note of two of these that are important to women in camps: (1) the struggle of widows to avoid remarrying so as to stay with their children and bring them up; (2) the struggle of young women against early, constrained marriage, and to continue their education. Further, the subordination of young married women to their mothers-in-law has been greatly diminished, partly through young women's insistence on separate households, but also through older women's self-restraint. This trend appears general in the Arab region but is most accentuated where high rates of urbanization and emigration place physical distance between parental and filial households. In the case of Diaspora Palestinians, we find contrary trends, on the one hand toward reaffirming family bonds, on the other toward reducing the authoritarian element in gender and age relations. Women now often insist during marriage negotiations on the right to continue work or political activities after marriage, and though such conditions cannot be written into contracts, and may even arouse disapproval, the fact that "conscious" men (often party comrades) increasingly accept such terms has increased variation within the sex/gender system, and weakened its force as a conformist model. Although pro-natalist pressures on women remain strong, they are not undisputed, and women can often be heard declaring their decision to limit family size. All these may seem small advances if we compare them with a utopian ideal of complete liberation, but camp women value them. Though partly the result of broader social change, they are also the fruit of women's daily contestation with kin and community, a struggle without manifestos, unnoticed.

It would be false to idealize Palestinian women's mass political activism, or imagine that it guarantees them equality and liberation in an eventual Palestinian society. To bring pressure on a state or national movement leadership, an organized women's movement is indispensable. Further, we must recognize the limits of the type of unorganized activism I have been describing. Sex/ gender systems appear to be a basic element in cultural identity, and thus unlikely to change radically in a prolonged struggle against ethnocide. Certain kinds of action are culturally legitimate for Palestinian women: for instance, when men are absent, or unable to act, women may replace them. Women have the right of access to powerful figures to invoke protection for their menfolk. Crisis or exceptional circumstances also legitimate women's political actions. Nonetheless, for the sake of future struggle, organized women might well revise their understanding of political action as exclusively undertaken within formal structures (unions, committees, Resistance organizations), and recognize the scope and readiness for many political activities of ordinary women within their own milieus, networks, and routines.

NOTES

1. D. Kandiyoti, "Emancipated but Unliberated? Reflections on the Turkish Case," paper presented at the MESA annual conference, 1984.
2. S. Joseph, "Women and Politics in the Middle East," *MERIP*, vol. 16, no. 1, Jan.-Feb. 1986.
3. H. Carby, "White Woman Listen! Black Feminism and the Boundaries of Sisterhood," in Center for Contemporary Studies, ed., *The Empire Strikes Back* (London: 1982).
4. Mai Sayigh, interview.
5. Leila Khaled, *My People Shall Live* (London: Hodder and Stoughton, 1973).
6. The writer and militant Ghassan Kanafani used to tell a story reflecting PFLP ideas concerning women and armed struggle: A woman *fedai* was walking on a road in Jordan when two men passing by commented that today's women have no honor.

The woman forced the men at gun point to crouch in a ditch, taunting them: "Now who has honor? You or I?"

7. See K. Abu Ali, *Muqaddamat hawl al-Waq'a al-Mar'a wa Tajribatuha fil-Thawra al-Filastiniyya* (Beirut: General Union of Palestinian Women, 1975).

8. Abu Ali, op. cit.

9. The GUPW is said to have received smaller allocations than the other unions, possibly a leftover from the habit formed by women in Palestine of fundraising for the national movement.

10. Information from a former member of both the Lebanese branch and the Executive Committee.

11. The much respected chairwoman, 'Issam Abdul Hadi, an Independent, remained from the earlier Executive Committee.

12. Leila Khaled, among others, came from the Movement of Arab Nationalists, and Mai Sayigh from the Ba'th.

13. Among them the Red Crescent Society, the Institute of Social Affairs, Samed, the Film Institute, the Chairman's Office.

14. Begun by a group of women in the GUPW, this study is a rare example of critical self-evaluation undertaken from within the Resistance Movement.

15. N.N., interview, March 1986.

16. *Al-Hurriyya*, March 8, 1982.

17. A.M., interview, April 1984.

18. M. Mogannam's *The Arab Woman and the Palestine Problem* (London: Herbert Joseph, 1937) is itself an example, and gives an account of information work carried out by the Palestine Arab Women's Association in Palestine.

19. See R. Sayigh and J. Peteet, "Between Two Fires: Palestinian Women in Lebanon" in Rosemary Ridd and Helen Callaway, eds. *Women and Political Conflict: Portraits of Struggle in Times of Crisis* (New York: New York University Press, 1987). (The chapter is in two sections, one pre-1982, one post-1982).

20. Peteet, op. cit.

21. Jihan Helou, interview, May 27, 1982.

22. Interview with Jihan Helou, *PFLP Bulletin*, no. 61, April 1982, p. 33.

23. Peteet, op. cit.

24. Peteet, op. cit.

25. Strong informal pressures prevented socializing and marriage across organizational boundaries.

26. Um Khaled is presented as a *mar'a nashita* (active housewife) by Peteet, op. cit.

27. See J. Bryce, *The Cries of Children* (Beirut: UNICEF, 1986); and Sayigh, op. cit.

28. Cf. T. Swedenburg, "Problems in Oral History; the 1936 Revolt in Palestine," *Birzeit Research Review*, no. 2 (Winter 1985/86): "in the absence of hegemonic state institutions, ideas about the nature of Palestinian history have neither been highly elaborated, nor have existing ideas generated by political leaders and the intelligentsia penetrated very deeply into the popular classes."

29. Interview with Rukeyya Huri, founding member of the Haifa Branch of the Arab Women's Association and leading member of the Palestinian Arab Women's Union.

30. See J. Peteet, "Women and National Politics: The Palestinian Case," in B. Berberoglu, ed., *Class, Power and Stability in the Middle East* (London: Zed Books, 1989).

IV

Gender Roles and Relations

X

THE ARAB FAMILY IN HISTORY
"OTHERNESS" AND THE
STUDY OF THE FAMILY

Judith E. Tucker

Despite the widely prevailing assumption that the family played an important part in the structuring of economic, political, and social relations in the Arab World, little historical study of the family has actually been done. The centrality of "family" to the history of the region is amply attested in studies of elite politics, for instance, where family ties and family alliances underlie both the solidarity and factionalism of the ruling group.[1] On other levels as well, the view of the family as a primary economic and social unit can be found in most of the historical literature on the peasantry or urban poor.[2] It thus remains all the more surprising that, upon closer examination, we find the almost total absence of any systematic study of family history in the Middle East, whether by region or historical period.

The neglect of family as the object of serious research can be traced to two rather different sets of perceptions, one belonging to the field of history of the family and one to the field of women's history. First, study of the family has been impeded by the untested assumption that the Arab family, whether in Egypt or Palestine, Algeria or Saudi Arabia, is one monolithic institution, variously termed the "oriental" family, the "Arab" family, or the "Islamic" family. This family is generally described as the mirror opposite of its Western European counterpart: it has remained basically unchanged, undergoing neither the signal historical transformations of family structure that paved the way for capitalism in Europe nor the process of "modernization" that promoted individualism at the expense of family control. Historical analyses of the European family now differ enormously on the very basic issues of the nature and timing of change in the family; most discussions of family in the Arab World, however, concur that it was (and is) an institution with a structure and function different from that of Western Europe and seemingly impervious to change until the very recent past.[3] This "otherness" of the Arab family, the notion that this family can be defined in historical opposition to the European family, still permeates most discussions of family life.

In the field of women's history, a palpable reluctance to focus on the history of women within the family springs from a very different set of considerations. With historical research on women in the Middle East still in its beginning stages, women's historians have directed their attention to correction of the pervasive neglect of women. Standard histories of the Middle East assigned women to the world of the household, thought to be far from the spheres of economic production or political and social power that mattered in society. Understandably, most women's historians therefore are engaged in research which will establish the historical roles of women as important economic producers and political actors.[4] The family, on the other hand, is likely to be perceived as the instrument of women's oppression, the mediator of values and customs that circumscribe women's activities and perpetuate an unequal distribution of power between genders. Study of the family reduces the woman to victim and obscures the multiplicity of ways in which she did participate in her society. While such a vision of the family holds more than an element of truth, it sidesteps the importance of the family to the history of the region in general and to women in particular. Women did live and act in familial contexts and, while we increasingly realize that they also enjoyed a multitude of activities and ties outside the family, there is little reason to doubt that family relations remained central to their lives.

In order to explore the critical role of family, we need to reclaim the history of the family, to study it in ways that intersect with the concerns of women's history.[5] The family in the Middle East was not an ahistoric institution expressing elaborate kin relations against which we can measure and highlight the dynamism of the European family. Rather, it was a unit of economic, social, and political relations situated within a particular historical context. The attempt to deconstruct this family in order to understand its importance for women must take into account the ways in which the family fit within the prevailing economic system as a unit of production and consumption, within the prevailing social system as an instrument of socialization and control, and within the political system as a means of recruiting support and forging alliances. Similarly, the woman's role within the family was not necessarily just that of victim. Women's perceptions and actions also shaped relations within the family and could affect how power was distributed and exercised.

The Arab Family as "Other"

In a preliminary attempt to raise questions about Arab family history, we focus here on four aspects of the "otherness" of the Arab family as it has been described that hold special significance for women's roles and power. First, the relationship between husband and wife is defined initially by the absence of consensual union. Marriage, in this "other" family of the literature, is not entered into by freely consenting adults who have developed affection for each other; rather, marriages are arranged to suit the interests or needs of the couple's respective families and the young people, particularly the young woman, may be forced to marry their families' choice of mate. Goody points out that consensual union was not always the practice even in Europe, for upper-class families with significant property at stake were careful to arrange proper marriages. Still the Catholic church early on viewed consensual union as a requirement of marriage and it was widely practiced among people outside of upper-class circles. While the high rates of divorce in "Islamic" society introduce a measure of doubt as to whether the absence of consent was always the rule among the Arabs, because of the freedom associated with the termination of one marriage and the selection of a new partner, Goody's discussion still implies that "Islamic" marriages were not based on free choice.[6] Thus, from its inception, the Arab marriage was a family affair in which the wills and emotions of the bride and groom had little place. Bonds of affection which tend to equalize conjugal relations were thus absent, and a young woman entered a marriage without any claim to her husband's affections.

Second, in the Arab family women bear the burden of family honor (*'ird*). Any female behavior explicitly or implicitly connected with sexual relations outside legal marriage reflected immediately and negatively on the good name of the woman's family. Although a woman's sexual conduct throughout her life was subject to close social scrutiny, premarital virginity had the greatest weight and any suggestion of loss of virginity before marriage the greatest shame. Fathers and brothers, whose responsibilities included the policing of their women and also their punishment if necessary, were therefore quite likely to favor severe restriction of unmarried female relatives, including their seclusion and early marriage.[7] One of the easiest ways to safeguard a girl's virginity was to marry her off at a young age, even before she had attained her legal majority at puberty. Again, the implications for female power loom large: a girlhood of seclusion and very early marriage thrust an inexperienced and hardly grown girl into a new setting where the possibilities of self-assertion appeared quite remote.

A third critical feature of the "other" Arab family was the importance of the patrilineal clan, a lineage structure that defined family relations in terms of several generations of descendants of a given male line. Economic and political relations were influenced, if not actually structured, by the patrilineal clan; as a result, the integrity and solidarity of the clan lay at the heart of both the economic prosperity and political power of its members. Whether this clan is described as a three-generation extended family or a group of families that could trace their origins up to ten generations to a common ancestor, endogamous marriage was one of the most important ways of maintaining economic integrity and achieving solidarity.[8] The prevalent form of endogamous marriage was cousin marriage, specifically that of the children of two brothers which would bind together the patrilineal unit. Here the implications for female power are somewhat mixed. On the one hand, marriage within a family, insofar as it allowed a young woman to remain within a familiar setting and close to her own parents, undoubtedly lent her greater leverage in her relations with her husband and his parents who were, after all, her own cousin, aunt, and uncle. Widespread cousin marriage, however, also may have heightened family control and narrowed marriage choices: certainly most cousin marriages were arranged with the interests of the wider family, not the young couple, in mind.

Finally, in the "other" family model, the woman is placed in a basically powerless position within the family. Although Islamic law reserves full property rights to women, married women exercised these rights only with difficulty because they lacked access to the public sphere. Often disinherited by their natal families in the interest of not dividing family property, women were then at the mercy of their husbands' management of whatever property they had acquired through inheritance or their *mahr*.[9] Perhaps the ultimate measure of such powerlessness was the practice of polygyny. With the legal right to marry up to four women concurrently, a husband could add wives to the household who could compete for material resources as well as affection, without the prior agreement or even knowledge of his present wife.[10] The practice, or even threat, of polygyny could be used as a form of social control, as an ever present threat to the position of a woman inside her own house and therefore as a means of enforcing submission.

The Arab family thus emerges as an extended family of patrilineal descent that preserved its integrity at least partly through the arranged marriage of very young women, often to their cousins. Within the family, male dominance was ensured by the practice of secluding the women, thereby effectively preventing them from exercising their property rights. Female submission and obedience was further enforced by the actual or potential practice of polygyny.

But was this family the reality or even the ideal for the majority of people in the region? The construction of the model itself presents problems, for it borrows heavily from prescriptive literature on the one hand and a small number of specialized empirical studies on the other. Are the discussions of polygyny and early marriage references to certain allowances under Islamic law rather than descriptions of actual past practice? Was forced marriage or cousin marriage really as widespread as the handful of available sources suggests?[11] The historical reality of the Arab family might, indeed, be far different from what this model implies: rather than one monolithic oriental family, Arab history may well present us with a number of different families, no one of which was the prototypical Arab family. In the context of eighteenth and nineteenth-century Egypt and Palestine, we can discuss at least two distinct "families," the family of the upper class, and the family of the urban lower class. Based on rather preliminary evidence, we would like to suggest that each type of family inhabited a different economic, social, and political environment, and evolved a different set of internal gender relations as a result, with distinct consequences for women.

The Upper-Class Family

Family life and gender relations in upper-class circles of eighteenth- and nineteenth-century Palestine and Egypt probably came closest to the Arab family as "other" model. In the realm of wealth and political power, upper-class concern for the integrity of property and the solidification of influence fostered a distinct vision of family life, a vision that tended to buttress the disparities of power between genders so clearly apparent in the "other" family model. In both the cosmopolitan milieu of the urban-based Egyptian upper-class, composed of government officials, wealthy merchants, and well-connected *'ulama* and among the rather more isolated elite circles of the Nablus region in Palestine, large landholders with strong rural ties who often held official positions, family ties were formed and defined in ways that emphasized the overweening importance of family solidarity and continuity to the social order. Marriage practices and the kinds of roles assigned to women within the upper-class family formed an important element of this family definition.

First, consensual union was not a current practice. Upper-class marriages were carefully arranged by the families involved to ensure that their economic and political objectives were achieved. One strong indication of scant attention to the wishes of the bride is marriage age: a girl who was married off before puberty certainly had small opportunity to exercise any kind of choice in the matter. Indeed, under Islamic law, a legally minor girl, that is, one who is prepubescent, enjoys no right of refusal of a marriage arranged by her guardian (*wali*), generally her father.[12] The Nablus area elite took full advantage of this law in the arrangement of its daughters' marriages. In the 107 marriage contracts that were recorded in the surviving registers of the *mahkama* (court) of Nablus in the eighteenth and early nineteenth centuries, only nineteen or roughly twenty percent of these marriages involved minor brides. Of these nineteen marriages, however, five were clearly lower class and four united members of the "middle" class of prosperous artisans, merchants, and *'ulama*; the remaining eight involved daughters of the ruling elite, who were thus far more likely to be married off while still below the age of reason or refusal.[13]

Once married, the upper-class woman tended to remain married to the same husband. In a society and under a legal system that recognized divorce and encouraged remarriage, the permanence of upper-class marriage is striking. In the Nablus marriage contracts, almost a quarter of the brides were marrying for at least a second time: twenty-three women were identified as *thayyib* (deflowered), meaning widowed or divorced. Of these twenty-three, however, only two were conceivably members of the upper class, while a full sixteen were clearly of lower-class origins. Such stability in upper-class marriage underscores the centrality of the institution to social and economic life in elite circles: when political alliance and property arrangements lay at the heart of a marriage arrangement, divorce could not be an option. The upper-class woman as well as the upper-class man had little freedom to change marriage partners.

Such severe limitations on consensual union were also linked to the upper-class practice of female seclusion. The *harim*, or separate women's quarters where wives, daughters, and female slaves and servants of the household were sequestered, was an upper-class institution. In Cairo, the daughters and wives of the official elite passed their lives in the confines of the household *harim*, or in visits to the *harims* of others. An array of services were brought to the *harim* by women of less lofty origins: special female peddlers (*dallalat*) and female musicians (*'awalim*) entered the harim, bringing their goods for sale and their talents for amusement.[14] Upper-class women themselves, however active an interest they might take in affairs outside the household, were physically restricted. Although wealthy Cairene women invested money in business ventures, founded *waqfs*, and bought and sold all kinds of property, they, unlike women of more humble background, never went to court for these transactions: the public aspects of their operations had to be entrusted to an agent (*wakil*).[15] Such isolation from all men, except close relatives they were forbidden to marry, certainly ensured that neither girls nor women would develop any inconvenient attachments that might disrupt family plans for marriage or disturb established marital bonds.

Thus, the idea and the practice of consensual union were indeed very distant from upper-class experience. Women were married early, sometimes before puberty, to mates of their family's choosing, and, despite the rather broad rights to divorce enjoyed by men, their marriages were seldom terminated before the death of one of the spouses.[16] The isolation of these women, away from almost any form of social intercourse with unrelated men, provided a critical key to the system: seclusion greatly reduced the opportunities for the development of desires contrary to family plans.

The practice of seclusion was also related to the second critical aspect of the Arab family, the view of women as the repository of family honor. Low marriage age and the many restrictions on the public movement of the upper-class woman served to safeguard family honor by ensuring that girls and women would have no opportunity, whether real or imagined, of transgressing rather strict sexual mores. The honorific titles commonly used for upper-class women were particularly revealing of the concern for sexual virtue, defined, in the case of a woman not previously married, in terms of guaranteed virginity. The daughter of Salih Basha, an Ottoman provincial governor of the early eighteenth century, is described in her marriage contract as "the pride of the guarded women (*mukhadarat*), the ornament of the venerable, the exalted veil, the inviolable temple."[17] Thick images of seclusion, of protection, of impregnability denote the value of the bride, a value directly correlated to her distance from the world of temptation and sexuality. Curiously enough, however, the attribute of virginity was far from being the most important determinant of a bride's worth. In the case of previously married brides of the upper class, the *mahr* specified in the marriage contract was not necessarily lowered by the prior "deflowering" of the bride. Two non-virgin brides of good family received *mahrs* of very ample proportions according to the contracts registered in Nablus.[18] While the virgin bride deserved the praise, representing as she did the ideal of absence of sexual experience, other considerations entered into the practical assessment of a bride's value including, we may assume, family connections and property ownership.

Third, the upper-class family, at least in Nablus, did indeed practice the cousin marriage of the "other" Arab family model. While not unknown in the lower class, cousin marriage, and specifically marriage between brothers' children, seems most common among the upper class in the Nablus district. Of the seventeen cases of cousin marriage in the 107 registered marriage contracts, eight of them involved upper-class families: roughly 25 percent of upper-class marriages were among cousins as opposed to 16 percent among the whole population. Cousin marriage occurred in the local families of greatest prominence: the Tuqans and the al-Hanbalis, two of Nablus's leading families, married among themselves in the eighteenth century as did the Abi Ghazalis in the nineteenth century.[19] Such marriage was highly valued, and the cousin brides received *mahrs* that were among the highest of the time. Sadiqah, the daughter of Hasan al-Hanbali, who married her cousin Najm, commanded a *mahr* which included a hundred gold sequins, a qaftan with special pinafore and belt, a rug, twenty white robes, twenty blue robes, twenty *ratls* of cotton, twenty *ratls* of wool, and a female slave for domestic service. Only in the relatively rare instance of an exchange, that is, of the simultaneous marriage of a daughter and a son of one brother to the son and daughter of another, was the *mahr* appreciably lower. In one such case of exchange, the *mahrs* were set at fairly low and equal amounts, reflecting the fact that the *mahr* was actually a token payment, each bride receiving immediately the amount her family had given to the other.[20] In general, however, cousin marriage, which served to knit families together and cement the social and economic ties central to the building of a strong extended family and therefore political power, was both practiced and highly regarded in upper-class circles in Nablus. There is less evidence for widespread cousin marriage among the Cairo elite: women tended to be married to the men of families in close association and alliance rather than to their first cousins, a practice which, of course, also underscored the importance of family to politics.

The fourth and final aspect of the Arab family model spoke to the powerlessness of women within the family. Subject to the erosion of her right to hold and dispose of property and ever at the mercy of her husband's decision to take another wife or wives, the woman of the Arab family supposedly could not exercise any real power. The lives of women in Cairene upper-class circles, however, suggest some modification of this picture of total subservience. Although secluded far from the world of the public marketplace, upper-class women did, in fact, control property and conduct business affairs of various kinds. Numerous wealthy Egyptian women joined commercial associations in the early nineteenth century where they invested their own money in various commercial ventures, including the lucrative sea trade in spices and the caravan trade in slaves.[21] Upper-class women were clearly acknowledged as competent managers of common forms of property: as holders of *iltizam* (tax-farm) land and as managers of *waqf* (religiously-endowed) property, they were entrusted with a significant proportion of both rural and urban productive property.[22]

On the other hand, polygyny was indeed practiced by upper-class men: the *harims* of the prosperous might contain multiple wives as well as concubines. In a random sample of sixty-two estates left by grown men in Nablus, all of which record surviving legal heirs, only ten listed two wives and only one more than two. It is striking that all of the polygynous men, except for one, were both wealthy and socially prominent: polygyny was not for the poor.[23] A woman might dislike the introduction of another wife or slave mistress, but she had no right of objection under the law. The *mufti* in Cairo, when presented with a case in which a woman and her relatives were applying pressure on her husband to sell his concubine, reminded everyone that the man was exercising a clear legal right and his wife had no grounds for protest.[24] Thus, while an upper-class woman might exercise considerable power within the family through her ability to control her own property, she was also vulnerable to the unwanted intrusion of other women, wives or concubines, whose presence would dilute her position, to say nothing of her material claims. Other wives and their children, as well as the children of concubines, acquired rights to material support and shares in the man's estate, all of which encroached on the resources available to the first wife.

On balance, the upper-class family, while it shared much in common with the "other" Arab family model, was not quite the same thing. Gender relations within the family were surely influenced by the absence of consensual union, by the strongly held view of women as the repository of family honor, by the social, economic, and political importance of the extended family, and by the practice of polygyny. But the upper-class woman was not the quintessential victim of male dominance, stripped of all rights in the service of the family. On the contrary, she remained capable of engaging in a fairly wide range of activities, albeit from within the "protection" of the *harim*. The family did serve to define and enforce one major dimension of her existence, the dimension of seclusion with all that it signified for her relations with men. It was within this same family context, however, that the upper-class woman controlled her own property and its disposal.

The Lower-Class Family

While discussion of the "other" Arab family does help to describe some critical aspects of upper-class family life, the urban lower-class family in the

Palestinian town of Nablus or in Cairo appears to have developed a significantly different lifestyle. Far from the circles of wealth and power, the family held less importance as a wielder of economic power or forger of political alliances. In the households of the modest artisans, small shopkeepers, service workers, and casual laborers, family ties also helped to organize economic and social life, but on a much more modest scale. With a good deal less at stake, some of the rigid controls, particularly over women, that characterized the upper-class family were greatly relaxed.

First, although we have no evidence for consensual union in the sense of a courtship period which might allow for an informed choice of mate, lower-class women in Nablus were more likely to have a say in marriage arrangements for a number of reasons. Fewer lower-class girls were married off in their minority: whereas 26 percent of upper-class marriages involved minor brides, among the lower class the percentage shrank to 15. Thus, a greater number of lower-class brides were in a position to exercise their right of refusal. More importantly, however, a lower-class woman was much more apt to marry more than once in her lifetime. Most of the marriages of non-virgin brides in the Nablus records clearly involved lower-class women: fifteen of twenty-three such contracts named brides whose families were neither part of the official elite nor of the merchant or *'ulama* communities. Indeed, such second- (or third-) time marriages represented almost half of the recorded lower-class marriages. When marrying a second time, the bride was most likely older, and better able to influence marriage arrangements. In addition, the impermanence of lower-class marriage suggests that far less, in the way of property or politics, was riding on marriage alliance in these social circles: the degree of family control over marriage arrangements could be correspondingly weaker.

Second, the lower-class lifestyle could not sustain female seclusion, the lynchpin of the preservation of female honor. The provision of *harim* quarters lay beyond the means of poorer families who could ill afford, in any event, the loss of female labor that strict seclusion entailed. Nablus marriage contracts recognized, indirectly, the lesser weight attached to honor, in the sense of the absence of female sexual experience, among the lower class: the bride is identified as simply "the woman" (*al-mar'ah*) in addition to her given name; there were no honorifics testifying to purity or protection. Similarly, the activities of the lower-class woman of Cairo precluded any strict adherence to an ideal of honor. Cairene women engaged in many professions which took them to the streets of the city: as petty traders or craftswomen, they labored in the public eye while as purveyors of varied services to other women, including those of midwife, bath attendant, weigher, etc., they passed through public space daily. Such women came to the Cairo *mahkama* in person with their business and their complaints; they purchased property, registered debts, and accused others of theft. Indeed, the upper-class female lifestyle was predicated on the mobility of these lower-class women who came and went from the *harims* in their capacity as servants, seamstresses, and peddlers.[25]

Third, lower-class families, at least in Nablus, appear to have practiced less cousin marriage. While a quarter of upper-class marriage contracts in Nablus involved first cousins, the proportion dropped to 12 percent among lower-class families. With less property at issue, we may assume that the families had a correspondingly lower motivation to marry endogamously. In addition, the forms of political alliance based on family ties so important to the upper class had far less relevance in lower-class circles. The politics of patronage integrated the lower classes into the political sphere, but integrated them vertically as the clients and followers of upper-class families. As such, horizontal linkages among the members of the lower class had less political significance and figured little in marriage arrangements.[26] In Cairo, there is much to suggest that lower-class economic and social life as well was based on a variety of popular associations. Men belonged to guilds, neighborhood groups, and religious brotherhoods while women maintained a range of informal social networks.[27] The fact that family ties played a rather minor role, as a result, in much of lower-class urban life helps explain a more casual attitude toward marriage arrangements.

Finally, lower-class women did manage, like their upper-class counterparts, to exercise considerable control over their property and their other affairs. Free of the trammels of the *harim*, lower-class women could assert their rights in person in court and use their control over property to forge a variety of economic relations. In Cairo, we find that men were often in debt to their wives. These debts were not merely formal: the women kept careful account of the loans of petty sums and resorted to the court, when necessary, to enforce repayment. Husbands and wives also bought and sold property together, as did, upon occasion, sisters. These women, then, were active in the employment of their property. In Nablus, on the other hand, lower-class women rarely appeared in court for business purposes: if they were doing business of any kind, they were settling their affairs outside the court. Estate records do demonstrate, however, that Nablus women also loaned money to their husbands: one lower-class man died owing his wife more than the entire, admittedly modest, value of his estate.[28]

Not surprisingly, male relatives at times attempted to defraud a woman of her rightful inheritance from a husband or father, hoping, no doubt, to avoid fragmentation of family property. In such cases, however, women were quick to resort to the court to invoke their rights as legal heirs and to call upon the judge to restore their property.[29] While the property at issue was usually meager—a few household goods, shares in modest houses, small sums of money—lower-class women did defend their property and the position of power it lent them within the family with considerable vigor. Nor did the lower-class woman have much to fear from the practice of polygyny: in these social circles, a second wife was an expensive rarity and there is almost no evidence of multiple wives or concubines among the lower class.

The lower-class family thus emerges as quite distinct. Weaker control of marriage, relaxed notions of honor, less pressure for the maintenance of family ties through marriage, and the absence of seclusion distinguish lower-class family life from that of the more affluent. The implications for gender relations are many. Because marriage practices played a far less important role in the construction of political and economic life, and female honor was not as publicly acclaimed, lower-class women need not have been controlled so strictly: their marriages, while not exactly consensual unions, probably did, at times, spring from the desires of the bride and groom. Once married, a woman of the lower class continued to live, in part, outside the family circle: her roles as worker and guardian of her own property took her into the world of the street, the market, the court—the antithesis of the *harim*. The court records do suggest that lower-class women in Cairo and Nablus did not have identical life styles: Nablus women are far less present, at least as independent craftswomen and traders, in the court; they were, however, well represented in real estate transactions. Overall, the images of female passivity and power-lessness fit rather poorly with the emerging outlines of lower-class family life.

Conclusion

On the basis of the rather fragmentary evidence we have so far, we would argue that the historical Arab family was far from being a monolithic institution. As part of the economic, social, and political landscape, the family evolved in response to variations in its role. On an economic level, the family of the wealthy appeared to function as an extended unit, keen to retain its property and economic influence within the family circle through carefully arranged marriages. Among the lower classes, on the other hand, the family, as an economic unit, was smaller: much economic activity rested on relations between husband and wife. In addition, business transactions and estates involved far less property and families appeared to be more relaxed about marriage arrangements. The family also operated differently as an institution of social control in different environments. Among the upper class, the overweening significance of family honor as vested in female behavior was manifest not only in the rhetoric of public testimonies to female purity, but also in the practice of confinement to the *harim*. Such a conspicuous display of honor was clearly beyond the means of the working poor: their women were very much part of a public work life which precluded all but the most formal adherence to the ideal of female seclusion. Finally, family politics also operated differently in class terms. Whether among the important landed families of the Nablus region or the urban elite of Egypt, marriage acted to buttress family solidarity or to forge needed political alliances. In either case, careful planning and control of marriage lay at the heart of the political system. The lower class, on the other hand, was integrated into the system primarily through material links of patronage or popular associations in which marriage played little role. As such, the lower class could afford to be far more flexible about marriage arrangements and tolerate changes of marriage partner.

The implications of such differences for women, for the ways in which they experienced family control and managed to carve out spheres of power within the family, surely lie at the center of any study of women's history in the region. As we attempt to understand the ways in which family helped structure gender relations, we need to pay close attention to variations in the idea, the structure, and the function of family that occurred across class and, most probably, across time. We have tried to suggest that the family of the upper class may have differed from the family of the lower class, a divergence obscured by reference to a monolithic model. We have certainly not exhausted the possible varieties of family in the region: the families of the peasants or nomadic pastoralists undoubtedly would display yet other differences in idea and organization. Nor have we tackled the critical issue of how families were changing, particularly in the context of the socioeconomic transformations of the eighteenth and nineteenth centuries. Family life, including the position and power of women, was part of a social world that was neither static nor absolute. As we begin to examine how families evolved over time, we will be better able to assess the significance of such historical change for women and understand how women themselves might have influenced family development.

NOTES

1. For a recent and most remarkably detailed study of this kind, see Linda Schatkowski Schilcher, *Families in Politics: Damascene Factions and Estates of the Eighteenth and Nineteenth Centuries*, Stuttgart, Franz Steiner Verlag Wiesbaden GMBH, 1985.

2. See, for example, Gabriel Baer, *Studies in the Social History of Modern Egypt*, Chicago, University of Chicago Press, 1969, pp. 210–11.

3. For a discussion of variant theses in European family history, see D. H. J. Morgan, *Family, Politics, and Social Theory*, London, Routledge and Kegan Paul, 1985, pp. 159–67. For a rather widely accepted vision of the Arab family as static, at least until very recently, see Halim Barakat, "The Arab Family and the Challenge of Social Transformation," in E. W. Fernea, ed., *Women and the Family in the Middle East*, Austin, University of Texas Press, 1985, pp. 31–32.

4. Recent or current research in women's history includes the work of Margot Badran on the Egyptian feminist movement, Margaret Meriwether on women and work in nineteenth-century Aleppo, Afaf Lutfi al-Sayyid Marsot on women's economic activities in eighteenth-century Egypt, Beth Ann Baron on the feminist press in late nineteenth-century Egypt, and Julia Clancy-Smith on female religious leadership in late nineteenth-century Algeria.

5. See Rayna Rapp, Ellen Ross, and Renate Bridenthal, "Examining Family History," in Judith L. Newton, Mary P. Ryan, and Judith R. Walkowitz, eds., *Sex and Class in Women's History*, London, Routledge and Kegan Paul, 1983, pp. 232–58, for a discussion of ways to integrate women's history and family history.

6. Jack Goody, *The Development of the Family and Marriage in Europe*, Cambridge, Cambridge University Press, 1983, pp. 24–26.

7. See William Goode, *World Revolution and Family Patterns*, New York, Free Press of Glencoe, 1963, pp. 89–90, for a standard discussion of the importance of honor to the Arab family.

8. See Goode, *World Revolution*, pp. 93–95; Goody, *Development*, pp. 31–32.

9. Goode, *World Revolution*, p. 139.

10. Goode, *World Revolution*, p. 123. In his discussion of polygyny, Goode notes that it remained the ideal, out of reach for many.

11. Goode himself deplores the absence of reliable studies of family life in the region, Goode, *World Revolution*, p. 87. Although over twenty years have passed since publication of his book, the situation he describes still holds true for historical studies of family in the Arab world.

12. See John L. Esposito, *Women in Muslim Family Law*, Syracuse, Syracuse University Press, 1982, pp. 16–22, for a discussion of the laws governing marriage arrangements.

13. Out of the 107 contracts registered in the incomplete Nablus records between 1721 and 1856 (*sijills* 4–5 and 9–12), 31 were clearly identified as contracts of the upper class, 38 as contracts of the comfortable "middle" class, and 33 as lower class. In addition, there were 2 contracts of freed slave women and 3 peasant contracts. Among the clearly identifiable ruling group who monopolized important official positions under Ottoman rule, 26 percent of recorded contracts named minor brides. We do not know why only some contracts, and surely a minority of the total number of marriages contracted in Nablus, were registered in the court.

14. See André Raymond, *Artisans et commerçants au Caire au dix-huitième siècle*, Damascus, Institut Français de Damas, 1974, vol. 1, p. 275; Edward Lane, *An Account of the Manners and Customs of the Modern Egyptians*, 5th ed., New York, Dover, 1973, p. 355; Edward W. Lane, "Description of Egypt," British Museum 34080, vol. 1, fol. 111; and Antoine Clot-Bey, *Aperçu général sur l'Egypte*, Bruxelles, Meline, Cans, 1840, p. 80, for comments on these professions.

15. See Judith E. Tucker, *Women in Nineteenth-Century Egypt*, Cambridge, Cambridge University Press, 1985, pp. 95–96.

16. Under Islamic law, a man enjoys a blanket right of divorce and need not show cause. See Esposito, *Women*, pp. 30–31.

17. Mahkamat Nablus, *sijill* 4, p. 11, 24 Dhu al-qaʻdah, 1135.

18. Mahkamat Nablus, *sijill* 4, p. 215, Shawwal 1137; *sijill* 11, p. 158, assume Shaʻban 1265.

19. Mahkamat Nablus, *sijill* 4, p. 127, 13 Rabiʻ I, 1137; *sijill* 4, p. 142, Jumada I, 1137; *sijill* 4, p. 297, Jumada I, 1138; *sijill* 11, p. 24, assume Rajab, 1263.

20. Mahkamat Nablus, *sijill* 9, p. 18, assume Jumada I, 1247: two contracts.

21. Mahkamat Bab al-Ali, Cairo, *sijill* 323, no. 628, 1216/1801–02; *sijill* 345, no. 196, 1226–27/1811–12.

22. See Tucker, *Women*, pp. 93–96.

23. Mahkamat Nablus, *sijills* 4, 5, 9–12.

24. Muhammad al-ʻAbbasi al-Mahdi, *al-Fatawa al-mahdiyah fi al-waqaʻi al-misriyah*, Cairo, al-Matbaʻah al-Azhariyah, 1883–84, vol. 1, 6 Rajab 1266/1850, p. 389.

25. See Tucker, *Women*, pp. 81–83.

26. For a detailed discussion of political alliance in the Nablus region with frequent reference to the mobilization of lower classes in the political system, see Miriam Hoexter, "The Role of the Qays and Yemen Factions in Local Political Divisions," *Asian and African Studies* (Jerusalem) 9 (1973), 249–311.

27. See Tucker, *Women*, pp. 102–15.

28. Mahkamat Nablus, *sijill* 9, p. 149.

29. See Tucker, *Women*, pp. 97–99.

XI

CHANGING GENDER RELATIONS IN A MOROCCAN TOWN

Susan Schaefer Davis

The topic of this chapter is especially well suited for a discussion of old boundaries and new frontiers for women in Arab society. The current state of gender relations between young people in a Moroccan town is itself a dynamic between old boundaries and new frontiers, especially in terms of acceptable behavior for females.[1] More generally, anthropologists have recently become interested in systems of meaning in different societies; an entire issue of one journal was devoted, tellingly, to several scholars exploring "how systems of meaning are currently contested and maintained in Middle Eastern contexts."[2] The focus on changing gender relations illustrates aspects of both contest and maintenance. Moroccan sociologist Fatima Mernissi commented on changing gender relations in urban areas that appeared in data she gathered in the early 1970s:

> In rural Morocco the access of young men to young women is subject to strict and apparently efficient control. In urban centers, access seems to be much less restricted. Young people meet each other frequently enough to fall in love and want to get married. . . . I believe that sexual segregation, one of the main pillars of Islam's social control over sexuality, is breaking down.[3]

The data presented here, gathered in a semi-rural area in the early 1980s, support her general point and illustrate that changing relations are not limited to urban areas. In what follows I will describe the old boundaries in terms of traditional norms and behaviors, and the new frontiers as reflected in changing ideals and behaviors concerning relations between the sexes, especially prior to marriage. The basis for these changes will be seen in several broader areas of the society.

The Research Site

To understand the implications of these data,[4] it is important to know something about the setting in which they were collected. The research site is the semi-rural community of Zawiya, a town of eleven thousand on the edge of a rich agricultural plain in north central Morocco near Meknes; the town is described more fully in my monograph *Patience and Power* (1983a). While earlier generations were raised in villages of fifty to seventy-five households in which subsistence was based mainly on agriculture and herding, many people lost their land during French colonization (1912–56). The economy is now more diverse, with people working in agriculture mainly as day laborers, or in commerce, transport, or trades like construction; a few men work in Europe. Although very few of the parental generation attended school, today virtually all children attend the town's primary school and many go on to secondary school in nearby "Kabar," a market town of about forty-five thousand. Until the early 1980s, all administrative services such as government offices, banks, and police were located in Kabar. This, in addition to the lack of running water and the unpaved streets, gives Zawiya the feel of a village despite its size. In fact, this semi-rural aspect of Zawiya makes it an ideal site to study change in gender relations. It is very different from the atypical westernized upper-class areas in the cities, and also from isolated rural communities which have experienced more limited change. Zawiya's proximity to both a larger community and to roads and railroads linking it to large cities, as well as the easy access to television, expose local youth to change while they are living in a traditional town. This situation is common in Morocco, where small towns are growing rapidly, and is probably found throughout the Middle East.

Traditional Gender Relations in Zawiya

Norms.[5] Especially with regard to female behavior, the norms concerning gender relations both before and after marriage were very restrictive, and in general fit the western stereotype related to the secluded Muslim woman. Marriages were arranged by parents, and the spouses may never have seen each other if they were not relatives, since females past puberty were not to speak to unrelated males. Older girls and women were to veil if they must go out before the public eye, but preferably they were to remain inside their homes, only leaving "to marry and to be buried," as one old woman said. A further restriction on females was that proof of chastity was required as part of the marriage ceremony. The test of virginity was practiced, in which hymeneal blood was displayed to wedding guests. If there was no blood on the marital linens, the marriage contract could be declared void and the bride sent away in sackcloth. All of these prescriptions for females served as a strong deterrent to interacting or forming relationships with unrelated men. In this regard, it should be noted that the term "sexuality" concerns a wider range of behavior in this Moroccan context than it would in the West. In a culture that traditionally has discouraged unrelated males and females from speaking to each other, most cross-sex interaction takes on a sexual tone.

Behavior. In attempting to move beyond traditional norms and discuss behavior, one encounters an obstacle: obtaining valid data on past heterosexual interaction is even more difficult than assessing it for a current group. Two types of data were especially useful. For the first I interviewed a long-time resident about "deviant" behavior in each of the approximately fifty families we worked with intensively in 1982, including accusations of crimes, illegitimate pregnancies, abortions, incidents of drinking (alcohol is forbidden in Islam) and drug use. Because the informant was young, the information only went back about fifteen years. She described eighteen cases of breaking sexual norms for the younger generation and ten in the parental generation. These included cases of young women being found alone with young men (suggesting intimacy), and also of girls becoming pregnant while unmarried.

My second approach was to ask an older woman for case histories of sexual behavior that violated norms in the nearby village where she had grown up. These data went back about forty years and showed that even then the norms were violated. In a village of about fifty households, the informant reported eight cases of illicit sexual activity, three for single women, four for married women, and one for a divorcee. Further, these were publicly known incidents; one expects there were others. This informant also reported the harsh local reaction to such cases: women were sent to jail, were banished from the village, or had their heads shaved. The only fatality was a man shot and killed by an aggrieved husband. An interesting note is that some of these "shamed" women have reformed and are currently materially well-off, accepted members of the community.

Although norms in the past proscribed heterosexual interaction outside the family, the data make it clear that, as is universally true, the norms were not always followed. However, ethnographic observation over the last twenty years suggests that deviation from norms was more limited in the past, and also that there has recently been some change in the norms themselves. For more details, we must examine the current situation.

Gender Relations in Zawiya Today

Norms. During our research in 1982, the restrictive traditional norms were still cited with general approval by most informants in Zawiya. It was shameful for an unrelated boy and girl to be seen talking together, girls should not be outside the household unnecessarily, and parents were still involved in arranging marriages. The display of hymeneal blood to prove virginity was still a part of marriage ceremonies. This quote from a young woman of eighteen shows that she recognizes the weight of these restrictions on her behavior: "A girl only stays home—that's all. It gets a little dark and she can't go out; she's not allowed to go out. She mustn't go to the movies . . . she shouldn't go out at night . . . she shouldn't do anything! As for the boy, it's no problem for him." We found direct evidence suggesting that females find their role limited when we asked Moroccan adolescents to "draw a person." Sixty percent of girls drew a male first, which is often interpreted as meaning the drawer prefers that role.[6]

However, there was also evidence that some of these norms are changing. One area of change is a decrease in the idea that females should not be seen by unrelated males, which can be inferred by changing behaviors. Girls do spend more time outside the home than they did in the past, mainly because a much larger number attend school. Veiling has decreased greatly in the past decade, so that while older adolescent girls always veiled in the past, now none do. This has also affected married women, so that currently only about one-third of them veil in Zawiya, while all did in the 1960s. We interpret these behaviors as reflecting changing social norms, because there was no comment on how certain persons were violating this or that norm by their behavior.

Another indication of changing norms is found in young people's responses to our questions about marriage. When we asked thirty-eight boys and fifty-three girls if they thought their parents, themselves, or both should choose their future spouse, 29 percent of the boys and 26 percent of the girls said they wanted to choose for themselves. This answer was related to their ages and their level of education, so that older adolescents were significantly more likely (at the .05 level) to want to choose for themselves, as were those with a higher level of education (at the .01 level of significance). Choosing one's own spouse necessitates some level of contact between the sexes, and this was indicated in these young people's answers to "What are the characteristics of an ideal spouse?" Although the majority of answers focused on characteristics that could be judged by one's parents—that a woman should be beautiful "in body and in mind," or that a man should have a good job—many responses were different. These noted the need for a good relationship, suggesting a desire to know the spouse before marriage in order to evaluate him/her. Sixteen percent of males and 33 percent of females defined the ideal spouse in terms involving their relationship, such as, "I have to like her—to agree with her," and "He should be good; he should have a good personality, and we should respect each other and be honest with each other, not insulting each other." These responses suggest that the traditional norm rejecting any relationship between unmarried boys and girls is being questioned, at least by some.

Behavior. When we move beyond norms and examine current practices, we find stronger indications of increased heterosexual interaction. This interaction appears to have increased in both the amount and the variety of different activities involving young men and women. We will first examine the different activities of young couples, and then discuss the frequency of interaction.

My taped interviews with young people are a valuable source of information about their own views on this topic. They include discussions of how young women think about developing relationships with boys, or the characteristics of a "platonic" as opposed to a "love" relationship, and of the usual stages in a developing relationship.

When I asked a girl of fourteen with a primary school education, "What's important to you these days? What do you often talk about with your friend, so that I can see what interests you? I want to know what you have on your mind, what preoccupies you most," she replied:

> F. What interests us [on some occasions, people use the "royal we," as here] is to see how girls date so that we learn too. We do want to start dating. However, if we do now, we won't know what to do. For example, they [boys] may say a word to us that we wouldn't know. We're still learning step by step.
> S. So what do you want to learn?
> F. I want to learn to hold a discussion, how to become shrewd.
> S. Who is going to teach you? How do you expect to learn? Do you want to date and learn gradually, or does your friend show you, or other girls who are knowledgeable, or what?
> F. No. She [the friend] watches girls from her own family and from my family and we teach each other. I learn from my relatives in cities; I do learn from them . . . I learned from my sister when she was still a girl. She was shrewd.
> S. Soumia?
> F. Yes. She on the other hand learned from her [older] sister and her sister's friends. To learn well, we teach each other.
> S. Did you discuss things with your sister before she got married or did you ask questions?
> F. No, I was just watching. . . . If I had asked her, it wouldn't have been appropriate. I would have looked bad.
> S. What do you mean you wouldn't look good? Why?
> F. She wouldn't like me. She would say "You are starting to learn at this age?" I have to be older so that becoming shrewd will help me accept what a boy would tell me. At the same time, one's parents won't fear for her. For example, we're too young and our parents worry about us. . . .
> S. Your girlfriend teaches you. Are you going to talk to boys to learn also?
> F. Little by little. You start first with young ones. You don't discuss with older ones. If you are young, you select your age so that you get trained. Once you learn from young boys, then you move to older ones.

Although most young women didn't begin to meet with boys until the age of fifteen or sixteen, this fourteen-year-old indicates that there is considerable attention to forming relationships before then. Her statement that she could not openly ask her sister about interactions with boys is an indication that the norms against interaction are still strong, even if belied by behavior.

Quite early on I learned that there are nuances in relationships between the sexes, so that two Arabic terms for friend (male), *sadiq* and *sahib*, have distinctly different meanings for girls. A *sadiq* is a platonic friend, usually someone you do schoolwork with, though uneducated girls sometimes said they considered a friend of their older brothers who regularly visited their homes as a *sadiq*. If a girl has a *sahib*, on the other hand, he is what we would call a boyfriend. Horriya, a young woman of sixteen in secondary school, described a dilemma she faced when a *sadiq* wanted to become a *sahib*:

> H. One day a boy told me "Come here; I want to talk to you." He's a neighbor of ours who lives up there. . . . Well, I did not suspect anything because I used to go and have him help me with schoolwork. I didn't expect him to tell me anything. So I went to his house. He helped me with my homework and then said to me, "I want to talk to you." I said, "What do you want to tell me?" He replied, "I want to talk to you and I want us to become friends."

She told him she had to think about it, and after talking it over with her best friend she decided not to accept his offer, and wrote him a letter saying so. Her explanation of why she made that decision shows the difference between the two types of friend, and also that to "talk" and to "laugh" with boys have different meanings.

> H. I don't want to be anybody's [girl]friend. I decided, and it is the right thing. I must really not talk to anybody. . . . It wouldn't be nice for me because everybody will know about it. It looks bad. That's why I want him to be like all our other neighbors' kids. We will laugh and all that. I don't want him to tell me that kind of talk. . . .
> S. This is what I don't understand—the difference between talking and laughing.
> H. The other guy [the *sahib*] will carry on, telling you "I like you, I love you, etc.," but with the other guys [*sadiqs*] we only talk about school, and we tell jokes. . . . What I like are talks about studies, jokes. I don't like anybody telling me "I like you" and then taking advantage of me as they usually do of others.

Thus one "laughs" or kids around with a platonic friend or *sadiq* and "talks" more seriously about romantic topics with a boyfriend or *sahib*. Horriya's account also suggests that norms are against the latter relationship when she says she turned her neighbor down partly because "it looks bad"; she wants to maintain a certain image of herself.[7]

A young woman in her twenties comments on "talking" in a way suggesting that while it was disapproved of in the past, the norms are changing.

S. Let's go back to the girl talking to the boy near the well. [You feel] this is the right thing to do, right? Why?

A. Listen, Susan, there is absolutely no girl on earth who would reach the age of twenty or twenty-four—the age of being asked for in marriage—without having felt the need at least to smile, talk and laugh with a boy, or even desire one in her own family. [Cousin marriage is approved.]

S. You are talking about this time now; before it wasn't so?

A. This time, not in the past.

If a girl decides she wants to pursue a relationship with a *sahib* or boyfriend, it will progress along a fairly regular course from casual meetings to an intimate relationship. Besides walking to school, the most likely settings for girls and boys to meet initially are the seven taps where the community of eleven thousand obtain their water. Girls between ten and twenty are the main water carriers, and they gather at the tap waiting their turn, while young men between roughly fourteen and twenty lounge against the walls of the surrounding houses, talking and watching the girls. Carrying all the water for a large family is an exhausting task, and a girl may carry 30 five-liter containers to her house in several relays. The whole process, including waiting, may take three hours a day. Given all this, I expected girls to despise fetching water, but few complained and several were even enthusiastic. Only when I understood the role of the water taps as meeting places was I able to explain this attitude. A boy who finds a particular girl attractive may ask her for a drink of water, toss a joke or compliment her way, or try to talk with her on her way home.

Once a couple has become acquainted in this way, if they decide to see more of each other they will arrange to meet in dark or isolated corners while the girl is running evening errands, buying mint for tea, or fetching the bread for her family. During these meetings they will talk about their feelings for each other and perhaps kiss. This phase may last several months before moving to the next stage.

If the couple desire a more intimate relationship, they arrange to meet outside town in a place where their activities will not be so easily observed. This may be the nearby town of Kabar, where they can walk together and window shop; the girl may suggest that the boy buy her a gift, which she will treasure as a souvenir. They may go to a shop to be photographed together, but both sexes are often wary of this because a photo provides concrete evidence of the relationship that may be used by a jilted lover. They may go to an empty house which the boy has arranged to borrow, or to the fields adjoining Zawiya; there they may engage in heavy petting, but the girl will attempt to preserve her virginity. Being discovered alone together, even just talking, is very shameful because it implies greater intimacy, so girls feel quite anxious when they agree to such meetings.

In fact, some girls do lose their virginity in these more isolated settings, although many couples use interfemoral intercourse or very shallow penetration and withdrawal before ejaculation to preserve the hymen. In the cases of lost virginity that I heard about, it was said that the male was drunk and had lost control of his behavior. It is interesting that no one ever reported a couple "getting carried away," but rather always cited an external cause, drunkenness, for the lack of control.[8]

A final indication of the commonness of heterosexual relationships was in the answers of my clinical informants to the question "How many girls your age have boyfriends?" (Early on I tried asking girls directly if they had a boyfriend, but since all denied it adamantly—again attesting to norms condemning such interactions—I used the more indirect question.) Of six girls between eleven and fifteen, one said no primary school girls (grades one through five, ages seven to fifteen) had boyfriends (but older girls did), while others answered "few" and one "many," often giving examples in their own classes. The change in estimates, which seems congruent with behavioral reality, comes around age sixteen. One sixteen-year-old who was not in school said "few" girls her age had boyfriends, while another who attended school said that although *she* had no boyfriends, "98 to 100 percent of girls do." Of the six girls seventeen and over, one said about 60 percent had boyfriends, and the rest said "all" or "nearly all" had boyfriends.

Thus while norms and practice did not and do not totally coincide, it appears that the proportion of young people involved in heterosexual relationships before marriage today is greater than in the past. It also seems that while couples in the past might have met in the field outside town, today's youth have a wider variety of options available. What are the reasons for the desired, and *de facto*, increase in these relationships? The answers are to be found in the wider society.

Causes and Consequences of Changing Gender Relations

Causes of Change. Several factors are responsible for the increase in heterosexual relationships, all related to the change from village to town life within the span of one or two generations. The majority of parents and grandparents in Zawiya grew up in small, kin-based villages that were much more isolated, by both distance and technology, from the modern world than Zawiya. Zawiya's size and heterogeneity, its integration in a national wage economy which encourages public education, and its effective integration into a nation-state all have the effect of making it more possible for boys and girls to spend time together. While young people most likely had the same desires in the past, getting together was more difficult in a village setting.

The greatest consequence of Zawiya's larger size is the attenuation of social control over heterosexual behavior. The town offers many settings in which the sexes can mix, either without being censured or without being observed. These settings include school, work place, and neighborhoods away from one's household. A girl can use the excuse of running an errand to meet a boy, and because of the large and varied population, she is unlikely to be seen with him by kin or family friends. Girls both went out less and were likely to be recognized and reported in small villages in the past. More adventuresome youths can even meet in larger cities because of Zawiya's access to transportation. Few of these possibilities existed for their parents.

Other reasons for change are at base economic, resulting from the fact that Zawiya is no longer a subsistence-based agricultural village, but rather tied into the national and international economy. This means that girls may now work in salaried jobs outside the household, and in some cases require education for these jobs. Another factor is worldwide inflation and national underemployment, which has led to what I call a "marriage crisis" for some young women. Finally, better transportation networks have been built, largely to move agricultural and mining products but resulting in greater general mobility.

In the past very few girls were educated, either because of lack of schools or of women's jobs requiring education, but this has changed for today's adolescents. Public schooling was not generally available until after independence in 1956, when it became a national priority; Zawiya opened its primary school in the 1960s. We see evidence of this lack of schooling in the parents of the adolescents we worked with: only two of a hundred parents had completed the five years of primary school. Even after schooling became available, parents educated sons more often than daughters for two main reasons. Girls were more helpful than their brothers, and thus were often kept home to do chores. Second, although schooling was free it required the purchase of books and clothing, and many families found even this minimal expense difficult to meet. When resources were limited, sons were educated because they were expected to use their education in white-collar jobs to contribute to the support of the family. Few women held such jobs in the early 1960s (and certainly not earlier, in villages), so parents did not see a similar payoff in educating girls.

By the early 1980s, educated young women were beginning to hold white-collar jobs, and many girls now aspire to them. Thus today virtually all children try to complete primary school. When we asked over a hundred adolescents what they hoped for in the future, about forty percent of boys *and* girls wanted to be teachers;[9] half of the Zawiya teachers are females. The school settings (which are not segregated by sex), especially the secondary schools outside the town, provide an opportunity for boys and girls to meet and talk unobserved by their parents. Uneducated girls also have opportunities to meet boys at work; those who work as agricultural day laborers are in settings away from their home villages (transported in trucks up to sixty kilometers) in groups that include males.

Another economically based factor is the "marriage crisis" for young women who are currently between about twenty-five and thirty-five. In the past, virtually all women in Zawiya were (or had been) married, but this is no longer true. The diversified economy that allows young men to have jobs and earn money independently of their families also ties them into the world economy, including inflation and the recent worldwide recession. This, in addition to local economic conditions, has led to a high rate of unemployment and made it harder for young men to amass a bride price and to maintain a new household. In support of this, anecdotal data indicate that currently young men living on family farms in the nearby countryside marry five to ten years earlier than their town cousins, since they can live and work with their families. When town men finally accumulate the money to marry, it appears they will skip their own generation and marry younger women. If the process were continuous, it would just mean that men married younger women, but this is not the case. This problem began in the early 1970s, and the women who were of marriageable age then were skipped over when their cohort finally married, because of cultural ideals encouraging both young brides (around twenty now) and beauty. A perhaps less conscious reason that men skip their own cohort is because those women have had ample time to develop their own personalities and are probably less malleable to a husband's taste. This marriage crisis causes some young women to fear that they will not marry, and they take action to maximize their chances, including increased interaction with males.

Change in the composition and functioning of the local political unit is an additional influence on changing heterosexual behavior. In the parental generation, people lived in isolated communities that were nominally under outside control, but they virtually ran their own affairs through a popularly selected council of village elders. These elders were also relatives, and their judgments were taken very seriously. In the past, infractions of sexual norms were first dealt with by the girl's parents or the father's male kin. If they did not put a stop to her behavior, the community elders would speak to the family and take action themselves if necessary. Punishments were common and often harsh, as described above. Today's situation is very different. People in Zawiya live within easy reach of a central government. Local officials are mainly people appointed from outside the area, and they are less involved in enforcing norms than in the past. People may still refer behavior that breaches norms to the authorities, but these authorities are less personally interested in the cases, less efficient (there may be long trials) and less harsh in meting out punishment. This means that another deterrent to heterosexual behavior, like the stronger social control of smaller communities, does not function as well today as it did in the past.

Consequences of Changing Gender Relations. What are the effects of this increase in heterosexual interaction? We see consequences in several areas including the physical, the affective, and the normative.

In physical terms, there does not appear to be the epidemic of teenage pregnancies that is found in the United States. This is due to several factors, including the fact that girls attempt to protect their virginity by avoiding full penetration. If a girl should become pregnant, she may resort to a traditional or modern form of abortion, although neither is strictly legal. Another physical consequence can be the loss of virginity, so that a girl would fail to produce hymeneal blood on her wedding night; this might cause severe social problems, like the cancellation of the marriage contract. However, this physical effect is seldom manifested. Beginning at least as early as the time of Harun ar-Rashid in the ninth century, chicken blood was used as a substitute in the bridal chamber, and this and other substitutes are currently in use.

The effect of increased heterosexual interaction on young people's feelings toward each other is rather ironically ambivalent. On the one hand, we have described how an increasing number of young people wish to choose their own spouse, and hope for a relationship of mutual affection and understanding. In this sense, they place higher affectional expectations on marriage than did most of their parents, who saw marriage more in terms of economic cooperation in raising a family. In the past, women's needs for affection were met by children and by other females, not to any large extent by husbands.[10] At this point I do not have data from young couples describing whether and how these expectations are met; this is an important area for further research.

However, I do have data on how young people currently feel about their interactions with the opposite sex before marriage, and these feelings are deeply ambivalent. Both sexes want to get together, and have romantic ideals about potential relationships. Once in a relationship, however, males distrust any girl who would let herself be dishonored by participating, and females fear young men will "love them and leave them," based on the experience of their peers. Hence these relationships operate on a profound "double standard." Further, if people hear about a relationship, a girl's chances for a good marriage might be decreased. These themes came up again and again in different sections of the interviews with clinical informants.

A young man in his twenties with quite a bit of education responded to a question about what love meant to him in a way that combined romantic ideals with the expectation of some problems—over which he expected to triumph.

> To love a girl is to give her, or to advise her, to help her, to take care of her, to show her the wrong things and the right ones. Not let her do the worst things but only the best and to be perfect. To tell her to ignore what people say to her because it's all lies and meant only to destroy her. . . . If that girl for instance is a good person, and she is working when people learn that I am going to marry her, they'll start gossiping about her. They will start telling me how bad she is, that she is not serious, she talks to many boys [i.e. goes out with them] and that I should reconsider and try to find another girl. . . . But the people don't really know what kind of relationship I have with her. I take what they say as lies because they may be just taking revenge for whatever misunder-

standing they may have had with her, or something of that nature. But I do what I like.

In another conversation, he presented a less idealistic view of relations between the sexes. I had asked him how a poor man could get expensive medicine for his dying wife (the Heinz dilemma used by Kohlberg, 1984). He said that it would be very hard for the man to get money, but much easier for a woman, who could use

> sex, for instance. And I know so many women who do that, and not even to buy medicine for their husbands, but only to buy a fancy dress to wear for a party or to buy a *jellaba* [long robe] or to buy new shoes or what have you.

The following edited excerpt from a taped interview gives a feeling for the young women's concerns. I had asked Amina, a single woman with a primary school education, to describe something that happened to her that was not right or was unfair:

> It concerns this matter of marriage. There's a boy—you trust him and he trusts you. He tells you "I care for you. If I don't see you, I'll go crazy; if you're away from me for only half a day, it feels like a year to me." And at that time the boy has feelings. He cares for you. Truly. Powerfully. But he doesn't have any money, and you just keep sacrificing yourself for him, talking to him, laughing with him. And you lose your value—and your family's. Okay, people see you together, but you say "They don't matter to me. Because even if I'm standing with him, he'll marry me, God willing."
> And finally, he doesn't marry you—how do you feel? It feels like a calamity, like a "psychological complex."[11] You feel angry at home, and you're always upset, because you don't trust anyone, even your parents. Since you sacrificed yourself for that boy, *even* in public you talked to him . . . and in the end he marries someone else; how do you imagine you would feel? You will remember your times together and what you went through in the past. You see how things happen. That a boy gives you his word of honor and later doesn't keep it is not right. That is what doesn't allow the girl who's become mature and responsible to trust a boy. She doesn't trust boys—never.

This excerpt reveals the common fear of being exploited by males in a relationship. It appears that males are mainly interested in the immediate sexual relationship, while females focus more on the long-term outcome, which they hope will be marriage. One wonders whether girls might say the goal is marriage because they do not want to admit enjoying sex, yet nearly all do want to marry, and being caught with someone who's "just for fun" may well decrease one's chances. It is interesting that girls in Zawiya do not see increased heterosexual interaction as part of a movement to greater general freedom, but as a means of attaining the traditional goal of marriage.

The different goals of males and females in relationships raises another interesting point. When my husband and I examined our data on heterosexual interaction, we found that most of the female data focus on relationships, while those for males focus more specifically on sexual behavior. This is interesting with regard to Carol Gilligan's recent work on the "different voices" she perceives in research on moral development. Although she says the different voices are "characterized not by gender but by theme," she notes that the association of one voice with women "is an empirical observation" although "this association is not absolute."[12] She identifies an ethic of care and an ethic of justice, the former more often associated with females and the latter with males in her research. "The logic underlying an ethic of care is a psychological logic of relationships, which contrasts with the formal logic of fairness that informs the justice approach."[13] "Instead of attachment [for females], individual achievement rivets the male imagination."[14] The greater concern of Zawiya girls with relationships, while boys are more interested in the specific activity (might it be seen as achievement?), is suggestive of different orientations by gender in Morocco. Recall also that twice as many girls as boys (33 percent vs. 16 percent) said they wanted a good relationship with their future spouse. However, this area requires much more systematic investigation; it will be pursued in future work, including the analysis of a set of "describe yourself" interviews developed in collaboration with Gilligan.

A final effect of increased heterosexual interaction is that Zawiya is beginning to experience some change in norms. As we saw above, heterosexual behavior is still usually viewed negatively, but this is less so than in the past. This is visible in two main areas. First, while all the factors which allow an increase in heterosexual interaction have put some pressure on the traditional restrictive norms, the "marriage crisis" described above is the primary factor, and it has mothers wondering how to maximize their daughters' chances of marriage. Edited excerpts from an interview with a mother of three teenagers highlight these concerns.

> S. Is there another issue that shows this [generation] gap?
> M. There are hundreds of issues. . . . Do you think our parents could mention marriage to us? If the word marriage was uttered in the street [about me], I would throw stones and hit our neighbors [who said it]. . . . Now talk to her [the daughter is sixteen] about marriage, and she won't object; she'll like it. . . . A neighbor girl argued that because girls like herself just stay home, nobody cares about them. . . . [She said] "A great many girls leave here and bring back a man, while we are staying home and nobody is checking us out." . . . She does not go out . . . always staying home, always covering her head. [Other] girls go out, they wear modern clothes . . . so they bring home husbands and we don't bring anything.
>
> Many girls want to get married. . . . [One] told me "If I could find a husband, I'd buy him with money. He wouldn't have to give anything [i.e. bride price]. . . . All he needs to do is to come and propose marriage to me. I'll buy clothes for him, do everything he needs, and go with him."

While this mother is partially disparaging of girls' current interest in marriage, her concern with it is telling. I heard the themes she raised on many occasions: girls who stay at home (the traditional norm) don't get married, while those who go out and are "seen" do. I had in fact noticed this during 1982, and by 1984, mothers and daughters were discussing it. While I know of no specific examples, other people mentioned girls' families offering to pay the bride price to ensure their daughters' marriage. Thus the motivation for girls to marry is very strong, and is encouraging the decline of the norm of female seclusion and isolation from males.

A second indication of changing norms is found in a recent change in marriage ceremonies. In the past, couples were legally married about a year before their families held a large party, at which evidence of virginity was displayed and after which the couple cohabited. Recently, some couples have stopped having the large party, and instead have a smaller family celebration at the time the marriage contract is signed. They note that this is inspired by economy; the large parties are costly and they prefer to spend the money furnishing a home. While this is certainly true, another characteristic of the smaller parties is that there is no test of virginity, then or later. Couples may cohabit immediately, since they are legally married, or they may wait. I suggest that this ceremonial change is a covert recognition that the norm of virginity for brides is declining. Instead of omitting the display of virginity from the usual ceremony (which is sometimes done), this new ceremony avoids a focus of attention on the omission, and is also economical.

I have examined how the Moroccan system of meaning with regard to heterosexual interaction is both contested and maintained. This was done by presenting an intensive view over time of both the norms designed to maintain traditional sex-segregated behavior and the activities that are challenging these norms. The current "marriage crisis" for some young women shows this sequence can also be reversed, providing an example of the pursuit of a traditional goal (marriage) leading to a movement away from traditional norms (little or no contact between the sexes before marriage).

Another motivation for more heterosexual interaction before marriage is the increasing expectation of affectional support from a spouse, whom one should thus know. Yet rather than leading to a supportive relationship, the effect of increased interaction is to give couples more realistic bases for their expectations than the romantic fantasies of secluded adolescents. At this point in Zawiya, increased interaction usually leads to distrust by females and disgust by males, hardly bases for a close relationship after marriage. I agree with Mernissi that the "direct confrontation between men and women brought up in sexually antagonistic traditions is likely to be, in this transitional period, loaded with tensions and fears on both sides."[15]

By the early 1980s, many growing semi-rural towns shared with Zawiya the larger population, greater educational and employment opportunities for females, and less immediate political control than in the past. In these conditions, we would expect heterosexual interactions to be changing in a similar way. One might note that even in a quite different and supposedly less antagonistic tradition, the attempts of many American couples to be "closer" are fraught with tensions.[16] However, in my experience Moroccan women have been very resourceful in dealing with problems, and their various responses to the current situation will be followed with interest. Currently, the young women of Zawiya appear to be learning to maneuver themselves skillfully between the old boundaries and the new frontiers.

NOTES

1. The research on which this paper is based was supported by grants from the National Institute of Mental Health and the William T. Grant Foundation. I would like to thank Professors Beatrice Whiting and Douglas A. Davis for helpful comments on an earlier version of this paper.

2. Dale F. Eickelman, "Introduction: Self and Community in Middle Eastern Societies," *Anthropological Quarterly*, 1985, 58:135–40.

3. Fatima Mernissi, *Beyond the Veil: Male-Female Dynamics in a Modern Muslim Society*, Cambridge, Mass.: Schenkman, 1975, p. 58.

4. These data were collected in 1982 and 1984 by myself and my husband, Douglas A. Davis, as part of research for the Harvard Adolescence Project directed by John and Beatrice Whiting and Irven DeVore. The data were collected from a sample of fifty families who had lived in the same neighborhood of Zawiya for at least ten years, including well-off, middle-class, and poor families (all in local terms). The data used here include self-reports from over one hundred youths aged ten to twenty-two, plus a psychological test "Draw a Person" on gender role preference taken by sixty adolescents. In addition, we conducted open-ended interviews with about twenty-five young people and a few parents; some of these were taped and provide an exceptionally rich source of data on how they feel about the current changes in heterosexual interaction and what it means to be male or female in Morocco today. We also obtained data in casual conversations about and observations of young people interacting. Direct questions on sensitive topics are difficult in any culture, and Zawiya was no exception. However, my work in the town over twenty years allowed me to develop sensitivity to local concerns, a basis for trust with many people, and to observe changes over time myself.

5. By norms, I mean what people *state* to be proper behavior rather than what they do. The traditional norms described here are based on statements of the parental generation in the neighborhood of Zawiya in which we worked. They refer to how people *should* have behaved in the past; actual behavior is analyzed below.

6. Susan Schaefer Davis, "Sexual Maturation, Cultural Constraint, and the Concept of the Self," paper presented at the Annual Meeting of the American Anthropological Association in Chicago, November 16–20, 1983.

7. It is interesting that apparently norms in the U.S. are just the reverse; boyfriends are approved, but boys as friends are often discouraged, as reported in a first-person account by a twelve-year-old (Spiro 1985).

8. This is interesting with regard to Frayser's (1986) finding that many American teenagers do not use birth control because they prefer to feel their sexual activity is a result of being "swept away" rather than premeditated.

9. Susan Schaefer Davis and Douglas A. Davis, "Adolescence in a Moroccan Town," in the series *Adolescents in a Changing World*, New Brunswick, N.J.: Rutgers University Press, 1989.

10. Susan Schaefer Davis, *Patience and Power: Women's Lives in a Moroccan Village*, Cambridge, Mass.: Schenkman, 1983.

11. The recent use of this term by Zawiya residents is striking, and suggests that western psychological concepts are entering Moroccan discourse along with the emotional consequences of "westernization."

12. Carol Gilligan, *In a Different Voice: Psychological Theory and Women's Development*, Cambridge, Mass.: Harvard University Press, 1983, p. 2.

13. Ibid., p. 73.

14. Ibid., p. 163.

15. Mernissi, p. 104.

16. Lillian B. Rubin, *Worlds of Pain: Life in the Working-Class Family*, New York: Basic Books, 1976; *Intimate Strangers: Men and Women Together*, New York: Harper and Row, 1983.

REFERENCES

Davis, Susan Schaefer
    1983a   Patience and Power: Women's Lives in a Moroccan Village. Cambridge, Mass.: Schenkman.
    1983b   Sexual Maturation, Cultural Constraint, and the Concept of the Self. Paper presented at the Annual Meeting of the American Anthropological Association in Chicago, November 16–20.

Davis, Susan Schaefer, and Douglas A. Davis
    1989   Adolescence in a Moroccan Town. In the series Adolescents in a Changing World. New Brunswick, N.J.: Rutgers University Press.

Eickelman, Dale F.
    1985   Introduction: Self and Community in Middle Eastern Societies. Anthropological Quarterly 58:135–40.

Frayser, Suzanne
    1986   Sex and the American Teenager. Paper presented at the Annual Meeting of the Society for Cross-Cultural Research in San Diego, February 14–16.

Gilligan, Carol
    1982   In a Different Voice: Psychological Theory and Women's Development. Cambridge, Mass.: Harvard University Press.

Kohlberg, Lawrence
    1984   The Psychology of Moral Development. New York: Harper and Row.

Mernissi, Fatima
    1975   Beyond the Veil: Male-Female Dynamics in a Modern Muslim Society. Cambridge, Mass.: Schenkman.

Rubin, Lillian B.
    1976   Worlds of Pain: Life in the Working-Class Family. New York: Basic Books.
    1983   Intimate Strangers: Men and Women Together. New York: Harper and Row.

Spiro, Jaala
    1985   Just Friends, Ms. September: 87–88.

XII

REBELLION, MATURITY, AND THE SOCIAL CONTEXT
ARAB WOMEN'S SPECIAL CONTRIBUTION TO LITERATURE

Evelyne Accad

Introduction

Fiction by women writers in North Africa and the Arab world goes back less than fifty years; yet in this brief period we can trace a remarkable pace—and breadth—of development in theme, form, and technique. Beginning with a preoccupation with bicultural anxiety and loss of identity (especially among the North African writers), the genre progresses to an egotistical orientation centered on the introspective consideration of personal problems and the search for the self. Although these works often seem to reflect the most self-centered aspects of western romanticism, this preoccupation is understandable. In the face of legalized oppression and social degradation, it is not too surprising that the first concern of these women novelists has been their female characters' private struggles for a personal identity, seen alternatively as a search for personhood or an escape from thinghood.

What is particularly interesting, however, is that the fiction of women writers in North Africa and the Arab world does not stop at this stage of development, even though it might be expected to, given the general powerlessness of the group from which the characters of the genre are drawn. Instead, the romantic egotism of the 1950s and 1960s gives way, in the works of many of these writers, to clear rebellion in the face of newly recognized oppression. Personal rebellion, however, is of little use when the entire structure of the surrounding society militates against the exercise of individual freedom. Much of the fiction of these writers ultimately escapes this impasse by universalizing the questions of individual freedom that confront the female characters in this genre. In addition, the social milieu begins to be explored with a new clarity and frankness that moves it from the background to the front of the fictional

224

stage. It becomes clear that not only individuals, but also the society in which they live, must be reborn. It is because of this progression that I suggest that the fiction of at least some of the women writers considered here has achieved a true maturity of vision, a realization that the self—and its freedom—cannot be separated from the entire social context. Obviously, this evolving vision has important political implications.

Because of their overwhelming concern with finding a personal identity, the early works of these women writers were not always warmly received by the critics. In the late 1950s and early 1960s there was a strong tendency to compare these works—either with outright disfavor or in an act of condemnation by association—with Françoise Sagan's *Bonjour Tristesse*. In fact, it may well be that adolescent rebellion and the search for identity are not the stuff of the great novels of tomorrow; whether or not this is the case is irrelevant. What matters is that, although the works of these women writers often fall into the melodramatic or prove to be embarrassingly autobiographical, they are in many ways authentic and necessary; you must know some basic things about yourself before you can begin to write about your place in the millennium.

The next stage in the evolution of the genre is rebellion in the face of the realization of the oppression that women must undergo in North Africa and the Arab world; this is a thing apart from the fairly universal human experience of rebellion on the way to maturity. The pattern is brutally simple in most parts of North Africa and the Arab world: women are born to fill the roles of daughter, wife, and mother, to be successively subservient to their fathers, husbands, and sons. Education for women is in most cases regarded as superfluous, few occupations outside the home are open to women, and in most cases the legal status of women is determined by the *shari'a* (Islamic religious code). In court, a woman's testimony is accorded only half the weight of a man's, a husband may divorce his wife without recourse to legal action, often merely by stating aloud that he repudiates her, and the law permits a husband or father to force his wife or daughter to remain at home, often literally under lock and key. Revolt against such customs and conditions leads to political awakening in the hope of finding solutions to women's problems through political commitment. Engagement is often mixed with a sense of nationalism and national identity, because the countries from which the women write are either struggling against foreign domination, or striving toward national identity and development.

Then comes disillusionment with the realization that political movements use women instead of serving them or working together with them for their liberation. Those novelists who find a productive solution to this impasse usually do so by universalizing the feminist cause and expressing women's problems in the context of Arab and North African societies.

Some of the writers, such as Assia Djebar, the acclaimed Algerian writer, exhibit all the stages mentioned above, but most of them exhibit only a few.

Some of the writers have stopped publishing (for example, Layla Baalbakki); others, such as Djamila Debeche, have stopped writing altogether; others are now dead (Marguerite Taos-Amrouche, Samira Azzam); and still another, Ghada al-Samman, has founded her own publishing house in order to be able to express freely what she has to say. It is not possible within this short study to cover all of the authors and works. I will limit myself to discussing the two later phases of development outlined above and the most representative authors. I will cover only authors from the *Mashriq* (Middle East).

Romanticism, Traditionalism, and Rebellion in the Works of Arab Women Writers between 1958 and 1965

The fiction of Arab women writers not only has broad thematic and stylistic range, but exhibits a multifaceted treatment of its subject matter. The works of the writers discussed here explore characters in their relationships to the prescribed elements of the Arab woman's tradition-bound life. Within this context of similarity, however, the writers exhibit striking differences of focus. One approach concentrates on the social or political aspects of the situation, another on its effect on individual development; yet another seeks to defend the status quo, and a fourth to use the social setting merely as a background for exploring general human problems. However, Baalbakki and al-Khuri, the two writers who deal extensively with the condition of women, emphasize the same social inequities as their North African counterparts. Again, we see the culturally determined unimportance of women from birth to death, punctuated only at regular intervals by the intrusion of harsh customs: brutally enforced virginity, arranged marriages, production of male children on demand, and finally, prolonged isolation from both men and the outside world during adulthood.

Most Arab women writers view the condition of women as one of oppression and deprivation. Nonetheless, writers such as Sufi 'Abdallah maintain that the Arab woman's role is capable of yielding a variety of enriching experiences that fulfill primary human needs within the context of Arab society. A more usual view is that of Samira Azzam, a Palestinian who lived in Lebanon. She describes women who fail in their attempts at self-realization because Arab society allows no scope for such endeavors.

In the works of such writers as Baalbakki (a Muslim from Lebanon) and al-Khuri (a Christian from Syria), the tradition-bound role of women is seen as an oppressive pattern, inimical to freedom of expression and development. Their various works of fiction, however, present rather different orientations toward the problematic condition of women. Baalbakki sees Arab women as trapped beings, and explores their consequent feelings of alienation and destructive rebellion. Her characters escape neither their self-absorbed view of woman's dilemma, nor the dilemma itself. Al-Khuri is concerned primarily

with the absence of freedom of choice for women. Perhaps because her characters are concerned with personal rather than political goals, they seek, and
often find, an inner strength that allows them to transcend social barriers.

The novelists considered here are located in the middle stages of the pattern
suggested in the introduction, that is, of personal rebellion, an intense search
for selfhood, and often a numb—or even despairing—resignation to intrac-
table forces of Arab society. An important difference between the works of
Mashriq women novelists and those of their *Maghrib* (North African) counterparts is the relative unimportance of biculturality and bicultural stresses in
the case of the former. For *Mashriq* women novelists, this is neither a major
theme, nor an available alternative in the fictional universe. For better or
worse, the resolutions of their fiction must take full account of Arab culture
and society.

Layla Baalbakki

A Lebanese writer of Shiite background, Layla Baalbakki is a woman who
has achieved much despite the cultural bias against her efforts. Baalbakki
published her first novel, *Ana Ahya* (I live), in 1958, at the age of twenty-two.
Her precociousness and the subject matter of the first novel are reminiscent
of the Algerian writer Assia Djebar. Then, in May of 1959, Baalbakki deliv-
ered her famous speech about Lebanese youth, "We without Masks," before
a Lebanese literary group. In this speech she urged others of her generation
to oppose hypocrisy and help Lebanon achieve its potential through honest
efforts at social reform. She explains how she understands freedom and what
the rebellion of her generation consists of: "We are more cruel, more violent,
more miserable than the youth of America and Europe because we are still
enduring a battle to gain our freedom as individuals, as a state, and as a
people, whereas they are practicing freedom."[1] She claims that Arab morality,
both Muslim and Christian, has created an impossible social dilemma by
making the body simultaneously vile and sacred, and that it is consequently
necessary to restore the body to the place it should hold, unified within the
totality of human relations. She also thinks that society will never discover
itself totally unless it does so on a "flesh" level, and that only through returning the body to its proper place in human affairs will the equilibrium of
Middle Eastern society be restored. On the personal level, Baalbakki advocates
what she calls "total love," an all-inclusive nondiscriminatory relationship
between two people. Quite clearly, such a relationship could only be achieved
following the breakdown of traditional prejudices and behavioral expectations
with regard to women.

In 1964, Baalbakki followed her first novel with a book of short stories
under the title *Safinat Hanan ila al-Qamar* (Spaceship of tenderness to the
moon). Readers of the work were outraged by its discussion of sexual subjects,
and the matter ended up in court: Baalbakki was accused of writing immoral,

provocative material offensive to public morality. Her lawyer won the case, but this example clearly illustrates the kind of persecution an Arab woman writer may encounter. A young Arab woman's discussion of "flesh" and sexual freedom could not be tolerated by an Arab audience. In fact, upon reading *Safinat Hanan ila al-Qamar*, the reader may wonder what caused such a strong reaction among the book's original audience. The title story presents a touchingly beautiful picture of a relationship between the sexes that manages to transcend the oppressive stereotypes of the culture. The action takes place in a bedroom, the husband is naked, and there is some suggestion at the end that sexual activity will follow. Coming from the pen of a female, it was too much for her audience. The line that caused the most uproar was: "He placed his hand on her stomach. . . ." Baalbakki's acquittal after a strenuous defense by her lawyer does not detract from the implications raised by the fact that she was indicted in the first place.[2]

According to the critic Rose Ghurayyib, this short story presents in an outspoken, suggestive manner the joy of sexual love between husband and wife. The woman plays the role of the convinced temptress. The fact that its publication aroused public protests which brought the author into court on an obscenity charge has led some to affirm that the whole event was arranged for the sake of publicity, because in a country like Lebanon, where freedom of the press has been a tradition, more so-called "immoral" stories have been tolerated.[3]

Despite such public outrage, Layla Baalbakki did not remain silent: her next novel, *al-Alihah al-Mamsukha* (The disfigured or monstrous gods), was published in 1965. In this novel, Baalbakki extends her theme of alienation and rebellion, revealing the constriction and frustration that the traditional expectations place on men as well as women. The central character, Aida, is married to a university professor, Nadim, who, despite his education and professed modernism, refuses to have sexual relations with her because she dared to marry him without being a virgin. This novel thus deals openly with one of the most sensitive topics in Arab society. Ultimately, all the characters suffer from the "monstrous gods" of tradition, but it is the women who are in the worst position, having the fewest alternatives.

Layla Baalbakki's first novel, *Ana Ahya*, illustrates the theme of rebellion, the second phase of development of Arab women writers. It describes the life of Lina Fayyad, a young woman who wants to rise above the hypocrisies of her environment. In order to do so, she rebels violently and self-destructively. The culmination of Lina's negative rebellion is an unsuccessful suicide attempt. The dual purpose of Baalbakki's portrayal of Lina, a criticism of die-hard traditionalism as well as of superficial modernity, has been pointed out by the critic al-Toma, who sees Lina as "An extreme example of a woman disenchanted with her existence as she seeks to find meaning for her life and asserts her identity despite the restrictions of a conservative society."[4] According to al-Toma, the portrayal of Lina underlines not only the absurdity of tradition but also the hypocrisy and dishonesty concealed by an anti-traditional facade.

Each person in Lina's world becomes an object of revulsion: her father, because she catches him watching the plump neighbor woman undressing; her mother, for submitting to the petty oppressions of her married life; one sister for wanting to get married, the other for wanting to amass learned degrees. She sees as typical of every Middle Eastern family an attitude unabashedly hypocritical or blindly passive. Lina's feelings toward her sisters show the extent of her alienation. She no longer has any compassion for other victims of society whose circumstances closely resemble her own. Limited by the tunnel vision of her personal rebellion, Lina even feels hatred for her own sisters.

Bored and frustrated, Lina takes a job in a press agency. Her parents violently object because it costs them a good deal of social status to have a daughter who goes off to work. At work she is not taken seriously: her job is to answer letters of complaint, but no such letters ever come in.

Still feeling empty and bored, she takes university courses in which she has no interest, and finally becomes an audience for Baha, a young Communist who sits in cafés, expounding his beliefs. As might be expected, although Baha is politically radical, he is socially conservative, does not approve of Lina's freedom of action, and eventually tires of her. Left alone once more, Lina throws herself in front of a cab, only to be rescued by a passerby. Thus, her empty life drags on. She can either rebel without goal or direction, or become a passive participant in the affairs of others; she cannot find the means to live an independent life and pursue her own ends.

The principal question remaining in the reader's mind at the end of *Ana Ahya* is why does Lina's alienation and attendant rebellion lead to inaction and withdrawal, rather than to positive action? As is the case with Assia Djebar's early female characters, the answer seems to lie in Lina's alienation from her female peer group. She cannot see beyond her own bitterness and boredom, and therefore cannot grasp the larger social problems that have resulted in her own condition. Like many of Assia Djebar's characters (Nadia in *La soif* or Dalila of *Les impatients*), she is stubborn, selfish, and spoiled— a true product of a culture that has a vested interest in producing women who are perpetual children in the emotional and intellectual sense. Furthermore, in spite of her rebelliousness, Lina acts out the passive social role that is expected of her: she rebels in superficial respects but plays a passive waiting game with the important aspects of her life.

Child-woman that she is, Lina is simply not in touch with the real-life problems of the world in which she lives. For instance, Lina attends a party where she meets a Palestinian guerrilla who has an open wound on his chest that cannot be healed, but which feels better when touched by cold objects. He asks Lina to put her metal bracelet against the wound to ease his pain. She does so reluctantly, with her eyes closed because the sight of the wound fills her imagination with the horrors of war. When she opens her eyes again, she finds the Palestinian gone and is left shaken by the incident. She had identified the Palestinian with the Communist Baha, and the guerrilla's disappearance foreshadows the eventual breakup of her relationship with Baha. Lina fails to recognize the significance of the Palestinian's disappearance, which is a symbol of her own inability to make meaningful contact with other human beings. With a little forcing, she can go so far as to soothe the guerrilla's wound, or provide an uncritical audience for Baha's political ramblings, but she cannot give either of them the moral strength and understanding that proceed from unselfish participation in another person's world. Baalbakki depicts Lina as a persona incapable of imparting such strength and understanding to others because she has never come to terms with her own inner self.

Like Djebar, Baalbakki has been silent for quite a long time now, but unlike Djebar she has not published any recent work, although she continues to write. This could be a result of the demoralizing effect that the long Lebanese war has had on its population. The fact that her prophetic warnings in her speech to Lebanese youth remained unheard, together with fear of censorship and repression, have perhaps prevented her from continuing her struggle in the open. It could also be due to the demands of raising a family. According to Rose Ghurayyib, it should be noted that Baalbakki's works are at least in part a reflection of the positions of the Syrian Socialist Party with which she has been connected.

> Baalbakki's novels reveal a defiant, independent and spontaneous behavior; a complete rejection of the past in form and thought. They carry a faithful presentation of the Syrian Socialist Party's principles, in vogue at the time (1950–1965), but in a personal, melodramatic and original style. The most outstanding of those principles were: anti-zionism, anti-communism, secularization of marriage, exaltation of the physical aspect of love.[5]

The waning influence of this party may be a factor in her silence.

Kulit Suhayl al-Khuri

Another woman who has dealt extensively with the position of women in Arab society is a Syrian, Kulit Suhayl al-Khuri, the granddaughter of the late Syrian statesman Faris al-Khuri. She comes from a wealthy Catholic family of Damascus and was educated in both French and Arabic. Although al-Khuri has written several volumes of poetry in French, her fiction—novels as well as short stories—has been written in Arabic. She published *Ayyam Ma'ah* (Days with him), a lengthy novel, in 1959. This was followed by another novel, *Laylah Wahidah* (A single night), in 1961. Since then, she has published numerous short stories—two collections appeared in 1961 and 1968—and the story "Dimashq Bayti al-Kabir" (Damascus, My Big House, 1969).

Al-Khuri deals with problems not unlike those treated by Baalbakki and her fictional techniques are similar; but her tone is less vindictive, if not less desperate. Like the North African Marguerite Taos-Amrouche, al-Khuri is a Christian in a Muslim country; however, the theme of religious alienation so evident in the work of her *Maghrib* counterpart is absent from al-Khuri's novels. Like Baalbakki and Djebar, al-Khuri is concerned with woman's freedom to make choices, but unlike these writers she does not choose to represent bored and selfish characters who will probably never be able to achieve real freedom or exercise it wisely. Al-Khuri's characters look for strength within themselves, as do the characters in Djebar's later works.

According to Rose Ghurayyib, Kulit al-Khuri, in her two novels, tries to revive the romantic idea that love is the only thing worth living for. Marriage means only a relation between a man and a woman who fall in love at first sight. Their love is predetermined, faithful, and eternal; this is the idea she tried to inculcate in one of her novels' protagonists, Ziyad, without success.[6]

In *Ayyam Ma'ah*, the central figure, Reem, reminds us of Lina in Baalbakki's *Ana Ahya*. The pattern of Reem's life closely resembles Lina's: she comes from a wealthy middle-class family; her parents are opposed to her working outside the home; and they also ally themselves with tradition in that they would like to have Reem marry a man of their choosing. Like Lina, Reem rebels against these wishes because she sees that they would lead her into a banal, ambitionless, self-sacrificing existence. Finally, as in *Ana Ahya*, *Ayyam Ma'ah* revolves around a love affair that ends as a fiasco. However, this is where the similarity ends. Whereas Lina almost destroys herself because of that experience, Reem emerges from her crisis as a stronger person. And although both Reem and Lina are trapped by men's view of them, Reem strives to break through the walls of her confinement while at the same time trying to help her male friend liberate his own thought toward her so that both can live fuller lives.

After she graduates from college, Reem's parents want her to marry a wealthy man of their choosing so that they can boast about the match to their friends. Instead, she rebels and goes her own way, publishing her poetry, studying, and taking a job in an office. These acts infuriate her parents, but they help her gain a sense of her own independence and potential.

Reem falls in love with Ziyad Mustapha, a musician whose crass materialism and libertine tendencies initially repel her. For a time she attempts to convert him to her romantic ideas of love, but he grows more and more impatient. Eventually, Reem begins to suspect that Ziyad is seeing another woman; when she follows him secretly, her suspicions are confirmed. Confronted with the true nature of the man, she is at first dismayed that she had never counted on the possibility that he might betray her. Instead of being devastated by the experience, as Lina was, Reem uses it as an impetus to drive her toward greater independence and self-assertiveness. She realizes that she has been misusing her energies in trying to change Ziyad instead of developing her own potential. Once she becomes her own woman and begins to withdraw from her relationship with Ziyad, Reem finds that the tables are turned: he now pursues her desperately, begging her to marry him. With her newfound inner strength, however, she is able to leave him and pursue her own interests.

In depicting Reem, al-Khuri has chosen a character who does not display the aberrations of character present in the dilettantish Lina, or the spoiled and selfish women of the early Djebar. In consequence, *Ayyam Ma'ah* is pervaded by a sense of rational optimism, an atmosphere in which a reasonable character can make reasonable gains in self-knowledge and independence. Al-Khuri also sidesteps the issue of the interrelation of alienation and rebellion, thus greatly simplifying the philosophical milieu of the novel.

In her second novel, *Layla Wahidah* (A single night, 1961), al-Khuri seems less optimistic about the acquisition of inner strength. In this novel, an Arab woman writer attempts for the first time to really penetrate the world of the women in the middle strata of her culture. The result is a spiritual bleakness much like that in Zoubeida Bittari's *O, mes soeurs musulmanes, pleurez!* (Oh, my Muslim sisters, weep!).[7] However, unlike Bittari's work, which is autobiographical, al-Khuri's story is told with the fictional perspective of an outsider.

Rasha, the central character, is the "barren woman" who appears so often in the fiction of North Africa and the Arab world. Her husband has sent her to every doctor in Damascus, but without success. Since he is going on a business trip to Marseilles, he decides to take Rasha along to be examined by the French doctors. In Marseilles, he puts her on a train to Paris, where she has an appointment with a famous gynecologist. On the train, however, she meets Camille, who is half-Syrian, half-French, and the two are irresistibly drawn to each other. They end up having a whirlwind, one-night affair, during the course of which Rasha realizes that she has found the love she dreamt of and yearned for, as well as sexual fulfillment.

The next morning, Rasha returns to her hotel room where she begins writing a long letter to her husband, which forms the bulk of the novel. The letter is in effect a confession by which she hopes to purify herself and return to her old life. She continues writing even while waiting for her appointment at the doctor's office.

When the gynecologist examines her, however, he pronounces her perfectly capable of having children. She is shocked to realize that her husband and all the Syrian doctors fooled her into thinking that the fault lay with her. With this shock comes the realization of the extent to which she has been victimized by her society. She decides to give up her old life and stay in Paris. Nevertheless, she has always been dependent on others, has no marketable skills, and is perplexed about her future. Distracted by her thoughts, she steps into the path of a car; as she lies dying in the ambulance, she thinks, "What is the use of years? . . . My whole life . . . was a single night" (p. 235).

In *A Single Night*, al-Khuri has managed to depict some of the severe dilemmas faced by a middle-class, Arab woman who attempts to escape from her situation. Social conditions are such that it is unlikely she will perceive the extent of her oppression in the first place. If she does come to a clear realization, it is likely to be a depressing experience because there is nothing in her background to prepare her for an independent life. Clearly the situation of such women is more desperate than that of the upper-class women depicted by Djebar, Debeche, Taos, Baalbakki, and even al-Khuri, in the case of Reem. For these women, wealth, advanced education and, in many cases, biculturality, provide both access to alternative lifestyles and the means to achieve them. A true picture of the condition of women in these countries would require that both the upper and lower levels of society be taken into account, a pattern that has been followed by some of the writers who represent the new trends in Arab women's fiction.

Political and Feminist Commitment: Trends in the Works of Arab Women Writers since 1965

The works of the novelists examined in this section represent more recent trends in the writing of Arab women. In contrast to previous works, they reflect a greater awareness of and commitment to the political, social, and sexual issues facing Arab women today.

Within this unity of concern, however, the writers exhibit a multifaceted approach to the problem, and great stylistic differences. Nawal al-Saadawi uses her experiences as a doctor and psychiatrist to express the internal and external conflicts brought about in women's lives through repression. Her style is direct and realistic, and her reflective thoughts often seem like theoretical works rather than fiction. Ghada al-Samman portrays women striving for self-realization through fantastic and occult plots in her first works, moves to romantic revolt against puritanical attitudes toward love and social hypocrisy in her middle work, and in her latest writing shows women revolting against being treated as sexual objects or slaves by despotic husbands or authoritarian parents. Her style exhibits the wide range of her thoughts: poetic and suggestive at times, surrealistic and irrational at others, and highly symbolic throughout. Hanan al-Shaykh approaches women's problems through an extreme sensitivity to her inner self and her sensual sensations that helps her grasp more acutely and fully the magnitude of women's oppression from within. Her style is poetic, sensual, and highly suggestive. Finally, Daisy al-Ameer and Emily Nasrallah portray with frankness and acute perception the evils that Arab society in general and Arab women in particular are facing today. Most of their work is in the form of short stories, particularly in the case of Daisy al-Ameer. Their style is usually realistic and thought-provoking.

In general, we can say that the various approaches taken by women recently are courageous and daring. They reflect a desire and concern not only to describe Arab women's problems and dilemmas, but also to find new ways for them to escape their trapped situations. This boldness is reflected in the lifestyles of the writers themselves, many of whom have tried to break away from the tradition-bound circles around them. They have asserted themselves as single women or divorcees despite the prejudices voiced against them, a path not easy to follow within the restrictions of Arab society. A few had to seek refuge in Lebanon, away from the persecution or lack of understanding they faced in their own countries. One must also note that most of the works discussed in this section were published in Lebanon, a country which has been torn by war for the last twelve years, but which, nevertheless, at least until the last two years, has continued to publish important works, thus demonstrating its leading cultural role even in the midst of its political turmoil.

Nawal al-Saadawi

Nawal al-Sayyid al-Saadawi was born in the village of Kafr Tahla, Egypt, on the 27th of October, 1931, near the Nile. She studied psychiatry at the Faculty of Medicine in Cairo, and received her doctorate from Cairo University in 1955. Between 1955 and 1965, she practiced as a medical doctor and psychiatrist in the University Hospital and in the Ministry of Health. Her practice in cities as well as in the countryside allowed her to deepen her understanding of matters related to Egyptian society, particularly women's condition.

After receiving a degree in Public Health from Columbia University in New York in 1966, she returned to Egypt and became the Acting Director General and later the Director General of the Health Education Department in the Ministry of Health. At the time she also founded the Association for Health Education, in addition to serving as the director of a popular magazine dealing with medical information.

She published *al-Mar'ah wa al-Jins* (Women and sex), where she dealt openly and courageously with the controversial issues of sex, religion, and politics in 1972. In it she uncompromisingly denounced women's economic and sexual oppression. It caused so much controversy that Nawal was dismissed from her job, the magazine she ran was shut down, and her books were censored. Later, the book was reprinted in Lebanon and became widely read throughout the Arab world.

Al-Saadawi is the author of six books on women in the Arab world, seven novels, six collections of short stories, two plays, and one memoir, all in Arabic, many of which have been translated into several languages, including English, French, German, Persian, Portuguese, Italian, Swedish, Norwegian, Danish, and Dutch. Some of these works have been adapted for the theater in various countries. The best-known titles are: *The Hidden Face of Eve, Woman at Point Zero, Two Women in One, God Dies by the Nile, Death of an Ex-Minister, She Has No Place in Paradise,* and *Memoirs from the*

Women's Prison. Her work has been crowned by two awards: the Literary Award of the Supreme Council for Arts and Social Sciences, Cairo, Egypt (1974), and the Literary Award of the Franco-Arab Friendship Association, Paris, France (1982).

Al-Saadawi uses her experiences as a doctor and psychiatrist to express the internal and external conflicts brought about in women's lives through repression. Her style is direct and realistic. In *al-Mar'ah wa al-Jins* (Women and sex), an Arab woman, a doctor, discussed frankly and scientifically the customs and taboos surrounding Arab women and their sexuality. She was not afraid to present new interpretations of such controversial issues as honor and virginity, work and education for women, marriage, polygamy, divorce, and "bayt al-ta'a" ("the house of obedience"), and finally, the importance of sex and women's right to orgasm, as well as the very touchy subject of genital mutilation.

Al-Saadawi presents some very daring ideas about Arab society. For instance, she asserts that if virginity is required of women, it should also be enforced for men, because the moral values of a society should be applied to all of its members regardless of sex, color, or social class. She claims that at present, the codes of honor imposed on women are like codes imposed by rulers on their workers and servants, rather than moral imperatives for the whole society.

Concurring with Simone de Beauvoir's thesis: "on ne nait pas femme, on le devient" ("one is not born a woman, one becomes a woman")—al-Saadawi is often said to be the de Beauvoir of the Arab world—she believes that the "differences" between men and women are not inherent in their "nature," but are learned within society. The social institutions and laws regulating Arab women's lives in marriage and divorce must be changed if the Arab world is to move toward an improved society. The cultural and media organizations, as well as all means of mass communication—television, radio, magazines, newspapers, the publishing industry—must take equal responsibility for bringing about the necessary social changes. They must, among other things, represent women in roles other than as cooks, dishwashers, beauty aids, and fashion models.

Concerning the taboos surrounding sexuality, she notes that the circumcision of girls is practiced as a means of ensuring their virginity by inhibiting their sexual impulses, thus making them frigid. With mutual sexual attraction more or less ruled out, marriage is usually based on materialistic considerations; it is a kind of business transaction or legalized prostitution in which the husband becomes the sole owner of his wife, with unilateral rights of divorce.

Another myth that al-Saadawi unveils is that of the traditional conception of love in Arab society. She points out that the most accurate model for this type of love is the love that is believed to consecrate the relationship between master and slave. Instead, al-Saadawi proposes a concept of "true love" that is devoid of the idea of ownership or selfish interests, and that is not marked by romantic self-sacrifice. She asserts that true love consists of respect and recognition of the other person's equality, freedom, and independence; it is characterized by mutual understanding and communication.

In her theoretical works, al-Saadawi asserts that the condition of Arab women can only be improved by structural means, by bringing about changes in the existing politico-economic system of the Arab world and by reforming the laws and regulations that oppress women in these societies. The sources of this constructive radicalism are made abundantly clear in al-Saadawi's fiction, much of which is based on her experience as a psychiatrist.

Firdaus, or *Woman at Point Zero*, is the inside story of a woman condemned to death for having killed a man. The narrator, a psychiatrist, goes to the prison to try to talk to this unusual woman who first refuses to see her, but later opens up and tells her story, which consists of one traumatizing experience after another.

The narrative unfolds like a horror film, beginning with Firdaus's childhood. She is born into a peasant family, her father unknown. Her mother slaps her when she asks about him. Her circumcision is described in vivid images: her mother brings a woman who holds a razor blade and cuts "the piece of flesh lodged between her thighs" (p. 17). She cries the whole night long from the painful experience. Her sexuality, which had been sensually described in previous passages, is thus eradicated, and the realism as well as symbolism of the scene comes out strongly: Firdaus's first wounds will leave scars on a life barely begun.

After the death of her mother, Firdaus's uncle takes her to Cairo, where he puts her in school. This is the first step toward Firdaus's self-realization, with the price such knowledge extracts. When her uncle remarries, his new wife does not want Firdaus to stay with them and therefore arranges a marriage for her with a sixty-year-old man (she is only nineteen). The man is not only old but miserly and brutal: he beats her so severely that she runs back to her uncle for protection, but his response to her is that all husbands beat their wives. His wife joins in and admonishes her that: "The man who knows religion well is the one who beats his wife, because religion allows the beating of wives and a virtuous woman will not reproach her husband—her duty is total obedience" (p. 51).

Finding all doors closed to her, Firdaus has no choice but to return to her husband, who rapes her once more and beats her again—so hard this time that she bleeds profusely. Her only way out is the street, where she becomes the prey of men who use her and profit by prostituting her. She goes from one bad experience to the next—even the police use her and abuse her.

One day she decides she has had enough and wants to become her own master, ruler of her body and mind. She ponders over the fact that a quarter of a century of her life has gone by before she was able to come to this realization: "How much of my life had gone before I got rid of other people's hold on me: to choose the food I would eat, the house I would live in, to refuse the man I didn't want, and to choose the man with a clean mind and body" (p. 78).

Nevertheless, Firdaus' aspirations and alternatives are not ones her society will tolerate. Her trials are not yet over. She gains a certain economic independence by working for an agency. She falls in love with one of the owners, who pretends to love her but uses her like the others: he betrays her and marries another woman. Firdaus is heartbroken by the experience. She feels a pain she has never felt before, and with the pain comes the realization that she hates men. Once more, she feels doors have been closed in her face. This time they belong to her inner self, the realm of her own feelings. This is even more difficult to bear.

The final incident of Firdaus's sufferings is with a man who tries to use her again, and then threatens her with a knife when she refuses to be his toy. In a gesture of despair and revolt, she grabs the knife raised against her and turns it back toward her oppressor, symbol of all the cruelties she had to endure: she plunges the knife into the man's body again and again. Condemned to death, her last words are loaded with meaning: "They condemn me to death because they are afraid of my life and they know that if I lived I would kill them. My life means their death and my death means their life . . . I am not afraid of death anymore . . . I am the ruler of my freedom" (p. 111). She emphasizes the symbolic nature of her act: "They are not afraid of the knife but truth. . . . The truth makes me unafraid of death and unafraid of life" (p. 113). Clearly then, Firdaus looks at her condemnation as a way to freedom. Her death is her only way out of an unbearable situation.

As for the psychiatrist, she goes away with a feeling of hopelessness and despair at the injustice done to a woman she sees as a victim. She reflects upon the inhumanity of a world that "kills truth," that sadistically gets rid of the "simplicity of the child who does not know lies, in the midst of a world which only knows lies. . . . Firdaus had to pay the price of truth" (p. 115). She goes away ashamed, ashamed of her own life.

In this poignant and vivid story, al-Saadawi gives us an account of some of the most painful problems facing Arab women today. Firdaus's revolt is not a selfish, self-destructive assertion of her personality, but an act of despair and an outcry against the oppression and servitude forced upon her. What al-Saadawi seems to be telling us is that Arab women's oppression today condemns all of Arab society to live in lies and inauthenticity. The judgments are harsh and the message strong: if the only way for Arab society to live is through the cloistering, veiling, and oppression of its women, its life is doomed to delusion. Dostoevsky once observed that one could judge the development of a civilization by the way in which it treated its prisoners; al-Saadawi implies that the same is true of a society's treatment of its women.

Through the simplicity of this story, al-Saadawi's prophetic voice gives us a warning. She lays on Arab society the responsibility for the crimes committed against its women; clearly, the society itself must be reformed if it is to move ahead. Refusing to limit the focus of her fiction to the struggles of the individual character, al-Saadawi instead uses her characters—like Firdaus—as a means of exploring the larger social context of individual oppression.

Ghada al-Samman

The importance of self-realization is central in the works of Ghada al-Samman. Originally from Syria, al-Samman studied, successively, medicine and English literature and has worked as a civil servant, journalist, and university lecturer. Although her early work is in French, her major work has been in Arabic. At an early age, she established herself in Lebanon, hoping to benefit from the relative freedom of the press. She is probably the most productive woman writer in the Arab world, having completed at least sixteen books in a period of twenty years with more ready for publication. She is a dynamic person who has founded her own publishing house and seeks to popularize her liberal ideas through a writing style that is by turns emotional, humorous, and even satiric. This is noteworthy because there are relatively few women writers in any culture who have attempted much humor or satire.

Her early short stories are semi-autobiographical, sometimes describing her world of fantasy. They often depict in a fantastic and symbolic style the conflicts of women who deviate into madness or perversion as an escape from their intense frustrations. The volumes of short stories from this early phase include: *La Bahra fi Bairut* (There is no sea at Beirut, 1963); *Layl al-Ghuraba* (The night of the strangers, 1966); *Rahil al-Marifi al-Qadimah* (Journey into ancient ports, 1973); and *al-Suqut ila al-Qima* (The fall toward the summit, 1975), all published in Beirut.

In "Ghajariyya bila mafa" (A gypsy without a haven), a story that appears in al-Samman's first collection, *La Bahra fi Bairut*, we see the ambivalent feelings of a woman toward the restrictions of her culture. Al-Samman describes a woman who is an orphan, her mother having died when she was five (as in al-Samman's case). The mother's death is attributable in part to her husband's desertion of her for another woman. The orphaned child, now grown to womanhood, is in love with a married man but has ignored her feelings and become engaged to a more eligible man, Kamal. She does this partly to spare the children of the married man the possibility of an ordeal like the one she herself suffered as a child. Her actions also are based on a strong desire to please her grandfather:

> My grandfather watches me with contentment in his eyes as I sit there beside my fiancé, Kamal; his glance steals to my hand lying lifeless in that of Kamal. Lying there only so as to bring a smile to that dear face at any cost. (p. 318)

Nonetheless, she is restless and cannot sleep at night. Her decision weighs upon her and she feels in conflict with her true nature, the real self that custom requires her to conceal for the benefit of the people she loves. Her uneasiness is all the greater because she is fully conscious of this real nature that she is violating:

> But this is my true face, the face of the gypsy who makes fun of other people's idealism. . . . Why do I contradict myself? How can I explain this overwhelming desire to bring a smile to the lips of my grandfather? . . . I really do live the life of a comet that loves its loneliness. Maybe it is only my mask that clings to them, the mask of a well-brought-up girl that has now molded itself to my face. Who knows what I would find underneath, if I were to peel it off? Has the gypsy's face decayed with time? If I were to fling off my mask would I find that I had no face at all? (p. 325)

Her problem, which has many counterparts in Arab fiction, is essentially an identity crisis. In this character we see that strict cultural requirements are at war with an essential drive for self-realization; the primary attachment of the human being for the culture that nurtured her during her development is at war with the individual's drive for independence and self-discovery. We see more of the central character's confusion when she says, "I felt like a puppet bound with invisible strings to the fingers of a madman who delights in moving us in exactly the opposite direction from that in which we want to go" (p. 325). She gets out of bed and walks in the streets of her city, following a blind man who thereby becomes her unwitting leader; she feels very much in tune with him, sensing a link that binds her firmly to him:

> And I, a lost tramp in a brazen city of legends, weep for a lost haven . . . weep for roads I am forced to tread and strangers with whom I must keep company on the journey through life . . . pretending I am happy and making believe I enjoy being with them. (p. 326)

In trailing her blind "leader," the female central character of this story symbolically mirrors the process by which human beings intermingle free will and determinism in their acceptance of social expectations; there is no question, finally, of accepting or rejecting the road she must travel in life. She must simply accept it, with the help of an illusion like that which allows her to accept the blind man as her leader for the duration of her stroll through the city.

Between 1967 and 1975, many of al-Samman's writings deal with the Arab national struggle against Zionism and imperialism. Her most important work on the subject is a book entitled *al-Raghif Yanbud ka al-Qalb* (The loaf beats like a heart, 1975). In it, she attacks virulently the diseases of Lebanese and Arab societies with a clairvoyance and a voice of warning much like that of the Moroccan woman writer Khanata Bannuna. She sees political corruption, fanaticism, apathy, social inequity, the unfair treatment of women, and lack of social consciousness as the sources of the Arabs' state of underdevelopment. Oppression is not merely an individual affliction: it pervades the whole social fabric.

Her most recent and important work is *al-A'mal Ghair al-Kamilat* (Unfinished works, 1979), which is composed of seven volumes of fiction and nonfiction dealing with a variety of subjects and bearing unusual and intriguing titles such as: *al-Jasad Haqibat Safar* (The body is a traveling suitcase), *al-Sibahat fi Buhairat al-Shaytan* (The swim in the devil's lake), *Khitm al-Zakirat bi al-Sham'a al-Ahmar* (The sealing of the memory with red wax), and *I'takalu Lahzat Haribut* (To grasp a fleeting moment). In *Unfinished Works*, al-Samman gives us vivid descriptions of her travels in Lebanon, in other Arab countries, and to various European capitals, among them London, Berlin, and Rome. She conveys critical, detailed reports, and her own analytical as well as satirical views of the places and the people she meets. These works also indicate the extent of al-Samman's wide reading and show an originality of expression and a reflective mind that never stops questioning.

In one of these pieces, *al-Jasad Haqibat Safar* (The body is a traveling suitcase), al-Samman criticizes the so-called "committed writers." She finds them to be merely tools paid to diffuse political propaganda, with no depth or sense of critical judgment. To her mind, authentic revolutionary works should be free from the clichés and prejudices of contemporary political parties; unfortunately, such works are all too few in Arab countries. She feels a certain loyalty toward Arabism, but would like to remain independent and free of political attachments that would narrow or devalue her writing.

As with other Arab women novelists discussed previously, al-Samman has been sharply attacked by the press and critics in the Arab world. They frown upon her ultraliberal ideas, her openness on sexual subjects, her eccentric style, her sweeping statements, her sharp sense of humor, and her gift for satire. It may be that her humor and satire are found to be particularly unforgivable, since these qualities suggest that she is a writer of true social vision and not merely a strident mouthpiece for a political position. In any case, she has refused to be intimidated or silenced and has founded her own publishing house to disseminate her works and avoid censorship. Her perseverance and hard work have made her one of the most widely read Arab woman novelists today. Her originality, her self-criticism and self-analysis, and her inner growth give a unique aspect to the voice of this courageous and daring woman writer, a voice that will continue to grow and must be heard.

Hanan al-Shaykh

Another woman writer who has contributed much to the unveiling of women's problems is Hanan al-Shaykh. Hanan al-Shaykh was born in 1945 and grew up in a strict Shiite Muslim family from the south of Lebanon. She studied in Beirut and later attended the American College for Women in Cairo, where at the age of twenty-two she wrote her first novel, *Intihar Rajul Mayit* (Suicide of a dead man, 1971). She then returned to Beirut and worked as a journalist at two magazines, *al-Hasna*, the major women's magazine, and *al-Nahar* (The day) newspaper supplement. After her marriage, she moved to the Arabian Gulf where her husband worked, and there she wrote her second novel, entitled *Faras al-Shaytan* (Satan's she-horse or The praying mantis, an insect common to the south of Lebanon, 1975), and her third one, *Wardat al-Sahra* (The rose of the desert, translated as The Story of Lulu, 1979).

The central character of al-Shaykh's second novel, Sarah, seems to be a partially autobiographical avatar of the author. Like al-Shaykh, she grows up in southern Lebanon, in a Shiite family, closely watched by her stern and fanatically religious father. Forced to undergo rigorous cleansing and prayer rituals every day of the year, she is savagely beaten for the slightest disobedience and, at the age of twelve, forced to don the thick black veil of traditional Muslim womanhood. The father's fanaticism is so extreme that, at least in Sarah's eyes, it is responsible for her mother's death: he refused to be disturbed from his prayers to fetch the doctor.

Although this portrayal is at times shocking, it is not self-pitying. The reason for this becomes clear in the second half of the novel, in which we see Sarah, now grown and married, on a visit to an unnamed desert region. Here she meets a woman who is a member of a *harim* of three wives and, after gaining her confidence, she gradually learns of the traditional ways and customs of the tribal people. By the end of the novel, Sarah realizes that, oppressive though her own upbringing may have been, she at least was able to see her own life in sufficient perspective to understand its limitations and eventually escape them.

Sarah learns that Lulu, the youngest wife, is considered barren, as are her two co-wives. The husband took the three wives in the hope of having children, but Sarah quickly perceives the real cause of the women's barrenness: the husband had intercourse with them anally, apparently ignorant of any other technique. The wives, for their part, know so little of their own bodies that they are unable to enlighten him. A similar veil of silence and oppression pervades other aspects of their lives as well. Even after Sarah becomes well acquainted with the oldest woman of the *harim*, she refuses to remove her veil in Sarah's presence, and Sarah later learns that none of the wives ever removes her veil, let alone undresses, in the husband's presence.

Bewildered by this glimpse into a strange, hidden world, Sarah ends her narrative on a pessimistic note. What, she wonders, would have to be done to break the cycle of ignorance and oppressive tradition that prevents the tribal woman from gaining the slightest perspective on her condition? When I questioned Hanan al-Shaykh in 1973 about the implications of her work, she replied that her only concern was with its aesthetic quality; she was not aware of the feminist message. Nevertheless, the message is there strongly: without at least a rudimentary sense of identity, is it possible to have any sort of rebellion? The important breakthrough in the case of al-Shaykh's work is that it brings to the literate classes of the Arab world the first open portrayal of the most degrading of traditional customs as they affect women in *all* classes of society.

It is often difficult to determine how involved Arab women writers are in the plight of women in the area. Many of them are insulated from the worst conditions in their countries by wealth, education, and social position. For the women novelists, the usual resolution is to allow female characters to escape through expatriation or some limited form of bicultural self-expression. Directly facing the odds against the liberation of women from the middle and lower classes, as in the case of al-Khuri's *A Single Night*, al-Saadawi's *Woman at Point Zero*, or al-Shaykh's *Satan's She-Horse*, seems to lead to equivocal and pessimistic results. Nevertheless, it is indicative of the evolving state of fiction by Arab women that these writers have even chosen to base some of their works on this bleak confrontation.

Hanan al-Shaykh returned to Lebanon but left when the war broke out in 1975, settling in London. There she wrote *Hikayat Zahrat* (The story of Zahra, 1980). Its explicit sexual descriptions, its exploration of taboo subjects such as family cruelty, women's sexuality, and its relation to the war, caused such a scandal that the book was banned in several Arab countries. Despite the censorship, the book has had wide circulation in the Middle East. Lebanese and Egyptian critics hailed the work for its strength, depth, and lyrical realism, and Hanan al-Shaykh is recognized as a forerunner among young writers expanding the scope of the contemporary Arabic novel. Her style is probably the most sensual of Arab women writers. With a sensitivity and an inner tone so far unequalled, she has managed to bring out a voice that is original, warm, and vibrant. The delicacy of her images and the lace-like quality of her descriptions are reminiscent of the French woman writer Chantal Chawaf. Her subject matter brings to light some of the most crucial aspects of sexuality as they relate to social and political problems, and more specifically to war.

The novel is divided into two parts. The first one, "The Scars of Peace," has five sections—"Zahra Remembers," "Zahra in Africa," "Uncle," "Husband," and "Zahra in Wedlock"—all dealing with Zahra's mental illness, the result of her oppression as a woman in a society that does not allow women to fulfill themselves as human beings. The second part, "The Torrents of War," shows Zahra overcoming her illness and oppression through the war, but it is an illusory, temporary freedom which masks the deeper problems of a society unable to solve its conflicts except through violence and death.

Zahra's first reactions to the war are to sleep, eat, and refuse to talk or to be sociable. Though she withdraws even further than before, the war gives her also a sense of relief: "I felt calm. It meant that my perimeters were fixed by these walls, that nothing which my mother hoped for me could find a place inside them. . . . My deep sleeping was a sickness, my devouring huge quantities of food was a sickness, my increasing weight, my wearing only my housecoat for two months on end were sicknesses. The scabs on my face that spread to my neck, to my shoulders, and my not caring about them, were a sickness. My silence was a sickness" (p. 107).

She is filled with despair and disbelief at what is going on in her country: the killings, the kidnappings, the disintegration, the slow death. . . . When she realizes her brother Ahmad had joined the fighters, she cannot accept it and reacts by screaming, grabbing at him, and actually passing out. The father seems to join her in these feelings and shouts at her mother who has just accepted two hundred liras from her son: "Who does he think he is fighting? His brother, his friend, his neighbor! We are all Lebanese, you foolish woman. We are all one family! Lebanon is a small country. . . . I wouldn't touch such cursed money. It belongs to martyrs and orphans. You did wrong in accepting it" (p. 112). It's the first time the father says something sensible and we feel sympathy toward him, just as we did when Zahra's uncle took Zahra's part over her virginity, telling her husband that times had changed, that such customs were trivial and stupid. This is Hanan al-Shaykh's genius: her ability to show unsympathetic characters nevertheless uttering wisdom, exhibiting complex personalities.

The major event of the novel is Zahra's relationship with the sniper. The reasons she throws herself into this adventure are not altogether clear to her. The war creates such contradictions within her she wishes somehow to find an answer—even in death. The afternoon she first goes to him, she really believes she is walking to her death: "I anticipated only one thing: hearing a bullet and then falling dead to the ground like the others the sniper had killed. . . . I could no longer feel my pulse and my body moved without thought or sensation. In that critical moment I said to myself, 'Well, here I am, I am about to lose myself forever'" (p. 125). It is evident from these lines that Zahra sees death as liberation. Death, war, and sexuality are closely associated in her walk toward the sniper. In that respect, her nihilism parallels that of her brother Ahmad and his comrades. They all seek liberation through death. While Zahra submits to it masochistically, as a result of her life of oppression, Ahmad and his comrades inflict it sadistically on others.

Zahra's first sexual encounters with the sniper are virtually rapes: he pounces on her and releases himself within her without consideration for her feelings, pleasure, sensations, or the fact that the bare floor hurts her back and side. However, as time goes by and she goes back to him every afternoon, they grow accustomed to each other, she relaxes, and he starts responding to her needs. She experiences orgasm for the first time in her life and cries out: "My cries became like lava and hot sand pouring from a volcano whose suffocating dust was burying my past life. It blotted out the door to Dr. Shawky's clinic [the doctor who had given her two abortions] and the door behind which we hid as my mother clutched at me in panic" (p. 130). The sniper's caresses unwind all the suffering from her past. The orgasm brings to the surface all the feelings she had buried deep inside her; it intensifies them while allowing her to forget them: "My cries as I lay in the dust, responding to the sniper's exploring fingers, contained all the pain and sickness from my past, when I had curled up in my shell in some corner, somewhere, or in a bathroom, hugging myself and holding my breath as if always trying to return to the state of being a foetus in its mother's womb" (p. 131). It is a kind of catharsis. She compares it to electro-convulsive treatment, and the image it conjures up is not positive, foreshadowing of events to come, coloring Zahra's pleasure with the specter of madness and death. She feels anxiety over the significance of her act and prospects for the future: "My body had undulated with pleasure as the sniper looked into my eyes. Was he really the sniper, this person who was now standing up and who had, for the first time, taken off his trousers? What had made him into a sniper? Who had given him orders to kill anonymous passers-by? Would I be thought of as the sniper's accomplice now my body had become a partner to his body?" (p. 132).

It seems as though, in Zahra's mind, the only way to have any kind of control over the elements of death ravaging her country is to become part of this violence through sexuality. She tried to help at the hospital but was unable to bear the stench and suffering. She tried to halt the militiamen from shooting the prisoners, but was held back by her parents and told she was mad, risking death herself. She tried to convince her brother to stop fighting, taking drugs, and looting, only to see him scorn her and masturbate in front of her! What choices did she really have? In light of all these barriers, her act of going to the sniper becomes more understandable, if not condonable. Like others in the war, Zahra is a victim. Deeply wounded in her past by a family and a society that do not allow their individuals, let alone their women, to fulfill themselves and develop into harmonious human beings, Zahra's "solution" is to sink even more deeply into sickness and destruction, while thinking she has become "normal and human." Even her assertiveness, her taking an active part by going to the sniper, is the result of her victimization.

Zahra is hit by a bullet as she crosses the street. He has killed her! "He kills me with the bullets that lay at his elbow as he made love to me. He kills me, and the white sheets which covered me a little while ago are still crumpled from my presence" (p. 183). The images used for the killing are explicitly sexual. It is the killer's ultimate "lovemaking" to Zahra, a metaphor of the Lebanese dilemma, illustrated with paradoxical images by al-Shaykh's powerful pen. Zahra has freed herself sexually through the anarchy that reigns because of the war. She was able to experience orgasm every afternoon in the arms of one of the worst perpetrators of violence in her country. All the taboos have fallen, the barriers and rules of morality have dropped; sexuality is loose, stark, brutal, and present not in love and mutuality but in domination, power relations, cruelty, masochism, and sadism. Zahra's acne and madness are cured. She, who in normal times might have led a traditional life with husband, children, and madness, never experiencing orgasm or any kind of ecstasy, suddenly finds the possibilities of her vibrant body. Unfortunately, this freedom is not a lasting or positive one because it is not based on solid ground. Its roots go deep into violence, war, death, and destruction. The sexual acts which freed Zahra at a certain level were not based on tenderness, love, and mutual respect, or a recognition of the other's dignity and pleasure as of one's own, and the result is not life and love, but death. Zahra becomes the target not only of the killer's sexual weapon, but of his Kalashnikov gun as well. She was able to tame the first, experience pleasure, and even create life, but can do nothing against the terror of the second, which reduces her to a cadaver.

Rape, as the sniper's first reaction to Zahra, is a way of proving his masculinity through control and domination. Along with his killing, it breaks his society's mores and emphasizes the state of chaos he has become part of. Fear is one of the primary motivations for such acts: fear of life, fear of women, fascination with death and destruction. As he grows accustomed to Zahra's daily visits, fear fades away; he starts responding to her sexual needs by caressing her, and to her physical comforts by bringing some sheets. He even becomes tender and shows some emotion. Nevertheless, at the announcement of her pregnancy and her question about his occupation, fear takes hold of him again. He cannot fulfill his promise to marry her and reintegrate into a "normal" life which he daily destroys. He cannot assume the life in her womb. In order to reestablish the chaos, the daily drug and only meaning of his existence, he must kill her.

The analysis of *The Story of Zahra* brings out other important elements. The youth in Lebanon use the war to revolt against tradition and authority, to break with the rules of the fathers and mothers. They want to destroy the old order which oppresses them. The boys or militiamen do it through cynicism, sadism, and cruelty. The women—in particular Zahra—achieve a certain autonomy through masochism and submission to cruelty and violence. Neither men nor women have any kind of vision that would help them out of the vicious circle: the patriarchal tribal system creates war, war is used to destroy the authoritarian system, war begets more war and violence.

Instead of destroying the old order and its tribal system of oppression, the *shabab* (young militiamen) gangs reinforce it and lead women a step further down. The youth may think they have gained a certain autonomy and freedom: men in the exhilaration of fighting, destroying, and looting; women in the excitement of sexual pleasure. As with drugs, however, it is a temporary, artificial nirvana. It does not really challenge the basic structure the youth are revolting against. It is an outlet, a diversion from hurt: pain fought with pain, violence attacked with violence, authority questioned with authority, power challenged with power. They seek liberation through death rather than through life and creativity, and the outcome is death. Only a different vision could break the circle of hell. Hanan al-Shaykh has successfully and sensitively portrayed the various dilemmas facing youth and women today. The war in Lebanon may be an extreme form of these conflicts; nevertheless, it illustrates some of the serious problems present in our world.

Emily Nasrallah and Daisy al-Ameer

The last two writers we will examine in this study are Emily Nasrallah and Daisy al-Ameer; the first is Lebanese, the second Iraqi. Both lived in Beirut until recently. Both have expressed themselves extensively in magazines and journals, and through the medium of the short story. Nasrallah's collections of short stories include *Jazirat al-Wahm* (The island of the imagination, 1973) and *al-Yanbu'* (The source, 1977). Al-Ameer's collections are *Thumma Ta'ud al-Mawjat* (And then the wave comes back, 1969) and *al-Bayt al-'Arabi al-Sa'id* (The happy Arab home, 1975). The form of the short story fits very well the content of these narratives, which often deal with the problems of women. Emily Nasrallah has also published several novels, among them *Tuyur Aylul* (Birds of September, 1962), *Shajarat al-Daflat* (The oleander tree, 1968), *al-Rahinat* (The bonded, 1974), and *al-Bahirat* (The blurring, 1977).

In a suggestive and realistic style, these two writers raise some basic questions about women's roles and the oppressive traditions surrounding their lives. "The Happy Arab Home," for example, a short story by Daisy al-Ameer in the collection by that name, is an ironic title for a story that actually deals with the problems of veiling and cloistering. One of the narrator's friends who had seemed very modern and progressive in his ideas had just gotten married to a veiled woman. This makes the narrator ponder over the double standards and hypocrisy surrounding some of the traditions in her country.

In another story entitled "The Cat, the Maid, and the Wife," Daisy al-Ameer continues her criticism of the double standards that men apply to women within Arab society. The narrator, a working woman, has gone to visit a friend who is the wife of a prospective general director and daughter of a minister. The wife talks bitterly about how every member of an Arab family (including the grandparents) feels the right to interfere in the way the children are raised. She spits out a virulent attack on how Arab society is structured and the way it exploits it own members, and how the husband and wife behave hypocritically toward one another, maintaining a facade of role-acting. At this point, the husband steps into the room and the wife changes her attitude completely, becoming docile and submissive. The husband praises the narrator for working outside her home, but when she asks if he would not like his wife to do the same, he replies that his wife is in a different condition—"protected and supported"—and that he would not like her to do that, showing again the double standards by which he judges women. The narrator goes away disgusted at what she just witnessed in both the man and the woman.

At this point, al-Ameer introduces two symbolic elements: the narrator's maid—who tells her that she is resigning in order to preserve her dignity and freedom—and a cat—thin, dirty, and starving—that wanders away from the narrator in spite of her calling to it. The cat, despite its starvation, and the maid, in spite of her humble position in society, seem to be more authentic and free than the rest of the characters, including the narrator, who must maintain a facade and move in the different circles of society with an air of politeness and concern.

Emily Nasrallah started her literary career in the 1950s by publishing prose poems reminiscent of Gibran in various magazines. She also practiced journalism. Her first novel, *Birds of September*, was published in 1962. Like the early novels of Baalbakki, al-Khuri, and Djebar, it deals with the familiar theme of romantic love that cannot be fulfilled and ends in fiasco. Three women in love are forced into suppressing their feelings and accepting the traditions imposed on them through arranged marriages. Unlike the earlier heroines, however, they silently submit to their fate: the men are the ones who rebel violently. Out of spite, one of them kills a girl he cannot marry. Another leaves the country and a woman he loves behind. Thus, the women are doubly oppressed; not only do they resign themselves to their fate, but this resignation leads to more suffering and loneliness. By shifting the focus to the fate of the men, Nasrallah also emphasizes that the effects of oppression in society are not limited to its obvious victims—it reaches and poisons all others as well.

In addition to the usual theme of frustrated love, Nasrallah introduces in this novel descriptions of the hard life of Lebanese villagers, in a way that is reminiscent of the North African writer Mouloud Feraoun. Poverty, superstition, ignorance, class, and religious divisions all act against the fulfillment of its inhabitants, who are forced to emigrate. As in the case of Feraoun's stories, the women are the ones who suffer the most.

In her second novel, *The Oleander Tree*, Nasrallah presents to us an unusual young woman whose rebellion leads her to suicide, a theme already discussed in many of the novels studied so far, and a theme found in much feminist literature throughout the world. The heroine is symbolized by the oleander tree, a tree beautiful to look at but venomous in nature. The woman's rebellion expresses itself through defiance of the village customs. She performs a wild dance at a wedding; this is considered obscene by the villagers, who blackmail her. It ruins her reputation, much to the despair of her mother, a widow who earns a meager living by cleaning people's homes.

Upset by the villagers' comments about her daughter's behavior, the mother seeks help from an old man known for his wisdom. Together, they secretly plan a marriage for her daughter. Having heard of the arrangements made behind her back, the young woman decides to defy custom once more. She proceeds to convince the intended husband to run away with her. The young woman's act is an interesting one in that it offers a solution not found in previous novels. Her revolt leads the woman to break customs by seeing through them and turning them against society. Unfortunately, this solution does not lead to positive results. The young people get married in a village nearby, but when they return to their home village, the young woman commits suicide. The village customs, instead of being broken, are reinforced through this turn of events.

As with al-Khuri's and Djebar's second novels, Nasrallah's concern in her second novel goes beyond the common litany of frustrations brought about by tradition. The plot's ending reminds us of al-Khuri's *A Single Night*, and the achievement of consciousness by a lower-class woman results in utter despair and suicide. Individual rebellion affords no escape from the cruelty, gossip, hypocrisy, and stagnation of village life.

Nasrallah's third novel, *The Bonded*, also deals with the oppressive customs of village life, especially as they concern women. Rania, the heroine, is also a poor peasant woman. She has been engaged since birth to a rich and powerful man named Namrood, who controls her and imposes his will on all her actions and behavior.

One element not found in the previous novels is the clash between modern and traditional values. Strangely enough, Namrood sends Rania to a college in Beirut where she is confronted with different ways of life and thinking. Having always followed her master's dictates, Rania is not prepared to take a different path, not even that of love in the form of a young student, Marwan, whose strong affection induces her to respond to him for a while. At that point, love appears to be the liberating force that could free Rania from bondage and servitude. Instead, she decides to return to her village and to slavery.

In this novel, Nasrallah subtly explores the more complex aspects of the meaning of liberation for Arab women. She explores the psychology of her heroine and finds that, even when given the choice and the chance to free themselves, young Arab women may not do so.

Another element that Nasrallah brings forth vividly is the notion of fatalism, which permeates the world of the village and its inhabitants' outlook on life. This notion has a greater effect on women than on men. According to the writer and critic Rose Ghurayyib: "The chains weigh so heavily on [women's] shoulders that they are like birds with broken wings."[8] This is to be expected since, even within the narrow confines of the village, men traditionally have more prerogatives and greater freedom of action and self-determination.

In the collection of short stories entitled *The Source*, Nasrallah expands her vision and deals with the Lebanese war. Again, she shows the evils of sectarianism, fanaticism, traditional customs, and hypocrisy that plague Lebanese society. She stresses the need for reform through love, courage, and sacrifice. She often uses symbolic elements and images from village life.

Rose Ghurayyib points out that Nasrallah's "gloomy vision of the Lebanese village shows how deeply the author feels the needs and the plagues of a sector which forms the backbone of Lebanon and includes more than half of the inhabitants." She adds:

> Emily Nasrallah has been called the "village woman poet." Her style contains a poetic flavour, probably inspired by the picturesque village atmosphere. It is hoped that in her future works she will try to present to her readers the strivings of militant women, and depict the efforts of those who follow positive ways of action, those who refuse to yield to accomplished fact.[9]

This does, in fact, appear to be an important next step for writers such as Nasrallah who have laid the groundwork by expanding the scope of their fiction to demonstrate that the oppression of women as individuals is inexorably tied to the nature—and fate—of the whole society.

In the writings of Nasrallah and al-Ameer, we witness an awareness of the more subtle social problems facing various kinds of women in a context that has already shaped their behavior very early in life, allowing them very little flexibility in moving toward authenticity and genuine behavior. In addition to the usual array of oppressive patterns, they also have to face all the ills that their environment has built into it. The style of these two writers is very much in tune with the message they convey: it is realistic and suggestive, with touches of symbolism used at the right moments to break the linear pattern of the narrative, emphasizing the search for truth, authenticity, and real freedom.

From this brief study of the more recent trends in the works of Arab women writers, we can conclude that there is a sense of greater awareness and commitment to political and feminist issues. The search for identity and self-realization is still present and it is not less desperate than in the other novels. However, it moves toward larger concerns. It is less individualistic and introspective, and it attempts to deal with the condition of women on all levels of society.

The Path of Arab Women's Fiction: Concluding Observations

The conclusions of the French critic Michel Barbot about the work of Layla Baalbakki seem to hold true as well for many of the other women writers discussed in this study. He points in her works to the threefold pattern of existentialist experience as described by Heidegger: the project, the leap, and the fall.[10] The female characters depicted in these works have as their project the desire to break away from the traditional model and assert themselves as individuals. To do so, it is necessary to make a leap, from their present condition of restricted consciousness, over the obstacles of tradition, hopefully to land in some brave new world of individual freedom. The leap, however, is in most cases too great to be completed, and instead the character falls.

An examination of the works discussed in this study reveals, however, that not all existential falls are of equal magnitude. For instance, the fall of Reem in al-Khuri's *Days with Him* is really a *felix culpa*, a fortunate fall through which Reem discovers her own inner strength. On the other hand, the fall of Baalbakki's Lina or of Nasrallah's female characters is more purely a fall in Heidegger's sense of a failure to achieve in actuality the leap that the imagination posits from the known to the desired. Most of the characters have the will—in varying degrees—to affirm themselves before what Heidegger calls "the others," the friends, families, and colleagues who are the other characters of the novels. In most cases this will toward affirmation is mixed with the realization of emptiness (*faragh*) and the desire to rebel, resulting in a mixture that Frantz Fanon finds to be characteristic of oppressed groups.[11] This is not to say that there is not a reality behind the urge to rebel; it is quite clear from most of the works discussed here that the characters are operating against a background of very real oppression, hypocrisy, double standards, and social injustice. It is in fact the existence of this negative social reality that gives to the projection, leap, and fall of the characters both literary depth and emotional poignancy.

Although the project, leap, and fall remain a satisfactory explanatory device for the recent fiction of Arab women writers, this should not be taken as an indication that these works are very much like those of the earlier writers. In some ways, the overall outlook is bleaker, and the project, leap, and fall more sharply defined in the recent works precisely because their authors have moved to a clearer sense of the magnitude of the task facing them.

The earlier works tend to use the social milieu as background, as the given underlying the individual struggles of the central characters who are the primary focus of the works. The blunter and more open treatment of the oppressive aspects of Arab societies that we find in the more recent works is not simply a more daring exercise of literary freedom—although we must never lose sight of the courage these authors have consistently shown. Rather, the increasing clarity and frankness with which the social context is presented suggests that it is no longer merely a backdrop for the action of the story. In these works, Arab society itself comes forth as a character in the play: a character complete with principles of choice and action, and with both trivial and tragic flaws.

This does not change the nature of the project, leap, and fall of the central female characters. Nevertheless, as the nature—and magnitude—of the obstacle becomes clearer, there is an increase in poignancy, anger, and at times, other-directed, even symbolic, rebellion. Even the negative responses of some of the characters in the later fiction—withdrawal, refusal to make the leap, suicide—appear to follow logically from an appreciation of the sweeping role of the social context in shaping individual behavior. What the characters discover is that they are not rebelling merely against a single custom, a particular oppressor, but are facing the complex and total interrelationship between their own beings and the society that has shaped them.

It is not necessarily the role of fiction to provide blueprints for concrete social action—and much bad fiction has resulted from attempts to do so— but the recent fiction of Arab women, with its greater openness and its integration of individual struggle into the larger social context, may well become a force for positive and creative social and political change in the Arab world. Even if this were not the case, the production of fiction by Arab women writers would be remarkable for its variety and its occasional aesthetic excellence, existing as it does in the face of a tradition that has supported no such ambitions or achievements.

NOTES

1. Layla Balabakki, "Nous, sans masques," *Orient* 11, no. 20 (1959): my translation.
2. For more information on this court case, see Elizabeth Fernea and Basima Bezirgan, eds., *Middle Eastern Muslim Women Speak* (Austin: University of Texas Press, 1977), 273–80.
3. Rose Ghurayyib's personal communication to Evelyne Accad, Beirut, December 2, 1982.
4. Salih al-Toma, "The Contemporary Arabic Novel," in *The Cry of Home* (Knoxville: University of Tennessee Press, 1972), 367.
5. Rose Ghurayyib's personal communication to Evelyne Accad, Beirut, January 8, 1982.
6. Ibid.
7. For a discussion of Bittari's work, see my earlier study, *Veil of Shame* (Sherbrooke: Naaman, 1978), 52–56.
8. Rose Ghurayyib, "Emily Nasrallah: A Novelist Who Has Portrayed the Beauty and the Misery of the Lebanese Village," *Asian Woman* (May 1979): 8–9.
9. Ibid., 9–10.
10. Michel Barbot, "Destineé de femmes arabes," *Orient* (1er trimestre 1965): 251.
11. Frantz Fanon, *Peau noire, masques blancs* (Paris: Seuil, 1952).

BIBLIOGRAPHY

'Abdallah, Sufi. *Alf Mubruk*. Cairo: al-Kaumiyah, 1965.
———. *Arusa 'ala al-Raff*. Cairo: Ma'arif, 1966.
———. *Baqaya Rajul*. Cairo: al-Tijari, n.d.
———. *Madrasat al-Banat*. Cairo: al-Zahabi, 1959.
Accad, Evelyne. *Coquelicot du massacre*. Paris: L'Harmattan, 1988.
———. "Entre deux," *Contes et nouvelles de langue française*. Sherbrooke, Quebec: Cosmos, 1976.
———. *L'Excisée*. Paris: L'Harmattan, 1982. English translation by David Bruner. Washington D.C.: Three Continents Press, 1989.
———. *Sexuality and War: Literary Masks of the Middle East*. New York: New York University Press, 1990.
———. *Veil of Shame: The Role of Women in the Contemporary Fiction of North Africa and the Arab World*. Sherbrooke, Quebec: Naaman, 1978.
Accad, Evelyne and Rose Ghurayyib. *Contemporary Arab Women Writers and Poets*. Beirut: Institute for Women's Studies in the Arab World, 1965.
al-Ameer, Daisy. *al-Balad al-Ba'id al-lazi Tuhib*. Beirut: Dar al-'Awdat, 1969.
———. *Thumma Ta'ud al-Mawjat*. Beirut: Dar al-'Awdat, 1969.
Azzam, Samira. *Ashya Saghirah*. Beirut: al-Ahliyya, 1963.
———. *al-Sa'ah wa al-Insan*. Beirut: al-Ilm, 1954.
———. *Wa Qisas Ukhra*. Beirut: al-Ilm, 1960.
Baalbakki, Layla. *al-Alihah al-Mamsukhah*. Beirut: al-Tijari, 1965.
———. *Ana Ahya*. Beirut: al-Tijari, 1958. In French, *Je vis*. Paris: Seuil, 1961.
———. "Nous, sans masques." *Orient* 11 (1959).
———. *Safinat Hanan ila al-Qamar*. Beirut: al-Tijari, 1964.
Bannuna, Khanata. *al-Nar wa al-Ikhtiyar*. Beirut: al-Tijari, 1969.
———. *Liyaskut al-Samt*. Beirut: al-Tijari, 1968.

Barbot, Michel. "Destinée de femmes arabes." *Orient*, 1er trimestre, 1965.
———. "Satire et pitié sociale chez Samira Azzam." *Orient*, 1er trimestre, 1965.
Beauvoir, Simone de. *The Second Sex*. London: Jonathon, 1968 [1948].
Beck, Lois and Nikki Keddie. *Women in the Muslim World*. Cambridge: Harvard University Press, 1978.
Bittari, Zoubeida. *O, mes soeurs musulmanes, pleurez!* Paris: Gallimard, 1972.
Boullata, Kamal. *Women of the Fertile Crescent*. Washington D.C.: Three Continents Press, 1978.
Debeche, Djamila. *Aziza*. Algiers: Imbert, 1955.
Djebar, Assia. *Les alouettes naïves*. Paris: Julliard, 1967.
———. *La'amour, la fantasia*. Paris: Lattes, 1985.
———. *Les enfantes du nouveau monde*. Paris: Julliard, 1962.
———. *Femmes d'Alger dans leur appartement*. Paris: Des Femmes, 1980.
———. *Les impatients*. Paris: Julliard, 1958.
———. *Ombres sultanes*. Paris: Lattes, 1987.
———. *La soif*. Paris: Julliard, 1957.
Fanon, Frantz. *Peau noire, masques blancs*. Paris: Seuil, 1952.
Farraj, Afif. *al-Hurriyyat fi Adab al-Mar'a*. Beirut: Dar al-Farabi, 1975.
Ghurayyib, Rose. "Emily Nasrallah: A Novelist Who Has Portrayed the Beauty and the Misery of the Lebanese Village." *Asian Woman*. May 1979.
Johnson-Davies, D. *Modern Arabic Short Stories*. London: Oxford University Press, 1967.
Khatibi, Abdelkabir. *Le roman maghrebin*. Paris: Maspero, 1968.
al-Khuri, Kulit Suhayl. *Ayyam ma'ah*. Beirut: al-Tijari, 1959.
———. *Laylah Wahidah*. Beirut: Dar al-Kitab, 1970.
Mernissi, Fatima. *Beyond the Veil*. Cambridge, Mass.: Schenkman, 1975.
Mikhail, Mona. *Images of Arab Women*. Washington D.C.: Three Continents Press, 1979.
Na'na, Hamida. *al-Watan fi al-'Aynain*. Beirut: Dar al-Adab, 1979.
Nasrallah, Emily. *al-Bahirat*. Beirut: Naufal, 1977.
———. *Jazirat al-Wahm*. Beirut: Naufal, 1973.
———. *al-Rahinat*. Beirut: Naufal, 1974.
———. *Shajarat al-Daflat*. Beirut: Naufal, 1968.
———. *Tuyur Aylul*. Beirut: Naufal, 1962.
———. *al-Yanbu'*. Beirut: Naufal, 1977.
Ossairan, Layla. *Qal'at al-Ustah*. Beirut: al-Nahar, 1979.
al-Saadawi, Nawal. *al-Bahitha an al-Hub*. Cairo: al-Haya al-Misriya Lilkitab, 1974. Beirut: Dar al-Adab, 1975 until 1986. Under the title *Imra'atan fi Imra'a*. Jerusalem: Manshurat Salah al-Din, 1976. In English, *Two Women in One*. London: al-Saqi, 1985. Seattle Press, 1986.
———. *al-Ghaib*. Cairo: al-Haya al-Misriya Lilkitab, 1967. Beirut: Dar al-Adab, 1980 and 1981. Cairo: Maktabat Madbuli, 1983.
———. *Hanan Kalil*. Cairo: al-Kitab al-Zahabi, 203 (2–39172), 1962. Beirut: Dar al-Adab, 1986.
———. *Imra'ah 'inda Niktat al-Sifer*. Beirut: Dar al-Adab, 1976. In French, *Ferdaous une voix en enfer*. Paris: Des Femmes, 1981. In English, *Woman at Point Zero*. London: Zed Press, 1983. Also in German, Italian, Dutch, and Swedish.
———. *al-Insaan*. Cairo: Maktabat Madbuli, 1983. In French, *Douze femmes dans Kanater*. Paris: Des Femmes, 1984.
———. *al-Kha'it wa al-Jidar*. Cairo: al-Shaab, 1972. Beirut: Dar al-Adab, 1980 and 1981. Cairo: Maktabat Madbuli, 1983. In English, *She has no Place in Paradise*. London: Methuen, 1987.

―――. *al-Mar'ah wa al-Jins.* Cairo: al-Shaab, 1972. Beirut: al-Mu'assassat, 1974 until 1988.

―――. *al-Mar'ah wa al-Sarah al-Nafsi.* Beirut: al-Mu'assassat, 1976. Cairo: Maktabat Madbuli, 1983.

―――. *Mawt Rajul al-Wahid al-Ard.* Beirut: Dar al-Adab, 1979. Cairo: Maktabat Madbuli, 1983. In English, *God Dies by the Nile.* London: Zed Press, 1985. Also in German and Dutch.

―――. *Mudhakirati fi Sijn al-Nisa.* Cairo: Dar al-Mustaqbal, 1984. In English, *Memoirs from the Women's Prison.* London: Women's Press, 1986.

―――. *Mudhakirat Tabiba.* Cairo: Dar al-Maaref, 1960. Beirut: Dar al-Adab, 1980. Cairo: Maktabat Madbuli, 1983.

―――. *al-Rajul wa al-Jins.* Beirut: al-Mu'assassat, 1967. Cairo: Maktabat Madbuli, 1983.

―――. *Ta'alamtu al-Hub.* Cairo: al-Nahda, 1958. Beirut: Dar al-Adab, 1986.

―――. *Ughniyat al-Atfal al-Da'iriyat.* Beirut: Dar al-Adab, 1978.

―――. *al-Untha hiya al-Asl.* Beirut: al-Mu'assassat, 1974. Cairo: Maktabat Madbuli, 1983.

―――. *al-Wijh al-Ari li al-Mar'ah al-'Arabiya.* Beirut: al-Mu'assassat, 1977. In English, *The Hidden Face of Eve.* Boston: Beacon Press, 1981. In French, *La face cachée d'Eve.* Paris: Des Femmes, 1982. Also in German, Dutch, Portuguese, Persian, and Danish.

al-Samman, Ghada. *al-A'mal ghair al-Kamilat.* Beirut: al-Samman, 1979.

―――. *I'takalu Lahzat Haribut.* Beirut: al-Samman, 1979.

―――. *al-Jasad Haqibat Safar.* Beirut: al-Samman, 1979.

―――. *Khitm al-Zakirat bi al-Sham'a al-Ahmar.* Beirut: al-Samman, 1979.

―――. *Layl al-Ghuraba.* Beirut: Dar al-Adab, 1966.

―――. *Muwatinat Mutallabissat bi al-Qira'at.* Beirut: al-Samman, 1979.

―――. *al-Raghif Yanbud Ka al-Qalb.* Beirut: al-Samman, 1979.

―――. *al-Sibahat fi Buhairat al-Shaytan.* Beirut: al-Samman, 1979.

―――. "al-Thawra al-jinsiyah wa al-thawrah al-shamilah." *Mawakif,* 12, 1970.

al-Shaykh, Hanan. *Faras al-Shaytan.* Beirut: Dar al-Nahar, 1975.

―――. *Hikayat Zahrat.* Beirut: Dar al-Nahar, 1980. In English, *The Story of Zahra.* London: Quartet Books, 1986. In French, *Histoire de Zahra.* Paris: Lattes, 1985.

―――. *Intihar Rajul Maymit.* Beirut: Dar al-Nahar, 1971.

―――. *Wardat al-Sahra.* Beirut: al-Mu'assassat, 1982.

Taos, Maguerite Amrouche. *La Rue des tambourins.* Paris: Table Ronde, 1960.

al-Toma, Salih. "The Contemporary Arabic Novel," *The Cry of Home.* Knoxville: University of Tennessee Press, 1972.

―――. "Westernization and Islam in Modern Arabic Fiction." *Yearbook of Comparative and General Literature,* 20, 1971.

Yetiv, Isaac. *Le thème de l'aliénation dans le roman maghrebin d'expression française.* Sherbrooke, Quebec: C.E.L.E.F., 1972.

CONTRIBUTORS

Evelyne Accad is Professor of French and Comparative Literature at the University of Illinois, Urbana-Champaign. Her many publications on women and literature include *Sexuality and War: Literary Masks of the Middle East* (1990); *Contemporary Arab Women and Poets* (coauthor, 1986); and *Veil of Shame: The Role of Women in the Modern Fiction of North Africa and the Arab World* (1978), which was awarded the 1979 Delta Kappa Gamma International Educator's Award.

Margot Badran is a historian specializing in women's studies who is currently a Visiting Fellow at Princeton University's Department for Near Eastern Studies. She recently completed a book on Egyptian feminism. Dr. Badran is coeditor of *Opening the Gates: A Century of Arab Feminist Writing* (1990) and editor and translator of Huda Shaarawi's *Harem Years: The Memoirs of an Egyptian Feminist* (1987).

Souad Dajani is Assistant Professor of Social and Behavioral Sciences at Antioch College. She has written widely on Palestinian society and is currently working on a book on strategies of nonviolent civilian resistance in the Israeli-occupied territories. She has been Research Associate with the Program of Non-Violent Sanctions at the Center for International Affairs, Harvard University, and has taught at Yarmuk University.

Susan Schaefer Davis is an independent scholar and consultant who specializes in Moroccan society and has a particular interest in the interrelation of gender roles, social change, and economic development. She is the author of *Adolescence in a Moroccan Town: Making Social Sense* (1989) and *Patience and Power: Women's Lives in a Moroccan Village* (1983), as well as several articles on Morocco. She received her Ph.D. in Anthropology from the University of Michigan in Ann Arbor.

Evelyn Aleene Early is an anthropologist who received her Ph.D. from the University of Chicago and has taught at the University of Notre Dame and the University of Houston-University Park. She is the author of *Baladi Women of Cairo: Playing with an Egg and a Stone* (1992) and several articles based

255

on field research on women in Cairo. She is also coeditor of *Everyday Life in the Muslim Middle East* (1993). Dr. Early is currently Press Attache at the United States Embassy in Rabat, Morocco.

Sondra Hale is an anthropologist who directs the Women's Studies Program at California State University, Northridge, and is also a Research Scholar at the Center for the Study of Women at the University of California at Los Angeles. She is currently working on a book on gender and politics in Sudan that is based on six years of fieldwork in Sudan. Her published articles deal with feminism and gender issues in Sudan and elsewhere in the Middle East.

Mervat Hatem is Associate Professor of Political Science at Howard University. She has written extensively on subjects relating to the Middle East, including nationalism, patriarchy, and the political economy of women in the region. She is currently working on a book on the rise and decline of state feminism in Egypt. Dr. Hatem, who received her Ph.D. from the University of Michigan in Ann Arbor, is a member of the Council on Women and Politics.

Margaret L. Meriwether is Associate Professor of History at Denison University. She is currently writing a book about family and society in Aleppo between 1770 and 1850 and is the author of articles and papers on different dimensions of the social structure of Aleppo in that period. Her fellowships and grants have included a Fulbright Islamic Civilization Grant and a Social Science Research Council Doctoral Dissertation Fellowship.

Julie M. Peteet is Assistant Professor of Anthropology at the University of Louisville. She is the author of *Gender in Crisis: Women and the Palestinian Resistance Movement* (1991). She has taught at the American University of Beirut and Georgetown University and is the author of several articles on Palestinian gender issues. She has carried out fieldwork in Lebanon, Jordan, and, most recently, the occupied West Bank.

Rosemary Sayigh is a sociologist and writer who has carried out extensive field research in Palestinian refugee camps. She is the author of *The Palestinians: From Peasants to Revolutionaries* (1979) and numerous articles about Palestinian social structure, sources of Palestinian nationalism, and the economic conditions of the Palestinian people.

Barbara F. Stowasser is Professor of Arabic at Georgetown University. She is the editor of *The Islamic Impulse* (1987). She has also published widely in both German and English on the subject of the early Islamic Hadith. Her recent research has focused on Quranic commentaries on the status of women and has included field research at theological faculties and schools in Turkey, Jordan, and Egypt.

Judith E. Tucker is Associate Professor of History at Georgetown University and Associate Director for Academic Programs at the University's Center for Contemporary Arab Studies. She is the author of many publications on the status of women in the Arab world, including *Women in Nineteenth-Century Egypt* (1985). She recently conducted extensive research into marriage and the family in Nablus in the eighteenth and nineteenth centuries. Dr. Tucker is a contributing editor to *Middle East Report*.

INDEX